Understanding Prejudice, Racism, and Social Conflict

Understanding Prejudice, Racism, and Social Conflict

Edited by
Martha Augoustinos and Katherine J. Reynolds

SAGE Publications
London • Thousand Oaks • New Delhi

Editorial arrangement and Chapter 1 © Martha Augoustinos and Katherine J. Reynolds 2001
Chapter 2 © Ian Walker 2001
Chapter 3 © Darren Garvey 2001
Chapter 4 © Drew Nesdale 2001
Chapter 5 © Julia Robinson, Rivka Witenberg, and Ann Sanson 2001
Chapter 6 © Patrick C. L. Heaven 2001
Chapter 7 © Vance Locke and Lucy Johnston 2001
Chapter 8 © Leith S. Baird and Julie M. Duck 2001
Chapter 9 © Deborah J. Terry, Michael A. Hogg, and Leda Blackwood 2001
Chapter 10 © Katherine J. Reynolds and John C. Turner 2001
Chapter 11 © Penelope J. Oakes and S. Alexander Haslam 2001
Chapter 12 © Michael J. Platow and John A. Hunter 2001
Chapter 13 © Amanda LeCouteur and Martha Augoustinos 2001
Chapter 14 © Mark Rapley 2001
Chapter 15 © John Duckitt 2001
Chapter 16 © Stephen Reicher 2001

First published 2001

Reprinted 2002

SAGE Publications Ltd
6 Bonhill Street
London EC2A 4PU

SAGE Publications Inc
2455 Teller Road
Thousand Oaks, California 91320

SAGE Publications India Pvt Ltd
32, M-Block Market
Greater Kailash – I
New Delhi 110 048

British Library Cataloguing in Publication data

A catalogue record for this book is available from the British Library

ISBN 0 7619 6207 7
ISBN 0 7619 6208 5 (pbk)

Library of Congress Control Number: 2001131841

Printed in Great Britain by Biddles Ltd, *www.biddles.co.uk*

Contents

Preface

As with most fields of social inquiry, the wider social and political climate over the last decade has been significant in shaping and influencing the research concerns and interests of this book: the psychology of prejudice and racism. Australia has witnessed an unprecedented period of public debate and controversy over matters of 'race', immigration, and national identity in the last decade. 'Race' has always been a central feature of the Australian political landscape since colonization. The treatment of Indigenous Australians throughout this period has been likened to genocide (Human Rights and Equal Opportunity Commission, 1997), and Australia maintained a race-based immigration programme known as the 'White Australia' policy until the early 1970s. Since the 1970s, however, 'multiculturalism' has been officially embraced by successive federal governments, and in line with this change Australia came to be recognized internationally as a 'successful' model of a multicultural society. More recently however, sustained attacks on 'multiculturalism' and racial politics emerged after the election of the conservative Howard government in 1996 and the rise of Pauline Hanson and the 'One Nation' party she founded. Since this time, Australia has witnessed a continual erosion of the 'liberal' social policies of the previous Keating Labor government. Indigenous people have borne the brunt of these attacks: their entitlements to land have been undermined by government policy, Prime Minister Howard has steadfastly refused to publicly apologize to Indigenous people for the forcible removal of Indigenous children from their families and communities (the Stolen Generations), and heated public debates have emerged over the nature of 'Reconciliation' that should be negotiated between Indigenous and non-Indigenous Australians. It has been this political and social climate, a climate that transformed Australia from a liberal society that embraced, officially at least, cultural diversity and difference, to one in which racial politics took centre stage, that Australian social researchers have tried to make sense of. How could the political and social landscape change so quickly and dramatically? Were Australians deep down 'really' racist, but had repressed such tendencies because of the norms of 'political correctness'? The 'chattering classes' the 'educated elite', conservatives argued, had stifled open and free speech about politically sensitive issues for too long and now 'mainstream Australia' was reasserting itself. One political analyst refers to this political backlash as 'the revenge of the mainstream' (Johnson, 2000).

While this book is largely a product of trying to understand and make sense of these political and social events within Australia, during the same period several Western countries experienced and witnessed similar political debates over 'racial' concerns, for example, Le Pen and the National Front in France, the proliferation of Neo-Nazi sentiment in a unified Germany, the electoral support of Joerg Haider and the Far-Right Freedom Party in Austria. Our book, therefore, should not be viewed as being concerned with parochial issues, to do with Australian political and social issues alone. Each and every chapter tries to grapple with prejudice and racism as not only a domestic concern, but also a pervasively international one.

Such shifts in the social and political landscape, where prejudice and racism become more or less culturally dominant, highlight the ephemeral nature of particular value systems and the interplay between the nature of the social system and individual attitudes and values. In our view, it is explaining this dynamic nature of prejudice that presents a significant and pressing challenge to the discipline of psychology. This point highlights our own theoretical biases. We believe that prejudice and racism as social phenomena, cannot be understood as the product of individual psychology. Of course prejudice is expressed discursively and behaviourally at the individual level, but an exclusive focus on the contents and processes of the individual mind ignores the structural context and the social identities within which people live out their everyday lives. In these terms, we believe that the interplay between the individual and the social system provides the most fertile ground for understanding the depth and complexity of social phenomena such as prejudice and racism. Judging from recent trends in social psychological research toward more asocial theories and research methods (e.g., information processing accounts, implicit prejudice measures, and personality approaches) ours is a minority view. However, this book reflects an attempt not only to represent current trends but also to emphasize their potential limitations and to highlight and advance more socially-based approaches to the study of prejudice and racism.

In terms of these aims, leading researchers were asked to provide an overview of theory and research related to their specific area of expertise and to identify strengths, weaknesses, and future directions. We also emphasized that the target audiences for the book were undergraduates, interested members of the general public, and academics looking for an introduction into prejudice and racism theory and research. We would like to thank all the authors for the enthusiasm with which they have embraced our vision and for their informative, thought-provoking, accessible, and up-to-date contributions.

We also would like to express our gratitude to Michelle Ryan and Lynette Webb for their assistance with organizing and compiling the references and the various indexes and for their careful attention to detail in formating much of the manuscript. The editorial team at Sage: Michael Carmichael, Naomi Meredith, and Ziyad Marer provided constant guidance, encouragement, and enthusiasm for the book. Finally, we would like to thank our families, Dave, Dylan, Tony, and Georgina, who yet again have demonstrated their patience and encouragement with respect to our academic endeavours.

Martha Augoustinos and Kate Reynolds, 2001

List of Tables

List of Figures

Contributors

Martha Augoustinos is Associate Professor in the Department of Psychology, Adelaide University. Her research interests are in the fields of discursive and critical psychology. Her most recent work has involved the analysis of everyday talk and political rhetoric on matters pertaining to 'race', social categories, and national identity.

Leith Baird is an Associate Lecturer in the School of Psychology and Counselling at Queensland University of Technology. She teaches in organisational, social, and interpersonal psychology and primarily researches the role of mood. Leith is also a military psychologist serving in the Australian Army.

Julie Duck is a Senior Lecturer in the School of Psychology at the University of Queensland. She received her PhD from the University of New England. Her primary research interests are in social identity and intergroup relations, with a special focus on the role of social identity in understanding media use and interpretation.

John Duckitt is a Senior Lecturer in the Department of Psychology at the University of Auckland in New Zealand. He is the author of *The Social Psychology of Prejudice* (Praeger, 1992/1994) and co-editor (with Stanley Renshon) of *Political Psychology: Cultural and Crosscultural Foundations* (New York University Press and Macmillan, 2000). He has authored more than 70 journal articles, reviews, and book chapters on topics such as prejudice, authoritarianism, racial and ethnic attitudes, and intergroup behaviour.

Darren Garvey is a Lecturer with the Centre for Aboriginal Studies at Curtin University of Technology, facilitating the Counselling and Mental Health specialisation of the health worker training course. Darren has recently co-edited (with Pat Dudgeon and Harry Pickett) *Working with Indigenous Australians: A Handbook for Psychologists* (Gunada Press, Curtin Indigenous Research Centre, 2000), and has written and spoken nationally and internationally about the role of psychology with Indigenous Australians, Indigenous youth suicide, and research methodology and ethics.

Alex Haslam is Professor of Psychology at the University of Exeter. Together with colleagues at ANU and elsewhere, his research focuses on social identity and self-categorization processes in groups and organizations. This work is related to the analysis of stereotyping and prejudice, but also to issues of leadership, communication, power, and politics.

Patrick Heaven is Associate Professor of Psychology at the University of Wollongong, NSW. He is interested in the extent to which individual differences and group processes affect psychological well-being, including prejudice and racism.

Michael Hogg is Professor of Social Psychology, Director of the Centre for Research on Group Processes, and Director of Research for the Faculty of Social and Behavioural Sciences at the University of Queensland. He is also a Fellow of the Academy of the Social Sciences in Australia. He has published about 150 books, chapters, and articles on group processes, intergroup relations, and social identity.

John Hunter is a Lecturer in social psychology at the University of Otago. He obtained his BSc and DPhil from the University of Ulster, Coleraine Northern Ireland. His primary research interests focus on intergroup conflict, self-esteem, and social identity theory.

Lucy Johnston is a Senior Lecturer at the University of Canterbury, New Zealand. Her research interests are in stereotyping, social perception, and sport.

Amanda LeCouteur is a Senior Lecturer in the Department of Psychology at Adelaide University where she teaches in the areas of qualitative research methods, gender, and metapsychology. Her research interests include discursive studies of racism and of medicine and women's health.

Vance Locke is a Lecturer at The University of Western Australia. His research interests include, stereotyping, prejudice, and thought suppresssion.

Drew Nesdale is the Foundation Professor in the School of Applied Psychology, Griffith University, Gold Coast Campus. His main research interests are in the areas of social cognition, intergroup behaviour , stereotyping, prejudice and discrimination in adults and children, and organisational culture, identification, and performance.

Penny Oakes is Associate Professor at the Australian National University, Canberra. Her major contribution has been in the area of social categorization and stereotyping. In particular, she has argued that group life rather than cognitive limitations drives the stereotyping process. She is co-author/editor of two books on stereotyping, and has contributed many chapters and journal articles in the area.

Michael Platow is a Senior Lecturer at La Trobe University in Melbourne, Australia. In his research, he examines distributive and procedural justice in both interpersonal and intergroup situations, adopting the perspectives of social identity and self-categorization theories. He has also conducted research other group processes, including social influence, leadership, prosocial behaviour, interdependence, trust, and organizational diversity.

Mark Rapley is Senior Lecturer in Psychology at Murdoch University. His current work applies discursive psychology to questions of power. Other work has examined the interactional and rhetorical production of persons with intellectual disabilities, the 'mentally ill', and Aboriginal Australians. He is co-editor with Alec McHoul of *How to Analyse Talk in Institutional Settings: A Casebook of Methods* (Continuum International, 2001).

Stephen Reicher is a Reader in Psychology at the University of St. Andrews. He has published widely on the relationship between social categorisation and collective action. He is co-author with Nick Hopkins of Self and Nation (Sage Publications, 2001).

Kate Reynolds is a Lecturer in Social Psychology at the Australian National University in Canberra. Her main research interests include prejudice, stereotyping, intergroup conflict and cooperation, and more recently, the interface between social and organizational psychology. Her current work focuses on issues of prejudice, diversity management, leadership, and power.

Julie Robinson is a Senior Lecturer in the School of Psychology at Flinders University in Adelaide, Australia. Her research and teaching interests are divided between developmental psychology and the application of psychology to palliative care. Her research interests in developmental psychology focus on the spatial representation and problem solving skills of infants and the influence of ethnicity on peer preferences and peer interactions among young children.

Deborah Terry is a Professor of Psychology at the University of Queensland. Her research interests are in the areas of attitude-behaviour relations, social influence, and intergroup relations. Recent research has focused on the effects of social norms on prejudice and discrimination on intergroup relations in organizational contexts.

Ann Sanson is an Associate Professor in Psychology at the University of Melbourne, and currently on secondment to the Australian Institute of Family Studies, where she is acting Research Manager. Her research interests revolve around the interplay of intrinsic child characteristics and family and social factors in the development of good and poor psychosocial adjustment. She has a particular interest in developmental pathways to positive outcomes such as social competence, conflict resolution skills and civic responsibility, as well as those leading to problem behaviours. Other research interests include psychological issues relating to peace and conflict, including racism, prejudice, conflict analysis and resolution, and tolerance. She is a member of the Committee for the Psychological Study of Peace of the International Union of Psychological Science.

John Turner is Professor of Psychology at the Australian National University, Canberra. He obtained his BA and PhD in social psychology from the Universities of Sussex and Bristol (UK) respectively. He collaborated with Henri Tajfel at the University of Bristol in the early 1970s in developing social identity theory, and also originated self-categorization theory in the late 1970s and 1980s at Bristol and elsewhere. His current research interests are in the nature of prejudice, social influence, leadership and the self.

Iain Walker is an Associate Professor in the School of Psychology at Murdoch University in Perth, Western Australia. His main research interests are in prejudice and racism, social representations (especially related to issues in biotechnology), and identity and acculturation. He co-authored *Social Cognition: An Integrated Introduction* (Sage, 1995) with Martha Augoustinos, and co-edited *Relative Deprivation: Specification, Development, and Integration* (Cambridge University Press, 2001) with Heather J. Smith.

Rivka Witenberg teaches Developmental and Cognitive Psychology at the Department of Psychology, School of Behavioural Science, University of Melbourne. Her main research interest is moral development and reasoning. Currently she is examining the development of racial tolerance, its dimensions and context specific nature.

Part I

Prejudice and Racism:
Defining the Problem,
'Knowing' the Experience

1 Prejudice, Racism, and Social Psychology

Martha Augoustinos and Katherine J. Reynolds

During the last years of the twentieth century, a range of international events has focused attention on issues of prejudice and racism: increasing ethno-nationalistic tensions in the former Yugoslavia and the Soviet Union; ethnic conflict in the Middle East and Africa; and a resurgence of debates and controversies concerning issues of 'race', racism, multiculturalism, nationalism, and immigration in western Europe, the US, and Australasia. In the 1990s alone we witnessed several sustained and systematic programs of genocide in Bosnia, Kosovo, and Rwanda. These sociopolitical events have led to a resurgence of research around issues of 'race', racism, and intergroup relations within the social sciences. With the publication of *The Authoritarian Personality* in 1950, by Adorno and his colleagues and Allport's *The Nature of Prejudice* in 1954, psychology, as a discipline, has contributed consistently and extensively to theories of prejudice and racism. While the common core of these theories has been to understand the psychology of prejudice, they have differed significantly in their theoretical approach and level of analysis. It is timely then, that as we enter the twenty first century we take stock and critically reflect upon what psychological theory has contributed to our knowledge of this pressing social issue, and offer some insights as to how the knowledge we generate may be put into practical service in understanding intergroup conflict and oppression. The present edited book has been written with this purpose in mind.

Most social researchers have argued that prejudice and racism manifest themselves at different levels, at the individual, interpersonal, intergroup, and institutional levels. As such, a variety of theoretical and conceptual approaches are therefore necessary to fully understand this social issue. Each of these perspectives is well represented by the contributors to this book, who outline significant and recent developments in relation to each approach. In presenting a variety of different analytic frameworks to understanding racism and prejudice, the present book also raises the difficult question as to whether it is possible to integrate these different approaches. This question has always been a bone of contention within psychology, as analytic frameworks differ significantly in their epistemological assumptions and orientations. As we will see, there are very different views regarding whether such a theoretical integration is possible or even desirable in understanding prejudice and racism.

This introductory chapter is designed to orient the reader to the conceptual and theoretical content discussed throughout this book. Firstly, we will define the concepts 'prejudice' and 'racism', by reviewing the historical and contemporary definitions of these constructs. Secondly, we consider the role of scientific racism within the discipline of psychology itself, and what implications this has had on psychological theory and practice throughout the last century and into the present. Thirdly, we provide a brief overview of prejudice research within psychology, identifying four broad and distinct levels of explanation into which psychological theories can be classified: the individual, the cognitive, the intergroup, and the socio-cultural. Similarly, we have organized the parts of this book to correspond to these different explanatory levels. Lastly, we describe the contents of each chapter in this book, detailing the central arguments and theoretical orientation of each.

Prejudice

A plethora of terms within social psychology have been used to describe the concept of prejudice including: discrimination, ethnocentrism, ingroup favouritism, ingroup bias, outgroup derogation, social antagonism, stereotyping, and social distance. Many of the definitions of prejudice that have been popular at various times in social psychology are consistent with different theoretical approaches. Typically though, prejudice or related terms refer to negative attitudes or behaviours towards a person because of his or her membership of a particular group. However, use of such terms also conveys, more or less explicitly, a value dimension that such treatment is bad and unjustified (Ashmore and DelBoca, 1981; Duckitt, 1992). For example, prejudice was defined as being, 'without sufficient warrant' (Allport, 1954: 7), 'a failure of rationality' (Harding et al., 1969: 6), and 'irrational, unjust, or intolerant' (Milner, 1975: 9).

Consistent with this view, prejudice traditionally has been understood as: (a) a negative orientation towards members of particular groups, (b) bad and unjustified, (c) irrational and erroneous, and (d) rigid. Irrational, because prejudice is not seen to be tied to the social reality of the perceiver. Erroneous, because such views are the outcome of cognitive distortions due to, amongst other things: information processing limitations, the impact of mood effects, and dysfunctional personalities (e.g., authoritarianism). Bad, because of the negative consequences such attitudes can foster, and rigid because of the belief that prejudiced people are unlikely to change their view even in the face of contrary information. Clearly then, 'prejudice' and 'discrimination' have largely been constructed as pejorative terms (Harding et al., 1969).

More recent work, however, has avoided the inherent value connotations associated with the term. This has led to the use of a range of more 'evaluatively neutral' definitions of prejudice such as 'ingroup favouritism' or 'bias' (Duckitt,

1992). For example, Tajfel defined prejudice as 'a favourable or unfavourable predisposition toward any member of a category in question' (Tajfel, 1982b: 3). Similarly, Brewer and Kramer defined prejudice as 'shared feelings of acceptance-rejection, trust-distrust, and liking-disliking that

characterize attitudes towards specific groups in a social system' (1985: 230). In general, the move towards less pejorative definitions has been associated with the rise of cognitive models of prejudice that have come to view prejudice increasingly as a natural and inevitable consequence of inherent cognitive processes such as categorization and stereotyping. However, in many instances this more neutral terminology means that the affect and *values* that characterize prejudice have become more difficult to detect and recognize in theories of discrimination and social conflict. Moreover, as many social theorists have argued, this has had the net effect of obscuring the political and ideological dimensions of prejudice.

Racism

There has been a tendency within the literature to use the terms prejudice and racism interchangeably. Jones (1972) however, makes the case that racism is distinct from prejudice. While prejudice is usually regarded as an individual phenomenon, racism is a broader construct that links individual beliefs and practices to wider social and institutional norms and practices.

The belief in a racial hierarchy between groups is a central defining characteristic adopted by many theorists to define racism. For example, Jones defines racism as a 'belief in the superiority of one's own race over another, and the behavioral enactments that maintain those superior and inferior positions' (1972: 5). The belief that the differences between racial groups are biologically driven implies that such variability is fundamental and fixed. These essentialist beliefs lead to the categorization of people into groups based on assumptions that surface characteristics reflect deeper essential features (Allport, 1954; Medin, 1989; Rothbart and Taylor, 1992; Yzerbyt et al., 1997). Such characteristics it is believed, are inherent, unchangeable, and reflect the 'real' nature of the groups they are established to represent (Miles, 1989).

It has been argued however, that this definition of racism is quite restrictive because contemporary racism is less about beliefs in the biological superiority/inferiority of groups, and increasingly about beliefs in a *cultural* hierarchy (Essed, 1991). Contemporary racism justifies and legitimates inequities between groups, not on the basis of biology or 'skin colour', but on claims that certain groups transgress fundamental social values such as the work ethic, self-reliance, self-discipline, and individual achievement. Another contemporary variant of racism, referred to as the 'new racism', rejects the notion of a cultural hierarchy altogether, but instead, emphasizes the need and desirability of the separate development of cultural groups, claiming that it is not in 'human nature' for us to co-exist peacefully with culturally different 'others' (Barker, 1981). This distinction between the 'old' and the 'new' racism(s) is a theme that runs throughout the book (see Chapter 2 in particular), but for now the important point is that racism has been defined and constructed variously, and often there are very fierce debates both within academe and in everyday life contesting what it is exactly that constitutes racism.

The second important difference between prejudice and racism relates to the role of power. At an individual level, a person can display race prejudice: 'a negative attitude toward a person or group based upon a social comparison process in which the individual's own ['racial'] group is taken as a positive point of reference' (Jones, 1972: 3), but this in itself does not necessarily constitute racism. In racism, the significance of ingroup preference (i.e., ethnocentrism) lies in the ingroup being able to exercise *power* over the outgroup (Operario and Fiske, 1998; Reicher, Chapter 16). If we define racism, without reference to power differentials between groups, it is clear that anyone can engage in ingroup preference and outgroup bias. 'Everybody is racist' is a counterclaim that is often used to counter accusations of racism (Hage, 1998). Indeed, this is often the implication of cognitive theories of prejudice: whether we like it or not, we are all prone to favouring our own group and discriminating against an outgroup. Importantly, the power one group has over another transforms race prejudice into racism and links individual prejudice with broader social practices (Jones, 1972, 1998).

Racism, practiced at a structural and cultural level, maintains and reproduces the *power* differentials between groups in the social system (Jones, 1998). Racism practiced at this broad societal level has been referred to as institutional and cultural racism. Institutional racism refers to the institutional policies and practices that are put in place to protect and legitimate the advantages and power one group has over another. Institutional racism can be overt or covert, intentional or unintentional, but the consequences are that racist outcomes are achieved and reproduced. For example, Jones (1972) highlights the entrance practices of university colleges in the US as an example of institutional racism. Universities relied on certain standardized tests to warrant entry despite the fact that African-American applicants had inferior training in the content that was assessed and in test taking. In this case, institutional practices are unequal and restrict the choices, rights, access, and opportunities of different groups.

Cultural racism occurs when those in positions of power define the norms, values, and standards in a particular culture. These mainstream ideals that permeate all aspects of the social system are often fundamentally antagonistic with those embraced by the powerless (e.g., African-Americans). In circumstances such as these the powerless, in order to participate in society, have to surrender their own cultural heritage and adopt new ones (e.g., those of the White majority).

Racism in Psychology

While psychology has contributed important insights to the study of prejudice and racism, at the same time it has not been immune from serious criticisms that the discipline itself has promulgated concepts and theories that are highly racist and ethnocentric. Psychology's 'racist' history is difficult to deny: scientific racism was taken up enthusiastically by many of the discipline's respected and eminent founding figures, including Sir Francis Galton, who also founded and promoted the discipline of eugenics. Influenced by Darwinian evolutionary theory, Galton believed that different 'races' reflected a natural evolutionary hierarchy, at the top of which were European peoples. Such views were widely held between 1850 and 1910, not only by psychologists, but also anthropologists, ethnographers, and biologists. The cultural, social and economic developments during this period, in particular European imperialist expansion and colonial rule over indigenous peoples, created the ideal conditions for the proliferation of such Social Darwinist beliefs (Richards, 1997).

It was in the US however, where scientific racism and the empirical investigation of psychological 'race' differences were vigorously pursued. Between 1910 and 1940, 'race psychology' came to dominate the concerns of US psychologists. The 'Negro education' question and immigration together shaped and influenced the interest in race psychology during this period. With the abolition of slavery, US government policy became increasingly occupied with how to 'manage' the sizable African-American minority. The systematic empirical study of 'race' differences, to identify and map the 'innate' personality characteristics and mental abilities of African-Americans, was central to the race psychology project, its primary goal being to develop educational policies and interventions for this population group. The first wave of large-scale intelligence testing occurred during this time, the results of which (poorer performance of African-Americans compared to Whites) were used to justify and promote segregationist policies. Similarly, race psychology was put into service for identifying which 'undesirable races' or groups should be excluded from migrating to the US. Eminent American psychologists such as Yerkes and Terman were very supportive of this work, adding their intellectual weight to the 'race differences' school. British psychologists were less directly engaged in empirical 'race differences' research during this time (except for Pearson, who founded the *Annals of Eugenics* in 1925). Nevertheless, the central tenets of scientific racism were enthusiastically embraced by prominent British psychologists such as McDougall, Cattell, and Spearman. Meanwhile, in Australia, Stanley Porteus was applying the 'race differences' paradigm to his research on Australian Aborigines (Richards, 1997).

There is little doubt, therefore, that psychology during this period contributed substantially to the legitimacy that was given to scientific racism. As Richards (1997) makes clear, however, while scientific racism was espoused by very influential and eminent psychologists during this period, it was by no means embraced universally. By the 1930s, geneticists had discredited the concept of 'race' as a scientific category, and by 1940, devastating and influential critiques of scientific racism and race psychology by anti-racist critics such as Otto Klineberg, led to the eventual demise of race psychology.

The advent of Nazi eugenics and the experience of the Holocaust during the Second World War, ensured that race psychology did not re-emerge during the post-war period. The civil rights movement in the US and the growth of a Black psychology also contributed to a post-war social and political climate that suppressed explicitly racist theories (Richards, 1997). This was to remain the case until 1969, with the publication of Arthur Jensen's paper in the prestigious *Harvard Educational Review,* 'How much can we boost IQ and scholastic achievement?' The race and IQ debate, one that psychologists and other social scientists had effectively refuted back in the 1930s, was about to be played out once again.

While it is beyond the scope of this chapter to detail the comprehensive critiques that have been made to refute Jensen's claims regarding the existence of reliable 'racial' differences in intelligence, one can only concur with Richard's comment (1997: 273) that supporters of this position, 'betray an inability to let go of the concept' of 'race', even though it had been discredited as unscientific long ago.

> There are quite simply, no stabilised, isolated, inbreeding gene-pools of any magnitude in the US [or elsewhere]. This point alone (totally separate from the heritability of IQ issue) surely comes close to being a clinching refutation of the race differences position. (Richards, 1997: 274)

Despite this, psychologists insist on resurrecting this debate, and recycling the same old arguments every so often. In the past decade alone, we have witnessed the furor and public controversy generated by Herrnstein and Murray (1994) and Rushton's (1994) claims regarding 'racial' differences in intelligence.

It is perhaps this debate on 'race' and IQ, more than any other issue, which has shaped the view that psychology as a discipline has contributed significantly to the justification and legitimation of racism. In his detailed history of racism and psychology, Richards (1997) contests this characterization of the discipline, arguing that throughout psychology's history, explicitly racist theorizing has always been a minority position, even during the 'hey days' of scientific racism in the early 1900s, and more recently, during the height of the race and IQ controversies. Indeed, Richards argues that it was the failure of scientific racism as a paradigm within psychology that 'enabled contemporary US psychologists to really begin to *see* racism (a term only dating from 1936) as a phenomenon ... to be recognized and articulated as a problem within and for Psychology' (1997: 112).

Other commentators, however, have not been so generous in their assessments, claiming that psychology has been and continues to be inherently racist (Bhavnani and Phoenix, 1994; Billig, 1979, 1985; Hopkins et al., 1997; Howitt and Owusu-Bempah, 1994). These critics are not only concerned with explicit and extreme forms of racist theorizing that attract considerable attention and criticism, but more subtle variants of racism that underlie mainstream concepts and theories that are widely accepted. Black psychologists such as Mama (1995) and Cross (1991), have argued that much of the anti-racism theorizing that took place in the US post-war period simply replaced the old stereotype of African-Americans as biologically inferior, with a new stereotype that viewed them as 'damaged victims' of White racism. This construction of African-Americans as primarily socially dysfunctional and culturally deprived persists today and is implicit in much contemporary psychology. A recent review by Garcia Coll and colleagues (1996), for example, has argued that research on children from minority cultures focuses overwhelmingly on what are theorized to be developmental 'deficits'. Perhaps one of the most insidious and persistent forms of racism within psychology is the uncritical acceptance of White middle-class values, behavioural patterns, and performance as 'norms' against which all other groups are measured and compared (Sanson, Augoustinos, Gridley, Kyrios, Reser, and Turner, 1998).

Like the distinction that has been made between old and modern forms of racism (see Chapter 2), critics have also argued that dominant mainstream theorizing on race and prejudice contain elements of the 'new racism'. Specifically, Hopkins, et al. (1997) draw parallels between some of the central tenets of social cognition research and the new racism. Both social cognition and the new racism assume that 'race' is a natural category which people automatically use to categorize self and others. Far from being socially constructed and strategically deployed for social and ideological ends (see LeCouteur and Augoustinos, Chapter 13), race becomes a 'non-problematic 'given' which is ... somehow inherent in the empirical reality of observable or imagined biological difference' (Hopkins et al., 1997: 70). Within the social cognition tradition, 'racial' categorizations are theorized to be similar to other kinds of categorizations, driven by our cognitive and perceptual need to simplify complex sensory information from the social environment. In this way, racial categorization becomes a natural and inevitable human cognitive process, not an ideological and social practice (Augoustinos and Walker, 1998). Social categorizations such as 'race' are conceptualized as laying the cognitive and perceptual foundations for stereotyping and ultimately, discrimination towards dissimilar others. Hopkins and his colleagues argue that there are disturbing conceptual similarities between this social cognitive approach to prejudice and the 'new racism' discourse, both of which construct intergroup differentiation and discrimination as 'human', based on a psychological preference for similar others who share the same values and way of life, and a 'natural' tendency to prejudge dissimilar others, especially those who are 'racially' different (for an alternative analysis see Billig, 1985; Turner, 1999a).

Overview of Prejudice Research

As Duckitt makes clear in his chapter to this volume, a variety of explanations for prejudice and racism have been advanced by social psychologists throughout the 20th century. The prevalence of particular kinds of explanations have shifted during this time depending on wider historical and social factors and the dominance of specific paradigmatic frameworks within social psychology itself. Researchers such as Allport (1954), Ashmore and DelBoca (1981), Simpson and Yinger (1985), and Duckitt (1992) have attempted, in different ways, to categorize the various types of theoretical explanations that have been advanced for prejudice. For example, Allport identifies six types of explanation (historical, sociological, situational, personality, phenomenological, and the stimulus-object level), Ashmore and DelBoca (1981) in their analysis of the stereotyping literature propose psychodynamic, cognitive and socio-cultural levels of analysis, and Simpson and Yinger (1985) identify three distinct levels of explanation for prejudice: the individual, group, and cultural levels. Consistent with these levels of analysis, the sections in this book are organized to reflect personality and socialization (Part II), cognitive (Part III), intergroup (Part IV), and socio-cultural (Part V) approaches.

Individual level theories dominated by the Freudian psychodynamic tradition were most prevalent between 1930 and 1960. From this perspective, prejudice, like other behaviour, was understood as being intrapsychically determined. Unconscious instincts primarily related to sexual and aggressive desires created psychological conflict within the person. In order to reduce tension, the person displaces their aggression onto certain groups and projects their own conflicts onto these targets in order to rationalize and justify their actions. For example, hostility towards members of a particular group is explained in terms of the outgroup's inferiority or violent nature.

Other individual level explanations of prejudice that locate prejudice within the personality are less psychodynamic in nature, placing less emphasis on unconscious and instinctual forces. Such personality-based theories link prejudice to child-rearing and socialization practices. Parent–child relationships with severe and punitive parental discipline can render offspring with an authoritarian personality that is characterized by, amongst other things, rigidity in thinking, intolerance of ambiguity, submissiveness to authority, and suggestibility and gullibility. Those with an authoritarian personality syndrome are also considered more prejudiced (see Heaven, Chapter 6).

Significant limitations have been identified with personality accounts of prejudice. Most notably is the issue of why certain groups rather than others become the target for prejudice by authoritarians or those with pent-up 'free-floating' frustration due to intrapsychic conflict. In addition, such theories neglect the potential interplay between individual psychology and social structural factors in the etiology of prejudice. While there is some recognition that economic and social factors may be elements that contribute to authoritarianism, these issues are never dealt with explicitly or integrated into the psychological analysis.

There is general agreement that cognitive theories of stereotyping have dominated the study of prejudice in the 1980s and 1990s. Ashmore and DelBoca (1981), among others, identify cognitive theories of prejudice as explanations that are primarily located at the individual level of analysis. These view prejudice and racism as inevitable consequences of 'normal' and functional cognitive processes such as categorization and stereotyping. Our limited cognitive capacities, it is argued, make the simplification and generalization of social information necessarily adaptive, so that a group's tendency to view outgroup members as 'all alike' is not surprising. Cognitive mechanisms are thus viewed as the essential foundations to stereotyping and prejudice. Social cognitive approaches place greater emphasis on how social information is encoded, processed, and retrieved from memory than on the specific content associated with particular social groups (Ashmore and DelBoca, 1981). Like the personality approaches, cognitive approaches tend to ignore or downplay the wider social context of intergroup relations.

Intergroup perspectives, such as social identity theory and self-categorization theory, place greater emphasis on the psychology of the group: the social context within which groups interact and the nature of the power and status differentials that shape group life. From this perspective, categorizing and stereotyping are functional not because these processes simplify and reduce information, but because they enrich and elaborate our perception of the social environment and our place within it. These cognitive processes, it is argued, orient us to the 'actualities of social life' and the nature of group relations that exist at any one time.

It is perhaps an irony that among many social psychologists there is a deep-seated denial of the functional reality of the group and its psychological properties. Group-based attitudes and behaviour are considered to be flawed and to represent a less accurate account of social reality than individual-related processes (i.e., personality, cognitive processes). Furthermore, the functional positive outcomes of group life are overlooked and negative human social conflict is understood as the main consequence of group-based identification and interaction (see Oakes and Haslam, Chapter 11; Reynolds and Turner, Chapter 10).

Groups are largely associated with negative features of social interaction (e.g., conformity and the loss of individuality and autonomy), rather than a force that contributes to and enriches social life. It is often assumed that group-based perception – perceiving individuals as group members rather than as individuals – is inherently bad, distorts social reality, and ultimately leads to all sorts of perceptual biases like stereotyping. Stereotyping and prejudice are often constructed within these models as the ultimate consequence of failing to perceive people as individuals with unique characteristics and traits. Group-based approaches, such as social identity and self-categorization theories, fundamentally question these central assumptions of social-cognitive models, by emphasizing the psychological validity of group-based perception.

In contrast to individual and group-based perspectives on prejudice, social psychology has contributed less to structural and institutional theories of prejudice and racism. Cultural theories of prejudice view the internalization of group norms and values and conformity to such norms (as a function of social rewards and punishments), as fundamental in the widespread adoption of prejudiced values within a society (Ashmore and DelBoca, 1981). Furthermore, the acceptance of such norms reinforces particular cultural patterns and relations of dominance. For example, theories of 'symbolic racism' share the common assumption that standards and values that are widely shared within a group can shape prejudice. The emphasis is on prejudice as a social or cultural norm. Even from this cultural perspective however, social psychologists have been more concerned with understanding how broader social and cultural norms are expressed and reflected in the psychology of individual perceivers.

One recent socio-cultural approach to racism that explicitly avoids making claims about the psychology of individual perceivers in its analysis of contemporary prejudice and racism is discursive psychology. Discursive psychology views racism as both interactive and communicative, and as located within the language practices and discourses of a society. It is through everyday language practices, both in formal and informal talk that relations of power, dominance and exploitation become reproduced and legitimated. The analytic site for discursive psychology is the way in which discursive resources and rhetorical arguments are put together to construct different social and 'racial' identities, and to provide accounts that legitimate these differences and identities as 'real' and 'natural'. Discursive psychology locates these language practices or 'ways of talking' at a societal level, as products of a racist society rather than as individual psychological and or cognitive products. The analytic site therefore is not the 'prejudiced' or 'racist' individual, but the discursive and linguistic resources that are available within an inequitable society. While this approach has been able to identify how linguistic resources are combined in flexible and contradictory ways to reproduce and justify racist outcomes, it says very little about the possible underlying psychological processes that are linked to the deployment of specific language practices in specific contexts. That is, it makes no claims regarding 'what is going on inside the person' when using racist discourse.

While Simpson and Yinger (1985) assume that these different levels of explaining prejudice and racism are unproblematic and complementary, others recognize the conceptual difficulties in reconciling the various assumptions that underlie the different approaches (Ashmore and DelBoca, 1981). For example, in what way can a personality approach to prejudice be reconciled with models with a group-based and institutional focus? If the norms of a culture change in a short time frame resulting in increased prejudice (i.e., at times of war) what implications does this have for the personality view? How does a group perspective account for stability in authoritarianism and therefore prejudice? How does the cognitive perspective deal with evidence that the use of stereotypes is not always associated with cognitively efficient outcomes? How does the discursive approach deal with individual subjectivity and accountability in everyday and formal talk around 'race' and difference?

More recently, Duckitt (1992) has attempted to provide a psychological framework for understanding prejudice and racism by integrating individual, group-based and structural approaches. For Duckitt, the psychological account of prejudice begins with the recognition that there are universal cognitive psychological processes that create a potential for prejudice. This potential is elaborated into socially shared patterns of prejudice through the reality of social and intergroup dynamics. Mechanisms of transmission are identified which translate intergroup dynamics to individual group members. However, individual differences in susceptibility to such transmissions are believed to explain why there are variations in the expressions of prejudice despite similar social influences. Several chapters in this book will pick up on the potential that Duckitt identifies for such theoretical integration.

Overview of this Book

Perhaps the clearest message that emerges from the above review is that prejudice and racism are multi-level phenomena that include individual, cognitive, group, and societal/cultural levels of analysis. The parts in this book are structured to reflect the range of analytic approaches in the social-psychological study of prejudice and racism. We should acknowledge however, that we have devoted less space than usual to socio-cognitive theories of prejudice and stereotyping that now dominate social psychology. We believe that these approaches receive considerable attention already within the available literature, while other approaches, in particular intergroup and socio-cultural theories, are under-represented within our discipline. Some of the chapters in this book, while recognizing the contribution that social cognition has made to the study of prejudice, aim to extend this approach by adding a more social perspective. For example, Chapters 7 and 8 in Part III both demonstrate how an intergroup perspective, emphasizing social identity processes, can extend and improve upon mainstream theorizing on the role of affect and attitudes in prejudice and discrimination. In contrast, other chapters are highly critical of the central assumptions of social cognitive theories, leading to a radical reconceptualization of concepts such as categorization and stereotyping (e.g., Chapters 9, 10, and 12). We hope, therefore, that this edited collection will reignite interest in the social and cultural dimensions of prejudice and racism.

Part I: Prejudice and Racism: Defining the Problem, 'Knowing' the Experience

The chapters contained in Part I are primarily descriptive and address the nature and personal experience of contemporary prejudice and racism. In Chapter 2, Iain Walker discusses what has been referred to as the changing nature of racism over the last century. Many social analysts and theorists, including social psychologists, have argued that 'old-fashioned' or 'blatant' racism, which was based on notions of racial superiority and open opposition to racial equality, has now been replaced with a more socially acceptable variant, known generically as 'modern' racism (McConahay, 1982, 1986). There are several theoretical variants of the nature of 'modern' racism which include 'symbolic' (Kinder and Sears, 1981, 1985), 'ambivalent' (Katz and Hass, 1988), 'aversive' (Gaertner and Dovidio, 1986) and 'subtle' racism (Pettigrew and Meertens, 1995). Walker details each of these distinct yet similar theoretical approaches to modern racism and evaluates the overall conceptual adequacy of the modern racism construct.

He then applies this construct to understanding the nature of racism within the Australian social and historical context, reminding us that theories of modern racism have by and large emerged in the US to account for the nature of race relations within that country. How adequate then, are these theoretical approaches in explaining and accounting for race relations in other countries such as Australia? In reviewing the empirical research that has addressed majority group attitudes to Indigenous Australians since the 1940s, Walker concludes that there is no clear, identifiable transition from old to modern racism over this time, but rather, both forms of racism have co-existed. Indeed, he suggests that ambivalence and contradiction have been central features of racist attitudes, beliefs, and practices in Australia since British colonization. Similarly, there is evidence in the US that old and modern forms of racism are not historically distinct but have co-existed.

In Chapter 3, Darren Garvey presents a reflexive analysis of the everyday lived experience of racism from an Indigenous perspective and raises the moral dilemmas majority group members face as observers to such instances. The 'data' that Garvey presents is not the usual data of social psychology: numeric averages on rating scales that measure attitudes or significant interactions drawn from laboratory experiments. Rather, Garvey's chapter contains a number of rich narratives or personal accounts of the everyday lived experience of Indigenous and non-Indigenous Australians. Social researchers have increasingly turned to the analysis of narratives or story-telling accounts to understand how people make sense of their experiences, and construct and negotiate their various social identities (Riessman, 1993). As Garvey emphasizes, as psychologists, we have been trained to be highly suspicious of such personalized accounts, questioning their correspondence to 'what actually happened' or their representativeness. Language-based, interpretative methods such as the study of narratives, however, have been instrumental in 'giving voice' to those individuals and groups who have been traditionally silenced or have gone unheard. The recent *National Inquiry into the Separation of Aboriginal and Torres Strait Islander Children from Their Families* (1997), was instrumental in giving voice to hundreds of Indigenous people whose stories of being forcibly removed from their families and communities brought to the Australian public's attention, the institutionalized racist practices of past government policies. As we write this chapter, the Australian Federal Government has declared that despite the Inquiry's findings, there was no such thing as a 'generation' of stolen children, since only one in ten Indigenous children were removed under these laws! This sentiment is echoed in the letter to *The Cairns Post* (1999) in Chapter 3, whose writer refers to the 'Stolen children' as 'the greatest fraud and con on the planet'. Clearly, such sentiments reflect the difficulty that many Australians have in coming to terms with a racist history.

One of the most recurring themes in the narratives that Garvey presents in Chapter 3 is that of Aboriginal identity. These narratives demonstrate the way in which an Indigenous identity is variously constructed and contested both by majority group members and within Indigenous communities. The writer to *The*

Cairns Post for example, sets up two contrasting categories, 'pretend Aborigines' and 'real Aborigines', in order to challenge and contest the 'authenticity' of those whom identify themselves as Aboriginal (see also LeCouteur and Augoustinos, Chapter 13). Likewise, the rhetorical question in the narrative 'Are you 1/8th or what?' provides a rich and detailed account of the constant questioning and scrutiny Indigenous people encounter over their identity. The narrative, 'Going back to school', again highlights the experience of negotiating and constructing an Indigenous identity in Australia today, the constant shifting from being constructed as 'different' and 'other' to being denied an Aboriginal identity when one's physical appearance 'belies' this categorization. Currently in Australia, 'reconciliation' between Indigenous and non-Indigenous Australians has been at the forefront of political and social debate. In this spirit, Garvey concludes his chapter by offering us some possibilities for 'bridging the divide' between Aboriginal and White Australia.

Part II: Development, Socialization, and Personality

Part II includes chapters that primarily deal with personality and socialization approaches to the study of prejudice and racism. It also aims to present the extensive empirical work that has been conducted on the development of prejudice and racism in children. In Chapter 4, Drew Nesdale reviews the now voluminous literature on prejudice in children. The dramatic 'Black doll/White doll' research by the Clarks in the 1940s clearly indicated that by age four children demonstrated racial awareness, could differentiate between different racial groups and identify their own group membership. Moreover, these young children also demonstrated a strong preference for their own group. The Clarks' work inspired a long tradition of research that was to follow in the measurement of ethnic prejudice in children. Nesdale reviews the various techniques and methods that have been used to measure ethnic prejudice in children, including the ethnic preference technique, trait attribution, interviews, unobtrusive observation and implicit measures. Clearly, the task of developing an ecologically valid method and instrument to measure ethnic prejudice in children still remains elusive as all methods have proved to be problematic. Nonetheless, most of this research has confirmed that children show an increasing preference for their own group up until seven years of age, with many studies reporting a decline in ethnic bias thereafter. The critical issue that remains unresolved however, is whether a child's ingroup preference should be equated with outgroup prejudice. We will see throughout this book that this is a conceptual problem that plagues much of the intergroup relations literature.

Nesdale then reviews the theoretical approaches that have been applied to understand the development of ethnic prejudice in children, the most notable of which are Aboud's (1988) socio-cognitive theory and Tajfel and Turner's (1979) social identity theory. Nesdale considers the relative strengths and limitations of these theories in accounting for the development of ethnic prejudice in children, concluding that while each offers critical insights that the other lacks, social identity theory is better placed to understand the development of a 'full-blown' prejudiced identity among older children.

In contrast to the development of prejudice and ethnic bias in children, Chapter 5, by Julie Robinson, Rivka Witenberg, and Ann Sanson, reviews the existing literature on the development of 'tolerance' in children. As Robinson, et al. make clear, this is no easy task, given the definitional ambiguities surrounding the notion of tolerance and the methodological problems associated with its measurement. While racial and cultural tolerance is often a value espoused in multicultural societies like Australia, there is a growing disaffection with this term and its implied meaning of 'putting up' with dissimilar others (Hage, 1998). Nevertheless, it still remains a widely used word that can shift from weak (putting up with) to strong (full acceptance) versions of the term.

The previous chapter documented the now long tradition of developmental research that has concluded that ethnic prejudice and bias is evident in very young children. In reviewing the same body of literature but focusing on the other side of the coin (the absence of prejudice), Robinson, et al., conclude that many of these studies 'have obscured evidence that an absence of ethnic and racial bias is also commonly observed among young children' (p. 78). By focusing one-sidedly on the presence of bias, many of these studies downplay the considerable individual differences that exist between children and how the presence or absence of bias varies contextually. As Nesdale indicated in Chapter 3, studies that focus on children's play interactions and friendship patterns, rather than trait attributions and preferences for abstracted stimuli such as dolls and pictures, show considerably less bias and evidence for ethnic tolerance and acceptance. This paints a much more optimistic and perhaps balanced picture of young children's capacity for ethnic acceptance. Robinson et al. next examine the cognitive factors and socialization experiences that appear to influence the development of tolerance in children. Finally, Robinson and her colleagues consider adolescence as a particularly important period for the development of political tolerance and tolerance for those with different beliefs, suggesting that this research may throw light on the development of ethnic tolerance and acceptance during adolescence. Their review suggests that education, cognitive skill, and moral development are factors that combine in complex ways to influence the acceptance of differences between groups.

As Patrick Heaven documents in Chapter 6, the publication of *The Authoritarian Personality* by Adorno and his colleagues in 1950 was an influential psychological contribution to understanding prejudice. Reflecting the intellectual influence of psychodynamic theory at that time, this groundbreaking book generated considerable interest in the idea that ethnocentrism, and more specifically prejudice, could be accounted for by intrapsychic processes and personality characteristics. While the early work demonstrated that authoritarianism, as measured by the F scale, was significantly related to ethnocentrism, anti-Semitism, and fascist tendencies, by the end of the 1950s, psychologists were beginning to question the extent to which personality could account for these. Pettigrew (1958), among others, pointed to the greater importance of social and cultural norms that in some societies, such as apartheid South Africa, tolerated and reinforced prejudiced attitudes. As Heaven details, these conceptual concerns, together with the proliferation of criticisms associated with the psychometric properties of the F scale, led to the eventual decline of interest in authoritarianism during the late 1960s and 1970s.

However, interest in authoritarianism was rekindled in 1981 with the introduction of Altemeyer's work on right wing authoritarianism (RWA). While clearly related to the original concept of authoritarianism, RWA referred more specifically to a rigid adherence to social conventions, submission to established authorities, and a strong rejection of outgroups who are perceived to be culturally and ethnically different. Unlike Adorno et al., whose work was heavily influenced by Freudian psychodynamic theory, Altemeyer viewed RWA as an individual personality characteristic that was predominantly shaped by social learning experiences. Heaven's review concludes that the instrument Altemeyer developed to measure RWA has proven to be a better predictor of racial and ethnic prejudice in a variety of different settings than the early authoritarianism scales.

Finally, Heaven introduces the most recent personality approach in understanding prejudice: social dominance orientation (SDO) (Sidanius, 1993), an individual difference variable that refers to a person's need to maintain their ingroup's superiority and dominance in the social hierarchy. Individuals who are members of dominant groups (e.g., White men) differ in the extent to which they hold attitudes and beliefs that preserve, maintain, and justify their dominance over members of outgroups. Heaven concludes that thus far, SDO has proven to complement the work on RWA, and used together can account for much of the variance (50–60 per cent) in predicting prejudice.

Part III: Social Cognition, Mood, and Attitudes

Part III includes theoretical frameworks that are central to socio-cognitive models of prejudice and attitudes. Gaining momentum in the 1980s, and becoming firmly established in the 1990s, cognitive processing models of stereotyping have been very influential in shaping psychology's approach to the study of prejudice. In Chapter 7, Vance Locke and Lucy Johnston review this tradition of research, outlining the conceptual rationale that has led many psychologists to view categorization and stereotyping as the cognitive bases to prejudice. As Locke and Johnston argue, such cognitive approaches have usually implied that prejudice is an inevitable consequence of our perceptual and cognitive processes. It was not until Devine's (1989) pioneering work that this 'inevitability of prejudice' perspective, inherent in most social cognitive approaches, was challenged. Devine's disassociation model argued that while everyone has knowledge of the stereotypes associated with particular social groups and that these are automatically activated; at a conscious level, high-

and low-prejudice people differ significantly regarding the use and application of these stereotypes in their judgements and evaluations. Low-prejudice people were argued to consciously inhibit stereotypes, whereas high-prejudice people did not because they usually agreed with the content of these stereotypes.

Despite Devine's more optimistic position on the relationship between stereotyping and prejudice, the disassociation model nevertheless continued to argue that everyone, regardless of his or her values and beliefs, was prone to having stereotypes automatically activated. In their review of more recent empirical work however, Locke and Johnston conclude that it is only the highly prejudiced that are susceptible to automatic stereotyping; those low in prejudice are less prone to stereotyping at both the automatic and conscious levels of processing. While this is good news, there is a growing body of literature that suggests that all of us, regardless of our beliefs, can be influenced by stereotypes when they are activated beyond our awareness. 'Implicit stereotyping' (Greenwald and Banaji, 1995) can not only influence our judgements, but also our behaviour. Locke and Johnston consider the situations in which such implicit stereotyping is likely to occur and how contextual cues shape its expression.

Finally, given the proposed centrality of stereotyping to prejudiced judgments, Locke and Johnston consider what the literature suggests about the possibility of changing stereotypes and thereby minimizing their prejudicial consequences. While much of this research has suggested that people are likely to subtype disconfirming instances of a category, concluding that stereotypes are highly resistant to change, Lucy Johnston's own work has demonstrated that under certain conditions people can resist their use and even change their stereotypes. Overall, Locke and Johnston's chapter illustrates how central theoretical constructs in the stereotyping literature that were originally shaped by a model of the ordinary perceiver as a 'cognitive miser' (Fiske and Taylor, 1991), have more recently shifted to the view that we are all 'motivated tacticians' (Fiske, 1998) who strategically process information in ways that best suit our motivational needs, attentional resources, and personal beliefs and interests.

Negative feelings and affect towards minority outgroups have always been viewed as central to prejudice, but the cognitive accounts of prejudice that came to dominate social psychology since the 1970s, either ignored or downplayed affective determinants. As Baird and Duck emphasize in Chapter 8, there has been a recent resurgence of interest in how emotions and mood influence social judgements and intergroup behaviour more generally. 'The politics of gut feeling' is back on the research agenda, suggesting, not surprisingly, that negative affect can increase stereotyping, prejudice, and discrimination (Esses and Zanna, 1995; Forgas and Fiedler, 1996; Mackie and Hamilton, 1993). In a series of four minimal group studies, Baird and Duck investigate the conditions under which a negative transient mood enhances discriminatory intergroup behaviour. Study 1 suggests that high-status groups in a negative mood are particularly prone to discriminating against low-status groups. Study 2 found that this tendency to discriminate against low-status groups was further accentuated in the high-status, negative-mood condition, if participants were given explicit instructions to favour their own group, thereby mitigating any social norms against discrimination. Moreover, these participants enjoyed the task more and reported feeling better after discriminating than those who were instructed to be fair or to favour the outgroup. This finding suggests that in negative moods, discriminating against an outgroup functions in the service of mood repair. Put simply, it makes people feel better. Study 3 demonstrated that the tendency for intergroup discrimination in negative mood conditions can be attenuated by instructing participants to deliberate over their intergroup judgements and to reflect upon how their mood may affect these judgements. Thus, in transient negative moods, intergroup discrimination can be minimized by longer, deliberative processing. Lastly, Study 4 examined more directly the view that discrimination is motivated by a need to regulate affect, specifically, to repair a negative transient mood. Participants in a negative mood who were led to believe that their mood would be labile after the ingestion of a drug (placebo) showed more discrimination, and felt significantly better after discriminating than those who believed their mood was temporarily fixed. Baird and Duck conclude that for high-status groups in a negative mood, 'discrimination against outgroups is a successful strategy of affect control' (p. 142): that is, discriminating makes high-status individuals in a negative mood feel better! Together, these series of studies demonstrate that the need to feel better can accentuate discriminatory behaviour in particular intergroup contexts.

In Chapter 9, Deborah Terry, Michael Hogg, and Leda Blackwood examine the role that social norms play in the expression of prejudiced attitudes and discriminatory behaviour. At least since LaPiere's (1934) classic study on racial attitudes and discriminatory behaviour, social psychologists have recognized that there is no simple and straightforward link between people's expressed attitudes and their behaviour. The theories of reasoned action (Fishbein and Ajzen, 1975) and planned behaviour (Ajzen, 1987, 1991) were formulated to understand this complex relationship more fully, recognizing that people's behavioural intentions were influenced not only by their attitudes but also by the subjective norms held by significant others towards the behaviour. Terry and her colleagues extend upon this formulation by applying the central theoretical constructs of social identity theory (Tajfel and Turner, 1979) and self-categorization theory (Turner et al., 1987). Together, these theories suggest that people are more likely to express prejudicial attitudes behaviourally if such attitudes are consistent with the social norms for a group to which the person belongs (ingroup), and with which they strongly identify. Such group membership conditions provide strong motivations for a person to express xenophobic or ethnocentric attitudes behaviourally because by doing so the person not only validates their own self-concept but also their status as an ingroup member. The motivation to express behaviourally such attitudes towards minority groups is further enhanced under conditions of status uncertainty and insecurity. Typically, members of dominant groups are likely to express ethnocentric attitudes and behaviour when they feel their social position is under threat in some way. This then provides the legitimation and justification for the expression of prejudicial attitudes and behaviour towards minority outgroups.

Terry et al. apply these ideas in a laboratory experiment and field survey, both of which provide support for the role of ingroup norms and salient group identity as determinants for the behavioural expression of ethnocentric attitudes. Importantly, Terry and her colleagues argue that these largely social and intergroup factors can account for the historical shifts and changes during the twentieth century in racial and ethnic 'tolerance'. Historical periods, such as the 1990s, that were characterized by increases in racism and ethnic intolerance in Australia and other Western countries, reflect shifts in the wider ideological or normative climate for the behavioural expression of such views. In such periods, members of dominant groups perceive ideological shifts in wider community norms regarding multiculturalism and ethnic tolerance that are then used to legitimate the behavioural expression of prejudice and intolerance.

Part IV: Prejudice and Group Life

The chapters in Part IV are all explicitly intergroup in their analyses of prejudice. One of the most influential analyses of intergroup discrimination stems from the minimal group studies (Tajfel et al., 1971). Several authors throughout this book refer to these studies in order to highlight that the division of people into two arbitrary groups is sufficient to stimulate discrimination that favours members of one's own group over members of the other group. Kate Reynolds and John Turner, in Chapter 10, provide a detailed description of these studies and their implications for understandings of intergroup discrimination. Both social identity theory and self-categorization theory have their origins in the minimal group research and these theories, their similarities and differences, are described in detail.

The theoretical and empirical focus of the chapter is the role of group-based processes and intergroup relations in understanding prejudice, discrimination, and social conflict. Groups are 'real' and have psychological significance for members. Consequently, individuals' collective psychology as group members, their social identity, in interplay with the realities of group relations within a social system are believed to be important in trying to understand both social antagonism and individual psychology.

It is argued that social antagonism is not an outcome of irrationality, cognitive deficiency, and personality-based pathology, as many theories suggest, but is rather a psychologically rational and valid outcome of the way members of certain groups perceive the social structure of intergroup relations. In these terms, prejudice can be viewed as an outcome of genuine political and social conflict. In line with this analysis, the authors question how theories that view conflict in the form of prejudice as an outcome of psychological deficiency can explain the important functional aspects of social disagreement and debate.

One of the central features of the self-categorization theory is its analysis of the categorization process. Penny Oakes and Alex Haslam use this analysis in

Chapter 11 to advance our understanding of a recurrent issue in prejudice and racism research, the relationship between categorization and prejudice. A widely accepted view is that because categorization enables people to be divided into ingroups and outgroups, 'us' and 'them', it is the primary source of intergroup hostility and prejudice. Such a position is reinforced by the belief that along with ingroup-outgroup categorization there is inevitably going to be evaluative bias – 'we are better then them'. Such discrimination is considered by many either to represent prejudice or to be the genesis of prejudice. For these reasons, the authors focus on the question of whether we are prejudiced because we categorize.

In trying to answer this question, Oakes and Haslam examine the nature of the categorization process. Theory and research that portrays categorization as a process that distorts and biases group-based social perception, is contrasted with work that argues that categorization is a sense-making, rational process that underlies all perception. This latter view is based on the self-categorization theory analysis that social life is an outcome of the actions of groups as well as individuals and that both must be able to be meaningfully represented psychologically. Four areas that are commonly used to support the contention that categorization compromises accuracy are discussed: accentuation effects, outgroup homogeneity, information construal, and ingroup favouritism or bias. In addition, for each, the opposite case, that such effects represent the functional and adaptive aspects of categorization, is also presented.

It is concluded that categorization has no special relationship to phenomena such as bigotry, intergroup hostility, and prejudice. Categorization is also demonstrated to be associated with individuated perception, prejudice reduction, and cooperation. Consequently, it is considered misleading to look to categorization itself as the culpable force in prejudice. Rather, the authors ask us to consider the reality of intergroup conflict and the extent to which political action has the potential to provide the real answer to racism and prejudice.

In line with a group-based analysis of prejudice, Michael Platow and Jackie Hunter in Chapter 12 ask 'doesn't real intergroup conflict over material and valued resources have anything to do with prejudice?' In order to reach the conclusion that 'it does' they review Sherif et al.'s famous boys' camp studies, known replications of this research, as well as work on social interdependence theory. The boys' camp studies demonstrated that negative attitudes and prejudice arise when groups (of similar power and status) are in competition for scarce resources and their interests are incompatible (e.g., negative interdependence – one group gains and the other group loses). However, tolerance and fairness prevail in situations in which group interests are compatible and complementary; where groups share superordinate goals (e.g., positive interdependence – one group gains only with the assistance of another group).

The conditions that drive competition or cooperation have been explored further within mixed-motive interdependence research. While such research indicates that groups are more likely to pursue competition than cooperation, findings also suggest that realistic conflict may not be a necessary condition for negative intergroup attitudes. Such conclusions find additional support from a number of areas including Tajfel et al.'s minimal group research.

Nonetheless, Platow and Hunter highlight that despite criticisms and limitations, realistic conflict remains a core source of prejudice. The way in which desired resources are distributed in social systems characterized by power and status differentials, raises issues about distributive justice rules and notions of fairness. In addition, the authors raise the paradox inherent in the realistic conflict work, namely that competition over resources can lead to unfair distributions within a social system, intergroup conflict and protest regarding the distribution, which can lead to prejudiced attitudes and behaviour. Therefore, there is a need to address the real conflict over valued outcomes rather than simply encourage superordinate goals and cooperation.

Part V: The Language and Rhetoric of Racism

Part V presents both discursive and rhetorical approaches to understanding social psychological phenomena such as prejudice and racism. In Chapter 13, Amanda LeCouteur and Martha Augoustinos provide an overview of the discursive approach. Discourse analysis focuses on the constructive nature of language and the role that the context of interaction plays in language use. Variability in language and the purposes such variability serve are of primary interest. It is argued that language is used to achieve certain ends and therefore is an active, dynamic, context-dependent outcome of social interaction. From this perspective, language is not simply the product of cognition, a medium through which to study the contents of the mind. Rather, language itself is the instrument of thought and therefore has no meaning independent of the context in which it is used. Consequently, on both philosophical and practical grounds that are elaborated in the chapter itself, discursive psychologists reject the experimental method and associated techniques such as surveys, attitude scales, and questionnaires. The preferred material for inquiry is text and talk, either produced in everyday conversation or via mediums of public communication (i.e., media, parliament).

This chapter also details the discursive approach to categorization – how categories are constructed in talk strategically to achieve certain social actions for the perceiver (i.e., blaming, accusing, justifying). As such, social categorizations are not treated as stable or fixed, reflecting 'real' and valid group entities in the world (such as 'race'), but socially constructed and negotiated in order to define the reality under discussion.

Chapter 13 also reviews the work that has been conducted thus far on racist discourse in New Zealand, The Netherlands, and Australia. This research has identified common patterns of talk and argumentative strategies that are used by majority group members to construct various minority groups negatively. In particular, such discursive analyses have found that liberal and egalitarian arguments are put together in ways that rationalize and justify social inequalities and racist outcomes. In this respect, there are similarities between these findings and contemporary theories of modern racism. However, unlike theories of modern racism that construct prejudice and racism as an internal psychological state located in individuals or groups, the discursive approach locates racism primarily within societal structures and the dominant discourse of a society. As such, discursive approaches have the potential to change institutional practices and unmake racist realities.

Chapter 14, by Mark Rapley, also highlights the unique contribution discursive psychology can make to matters of 'race' and racism. As well as outlining the interest and scope of discursive work, this approach is contrasted with mainstream social cognition and self-categorization theory analyses of prejudice and racism. It is maintained that both social cognition and self-categorization theory portray prejudice as an inevitable outcome of human cognitive structure and therefore excuses racists from being accountable for their attitudes and actions (but see Fiske, 1993; Oakes, Haslam, and Turner, 1994; Oakes and Haslam, Chapter 11).

In addition, an analysis is provided of the way the meaning of categories such as 'racist' and 'racism' is contested and actively negotiated. Along these lines, detailed examination of speeches by two Australian politicians, Pauline Hanson and John Howard reveals that issues of racism are explicitly addressed in order to recast the meaning of the term 'racist'. Amongst other things, racially negative views are redefined as the ordinary, common sense response of Australians to difficult and complex 'racial' issues such as Indigenous land rights.

Furthermore, there is evidence that racism is linked to principles such as 'colour-blind' equity and fairness and also that being able to talk about race issues is a sign of maturity, reasonableness and common sense on the part of the speaker. In Rapley's terms, 'doing equity' accomplishes discrimination without 'being racist'. In this way, Rapley demonstrates that aspects of political talk are consistent with the sentiments of modern racism, but that explicit engagement with the topic of racism itself is inconsistent with this analysis.

Part VI: Future Directions

The emphasis of this book is to present different social psychological approaches to understanding prejudice. Thus, an understanding of personality, cognitive processes, intergroup dynamics, and the discursive practices of a society is fundamental to developing effective interventions aimed at moderating prejudice. The chapters in Part VI aim to piece these different perspectives together with the hope of providing an integrated framework for understanding the psychology of prejudice and racism.

In Chapter 16, John Duckitt examines the question of whether it is possible to reduce prejudice and racism. Three causal processes, each relevant to a different level of analysis, (a) individual-differences in susceptibility, (b) interpersonal contact experiences and exposure to certain social influences, and (c) intergroup relations and changing social conditions, are identified as being central to modification of prejudice attitudes and actions.

In this chapter, the multi-level analysis of prejudice that stems from Duckitt's historical analysis of the study of prejudice is used to explain prejudice reduction. At the individual level, programmes aimed at changing individuals' (a) prejudiced attitudes (e.g., racism awareness training) and (b) potentiality for prejudice (e.g., authoritarianism) are discussed. Interventions designed to change social norms of prejudice and discrimination (e.g., mass media, education curricula) are reviewed in the section on interpersonal level interventions. Mass persuasion campaigns and the success and failure of intergroup contact in work and school settings, both examples of interventions at the interpersonal level, are examined. Duckitt highlights that social structure has the most powerful influence on the parameters that govern interventions at lower levels. Societal norms, defined through institutional practices, are identified as central to prejudice reduction. Along these lines, anti-discrimination legislation, equal opportunity programmes, affirmative action, a society characterized by security and social stability, as well as social justice, are all social-structural mechanisms that can reduce prejudice. In addition, there must be political processes in place that call for social change (e.g., democracy, non-corrupt government, open media, freedom of speech).

In the concluding chapter, Steve Reicher critically reflects upon the different theoretical approaches to prejudice and racism that psychology as a discipline has generated. Rather than adjudicating between each perspective and arriving at a final answer as to which approach is best in accounting for prejudice and racism, Reicher demonstrates how the ways in which we conceptualize and explain these social phenomena have different social and political consequences. Far from being abstract intellectual arguments, there is a lot at stake in the ideas and theories we as social psychologists embrace regarding prejudice and racism. Our theories and concepts have practical consequences that can either contribute to the fight against racism, or alternatively, contribute to the reproduction of racism within our societies. Too often, psychological theories of various persuasions have simply reflected common sense beliefs that intergroup conflict or racism is an inevitable part of human nature, or part of our cognitive 'hard-wiring'. All our theories, argues Reicher, need to be critically examined for taken-for-granted assumptions about the nature of our social world.

A pervasive assumption throughout most psychological theories is that racial categories or racial groups are self-evidently real and therefore it makes sense to categorize people along this 'natural' dimension. As Reicher points out, most individual and social cognitivist accounts of prejudice and racism rarely question this premise at all. In contrast, a social contextual analysis would investigate when, how and why racial categorization (classifying people into racial categories) became a dominant and pervasive social and institutional practice within particular societies. What forms of social and structural organization have encouraged and facilitated such practices and whose interests has it served? The warning is that it is all too easy to view racism as a psychological phenomenon alone, when we ignore the social and historical contexts within which racialization has occurred. Thus, there is nothing inherently natural about 'race' that makes it such a salient form of social categorization. Rather, the 'reality' of a social world organized 'racially' makes it so.

From intergroup perspectives such as social identity and self-categorization theories, the reality of a social world marked by racial categories provides the contextual framework for understanding prejudice and racism. However, these theories have paid less attention to the ways in which our categories construct and shape our understandings of the world. While social constructivist and discursive approaches specifically address this issue, they sometimes neglect to consider how existing forms of social organization and structure provide us with the categories we use to construct and understand our social realities. What are needed, are innovative models and theories that can articulate the complex relationship between racial categories and social reality. In Reicher's view, this will require social psychologists to move beyond the simple use of fixed quantitative methods and techniques, to study the complex and subtle qualities of implicit racial theories and racist action. Overall then, there is more work to be done before we develop an integrated understanding of prejudice and racism. We hope that this book stimulates enough interest among new scholars and researchers to take up this important and exciting challenge.

2 The Changing Nature of Racism: From Old to New?[1]

Iain Walker

The inhabitants of this country are the miserablest people in the world ... [they] have no Houses and skin Garments, no Sheep, Poultry, and Fruits of the Earth, Ostrich Eggs etc ... and setting aside the Human Shape they differ but little from the Brutes ... they have no Cloathes ... their only food is a kind of fish ... I do not perceive that they did worship anything...But all the signs we could make were to no purpose, for they stood like Statues, with no motion but grinned like so many monkeys. (Captain William Dampier, 1688, cited in Stone, 1974: 15)

From what I have seen of the Natives of New Holland they may appear to some to be the most wretched People upon Earth; but in reality they are far more happier than we Europeans, being wholly unacquainted not only with the superfluous, but with the necessary Conveniences so much sought after in Europe; they are happy in not knowing the use of them. They live in a Tranquility which is not disturbed by the inequality of Condition. The Earth and Sea of their own accord furnishes them with all things necessary for Life. They covet no Magnificant Houses, Household stuff, etc; they live in a Warm and fine climate, and enjoy every Wholesome Air, so that they seem to be fully sensible of, for many to whom we gave Cloth, etc, left it carelessly upon the Sea Beach, and in the Woods, as a thing they had no manner of use for; in short they seemed to set no Value upon anything of their own nor any one Article we could offer them. This in my opinion Argues, that they think themselves provided with all the necessarys of Life, and that they have no Superfluities. (Captain James Cook, 1770, cited in Stone, 1974: 15)

There can be no doubt that extreme forms of discriminatory behaviour against Aboriginal Australians have abated over the last fifty to one hundred years. Massacres, systematic poisonings, lynchings, and other forms of brutality against Aboriginal Australians have been well-documented (e.g., Elder, 1988; Tatz, 1999). The general pattern is one of attempted genocide of an Indigenous population by an invading, colonizing, foreign power. Direct brutality generally characterized White settlers' behaviour toward Aboriginal Australians from the time of White invasion until the early decades of the 20th century. Some forms of genocide, such as the forced removal of Aboriginal children from their families and communities, persisted until the 1970s (National Inquiry into the Separation of Aboriginal and Torres Strait Islander Children from their Families (Australia), 1997). Aboriginal Australians were not able to be citizens of Australia, to vote, to hold a passport, and were not counted in the national census until after a 1967 federal referendum (see Bennett, 1985). Indirect brutality persists today, though, as the following statistics attest (ATSIC, 1998). Aboriginal life expectancy is 15–20 years less than for non-Aboriginal Australians. Aboriginal infant mortality rates are 2–4 times higher, and Aboriginal babies are 2–3 times more likely to be of low birth-weight, than for non-Aboriginal Australians. Aboriginal people are over-represented in the criminal justice system by a factor of at least 15. Fewer than one-third of Aboriginal or Torres Strait Islander people complete secondary education, compared with about 70 per cent nationally. The unemployment rate for Aboriginal people is 26 per cent, compared with about 8 per cent nationally. The Aboriginal home-ownership rate is about 30 per cent, compared with about 70 per cent generally.

In this chapter, the general proposition is reviewed and examined that racism has changed from being blatant, direct, and hostile into being subtle and indirect. Social psychology has developed several different analyses of this 'new' racism, and these are briefly presented. The limited available evidence from Australia is then examined for signs that racism against Aboriginal Australians has evolved into a 'kindler, gentler' racism (Bobo et al., 1997; or, following Australian Prime Minister John Howard's lead, a 'more comfortable and relaxed' racism), wary of the limitations on extrapolating from the case of intergroup relations in the US to the case in Australia.

The Changing Nature of Racism?

In the early 1970s, American social psychologists claimed that the nature of European American racism against African-Americans was changing (e.g., Sears, 1988). Once, race relations were characterized by 'red-necked', blunt, hostile, segregationist, and supremacist views. But these views apparently became less openly acceptable to European Americans in the 1960s, coinciding with the rise of the civil rights movement in that country. Instead, European Americans endorsed egalitarianism. They always had, of course, at least in rhetoric. The flight from persecution in the Old World led to a commitment, enshrined in the US Constitution, that 'all men are equal'. Myrdal (1944) noted this feature of American life in his famous work on the 'American dilemma' in the 1940s. The other horn of the dilemma was the unconscionable treatment of African-Americans, and others, as somehow less than human (and hence not equal).

Prior to the American civil rights era of the 1950s and 1960s, the latter of the two horns of the American dilemma dominated European Americans' views of African-Americans. But by the early 1970s, several researchers discerned a notable change, from what came to be known as 'old-fashioned racism' to what was called 'modern racism' (for reviews, see Brown, 1995; Duckitt, 1992; Fiske, 1998; Jones, 1997). Old-fashioned racism was, as already noted, blunt, hostile, segregationist, and supremacist. The 'new' racism was a kind of racism which, paradoxically, endorsed egalitarianism. Social psychological analyses in the US have identified several different, but substantially overlapping, versions of new racism, and these are briefly reviewed in the next section. The idea that racism was/is changing is unique neither to social psychology nor to the US (see, for example, Barker, 1981; de Benoist, 1999; Miles, 1989).

Symbolic Racism and Modern Racism

The first social psychological conceptualization of the 'new' racism was termed *symbolic racism* (Sears and Kinder, 1971; Sears and McConahay, 1973). The construct of *modern racism* was developed by McConahay out of the symbolic racism notion (McConahay, 1982, 1986), and led to the development of the commonly used 'Modern Racism Scale' (McConahay and Hough, 1976). The two approaches are essentially the same, although there are some minor differences. The label 'symbolic' implies that the racism it describes is not quite 'real', although this was far from the intention of Sears and McConahay, who coined the phrase because of the theoretical backdrop of symbolic politics. The term 'modern racism' will be used here to refer to both approaches.

Modern racism has two distinctive features. The first is an outright rejection of the principles of old-fashioned racism. Modern racism rejects segregationism and supremacy, and endorses egalitarianism. But, secondly and somewhat paradoxically, it also rejects African-Americans (and other outgroups). Rejection is a function of anti-Black affect and a strong adherence to traditional values of individualism.

Although many, perhaps even most, European Americans endorse egalitarianism, they retain cultural vestiges of anti-Black affect. Whereas once that affect may have been plain dislike or even disgust, it is now more likely to be anxiety in the presence of African Americans, distrust, fear, hostility, or perhaps just arousal (Stephan and Stephan, 1985, 1993). These affects may not be as strong as earlier forms, but they are, none the less, still negative. This negative affect colours behaviour.

European Americans have often resisted attempts to introduce measures designed to remedy social inequalities which disadvantage African Americans. Affirmative action and busing to desegregate schools are probably the two most notable examples. The net effect of such resistance is continued inequality and disadvantage. Resistance has a racist outcome. Yet the resistors disavow the traditional, old-fashioned form of racism, and claim to be egalitarian. The source of the antagonism is not (usually) a desire to maintain segregation in employment or education. Rather, it is because social programmes such as affirmative action and busing, violate deep-seated, cherished, traditional values. The most important of these values are '...individualism and self-reliance, the work-ethic, obedience, and discipline' (Kinder and Sears, 1981: 416). A modern racist reaction to affirmative action and busing stems from the belief that

African-Americans are benefiting unfairly from social programmes that violate individualism, self-reliance, the work-ethic, obedience, and discipline – all the things that, in a sense, make up the 'American character'. Such programmes are 'unAmerican'.

Modern racism is seen most often and most easily in situations where European Americans are able to discriminate against African-Americans and, simultaneously, maintain an image as non-prejudiced. Thus, opposition to affirmative action or busing programs is because 'I am against reverse discrimination' or 'It is unAmerican', but not because 'I am a bigot'". To paraphrase the title of one influential article in the area, 'it's the buses, not the blacks' (McConahay, 1982).

Most of the research and theoretical work on modern racism has focused on relations between European Americans and African-Americans. However, the concept has been applied in other intergroup contexts – for example, to gender relations (Swim et al., 1995; Tougas et al., 1995), and to 'race' relations in South Africa (Duckitt, 1991), the UK (Brown, 1995), and Australia (Pedersen and Walker, 1997).

Ambivalent Racism

The modern racism perspective assumes unidimensionality in racist attitudes. This has been challenged both empirically, using re-analyses of the data used by modern racism theorists (e.g., Bobo, 1983), and conceptually. Katz and Hass (1988) and Katz et al., (1986) have argued that (majority group) racist attitudes are complex, contradictory, and multidimensional. In the case of prejudice against African-Americans, pro-Black and anti-Black sentiments co-exist within the one (White) individual. The co-existence of positive and negative attitudes constitutes *ambivalence*, which makes individual behaviour patterns unstable, and amplifies both positive and negative reactions to African Americans (Katz and Glass, 1979). The co-existing pro-Black and anti-Black attitudes rest on different value structures held by the individual. Pro-Black attitudes reflect humanitarian and egalitarian values which emphasize equality and social justice; anti-Black attitudes reflect individualistic, Protestant Ethic values of freedom, hard work, individual achievement, and self-reliance.

As Augoustinos and Walker (1995: 233) point out, the ambivalent racism position suggests that racism may be enduring because it is tied so strongly to central cultural values such as individualism and egalitarianism, which themselves may be contradictory. At a practical level, the ambivalent racism position also indicates that interventions designed to increase positive attitudes in the community may work, but will leave prevalent negative attitudes unchanged. Similarly, attempts to decrease negative attitudes will not necessarily lead to strengthened or more prevalent positive attitudes.

Aversive Racism

The ambivalent racism perspective develops a multidimensional, dynamic model of how individual European Americans express attitudes toward African Americans. Developed more or less contemporaneously, the aversive racism perspective provides an alternative, but similar, account of the same phenomena. Building on the psychoanalytic position of Kovel (1970), Gaertner and Dovidio (1977, 1986) distinguish between aversive and dominative racism. *Dominative* racism resembles what the modern racism perspective calls old-fashioned racism: it is blatant, 'red-necked', and overtly discriminatory. In contrast, people who are described as *aversive* racists:

> sympathize with the victims of past injustice; support public policies that, in principle, promote racial equality and ameliorate the consequences of racism; identify with a more liberal political agenda; regard themselves as nonprejudiced and non-discriminatory; but, almost unavoidably, possess negative feelings and beliefs about blacks. (Gaertner and Dovidio, 1986: 62)

The description of aversive racism resembles that of ambivalent racism. Both aversive and ambivalent racists strive to maintain an image, to themselves and to others, of being non-prejudicial. Both accounts are built upon the notion of intra-individual conflict, and both accounts imply that the resolution of the conflict is largely non-conscious. There are differences between the accounts, though. The site of the contradictions is different. From the ambivalent racism perspective, the conflict is between pro- and anti-Black attitude structures and their underlying value systems; from the aversive racism perspective, it is between an openly endorsed egalitarian attitude and value system and negative feelings of 'discomfort, uneasiness, disgust, and sometimes fear, which tend to motivate avoidance rather than intentionally destructive behaviors' (Gaertner and Dovidio, 1986: 63). Gaertner and Dovidio also are not as generous or optimistic as Katz and Hass about the prevalence of genuinely pro-Black attitudes.

Subtle Racism

Building on Allport's (1954) classic analysis of prejudice, Pettigrew and Meertens (1995) and Pettigrew et al. (1998) distinguish between *blatant* and *subtle* prejudice. Derived from theoretical analysis, rather than deduced empirically, Pettigrew and Meertens posit a multidimensional model of both blatant and subtle prejudice. Blatant prejudice, which is 'hot, close, and direct' (Pettigrew and Meertens, 1995: 58), has two components: threat and rejection, and opposition to intimate contact with the outgroup. Subtle prejudice, which is 'cool, distant, and indirect', has three components: the defence of traditional values, the exaggeration of cultural differences, and the denial of positive emotions. Using survey data from almost 4,000 respondents in seven independent probability samples, from four western European countries, Pettigrew and Meertens demonstrate that blatant and subtle prejudice are 'separate but related' constructs, and report evidence from structural equation modelling supporting the proposed multidimensional structure. They also cross-categorize respondents using their scores on blatant and subtle measures, forming distinct categories of *bigots* (high on both), *subtles* (high on subtle, low on blatant), and *equalitarians* (low on both). The category constituted by low scores on subtle and high scores on blatant is assumed to be an error category. Pettigrew and Meertens report large differences across bigots, subtles, and equalitarians in their responses to several different public policy questions dealing with immigration. This type of categorical analysis, joining responses on different scales, seems to be profitable, and one wonders why other researchers using concurrent measures of 'old-fashioned' and 'modern' prejudice have not gone down this analytic path.

Summary

All of the different approaches listed above have somewhat different conceptualizations of the features of contemporary racism in the US. They also have a common core. It is this core that I concentrate on in this chapter, and I avoid the necessarily lengthy and difficult work of trying to integrate these different perspectives or of trying to arbitrate among them. In this chapter, the term 'modern racism' is used to refer generically to the family of similar approaches. In doing so, McConahay's account is not endorsed more than any of the others. Rather, the term is used because of its common currency, and because one of the features of all these approaches is an emphasis on, literally, *modern* racism.

I turn now to a critical evaluation of the construct of modern racism itself, and then examine Australian social psychological evidence on changing patterns of prejudice to see whether the old versus modern distinction makes sense in the Australian context.

Conceptual Adequacy of the Modern Racism Concept

Several criticisms can be, and indeed have been, made of theories of modern racism (see, e.g., Bobo, 1988; Schuman et al., 1985; Sniderman and Piazza, 1993; Sniderman and Tetlock, 1986; Weigel and Howes, 1985; but see also Meertens and Pettigrew, 1997). I briefly summarize some of the more cogent ones here.

1) Proponents of the modern racism perspective often rely on empirical evidence to support their position. This evidence is far from unequivocal however. Generally, measures of old-fashioned and modern racism correlate somewhere between .5 and .6, uncorrected for attenuation due to measurement unreliability (e.g., Hughes, 1997; Pedersen and Walker, 1997; Pettigrew and

Meertens, 1995). In many other areas of psychology, a correlation this size would be taken as evidence for the *similarity,* not *difference,* of the two constructs being measured. Similarly, these same studies often look for different patterns of association between old-fashioned racism and modern racism, on the one hand, and other key criterion variables, on the other. Almost always, the pattern of correlations is the same, but generally measures of modern racism correlate a little more strongly. This may be due to measurement adequacy, and not conceptual clarity, though. Modern racism measures are often claimed to be less reactive than old-fashioned racism measures, and this difference could account for the stronger correlations involving modern racism.

2) The concept of modern racism is supposed to hinge on 'a blend of anti-black affect' and violation of deep-seated norms, at least in Sears' and McConahay's accounts. Studies of modern racism, however, almost invariably neglect affect, and focus exclusively on cognitive judgements. None of the items in McConahay's widely-used Modern Racism Scale (McConahay, 1986), for example, refer to anything that could be construed of as 'affective'. From a measurement perspective, the only exception to this criticism is work only recently done (Hughes, 1997; Pettigrew and Meertens, 1995).

3) Even if we accept that the expression of racism has changed from being blatant, hot, segregationist, and supremacist, to subtle, cool, and with a veneer of egalitarianism, the modern racism approach fails to explain *how* or *why* the expression of racism has changed in this way. It simply describes, and defers the difficult explanatory questions. For this reason, Bobo et al. (1997) explicitly locate their analysis of prejudice within a structural analysis of socioeconomic change (see also Bonilla-Silva, 1996).

4) The modern racism approach tends generally to oversimplify the form and expression of 'old' and 'new' racism, and neglects the multifarious forms of racism at any time. How, for example, could Myrdal have talked of the American dilemma, unless there already existed in the US of the 1930s and 1940s (and, arguably, earlier, dating to the US civil war) egalitarian attitudes, beliefs, values, and ideologies which Sears, McConahay and others later recognized in public opinion?

5) Even if we accept that the modern racism account was a fair depiction of the nature of racism in the US in the late 1960s and 1970s, do we still, a quarter of a century later, want to accept it as a fair depiction of 'modern' racism? Or is it itself now 'old-fashioned', supplanted by something even more modern (postmodern)? If so, why has the dominant theory of racism in social psychology not kept up with the times? And what should it look like now?

Racism in Australia

Difficulties in Importing Concepts

Most of the theoretical and empirical work related to the modern racism concept has been done in the US. As with many other things, there has been a tendency to import and use this concept uncritically. There are many cultural, historical, and social reasons why importing concepts such as modern racism should be done circumspectly (see Banton, 1999, for an elaboration of US 'exceptionalism' in racism and intergroup relations). Although the points I list below refer specifically to the Australian context, they, and other similar points, limit the extent to which US research can apply to *any* other context.

1) African-Americans have a history of transportation into slavery in the US, whereas Aboriginal Australians are Indigenous.

2) Aboriginal Australians were conquered through English invasion; they were not imported to Australia as a cheap labour force (though they were certainly used as such).

3) The genocidal acts accompanying the English invasion were more widespread, and more recent, than the officially sanctioned oppression of African-Americans. Indeed, official acts by state and federal governments in Australia, which are now defined as genocidal, occurred as recently as the 1970s – the same time that authors in the US were noting how old-fashioned racism had declined and was being replaced by modern racism!

4) African-Americans constitute a larger proportion of the US population than Aboriginal Australians do of Australia's population. [2]

5) Despite persistent segregation and discrimination, African-Americans are more visible in everyday life to the European American majority than Aboriginal Australians are to the Anglo Australian majority. However, Aboriginal Australians are perhaps more visible in a 'symbolic' form because of various forms of government services provided to Aboriginal Australians clearly labelled as such (for example, there are no US equivalents of the Aboriginal Affairs Departments which exist at state level in Australia), and because of the official and unofficial expropriation of various Aboriginal cultural symbols, ceremonies, and practices, such as Aboriginal artwork and dancing.

6) The issue of land rights is another notable difference between African-Americans and Aboriginal Australians. Aboriginal claims to land title have featured prominently in the federal and state parliaments and courts, as well as in the media and the public consciousness, throughout the 1990s. African-Americans do not claim any prior 'ownership' of land stolen from them. This issue, and others, constitutes a formidable 'realistic' basis for intergroup

hostilities (see Platow and Hunter, Chapter 12, for a discussion of realistic group conflict theory).

7) Indicators of health and of economic and social well-being are much worse for Aboriginal Australians relative to Anglo Australians than they are for African-Americans relative to European Americans, though the general health and well-being of African-Americans is worse than that of European Americans (Taylor and Repetti, 1997; Williams and Collins, 1995).

8) The US and Australia have different histories of immigration, providing different social climates in which different ethnicities, nationalities, religious groupings, and other social categories interact. Whereas the US had massive waves of migration from Europe in the latter years of the 19th century and the early years of the 20th century, Australia's largest influx of migrants came after the Second World War from Europe, and, since the 1970s, from South-East Asia. The US had no formal equivalent of Australia's White Australia policy governing immigration (though it certainly had other mechanisms to ensure the same ends). The White Australia policy only ended officially in the 1960s.

All these factors, and probably many more, constitute major differences between the US and Australian contexts, and, indeed, between the US and any other context. The social position of Aboriginal Australians resembles that of Native Americans more than that of African-Americans. It is noteworthy that very few studies of prejudice in the US have examined prejudice against Native Americans, and that the edifice of social psychological theories of prejudice (old and new) rests almost completely on relations between European and African-Americans. These factors may make American concepts such as that of modern racism, irrelevant or redundant to Australia, to other countries, and even to relations in the US between dominant and minority groups other than African-Americans. However, assessing this relevance is an empirical question.

An Overview of Australian Research

Social psychology in Australia is a relatively recent development, dating only from the 1950s, and not expanding until the 1970s and 1980s. Consequently, there is not the same wealth of research that there is in the US, documenting patterns of stereotyping, prejudice, and discrimination over the decades. However, there is some pertinent research, which is reviewed in this section with the aim of examining whether and how patterns of prejudice against Aboriginal Australians have changed over the years. In reviewing this evidence, only some relevant representative material is included. Also, in this review, it is important to examine the evidence for *disconfirmatory*, as well as confirmatory evidence. The modern racism literature generally suffers from a tendency only to seek evidence that racism has become more benign, and neither looks for, nor sees, possibly disconfirmatory evidence. As will become apparent, the extant Australian literature contains evidence that 'old-fashioned' and 'modern' forms of racism have co-existed for some time – perhaps, as illustrated by the quotes at the beginning of the chapter, since the first contact between Europeans and the original inhabitants of 'Terra Australis'. Although not documented here, a similar argument could be established using evidence from the US, or from other developed countries. The examples presented in this chapter are local, but the argument holds generally.

Two large studies by Oscar Oeser (Oeser and Emery, 1954; Oeser and Hammond, 1954) almost defined the beginning of Australian social psychology. Oeser and Hammond (1954) examined a sample of 370 people drawn randomly from the electoral rolls in Melbourne in 1948. Conducted just after the end of the Second World War, when Australia's vulnerability to foreign attack and its inability to defend itself were exposed, and soon after the Australian government embarked on a programme of immigration, respondents were asked to indicate how favourably they felt towards particular nationalities as immigrants to Australia. As Table 2.1 reveals, there is a clear social distance hierarchy among the target groups, roughly reflecting the Anglophilic nature of Australia at the time. The position of the Chinese is anomalous here, which Oeser and Hammond (1954) try to explain by turning to the long history of the Chinese in Melbourne, dating from the goldrushes of the 1870s. Since this study concerned immigration, Aboriginal Australians were not included. However, the authors write that:

> Comparable data from children show the same sort of picture with respect to all race groups, including the Chinese groups. The positions of Chinese and of the Australian Aborigine in terms of favourable attitudes seem to be closely similar. It is possible that in general the Chinese and the Aborigines are regarded in some way as *'our local coloured groups'* ... (Oeser and Hammond, 1954: 56, emphasis in original)

Table 2.1 Attitudes to immigration to Australia by different groups

Group	Keep them out	Let only a few in	Allow them to come in	Try to get them to come in
Negro	77%	13%	8%	2%
Jew	58%	25%	13%	4%
Italian	45%	34%	17%	4%
Greek	32%	42%	19%	7%
Chinese	26%	44%	22%	8%
German	30%	34%	24%	12%
Irish	15%	21%	39%	25%
English	1%	8%	29%	62%

Source Based on Oeser and Hammond, 1948: 55, Figure 4. The group names in the table are those presented in the original report.

This point, paternalistic as it is, that the Chinese and the Aborigines are 'our local coloured groups', suggests yet another point of difference between the Australian and US contexts. More important to our present purpose, it implies a degree of (condescending or paternalistic) favourability – *not* outright rejection or hostility – that would not be conferred on a similar group that were 'not ours'.

The data from the children that Oeser and Hammond refer to, come from a study reported by Oeser and Emery (1954). This study was conducted soon after the Oeser and Hammond study, and sampled children from a large town in rural Victoria. The children were asked to describe 'The things I *like* about X are...' and 'The things I *dislike* about X are...', where the Xs were Australians, British, Americans, Aborigines, Chinese, Russians, Jews, Germans, and Japanese. For each target group, responses were classified as either 'acceptance' (some things liked, but nothing disliked), 'rejection' (some things disliked, but nothing liked), or 'ambivalence' (some things liked and disliked).

Table 2.2 shows almost *no rejection* of Aboriginal Australians, but substantial ambivalence. Consistent with the Oeser and Hammond (1954) study, the Chinese were not rejected either. Oeser and Emery concluded:

(i) Racial differences do not appear to be an important dimension [of judgement] (Chinese and Aborigines accepted; Japanese and Jews rejected). (ii) Opposition or potential opposition in war appears to be of major importance for rejecting nations (all the rejected groups have fought in wars against Australia, or are seen as threatening to make war, and even the Jews fought against the British in Palestine during the period of this survey and just before). (iii) There is no consistent anti-minority attitude (Aborigines accepted, Jews rejected).

Table 2.2 Attitudes to different nationalities

Nationality	Acceptance	Ambivalence	Rejection
Australians	49%	51%	0%
British	45%	51%	4%
Americans	33%	54%	13%
Aborigines	26%	72%	2%
Chinese	24%	70%	6%
Russians	15%	28%	57%
Jews	11%	42%	47%
Germans	4%	29%	67%
Japanese	6%	45%	49%

Source Based on Oeser and Emery, 1954: 67, Table 22. The 'nationalities' are referred to here as they are in the original, even though some of the groups do not constitute nations.

(iv) Acceptance appears to be based in some dimension such as common history, rather than on future interdependence or racial similarity (thus Aborigines are more acceptable than Americans). (1954: 68–69)The two Oeser studies show that in the post-war years, non-Aboriginal Australians (or at least those in Victoria) were *not* unambiguously hostile or negative in their views of Aboriginal Australians. They were not overwhelmingly positive, to be sure, as they tended to be about the English, but neither were they overwhelmingly negative. Oeser's data suggest either an indifference or, perhaps more likely, an ambivalent tolerance. A similar conclusion follows from an early study by Ron Taft (1970), in Western Australia (WA).

In 1965, Taft interviewed a random sample from three WA localities: *Bigtown* (a provincial city with a population of about 5,000, including 300 Aboriginal Australians, with a bad record of racial conflict); *Smalltown* (a provincial town of about 1,500 people, including about 75 Aboriginal Australians, and with no record of racial conflict); and *Perth* (the capital city of WA, with a population then of 450,000, including about 1,000 Aboriginal Australians).

Table 2.3 presents a clear social distance hierarchy. 'It is quite clear that Italian immigrants were preferred over Aborigines in all three towns and the general trend is for part-Aborigines to be more acceptable than full-bloods' (Taft, 1970:12).

Table 2.3 Social distance choices (in percentages)

	Part-Aborigines			Full-bloods			Italians		
	Perth	Small	Big	Perth	Small	Big	Perth	Small	Big
Relative by marriage	35	20	24	24	10	14	76	58	64
Friend	76	64	76	62	56	61	93	90	78
Eat at same table	81	82	82	62	60	80	94	96	94
To serve food	83	74	74	66	58	76	98	100	94
Neighbours	78	80	62	63	66	64	94	98	94
Same job	88	92	84	79	74	84	94	96	88
To serve in shop	85	86	84	75	76	84	98	100	98
Live in the state	90	96	94	82	92	96	97	98	98

Source Based on Taft, 1970: 11, Table 1. The group names are those used in the original report.

Also, there was clear evidence of a fairly substantial desire for segregation:

> In all three towns the same places (with one exception) were chosen for segregation. These places might well be seen as the ones in which lack of hygiene would be particularly distasteful, and many of the respondents indicated that if it were not for questions of hygiene they would not advocate segregation at all. (1970: 13)

This response appears to be a curious amalgam of old-fashioned and modern racism. Simultaneously, respondents indicated they thought Aboriginal Australians were unhygienic (an 'old-fashioned' statement'), but were also attempting to express rejection on grounds which were ostensibly not racial (a 'modern' sentiment). Other responses in the study indicate a general acceptance or tolerance of Aboriginal Australians and a belief in equality (see tables in Taft, 1970: 13, 17, and 18). Again, this appears to indicate modern racism. A series of studies conducted by Bochner (1971, 1972; Bochner and Cairns, 1976), using unobtrusive measures to examine prejudice and discrimination, provides mixed evidence. Bochner (1971, Exp. 1) had two young women, one Aboriginal and one 'White', walk a dog on a leash through Hyde Park in Sydney. They were followed by two observers, who recorded 'the frequency of smiles, verbal approaches, and nods directed at the dog-walkers ... Joanne, the 'White' girl was a much more frequent target for communication than Gwenda, the Aboriginal girl' (1971: 111), receiving 50 responses compared to 18 responses in two equal-timed intervals. In the second experiment, two women, one Aboriginal and the other 'White', asked for ten cents' worth of dog bones at 14 different butchers' shops throughout a busy, middle-class shopping centre in eastern Sydney where Aboriginal people did not normally shop. The bones were weighed and rated for quality on a three-point scale by an experienced dog-lover blind to the purposes of the experiment. The mean weight and quality were not significantly different between the two women, although the slight differences did favour the White woman. Together, these two studies fail to provide unequivocal evidence either way about old-fashioned or modern racism: one provides evidence of discriminatory behaviour, the other not.

Bochner (1972) placed two advertisements for accommodation in the 'Wanted to Rent' column of a Sydney paper. Both advertisements read the same, except for a single crucial difference: viz, 'Young [Aboriginal] couple, no children, want to rent small unfurnished flat up to $25 per week. Saturday only. 759-6000 [759-6161]' (1972: 335). A total of 22 phone calls were received, 17 to the 'neutral' and 5 to the 'Aboriginal' advertisement. Three of these 22 had responded to both advertisements. These differences were significant, indicating a bias against Aboriginal accommodation seekers (i.e., blatant discrimination).

Finally, Bochner and Cairns (1976) adapted the lost-letter technique of Milgram et al. (1965), and included with the letter a photograph to vary 'race'. The study had a 2 x 2 design, varying 'race' of letter-loser, and status of suburb the letter was lost in (high status or low status). They expected that 'suburb status' and 'race' would interact such that fewer 'Black' than 'White' envelopes would be returned in the low-status suburb, and the same proportions would be returned in the high-status suburb. But, the interaction was somewhat different. The low-status suburb only returned 30 per cent of the lost letters, but favoured 'White' (60 per cent) over 'Black' (40 per cent) envelopes. About half the letters lost in the high-status suburb were returned, and twice as many 'Black' envelopes (66 per cent) than 'White' (34 per cent) were returned. In terms of old-fashioned and modern racism, we again have mixed evidence: the low-status suburb demonstrated blatant discrimination against Aborigines; but the high-status suburb discriminated in *favour* of Aborigines.

A group led by Vic Callan and Cindy Gallois at the University of Queensland conducted several studies throughout the 1970s and 1980s on stereotypes and prejudice. In one such study, Gallois et al. (1982) used a large sample of psychology undergraduates to look at the relationship between ethnocentrism (measured with the Beswick and Hills, 1969, scale) and evaluations of Aboriginal Australians, Russians, Greeks, and Anglo Australians. They reported consistent differences in favourability ratings and social distance ratings of these four groups across people categorized as high, medium, or low in ethnocentrism (using a tritile split). Rather than focus on these differences here, I want to make a point about the absolute levels of the different ratings. The lowest favourability ratings given by any subjects were by the high ethnocentrics toward Australian Aborigines ($M = 2.59$) and Russians ($M = 2.49$). These means are on a four-point scale, from 1 = low favourability to 4 = very favourable. These two means are at about the midpoint of the scale (2.5) – that is, these highly ethnocentric subjects were not negative in their ratings, they were just neutral, or rather, they were not as positive in their ratings as they were for the other groups. Similarly for the social distance ratings. The lowest ratings were once again provided by the high ethnocentric subjects rating Australian Aborigines ($M = 3.15$) and Russians ($M = 3.08$). These ratings are on a five-point scale, where 1 = 'I would prefer not to associate with this group at all', 3 = 'I would be happy to work with or do business with someone who is a member of this ethnic group', and 5 = 'I would be happy marrying, or having a family member marry, a member of this ethnic group'. The means are just above the scale midpoint, representing 'moderate closeness', and do not represent antipathy to these groups at all. So, once again, there is evidence of tolerance or acceptance of Australian Aborigines, but simultaneously also evidence of discrimination. However, the discrimination does not involve greater negativity, but rather less positivity (see also Fiske, 1998; Gaertner and McLaughlin, 1983).

The studies by Oeser and Hammond (1954), Oeser and Emery (1954), Taft (1970), Bochner (1971, 1972), Bochner and Cairns (1976), and Gallois et al. (1982) all demonstrate a degree of tolerance and acceptance of Aboriginal Australians since the Second World War, but also demonstrate evidence of prejudice and discrimination. These studies use a variety of cross-sectional methods and measures that make difficult the task of discerning any change in prejudice over time. To my knowledge, there are no longitudinal studies of prejudice in Australia. However, some survey studies use comparable sampling methods and ask the same or similar questions at different times, and these studies are better able to reveal broad social changes in prejudice over time.

Some questions have been asked repeatedly in surveys by the Gallup organization (Gallup, 1974, 1976, 1978, 1981). I report here results from a couple of questions, over the period in which the greatest change in racial attitudes purportedly occurred (according to modern racism theorists). Table 2.4 shows a breakdown of responses to the questions 'Do you believe Australia's Aborigines suffer from unjust treatment a lot, or a little, or not at all?', in 1974 and 1981, and Table 2.5 shows responses to a question asking about the amount being done for Aborigines by Australian governments, in 1976, 1978, and 1981. Responses to these two questions show that a clear and sizeable majority (more than three-quarters) of Australians believe that Aboriginal Australians suffer from unjust treatment, and that only a minority (less than one-fifth) believe that the governments are doing too much for Aboriginal Australians. Responses also show a remarkable stability across time – a time when beliefs about racism and prejudice were purportedly changing rapidly. These two poll questions, then, suggest a fair degree of tolerance that did not change much through the 1970s.

Table 2.4 Responses to the question 'Do you believe Australia's Aborigines suffer from unjust treatment a lot, or a little, or not at all?' in nationwide Gallup Polls in 1974 and 1981.

Aborigines suffer from unjust treatment		
	1974	1981
A lot	38	
A little	40	79
Not at all	19	19
Don't know	3	2

Note The 1981 poll combined the two response categories of 'a lot' and 'a little' into a single category. The 79 per cent at the top of the 1981 column therefore should be compared with the 78 per cent combined totals of the 'a lot' and 'a little' categories in the 1974 poll.

Table 2.5 Responses to the question 'Is the amount being done for Aborigines by governments ...?' in nationwide Gallup Polls in 1976, 1978, and 1981.

Amount being done for Aborigines by governments is:		
	1976	1978	1981
Too much	16	17	18
Not enough	50	44	50
About the right amount	25	28	25
Doing nothing right/ What they're doing is done in the wrong way	2	2	–
Don't know	7	9	7

A series of studies by Western (1969), Larsen (1978, 1981), Walker (1994), and Pedersen and Walker (1997) uses the same or similar questions in surveys of different communities throughout Australia and at different times over the last three decades. Table 2.6 summarizes the percentage of respondents in each study agreeing with items common across these studies. The two surveys reported by Western (1969) reveal high levels of prejudice – much higher than in any of the other studies, and certainly much higher than in Walker (1994) using the same questions. The Western (1969) surveys were both conducted in country towns in New South Wales, and were both conducted earlier than the other studies and at about the same time as the nationwide referendum allowing the federal parliament to pass laws for the welfare of Aboriginal Australians. The studies by Larsen (1978, 1981) and Walker (1994) reveal fairly stable patterns of prejudice, especially between Larsen's (1981) study and Walker's (1994) study. Generally, these survey studies reveal substantial amounts of prejudice in Australian communities. Most of the items reported in Table 2.6 are blatantly prejudicial, and responses to them ought to be susceptible to various reactivity and social desirability effects. If anything, then, the percentage agreement data in Table 2.6 underestimates the prevalence of prejudice in the various communities surveyed. Normally, self-report data on questions such as these should reveal much lower levels of prejudice than is obtained using various subtle or unobtrusive measures of prejudice (Crosby et al., 1980). However, these surveys tend to paint a bleaker picture than do the studies mentioned earlier in this chapter.

The stability in negativity apparent in the surveys summarized in Table 2.6 conflicts with the central premise of modern racism theories. In addition, Pedersen and Walker (1997) tested some of the other central premises of modern racism theory. First, items from measures of old-fashioned and modern prejudice loaded clearly and separately on two different factors. However, these two factors correlated .55 with one another. This correlation fits with other research over the years, generally indicating that old-fashioned and modern racism measures are 'separate, but related'. More important, though, is the absence of a link between the modern racism measure and a measure of individualism, which is purportedly a core value in the modern racism concept. The measure of individualism in the Pedersen and Walker (1997) study correlated .06 with old-fashioned racism, and -.13 with modern racism (both n.s.). This pattern of results was confirmed in a more recent study by Fraser and Islam (1999), who used different measures of old-fashioned and modern racism developed specifically for their study, but conflicts with correlations between the MRS and Protestant Work Ethic (-.31) and Humanitarianism-Egalitarianism (.43) reported by Augoustinos et al. (1994).

Table 2.6 Percentage agreement to particular items in prejudice scales, across four samples.

Item	Western 1969[a]	Larsen 1978	Larsen 1981	Walker 1994
If an Aborigine sat next to me on a bus or train I would feel uncomfortable.	94.0 91.0			20.1
No matter how much one might support it on idealistic grounds, there have been too many unfortunate consequences of racial mixing for me to be willing to agree with it.	66.0 38.0			34.9
One reason why the White and Black races can never merge is that the White culture is so much more advanced.	64.0 44.0			26.5
If I had decided to vote along party lines in an election, I would still vote for my party even if they chose an Aborigine as the candidate.	91.0 88.0			13.1
Most Aborigines are dirty and unkempt.		33.1	42.5	45.7
I don't like Aborigines.		34.8	19.0	19.4
On the whole, Aborigines are a loud and noisy lot.		24.1	32.5	29.2
I admire the peaceful and gentle nature of the Aboriginal people.		37.6	45.0	31.5
White Australians could learn a lot from Aboriginal people.		29.9	31.0	29.4

Source The 1969 survey is reported in Western (1969), the 1978 survey in Larsen (1978), the 1981 survey in Larsen (1981), and the 1990 survey in Walker (1994). For the 1969 survey, the first responses are from a small country city, and the second responses are from a small country town.

Summary

The evidence from the Australian studies reviewed here does not lend itself easily to a conclusion that patterns of prejudice against Aboriginal Australians have changed in a systematic way from old-fashioned, red-necked, blatant, segregationist, supremacist views to modern, apparently egalitarian, views based on anti-Black affect and perceived violation of deep-seated, cherished values such as individualism and the Protestant work ethic. Rather, the evidence supports the view that both 'old-fashioned' and 'modern' racism have co-existed at least since the end of the Second World War. Extrapolating from the direct evidence of particular studies, we can argue that this co-existence of conflicting views occurs at a societal, ideological level as well as within the heads and hearts of individual men and women. 'Old-fashioned' and 'modern' racisms co-exist, today as much as any other day, as social representations, as cultural products and cultural repertoires informing current social relations as much as describing pre-existing ones. As co-existing but conflicting representations, they provide the dilemmatic background against which individual attitudes, beliefs, and values, and social and political structures, policies, and practices are played out.

Conclusions

The evidence from Australia suggests that there has always been ambivalence among Anglo Australians in their views of Aboriginal Australians. If we look more broadly than just the level of the individual, we see expressions from long ago which may be classed as 'modern racism', and we see expressions from not so long ago which are clearly 'old-fashioned racism'.

Extreme behaviours (shootings, ration poisonings, etc) are not as prevalent now as they once were, but rather than attribute that to changes in the nature of attitudes held by Anglo Australians, it is perhaps more likely that the attitudes are, as usual, a consequence, not a cause. One of the central tenets of realistic group conflict theory is that changes in intergroup attitudes reflect changes in the 'real' relationships between groups (Levine and Campbell, 1972; Platow and Hunter, Chapter 12; Sherif, 1967) – a point made by Oeser and Hammond (1954) when reflecting on how attitudes towards different groups are more a function of wars between nations than of race, religion, or ethnicity. Shootings and poisonings of Aboriginal Australians may not be as prevalent as they once were, but acts of racist violence still occur in Australia today (National Inquiry into Racist Violence in Australia, 1991). Following Deutsch's crude law of social relations (Deutsch, 1985: 69), if the 'real' relationship between Anglo- and Aboriginal Australians shifts to become more overtly competitive, then we would expect corresponding increases in hostilities. If, for example, Aboriginal Australians secured significant rights to land currently occupied by pastoralists or miners, then the easy tolerance of many Anglo Australians would disappear. The rise to prominence of Pauline Hanson and the One Nation Party can be seen as a backlash against recent political gains made by Aboriginal Australians (e.g., the success of the Mabo and Wik land rights claims).

Modern racism, and indeed also old-fashioned racism, is usually theorized as an individual phenomenon, a characteristic of individual European Americans or Anglo Australians. This ignores important aspects of racism, and has politically conservative ramifications. Jones (1997) distinguishes between individual, institutional, and cultural racism. Racism is as much, or more, a feature of institutions and cultures as it is of individuals. Focusing only on the individual aspects of racism ignores the important roles played by institutions and cultures in reproducing racist social relations, and directs attention away from institutions and cultures and towards individuals in the search for effective interventions to disrupt the reproduction of those racist social relations. By focusing almost exclusively on individual prejudice, and individual differences in prejudice, social psychology helps reinforce and reproduce the location of prejudice within the individual (Hopkins et al., 1997). This ignores the social, structural, institutional, historical, and cultural forces propelling the individual towards prejudice. It deflects attention away from social psychological analyses which may offer fuller accounts of the production and reproduction of prejudice, and, more importantly, makes less likely the development of strategies of change. In stressing the social, and not the individual, aetiology of racism, I hasten to add that the individual is not thus relieved of a moral responsibility for how he or she thinks or acts.

In reviewing some past Australian social psychological studies in the area, I have tried to convey an impression that aspects of what is now called modern racism have existed at least since the end of the Second World War – they are not particularly 'modern'. I do not want this to be taken to mean that all was rosy then, or now, for Indigenous Australians, or indeed for any one else not of northern European, non-Jewish, non-communist stock. Far from it. The brutality of racism has certainly abated in this country in the last half century. But my point is that, just as racism today is still brutal, in its consequences if not in its form, so too was 'old-fashioned' racism, not so uncomplicated by dilemmas of conscience and egalitarianism.

Notes

1. I thank Martha Augoustinos, Mike Innes, Anne Pedersen, Mark Rapley, and Kate Reynolds for their thoughtful and helpful comments on earlier drafts of this chapter. This chapter has been aided by grants from the Australian Research Council and from Murdoch University.

2. Poll data suggest that most Anglo Australians greatly overestimate the percentage of Australia's population which is Aboriginal. In a 1993 poll (Morgan Poll, 1993), respondents were asked 'To the best of your knowledge, what percentage of the Australian population are Aborigines?' 18 per cent of those surveyed estimated 1 per cent or 2per cent, 17 per cent 'couldn't say', 41 per cent indicated more than a quarter, and the mean of those who gave an estimate was 13 per cent. The official answer at the time was about 1.4 per cent.

3 Boongs, Bigots, and Bystanders: Indigenous and Non-Indigenous Experiences of Racism and Prejudice and their Implications for Psychology in Australia.

Darren Garvey

Coming to Terms

Driving through the shopping centre car park (made slower by the additional Christmas shoppers), we paused at the intersection to allow two young cyclists by. The older boy (around 15 in my estimation) peered into the car as he rode past, staring straight at me.

'Fuck you nigger!' were his only words as he and his mate peddled nonchalantly away with cheeky grins on their faces.

In what amounted to a minute of shock and disbelief, we paused a moment longer at the intersection, checking with each other to see if what we had experienced had in fact happened – checking with each other to see if what we had heard had in fact been said. Indeed it had.

Following the shock came realization. What to do? The need to drive on became the immediate priority as the line of cars behind us grew longer. I do remember thinking that despite my knowledge and experience as a university lecturer facilitating courses in counselling and mental health, Indigenous, and cross cultural psychology and cross cultural awareness, my thoughts at that moment were far from understanding, humanitarian, or peaceful towards the source of this season's greeting.

By means of introduction, I share this recent event in my life. It helped clarify for me my uneasy relationship to the issues and experience of racism and prejudice. Part of this is a critical and ongoing tension between the 'personal and professional' as several more questions about the incident and my responses to it emerged. I asked myself why I felt so helpless at the moment of attack and angry at the moments shortly after. Surely my psychological and academic training should immunize me against such attacks or at least minimize my unpleasant feelings? I considered whether I was able to profess about

Indigenous issues and cross-cultural awareness when my own responses to racist attacks were so heated and potentially prejudiced. How could I hope to provide a reasoned, rational, and objective commentary in the classroom, or for that matter, on the page?

Remnants of these anxieties remain, sometimes serving to undermine my confidence in those professional endeavours and at other times acting as a potent motivation to confront and understand them. It is this latter role that fuels the present discussion. It is from this place that I write the following chapter with both experience and questions. It is this place and these uncertainties that I wish to explore because I think they reflect much of the current discourse relating to racism and prejudice, particularly in relation to psychology, psychologists, and the Indigenous people of Australia. This chapter provides a range of perspectives on the issues of racism and prejudice that have not yet received substantial attention, point to the detail and expanse of racist and prejudicial experience, and perhaps represent situations which readers have (or stand to) encounter.

It shares experiences felt by Indigenous and non-Indigenous Australians to contain racist or prejudicial intent. Stories such as these illustrate the complexities of often difficult, everyday lived experience and of the strategies used to negotiate such terrain. They include examples of targeted accusation and the recipient's responses to it, raise the question of whether one remains a silent 'observer' to racist behaviour, and highlight one psychologist's journey from the perspective of reconciling his experiences of racism and prejudice while working with Indigenous people. As a background to these stories, this chapter begins by discussing historical contexts to racism and prejudice in Australia. It considers the origins of these phenomena in this country by proposing possible trigger events, describing their consequences, and highlighting aspects of psychological comment and involvement amongst these.

New Beginnings?

Identifying the origins of racism and prejudice in Australia is an interesting and vexing proposition. The beginning is hard to determine, elusive and perhaps unable to be pinpointed exactly. I remain uncertain as to when racism and prejudice began in Australia, whether it existed precolonization or is primarily a postcolonial phenomenon. Perhaps it is found in the assertion of Terra Nullius: that at the time of European colonization a little over two hundred years ago, Australia was in fact an empty land, devoid of human life (or comparably 'civilized' human life to be more precise). Maybe it started with the actions that followed such an assumption: categorization, separation, disregard, and extermination? Some instances have even been described as 'genocidal' in their impulse and intent (e.g., Coe, 1993; Flick, 1998).

Attempts to facilitate these processes for a 'race' not long for this world were premature, however, as Indigenous people failed to fade away under the pressure of introduced policies, poor nutrition, and disease. 'Smoothing the dying pillow' was a term coined in reference to an attitude pervasive during the period of the Protection Policy (1890s to mid 1900s) in which Aborigines were seen as a 'dying race'. While this was viewed by many as inevitable, the concern that this should take place humanely was felt by many as part of the 'White man's burden' to make the passing as smooth as possible.

Policy and action targeting Australia's Indigenous inhabitants specifically (and for their own good) yielded results whose repercussions are still being felt today. Even good intentions in the face of such destructive pressures proved ineffective, and at times, equally destructive to Indigenous cultures tens of thousands of years in the making. Arguably, the trend continued when assimilation replaced segregationist policies as official sociopolitical imperatives during the 1950s. Its objectives directed that Aborigines shall obtain the same manner of living as other non-Indigenous Australians, enjoying the same rights and privileges, accepting the same responsibilities, observing the same customs and being influenced by the same beliefs, hopes, and loyalties. It was redefined in 1965 to urge that all persons of Aboriginal descent choose to attain a manner of living similar to that of Australians and live as members of a single community. The newly introduced element of choice did little to alleviate the cultural pressures on Aboriginal groups to be 'just like us' (Eckermann et al., 1992). Pressure to assimilate therefore was not only felt socially but had taken the form of legal pressure, enforced by bureaucratic structures in each state and their agents.

The attitudinal remnants of this history remain for many non-Indigenous Australians. The following, recent excerpt from a letter to the editor (*The Cairns Post*, 1999) captures many salient attitudes still held about Australia's Indigenous people today.

Native title is starting to screw the rural and mining sector. It is the con of the highest degree run by a group of 'pretend White Aborigines'. The real Aborigine is the one who misses out.

It appears everything comes to an abrupt halt as our politically correct, do-gooders have sided with these 'pretend two-sided so-called Aborigines' in dragging the bush down to its knees.

For example, one has to get a permit to cut a post, dig a hole, plant a tree and this process takes anything from two–six years to achieve as the 'pretend Aborigines' have the last say on everything – they have to give the go-ahead.

Mining companies have difficulties in extending their leases, and in most cases they can't, as these greedy few demand astronomical compensation for something they don't own.

This country, whether you like to believe it or not, belongs to all Australians, no matter what your colour or creed. It does not belong to the Aborigines, and never has. It belongs to us all.

All countries on the planet went through a process of conquer and take-over strategies. The Whites of this country conquered and won, then shared our great country with our indigenous Australian people.

In the past, if someone committed a misdemeanour they were 'kicked up the backside' whether they were Black or White.

What was done in the past is in the past. 'Stolen children' is the greatest fraud and con on the planet. One must remind the ignorant do-gooder that before we, the stupid Whites arrived here, the Aborigines had a life expectancy of 25–28 years. One in 10 kids survived.

Under no circumstances did they even attempt any form of agriculture or construct any form of abode other than a gunya. They were hunters and gatherers and they were nomadic. That shoots down in flames their claim of cultural love of the land.

Two points are worth making about this letter. As much as we might disagree (or agree) with the sentiments in this letter, consideration still needs to be given to the position these statements represent, particularly in terms of a broader reconciliation between Australia's Indigenous and non-Indigenous peoples. As we tread an uncertain path towards reconciliation, to deny or reject people expressing such views would also exclude them from a process of which they are a part.

Secondly, the comments exhibit several prevailing attitudes that perpetuate the stereotype of a 'passive, simple, unsophisticated people', bereft of agriculture or of the sense to 'roll over' and 'take defeat on the chin'. Furthermore, contemporary Indigenous identity is questioned, ownership and relationship to the land denied, and 'stolen children' are described as a 'con' rather than a concern.

It could be said that it is the 'breaking free' and placing of history in perspective by Indigenous people that characterizes much of our current endeavours and aspirations. It sees us more so than ever, speaking out, confronting, challenging, and re-examining our history and present circumstances with a view to the future. Empowered action of this type represents contemporary Indigenous reality reflecting the age-old process of adapting to and living in an ever-changing and often harsh environment. Difficulty arises when such self-determining actions conflict with long held and entrenched attitudes about Indigenous people or are felt as 'inconvenient' to others' agendas. Ironically, however, by describing Indigenous people in such terms, we are expected to remain part of a history it is suggested we leave behind!

In Australia, and no doubt in other locations, relationships between Indigenous people and researchers (including psychologists) have followed a similarly rocky path. Psychological involvement with Australia's Indigenous people continues to be a much debated and inconclusive proposition. Historically, Indigenous Australians have been examined as 'research oddities', deviants, and anthropological relics. It is only recently that the role of Indigenous people has been reconsidered, with the transition from passive subjects to empowered participants in psychological research slow, and by no means complete. A poignant Indigenous perspective was provided by Bailey at the 1993 National Aboriginal Mental Health Conference. While psychology is not specifically mentioned, the points she makes are relevant and help explain an enduring suspicion of many 'helping' professions and the associated reluctance of Indigenous people to access them.

It's peculiar also to say the least that as one of the most consulted and researched people in the country, we are the least listened to. We have to go continually to the government with cap in hand, bowing and scraping and proving that we're here. Justifying our existence and our numbers. And our needs of course. As Koories we are born into a situation according to our report, where our communities are in isolation. We are subjected to a constant procession of academics, researchers, government agents, anthropologists, archaeologists, and sociologists who come to our door requiring information. As sure as one leaves, another arrives. We rarely see the report and often too late. We sometimes get quoted out of context or not at all, to our detriment. And there are no improvements in our conditions or benefits for our efforts. They, on the other hand, have either tidied up their files, made a decision on our behalf, made a scientific breakthrough, attained doctoral status, published their opinions, become experts in the field. Provided a consultant's report, moved onto another job on the basis of their knowledge in Aboriginal affairs. Proffered a whole new theory, gained a new, more prestigious portfolio, attracted lucrative publicity, gained political kudos, altered legislation, made an impressive speech, attacked our credibility, denied our Aboriginality, advised us as to what we should be doing, or created another problem for us on which we will soon be consulted. Quite an expansive industry. (Bailey, 1993)

At the centre of much contemporary debate within psychology lies the question of whether 'races' in fact exist. It has identified the metamorphoses of prejudice over time while joining the push to eradicate 'race' from everyday discourse and research. Typical of recent discussion at a Congress of the International Association of Cross-Cultural Psychology: 'An emerging consensus among population geneticists and physical anthropologists is that race is not a useful biological concept at the human level. Psychologists in the main don't seem to understand this. Nor do laypersons in many societies who view the world as if it contained "races"' (Segall, 1998). The logical conclusion offered was that if races were no longer a reality, is there such a thing as racism? It seems that for some sections of psychology, the answer to the question of 'when did racism begin', is answered by 'does racism really exist?'

Unfortunately though, the news of the impending end to 'racism' comes too late for many and remains slow in the translation to non-prejudicial behaviour by psychologists and others. While there may be a concerted push to eradicate the terminology of 'race and racism' from psychological discourse, their presence in popular descriptions remain abundant and meaningful. The legacy of inappropriate and disrespectful prior involvement lingers in the minds of many indigneous Australians and as suggested by Bailey, one does not have to delve far into the past to be reminded. This leads me to suggest that in fact, what is experienced, felt and described as racism and prejudice begins everyday. What I (and others) know and experience, are old and new forms of racism and prejudice, (see Augoustinos et al., 1999) and the prospect of those occurring daily, in the car park or the classroom, the boardroom, or the train as the following stories illustrate.

'Going Back to School'

The suggestion that racism and prejudice are reincarnated daily and that the experiences of the past are not easily forgotten brings us to our first story. It suggests that the lessons learned at school do prepare people for adulthood but sometimes for the wrong reasons.

> I didn't realize there was a difference until I went to school or at least that's where the difference was made and became more obvious. I got suspended once. One of my classmates called me a 'Black slut'. I punched her – I got suspended.
>
> My awareness grew from there. When things stuffed up, the 'boongs, half castes, and niggers' were to blame. Then, if we tried to assert our rights and demand some recognition, we were told that 'we were too White to be Aboriginal'.
>
> Thinking back, I can see how you could get a reputation for being a 'Black slut' or a troublemaker and how you could start to see yourself as that – like a self-fulfilling prophecy. I know some of my friends went that way.
>
> When justification is an almost daily thing, it can become very tiring. I've noticed that my responses have changed over time. At school or when I was younger, I was more aggressive, violent – verbally at least. Mind you I wouldn't back away from a fight. I realized that that wasn't getting me anywhere though.
>
> Now I tend to be more choosy of who I respond to and how I do. If a person looks to be sincere, I'm likely to try and communicate with that person. If it looks like that person isn't listening or hearing, I'll probably choose to say nothing. There have been times when I've shared things that have then been used against me or used inappropriately. So now I choose my circumstances more carefully.
>
> I still realize my right to say something but sometimes I'll remain quiet. Probably for my own safety or for the safety of others I am with. It is hard to verbalize something very deep, and risky if it looks like the person isn't going to understand. Therefore I usually do it after I've established trust and rapport with a person.
>
> This is a situation I have since been in with other Aboriginal people. My appearance belied my Aboriginality. I was questioned, asked to defend or explain my identity. When the misunderstanding comes from within your own, it can do the most damage.
>
> My mum was a good role model for me and she helped explain these situations to me. She told me this story about how we develop an armour to these attacks – like a turtle. A barrier to protect yourself, to survive. But when the attacks come from other Aboriginal people, I find that it hits a 'soft spot' like the belly. I assume that other Aboriginal people will understand and respect the Aboriginality of others. But I guess this is an assumption on my part. Belonging to a particular cultural group doesn't ensure respect, but out of all the people in the world you want to have respect you, it is your own that are the most important. I could brush off non-Aboriginal comments as 'ignorant', but when it's your own people …
>
> Some Aboriginal people have said to me that I have an advantage because of my appearance – that I can choose not to engage in a discussion or an argument. I remember a time when a taxi driver was making some racist comments about Aboriginal people. Deep down I wanted to respond but my energy at the time meant that I chose not to. This isn't really an advantage though because it means that I often get confronted by the blatant, 'in your face' racism because people don't realize my Aboriginality. Mind you, it also means that people are more likely to express themselves and their attitudes more openly if they don't realize

I'm Aboriginal. It still means I get confronted with a lot of that in your face racism but at least I know where that person stands. I think they'd be more likely to cover up their real feelings if they knew I was Aboriginal.

I'm also asked why out of all the parts of my heritage, that I choose to identify more as Aboriginal. Why not another culture? I say that who I am is not just a blood thing, it's how I grew up, how I was brought up. My Aboriginality was given prominence in my upbringing, it was supported. Other Aboriginal people have said that I had an advantage in this respect.

Moving out of your area, away from your connections to a place where you are not known exposes you again. This is a geographical and social dislocation and means that you have to go about establishing yourself, your identity again. I guess this is what it was like when I first went to school. Once you move out of your familiar surrounds, your comfort zone, you're faced with the same type of questions and attacks that you've just gone through and dealt with. It's like going to school all over again …

There seems to be no age restriction to insults. That they should occur so young, contain such venom and focus on the 'racial' characteristics of another child is a sobering reality. This story also highlights the anguish associated with being challenged about your identity by those of whom you least expect. What does it mean when this harsh scrutiny is carried out by other members of your own group? Dudgeon and Oxenham (1989) identify a process they call 'internalized oppression' which helps explain this occurrence. They suggest that an insipid cycle of oppression is perpetuated when a dominant group's oppressive messages are internalized and enacted by and within an oppressed group. Dudgeon and Oxenham describe it as a destructive element in not only the psyche of some Indigenous Australians, but also in the behavioural manifestations that the accompanying attitudes promote, such as the oppression of 'same group' members.

'Are You 1/8th or What?'

The second story develops the theme of 'doubt' expressed about the authenticity of a person's identity. It also reveals a process of developing responses to racism as suggested in the first story.

Bus travel was exciting. Going home for a study break from the 'big city'. We stuck together, my brother, sister and I. They couldn't have been more than 10 or 8 at the time. I remember putting them in the seats side by side and I sat in the seat in front of them. My travelling companion was a White, middle-aged man who took an almost immediate interest in me and my background.

'Where are you from?' he asked.

'Australia,' I replied (with a sense of where this was heading).

'No, I mean what are your parents?'

'Australian,' I assured him (more certain of where this was heading).

Momentarily stumped, he then went on to talk about his experience of 'boongs' and 'niggers' and that he was surprised that I was well dressed and well spoken. I didn't fit his understanding of an 'Aborigine'.

I wondered whether to go into 'educative mode' but also remember not wanting to get upset and felt extra vulnerable because I didn't want my brother and sister to get upset either. I didn't want it impacting on them, but there is only so much protection you can give. I remember that I spoke with them later about the incident explaining that some people are ignorant and racist.

As I reflect on this now, I can see that I have gone through several stages in my life with respect to this type of situation. I've found that I've become more aware and more strategic about the type of response I give to such questions and accusations. This is very much on a 'person-by-person' basis. I see my options as including:

Ignoring – to walk away

Confronting – to take up the question and challenging the questioner as to their agenda and assumptions

Humour/satire/critique – for example: Question: So, are you 1/8th Aboriginal? Answer: Yeah, my big toe.

Educating – to discuss the diversity of contemporary indigenous identity.

These are combined with varying levels of restraint or retaliation – from a 'fuck off!' to a more measured conversation in which I try to talk with them as another human being and hope that I will somehow change their opinion. I feel that I have gotten to this point because of the continual and sustained occurrence of these types of situations. I feel like I've experienced more blatant racism in the city – my identity continually being questioned and challenged. I still feel that in doing so, they are trying to work out whether I am a 'good or bad boong'. At least when I'm home, I'm known and don't come under the same type or amount of scrutiny.

I felt my political, educative, and lecturing roles never ceased. I found that I was in situations where I was continually needing to educate. Wherever I go, I'm Aboriginal and that's how people related to me. After a time of continual engagement and response, I began to feel worn out. It was relentless. It felt like there was no relief. I got really depressed about four year ago. Sooner or later, it always came up, at work or after hours. Now I consider which battles I'm going to fight. I base this on a gut reaction and how the person speaks. I also base this decision on how they respond to my initial response to their question.

As it did so many years ago on the bus, what I find most offensive is the assumption of 'normality' on which these questions are based. Because I was seen as different to that norm, I felt like I was made to feel abnormal or 'something less than'. Being in that position of having to continually justify and validate myself to others was draining. I have developed and 'grown up' since then and have other ways of dealing with these situations now. I just wish it would cross other people's minds to do the same.

This piece suggests that the position from where one speaks to address racist or prejudicial attacks is not arrived at naively. On the contrary, continued and repeated attacks provoke a range of defensive mechanisms and strategies that contribute to the person's existing repertoire.

Several types of cognitive, affective, and behavioural responses are evidenced in this story. They include: confusion and shame, confrontation and resolution, in terms of a new repertoire of responses to such challenges, and education or a challenge in return.

The choice is based on this speaker's assessment of the situation and the protagonist, and perhaps the cost of expending the effort associated with a particular reply. It is telling that there seems to be a palpable sense of frustration in the words of this speaker with having to engage and re-engage in this assessment process. Notably, it also seems that the uncertainty of encountering racism or prejudice that proves to be as, if not more, stressful than an actual encounter.

'Side by Side'

The next story highlights the position that a non-Indigenous person may find themselves in when conducting business with an indignenous colleague in a non-Indigenous setting. This scenario raises several important questions, relevant not only to the boardroom, but for the classroom, the clinic, or community. They include: Who is the significant person in this situation? Who has the right to speak? What is my role within this situation? If I am uncomfortable with what is going on here, will I do anything about it?'

The story suggests that even as 'observers' to racism or prejudice, an individual, a group, or profession assumes a role via inaction. This type of informed non-involvement, while not directly contributing to the perpetration of racism or prejudice, nonetheless contributes indirectly to the broader social milieu of acceptance that maintains and sustains prejudicial behaviour and attitudes.

We had gone to discuss training issues for a large organization. How best could their employees be prepared, especially when it came to dealing with the Aboriginal people who made up a significant portion of their clientele. The meeting took place with a senior administrator within the organization, obviously keen to facilitate an agreeable training arrangement. My Aboriginal colleague and I sat side by side. The superintendent sat on his side of the desk.

It became apparent quite quickly that the superintendent was directing his inquiries and discussion to me, rather than to my Aboriginal colleague, who happened to be my superior from work. Trevor and I had experienced this type of selective communication on previous occasions and had developed a type of system whereby I would deflect and redirect questions and comments away from myself towards Trev. This was done verbally, for example, 'What do you think of that Trevor?' And non-verbally by a not so subtle rearrangement of my posture and body so that I faced Trevor which effectively gave the superintendent my shoulder to speak to.

One can often pick up quite quickly as to whether there is antagonism motivating the words and behaviour of others in a meeting. This didn't seem to be the case in this instance. I did not feel that the superintendent was directing his communication to me because he felt bad about Trevor due to his Aboriginality. Instead, a more likely explanation was that the context of 'business' and the position of authority which the superintendent held, meant that he was looking for his 'counterpart', his equal, the suitably qualified and experienced person with whom he could appropriately discuss the important business issues to hand. I apparently fit that description better than my Aboriginal colleague, hence, the focus of attention on me.

I have experienced this type of 'prejudgement' many times and in a variety of contexts. So much so that I have developed a set of verbal and behavioural cues meant to shift appropriately, the focus of attention to my equally, if not better qualified colleague.

As the story above describes, choosing not to be a bystander can begin at an individual level in what might even be considered mundane circumstances. Reconciliation on a larger scale, however, also has at its most fundamental requirement, the participation in a process of respectful communication. Psychology's reconciliation with the Indigenous people of this country must also engage in this process. It is reasonable to conclude that if professions are seen to be tolerant of such inappropriate behaviours, the people whom the profession is meant to serve, retain a healthy sense of apprehension regarding that profession (and its representatives). Echoes of Bailey's earlier sentiments re-emerge at this point.

The final story comments on the changing nature of psychology in relation to Indigenous issues and of one person's experience and involvement within this.

A Way Forward . . .

My experiences and interests have led me to see my involvement with indigenous issues and people as 'an engagement in a mutual struggle.' The notions of partnership and mutual benefit are central – 'being part of and partner in the process'.

I see the establishment of the partnership relationship as a process in itself and as important as addressing the issue itself. It is important because I see that there are risks in assuming a place in the process or assuming one's place in the process. At an extreme point, a presumption of knowledge, competence or understanding, or of the right to be involved centrally with an issue is not only inappropriate, but also disrespectful. Doing so can see us as perpetrators of disempowering practice and behaviour. Perhaps our role is developed and established over time, and through an active process. Acceptance into the struggle must be earned as does finding a 'negotiated place'.

I see sections of psychology as beginning to engage in a fundamental paradigm shift. From viewing others as 'objects of inquiry and the recipients of well-intentioned advice' and remaining as a scientifically objective observers and unaffected, to one where the psychologist is more critical of his or her role and practice in psychological interventions. From being the appliers of a process or scientific method, to a consultative and negotiated way. Objectivity remains fundamental but is tempered with compassion and the need to negotiate the terms of involvement together.

Working and relating as a non-Indigenous person with Indigenous people is perhaps individually, a small-scale version of a larger scale process of reconciliation. I would argue that this process is best carried out with depth and engagement from both parties, each respectful of the other.

There are arguably many levels to reconciliation, from a 'polite' or surface reconciliation to what I refer to as 'depth reconciliation'. In my opinion, psychology and psychologists have a role to play at the different levels of this process but it is up to each psychologist to decide to what depth he or she goes. Thus, there are varying levels of commitment and engagement. At the deepest levels, the question changes for the psychologist. It changes from inquiring of indigenous people, 'who are you?' to, 'who are we together?'

Psychology's interest in issues of racism and prejudice is something of a double-edged sword. Psychological involvement has the potential to demonstrate our progress as a socially responsive discipline and expand our understandings of racism and prejudice in Australia, yet ironically stands to perpetuate them via inappropriate, insensitive and disrespectful conduct. The notion of partnership is highlighted in the preceding story – of the need to examine not only the policy and philosophy that directs and defines our profession, but to reflect on what this means in our own conduct with others.

Some Words of Caution

Moore and McCabe (1993) remind us that anecdotal evidence is based on haphazardly selected individual cases, which often come to our attention because they are striking in some way. Furthermore, these cases may not be representative of any larger group of cases. The small sample of a few individual cases is rarely trustworthy. Therefore, the preceding stories should be read with this caution in mind.

It is also worth remembering however, that in Australia, the gradual collection of stories relating to Indigenous experience has no doubt contributed to our awareness of other issues – Aboriginal deaths in custody (Royal Commission into Aboriginal Deaths in Custody, 1991) or the plight of forcibly 'removed' Indigenous children (Human Rights and Equal Opportunity Commission, 1997; After the Removal, 1996; Telling Our Story, 1995). Our appreciation of these might not be so great were it not for the repeated and concerted telling, collection and sharing of such strikingly personal accounts. Such narrative or story-telling approaches can have real value as we continue to struggle with our understandings and awareness of racism and prejudice in our own country.

Furthermore, it is not 'despite' these concerns, but because of these, that these stories were included. The lack of statistical significance does not render these stories personally insignificant. Future investigation may point to the idiosyncrasies of the particular respondents in these cases or as representative of more general experience. In either case, we must remember that psychologists are still required to consider and listen to the individual's story.

Bridging the Divide

While the origins of racism and prejudice in Australia are unclear, and the meanings of these terms debated, it is reasonably certain that their manifestation is a regular occurrence for many people. Chosen because of their distinctiveness, these stories represent both Indigenous and non-Indigenous perspectives as recipients, witnesses, and challengers to racist or prejudicial attention.

As research continues to examine the nature and extent of racism and prejudice in Australia, the illustration of these experiences is surely most poignantly expressed in the stories of those most intimately affected. They illustrate how people have confronted, addressed and reconciled the professional and personal aspects of racism and prejudice and how that experience has affected, shaped, and influenced them personally and professionally. In doing so, numerous themes and lessons have emerged that may become the topics of future investigation and provide directions for their amelioration as do the other contributing chapters to this book.

Attention has been paid to considering the implications and challenges for psychology and psychologists. To it's credit, The Australian Psychological Society as an organization has become proactive in its attention and consideration of racism and prejudice and is distinctive and progressive in this attention, particularly through several recent works including *Racism and prejudice* (Sanson et al., 1998) and the *Guidelines for the provision of psychological services for and the conduct of research with Aboriginal and Torres Strait Islander people of Australia* (Australian Psychological Society, 1997).

It is notable that psychology as a profession continues to challenge, re-evaluate, and deconstruct concepts such as race, racism, and prejudice, and that it continues to play a part in defining and researching these shifting phenomena. It is important that this discussion translates into effective and appropriate practices that are considerate and respectful to those to whom we provide professional services. As Steve Reicher argues in the concluding chapter to this book, psychology's theories and concepts have practical consequences: they can either help to undermine and fight against racism, or they can contribute to its reproduction. Ultimately though, as it is for me, an Indigenous psychologist, the way forward is not merely an intellectual exercise. Progress will be achieved only through an ongoing and gradual reconciliation of the personal and the professional, and by coming to terms with the past and the everyday.

Note

Sincere thanks to Jo Cameron, Darlene Oxenham, Dr. Ernest Stringer, and Harry Pickett for their honest contributions.

Part II:

Development, Socialization, and Personality

4 The Development of Prejudice in Children

Drew Nesdale

Beginning in the 1930s, a vast amount of research has addressed the development of ethnic prejudice in children, together with related issues such as the acquisition of ethnic awareness, ethnic self-identification, and ethnic stereotyping (see reviews by Aboud, 1988; Brown, 1995; Davey, 1983). Although there is a tendency to think of ethnic prejudice (i.e., unjustified feelings of dislike or hatred towards members of ethnic groups) as an adolescent or adult phenomenon, the extent of interest by researchers in children's prejudice reflects the importance attributed to it. Firstly, there is research suggesting that prejudice may be widespread among school-age children (Aboud, 1988). Secondly, since middle childhood is an important period for the formulation of social understanding and social attitudes, values established or crystallized during this phase of development may endure into adulthood. Thirdly, there is the possibility that tackling ethnic prejudice in children may actually comprise one of the few viable options for minimizing the development of ethnic prejudice in adolescents and adults.

Finally, the development of ethnic prejudice in children is simply intriguing because a clear picture of the nature of the developmental process has yet to emerge. There is currently little clarity on issues such as when ethnic prejudice emerges in children, whether or not there are age-related phases or stages through which prejudice develops, what are the psychological processes or mechanisms which govern the acquisition of ethnic prejudice, and what impact children's emerging linguistic and cognitive abilities have upon their acquisition and retention of ethnic prejudice.

This chapter reviews theory and research on the development of ethnic prejudice in children, with a particular focus on the findings relating to dominant- or majority-group children since it is this group that most commonly expresses prejudice towards members of ethnic minority groups (Verkuyten and Masson, 1995). The chapter commences with a consideration of the array of methods which have been used by researchers to measure children's prejudice, together with the findings which have been revealed.

Measuring Ethnic Prejudice in Children

The task of devising an ecologically valid measure of young children's ethnic prejudice has proven to be a considerable challenge for researchers. Not only is prejudice an internal affective response which is neither directly observable nor immediately accessible, but very young children, in particular, also lack the cognitive and linguistic apparatus necessary to respond to measures (e.g., questionnaires and scales) which might be used effectively with adults (Milner, 1996). A measure is needed in which ethnicity is represented in a concrete, recognizable way to children, the task is comprehensible, and the response(s) required reflect children's level of affect towards members of the particular ethnic outgroup(s) represented in the stimuli.

Researchers have responded to the challenge by utilizing a variety of techniques, including ethnic preferences, trait assignments, structured interviews, behaviour observations, questionnaires, sociograms, and projective tests, although the first two – ethnic preferences and trait assignments – have dominated the field. This chapter will focus on these techniques, together with interviews and behaviour observations, since these exhaust the great majority of the research activity.

Ethnic Preference

This technique emerged from the separate but overlapping work of Horowitz (1936), Horowitz and Horowitz (1938) and Clark and Clark (1947). The procedure devised by Horowitz involved presenting children with a page displaying an equal number of photos of White and Black children (previously judged for 'racial typicality' and 'pleasantness') who were asked in one version, the Ranks Test, to select the person they '... liked best, next best, next best ...' and so on. In the second version, the Show Me Test, the children engaged in a social distance-type task, being asked to indicate '... all those that you want to sit next to in a street car', '... want to be in your class', '... want to play ball with', '... want to come to a party', and so on. Pro-White bias/anti-Black rejection in both tests was then based upon the proportion of ingroup versus outgroup children selected.

Both versions of the test have proven to be popular with researchers with more than 30 studies being reported in which children's ethnic preferences were estimated based on their responses to photos or drawings of two or more children representing different ethnic groups (e.g., Boulton, 1995; Clark and Clark, 1939; Davey and Mullin, 1980; Newman et al., 1983; Radke et al. 1950; Rice et al., 1974; Vaughan, 1964a; Zinser et al., 1981). In addition, a further 20 or so studies have used some type of social distance scale as a technique for estimating children's intercultural attitudes (e.g., Bird et al., 1952; Katz, 1973; Moore et al., 1984).

In a similar, but more dramatic vein, the Clarks devised a dolls task in 1940/41 in which children were presented with a pair of dolls which were identical except for skin colour, being clad only in brief diapers in order to expose maximum skin surface (Clark and Clark, 1947). Children were then asked a series of eight questions: 'Give me the doll that you want to play with', '... that is a nice doll', '... that looks bad', '...that is a nice colour', '... that looks like a White child', '... that looks like a coloured child', '... that looks like a Negro child', '... that looks like you'. Responses to questions 1–4 were considered to be evaluative responses that reflected the child's ethnic preference (questions 5–7 were included as measures of ethnic awareness or knowledge, and question 8 was a measure of ethnic self-identification). This technique has also been used extensively with more than 20 studies being reported, albeit with variations in the number and type of dolls and the questions addressed to the children (e.g., Asher and Allen, 1969; Branch and Newcombe, 1980; Vaughan, 1964b).

Despite the topological variations, each of these techniques measures children's *preference* for one ethnic group over another. The strengths of the technique are that it is easy to administer and consumes little time, race is presented graphically and/or concretely, and the questions accompanying the stimuli are comparatively simple and straightforward, thus making the task both comprehensible and engaging to children, even as young as three years.

On this basis, it is perhaps not surprising that a remarkably consistent set of findings emerged, especially in relation to dominant-group children. There is clear evidence that these children can differentiate among people based on racial cues from a very early age and certainly by around four years their racial awareness enables them to distinguish explicitly among members of different racial groups. There is also extensive evidence that from four years onwards, children from the ethnically dominant group can accurately identify their ethnic group membership and that they reveal increasingly strong ingroup bias in an ethnic preference task (see reviews by Aboud, 1988; Goodman, 1964; Katz, 1976; Proshansky, 1966). Based on her review of the literature and her own more recent findings, Aboud (1988) further concluded that this bias actually peaks at around age six to seven years, and then gradually declines during middle childhood.

The major weakness relating to the ethnic preference technique concerns the uncertainty over whether it actually comprises a valid measure of children's prejudice towards members of ethnic outgroups (e.g., Aboud, 1988; Brigham, 1971; Gregor and McPherson, 1966; Hraba, 1972; Proshansky, 1966) or whether it is simply a measure of ingroup bias or preference (e.g., Brand et al., 1974; Davey, 1983; Katz, 1976; Stephan and Rosenfield, 1979).

There are a number of arguments and findings which support the latter view. Firstly, the ethnic preference technique calls for a choice response, frequently a forced response between only two alternatives, which does not necessarily imply dislike for, or rejection of, the unchosen stimulus figure (e.g., Brand et al., 1974; Katz, 1976). Secondly, preference responses are undiscriminating because they do not provide a sensitive assessment of children's intensity of affect for either the ingroup or the outgroup (e.g., Aboud, 1988; Williams et al., 1975). Thirdly, by stripping away all individuating information until only the skin colour cue remains as a basis for choice, the technique artifactually and unrealistically enhances the salience of the ethnicity category over other socially relevant categories such as gender and age. Fourthly, and related to the previous point, race is simply not a salient category to the majority of dominant group children until nine or ten years – younger children invariably respond to gender before race (e.g., Boulton, 1995; Epstein et al., 1976; Goldstein et al., 1979), unless the intergroup situation is one of tension or conflict (Radke et al., 1949). Indeed, Epstein et al. (1976) demonstrated that cleanliness was a more potent determinant of preferences than was race in second to fourth grade children, while Richardson and Royce (1968) reported that physical handicap was a greater deterrent to young children's friendship than race.

Fifthly, given the transparency of the ethnic preference technique, there is a distinct possibility that children may give socially desirable responses, especially with increasing age (e.g., Clark et al., 1980; Katz, 1976).

Sixthly, a number of studies have reported a lack of correspondence between ethnic preferences and race of friends and playmates (e.g., Boulton and Smith, 1993; Fishbein and Imai, 1993; Hraba and Grant, 1970) and that if racial cleavage does occur, it tends not to be before children are ten or eleven years of age (e.g., Brand et al., 1974; Proshansky, 1966; but see also Lambert and Taguchi, 1956).

In sum, while the ethnic preference technique provides reliable estimates of the ages at which children acquire ethnic awareness, ethnic self-identification, and ethnic preferences, the major weakness of the technique relates to its doubtful validity as a measure of children's ethnic prejudice.

Trait Attribution

The trait attribution technique contains considerable similarities to the ethnic preference technique, presumably because its genesis can also be traced to the early work of Horowitz and Horowitz (1938). In this technique, children are asked to assign positive (e.g., good, clean, nice) and negative (e.g., bad, dirty, sad) traits and attributes to one of two stimulus figures (e.g., photo or drawing) representing the ingroup and ethnic outgroup (e.g., 'which child is the dirty boy?', 'which child is the smart boy?'). The children's intergroup attitudes are then based upon the ratio of positive to negative traits chosen for the ingroup versus outgroup stimulus figures. One variant of this technique has been formalized as the Preschool Racial Attitude Measure (PRAM) (Williams and Roberson, 1967), with a subsequent lengthened version (incorporating equivalent short forms) presented as PRAM II (Williams et al., 1975).

More than 30 trait attribution studies have also revealed a remarkably consistent set of results with dominant group children displaying an increase in ingroup positivity/outgroup negativity from three years, followed by a decrease after six or seven years (Horowitz and Horowitz, 1938; Williams and Morland, 1976; Williams and Roberson, 1967; Williams et al., 1975) although there have been some exceptions (e.g., Blake and Dennis, 1943; Goldstein et al., 1979).

While the trait attribution technique enjoys the strengths of the ethnic preference technique, it also shares many of its weaknesses. For example, the child is again forced to make a preference choice between the two stimulus figures in attributing each trait. Although it might be argued that the confound of preference and rejection entailed in a forced choice is moderated to an extent by the requirement of assigning a series of positive and negative traits to one or the other stimulus figure, a forced choice is still required in relation to each trait, and most scoring methods still aggregate across the children's trait attribution responses to the two figures (e.g., see Williams et al., 1975).

Some recent attempts have been made to tackle the problems entailed in the forced choice and aggregated scoring. For example, researchers have extended the range of choice in assigning traits to include three or four possibilities; that is, the ingroup and outgroup figures, both figures, and/or neither figure (e.g., Black-Gutman and Hickson, 1996; Boulton, 1995; Doyle et al., 1988). In addition, some researchers are now disaggregating the children's trait assignment responses so as to provide measures of children's ingroup bias/outgroup rejection and ingroup rejection/outgroup bias (or, 'counterbias'; Black-Gutman and Hickson, 1996: Doyle and Aboud, 1995).

In the final analysis, however, there remains the critical question of whether the common finding of ingroup positivity/outgroup negativity which is increasingly revealed by children on the trait assignment task from three years, followed by a decrease after seven years, is indicative of the level of children's dislike or hatred for members of ethnic outgroups, or is simply indicative of children's level of ingroup preference (with, again, the responses of older children reflecting decreased ingroup preference or social desirability).

Consistent with the former view is the possibility that the trait attribution measure actually loads on to children's negative stereotypes of ethnic outgroups. However, a number of writers have argued that up to six or seven years, children are still involved in learning the prevailing racial 'facts' concerning the group to which they belong and the groups to which they don't belong (e.g., Milner, 1983; Proshansky, 1966; Radke and Trager, 1950; Vaughan, 1987). Importantly, while most dominant-group children can typically verbalize these 'facts' or stereotypes by six or seven years, they are usually not held as the child's own, and especially when the local situation is devoid of intergroup tension or conflict (Chyatte et al., 1951; Goodman, 1946; Proshansky, 1966; Radke et al., 1949). Accordingly, if the trait attribution technique does not load on to ingroup ethnic stereotypes, at least for the younger children, then it appears to be simply another measure of ethnic preference; at each choice point, the child merely accepts the good traits for the preferred ingroup and rejects the bad traits (i.e., assigns them to the available comparison outgroup). In terms of children older than six or seven years, the position is even less clear cut. With increasing age, the children's response to the trait attribution technique might reflect ingroup preference, or knowledge and/or acceptance of the prevailing ethnic outgroup stereotype, or desire to give socially desirable responses.

In sum, as with the ethnic preference technique, the trait attribution task does not provide an unambiguous estimate of children's level of prejudice towards members of ethnic outgroups. As with the former test, it may well provide a reliable estimate of children's ingroup preferences, at least up until six or seven years of age. Beyond this age, however, there is less certainty as to the interpretation to be placed upon the findings obtained from the trait assignment technique. On this point, it should also be noted that the issue of whether prejudice is ingroup favouritism or outgroup derogation is also controversial within the adult literature (Fiske, 1998).

Interviews

A number of researchers have utilized in-depth interviews with young children as a mechanism for accessing their developing intergroup attitudes, although most such studies were reported prior to the 1960s (e.g., Chyatte et al., 1951; Hartley et al., 1948a, 1948b; Radke and Trager, 1950; Radke-Yarrow et al., 1952; but see also Boulton, 1995). Undoubtedly contributing to this underuse of interviews are their well-documented disadvantages (Neuman, 1994). For example, interviews are time-consuming and, as a result, only comparatively small samples tend to be tested, with consequent reductions in generalizability. Interviews also draw more heavily than any of the other techniques on children's developing cognitive and linguistic abilities. In addition, the face-to-face interview situation enhances the possibility of social desirability responses by children and bias by the interviewer. Finally, the range of response options available to the respondents enhances coding difficulties, reduces the sharpness of intensity estimates, and consigns the data analysis to nonparametric statistics.

Against this, however, the great strength of the interview technique resides in the richness of the resulting data protocol. Moreover, the variance and coding problems can be minimized by the use of structured formats (e.g., Hartley et al., 1948b; Horowitz and Horowitz, 1938; Radke and Trager, 1950) and, as with the previous techniques, the use of photos and drawings (e.g., Hartley et al., 1948a; Radke et al., 1949) and formboards, puzzles, and models (e.g., Radke and Trager, 1950) to represent race graphically and concretely, and to engage the child's interest.

The important findings revealed in the comparatively few interview studies which have been reported illustrate the benefits of the technique. They indicated that, from as young as three years, children in multiracial communities have a developing awareness of the social structure in their community and the nature of majority–minority group relationships (Radke and Trager, 1950). At the same time, the data suggested that race was not a salient category to most dominant-group children prior to middle childhood (Radke et al., 1949).

In sum, the evidence suggests that interviews comprise a considerably underused research tool, given the richness of the data which can be realized and the disadvantages of other techniques.

Unobtrusive Observations and Other Implicit Techniques

A shared weakness of each of the preceding measurement techniques concerns their transparency of intent, even to young children, with the resulting problem that each invites children to construct responses which they consider to be more socially acceptable. One solution to this problem is to take unobtrusive measures of children's actual behaviours towards ethnic outgroup members on the assumption that if the children do harbour feelings of dislike or hatred, their feelings will be revealed in their interactions. Surprisingly, given the size of the literature, and the number of studies with adults in which this technique has been employed (see Crosby et al., 1980, for a review), unobtrusive techniques have been little used.

Studies by Goodman (1946), Stevenson and Stevenson (1960), and Fishbein and Imai (1993) are among the few that have unobtrusively recorded the social interactions of culturally mixed groups of children, primarily of children between two and five years of age. No evidence was reported in these studies of a systematic relationship between play-partner preferences and race. Little data is available, however, concerning the impact of race on the actual social interactions of older children.

Another approach to handling the transparency problem is to examine children's responses on measures which are psychologically relevant to the research question, but of which the children are unaware; that is, to focus on measures which are implicit rather than explicit (Nesdale and Durkin, 1998). For example, recent work by Maass and Arcuri (1996) and their colleagues has focused on what has been termed the Linguistic Intergroup Bias (LIB). This is a tendency for people to describe behaviours attributed to an ingroup or an outgroup at different levels of linguistic abstraction. Specifically, since desirable ingroup and undesirable outgroup behaviours are expected, they tend to be perceived as reflecting quite general properties of the groups and hence are described in relatively abstract terms. In contrast, undesirable ingroup and desirable outgroup behaviours are unexpected, hence not perceived as reflecting stable qualities of the groups and, as a result, are more likely to be described in less abstract terms. LIB has potential as an implicit measure of intergroup attitudes because it comprises an affective index of which the participants are typically unaware, as they complete their response descriptions. However, whether LIB is relevant to assessing ethnic relations in young children remains to be assessed.

A third approach is to reduce the focus on prejudice by, firstly, providing a range of additional and more realistic information concerning the target stimulus and, secondly, seeking responses from children on a number of other context-relevant indices, in addition to affect or liking. An example of this approach is provided by the Intergroup Narrative Test (INT) (Nesdale, in press-a; Nesdale and McLaughlin, 1987). The INT involves children reading (or being read) a short story involving two characters, one being of the same, and the other different, ethnicity to the participant. The story is thematic (e.g., 'a day at the zoo') and each character reveals a mixture of positive and negative traits and behaviours as the story unfolds. Thus, ethnicity and prejudice are de-emphasized and the task is made more familiar and realistic because of the array of information presented, as well as the other issues addressed (e.g., the participants' recall of what happened, judgements, and attributions of story character behaviours), in addition to their liking for the story characters. Importantly, the INT technique has also been found to be suitable for use with children as young as five years (Nesdale and McLaughlin, 1987).

In sum, there is evidence that researchers are beginning to appreciate the need for more implicit rather than explicit measurement techniques, in order to minimize social desirability effects. However, although some promising techniques have been reported, this trend is currently only in its infancy.

Conclusions

Researchers have primarily used two techniques to measure children's ethnic prejudice – the ethnic preference technique dominated the field until the mid-1980s, with trait assignment being more predominant since that time. Although the shared strengths of these techniques are that race is presented in an uncomplicated and graphical way and children are required to make comparatively simple responses, their weakness is their transparency of intent and hence their susceptibility to response construction. This is also a serious flaw in using structured interviews although, in comparison, that technique provides greater opportunities to pursue issues in depth and hence test for response construction by children.

It seems that an enhanced understanding of children's prejudice will depend upon the development of creative implicit measurement techniques, in conjunction with structured interviews. Importantly, ascertaining the concurrent validity of such techniques will need to be central to these endeavours.

Bearing the limitations of the existing techniques in mind, it is reasonable to conclude that dominant-group children (particularly those in multiracial societies) are racially aware by four years, that they can identify their own racial or ethnic group shortly afterwards, and that their ingroup preference increases thereafter, at least up to six or seven years of age. What is less clear, however, is whether ethnic preference (as measured to date) is synonymous with ethnic prejudice. If not, the question remains as to when preference becomes prejudice in those children so afflicted.

Theoretical Approaches to the Development of Children's Prejudice

There are four major approaches to accounting for the development of ethnic prejudice in children, including emotional maladjustment, social reflection, sociocognitive development, and social identity. Since the first two approaches are dealt with in other sources (e.g., Aboud, 1988; Brown, 1995), and currently hold less sway, their treatment here will be somewhat cursory with greater emphasis being placed on the latter two approaches.

Emotional Maladjustment

This approach links the acquisition of prejudice to the development of a particular personality type, the authoritarian personality (Adorno et al., 1950). Much influenced by Freudian thinking, children's prejudice was considered to stem from emotional maladjustment arising from a repressive and harshly disciplined upbringing. Under these circumstances, the child's resulting frustration, anger and hostility towards his/her parents was considered to be displaced away from the parents towards scapegoats who were weaker and lacked authority and power, such as members of minority groups.

While a strength of this theory is that it provides an account of differences in levels of prejudice between individuals (Aboud, 1988), it does not account for the uniformity of prejudice across whole groups of people in particular places and times, nor why some groups are the recipients of prejudice but not others (Brown, 1995). The approach generally ignores the importance of the social environment in influencing people's (including children's) intergroup attitudes and behaviour.

Social Reflection

The social reflection approach takes the latter point as a fundamental premise – children's prejudice simply reflects the community's attitudes and values, which are typically transmitted to children by their parents. According to this social learning-type approach (Bandura, 1977), which has appeared in the literature over many years (e.g., Horowitz and Horowitz, 1938; Kinder and Sears, 1981), children learn their attitudes towards particular ethnic groups, either by direct training or by observing and imitating their parents' verbal and non-verbal behaviour. Presumably, such learning occurs because the children are rewarded for their imitative behaviour, identify with their parents, and/or want to please them.

Consistent with this approach are findings that children from three to four years begin to develop an awareness of the nature of intergroup relationships in their community (Radke and Trager, 1950; Vaughan, 1987); that positive correlations have been reported between the ethnic attitudes of children and their parents (e.g., Bird et al., 1952; Goodman, 1952; Radke and Trager, 1950) and that there are similarities in the statements of parents and their children concerning ethnic minority groups (e.g., Radke-Yarrow et al., 1952).

However, the correlation between the attitudes of children and their parents have typically been low (e.g., Bird et al., 1952; Frenkel-Brunswik and Havel, 1953) and sometimes non-existent (e.g., Aboud and Doyle, 1996b; Pushkin, as cited in Davey, 1983). These findings emphasize the point that it would be incorrect to assume that children should simply be regarded as empty containers into which prevailing societal prejudices are poured, or as sponges that soak up dominant ethnic attitudes (Brown, 1995; Davey, 1983; Milner, 1996). As a considerable amount of developmental research has made clear, children's intellectual and social abilities reveal dramatic development through the middle childhood years and they are active participants in seeking to understand and control both their cognitive and social worlds (Durkin, 1995).

Sociocognitive Theory

The most complete and explicitly developmental account of children's acquisition of prejudice is provided in Aboud's (1988) sociocognitive theory. According to this approach, a child's attitude to other groups of children depends upon his/her levels of development in relation to two overlapping sequences of perceptual-cognitive development. One sequence involves the *process* that dominates a child's experience at a particular time. The child is initially dominated by affective-perceptual processes associated with fear of the unknown and attachment to the familiar. Perceptual processes subsequently dominate, preference for the (similar) ingroup and rejection of the (different) outgroup being determined primarily by physical attributes (e.g., skin colour, language, body size). Thereafter, cognitive processes take ascendancy with the advent of the concrete operational stage of cognitive development around seven years of age and, later, formal operational thinking (Flavell, 1963). The effect of the transition to cognitive processes is that the child is increasingly able to understand the individual rather than the group-based qualities of people. The second sequence of development is concerned with changes in the child's *focus of attention*. Whereas very young children mostly focus on themselves and their preferences and perceptions, older children emphasize categories of people such that individuals are seen as members of these categories or groups. Still later, however, children focus on individuals, who are liked or disliked for their personal rather than group qualities.

Based on these sociocognitive developments, Aboud (1988) argues that ingroup bias and outgroup prejudice increase to a peak at around seven years of age, when group differences are paramount. However, with a subsequent increase in the child's cognitive abilities, occasioned by the onset of concrete operational thinking around seven years of age, Aboud claims that there is a systematic decline in group-based biases, which is further enhanced when the child's ever-increasing cognitive abilities allow him/her to attend to the differences between individuals.

Sociocognitive theory comprises the first attempt at providing an age-related account of children's prejudice and of the specific processes that are responsible for those changes. Of particular note is Aboud's recognition, together with others (e.g., Katz, 1976; Milner, 1996; Vaughan, 1987) of the contribution made by perceptual-cognitive processes to the acquisition and change of ethnic attitudes during childhood.

Consistent with the theory are the results of studies reviewed earlier on the development of majority group children's ethnic awareness and ethnic self-identification (e.g., Aboud, 1977, 1980; Newman et al., 1983; Vaughan, 1963), and their ethnic preferences and attitudes (e.g., Aboud and Mitchell, 1977; George and Hoppe, 1979; Vaughan, 1964a). In addition, research has revealed evidence of apparent linkages between the development of children's cognitive abilities from three to 12 years of age and several types of ethnic cognitions. For example, children's understanding of conservation (an achievement of the concrete operational stage of cognitive development) is correlated with ethnic flexibility, the understanding that ethnically similar and different individuals can have different and similar attributes, respectively (e.g., Doyle et al., 1988). Further, research by Aboud and her colleagues (e.g., Doyle and Aboud, 1995; Doyle et al., 1988) has revealed that the acquisition of concrete operational thinking coincided with a decrease in ingroup prejudice (using the trait attribution measure), and that the mastery of conservation preceded the reduction in prejudice.

However, there are also issues and research findings which provide a challenge to key aspects of the theory. Firstly, while it is now widely accepted that cognitive developmental changes are implicated in the acquisition and expression of many social behaviours (Durkin, 1995), their importance in children's ethnic prejudice remains unclear. For example, although Doyle and Aboud (1995) found a linkage between children's conservation and prejudice, up to 50 per cent of the children who could conserve, still displayed prejudice. In addition, Doyle et al. (1988) found that children's prejudice continued to decline long after they could conserve, again suggesting that additional factors are implicated in the expression of prejudice, beyond the merely cognitive.

Secondly, while the theory proposes that a young child's initial fear reaction to a strange person (from an ethnic minority group) is extended to all individuals from that minority group through the process of generalization, it is silent on how fear turns into the dislike and hatred which are the defining characteristics of prejudice, and why it should persist in the absence of contact. Indeed, the theory does not encompass the possibility that children (and adults) may well develop long-lasting prejudices in the absence of any (negative) contact with an ethnic minority group member (e.g., Brown, 1995).

Thirdly, sociocognitive theory has been proposed to account for a pattern of findings in which the level of prejudice in young children first increases to a peak at around five to seven years, and then gradually declines during middle childhood. Indeed, Aboud's account might be taken to indicate that ethnic prejudice ceases to be a problem during the primary school years, or at least is substantially ameliorated. However, there are findings which suggest that this may not be so. While there are certainly a number of studies which have reported an unambiguous decrease in prejudice after seven years, as sociocognitive theory would predict (e.g., Aboud and Mitchell, 1977; Williams et al., 1975; Zinser et al., 1981), other studies have reported not only that ingroup preference remained at the same level from seven to 12 years (e.g., Asher and Allen, 1969; Davey, 1983; Milner, 1973), but that ingroup preference actually increased during these years (e.g., Hraba and Grant, 1970; Rice et al., 1974; Vaughan and Thompson, 1961). Having said that, of course, as the earlier review has made plain, there are good reasons for questioning whether the ethnic preference data upon which sociocognitive theory is founded, and which it seeks to explain, actually comprises ethnic prejudice.

Fourthly, and most importantly, sociocognitive theory offers a developmental account which is largely indifferent to the social context and motivational considerations. For example, it is unlikely that the initiation of prejudice in children is governed simply by the child's affective-perceptual processes associated with fear of the unknown (and attachment to the familiar). Some, but not all, physical differences are associated with prejudice in both children and adults and the physical differences young children respond to are also those of racial significance to adults (Katz et al., 1975). Further, strong prejudices (e.g., towards particular national groups, religions, homosexuals) can occur even in the absence of physical differences (Tajfel et al., 1972). Thus, the cues to which even young children respond have a distinctiveness which is socially determined, particularly by the labels and evaluative statements applied to groups by peers and adults (Katz, 1976; Marsh, 1970; Vaughan, 1987).

In sum, while sociocognitive theory provides a theoretically consistent account of children's acquisition of ethnic prejudice in terms of their developing perceptual-cognitive processes, the theory is ultimately severely limited by this overwhelming emphasis on these processes to the exclusion of social and motivational considerations.

Social Identity

An approach which places considerable emphasis on motivational considerations and awareness of social structure in accounting for ethnic prejudice is provided by social identity theory (SIT) (Tajfel and Turner, 1979) and its more recent elaboration, self-categorization theory (SCT) (Turner et al., 1987; see Reynolds and Turner, Chapter 10). According to SIT, prejudice and discrimination towards members of ethnic outgroups derives from the desire of individuals to identify with social groups which are considered to be positively distinctive or comparatively superior to other groups, in order to enhance their own self-esteem. The consequences of group identification are that ingroup members are perceived to be similar and to possess positive qualities and hence are subject to positive bias. In contrast, outgroup members are perceived to be different and to possess less favourable qualities and hence may attract prejudice and discrimination. Numerous studies of adults and adolescents have provided support for SIT (see reviews by Brown, 1995; Hogg and Abrams, 1988; Mullen et al., 1991), especially in research using the minimal group paradigm (Tajfel et al., 1971).

However, while SIT provides arguably the most widely endorsed social psychological account of ethnic prejudice in adults at the present time, the theory is virtually mute on the issue of the development of prejudice in children, although several researchers have emphasized the relevance of SIT to accounting for ethnic prejudice in both children and adults (e.g., Davey, 1983; Milner, 1996; Nesdale, in press-a, in press-b; Vaughan, 1988). Firstly, consistent with the theory are findings indicating (a) that children from as young as three years have a developing awareness of which groups are better off and more highly regarded than others, and (b) that they make comparisons between their standing as a member of one social group versus other ethnic groups (e.g., Milner, 1996; Radke and Trager, 1950; Vaughan, 1987).

Secondly, the findings of the ethnic preference studies reviewed earlier are consistent with SIT's assumption that people, including children, seek the positive distinctiveness conferred by membership of higher rather than lower status groups in order to enhance their self-esteem. Thus, whereas dominant group children rarely misidentify their ethnic group, members of low-status minority groups (e.g., Black, Native, and Hispanic Americans) frequently misidentify with the dominant (e.g., White American) cultural group (e.g., Asher and Allen, 1969; Hunsberger, 1978).

Thirdly, SIT provides a ready account of both the differences which may occur between individuals in their levels of prejudice, as well as the considerable similarity in prejudice which can occur across large groups of people at a particular place and time. In both cases, the explanation, according to SIT, lies in the values and attitudes of the particular social group with which the individual chooses to identify. The individual takes on a particular intergroup attitude because it fits with his/her view of him/herself as belonging to a particular group and deriving positive distinctiveness from it (Milner, 1996). This same explanation also accounts for the fact that some minority groups, but not others, are the recipients of prejudice, that children (and adults) can acquire ethnic prejudice without having come into contact with the target group, and that it can persist across generations (Brown, 1995).

Fourthly, since ethnic prejudice, according to SIT, primarily reflects motivational and contextual rather than cognitive considerations, the theory would not predict specific age-related changes in children's prejudice – it might increase, decrease, or remain stable, depending upon the child's prevailing social group identification, as has been reported. Indeed, the implication of this analysis is that, contrary to sociocognitive theory, the child (and the adult) may never acquire ethnic prejudice because he or she chooses not to identify with the social group which holds ethnic prejudice as a value.

Fifthly, a further implication of SIT is that a positive correlation between the intergroup attitudes of parents and their children is not necessarily to be expected, particularly as children increase in age and their social environment expands. Consistent with this are the findings noted earlier of low or non-existent parent–child correlations (e.g., Aboud and Doyle, 1996b; Bird et al., 1952; Frenkel-Brunswik and Havel, 1953; Pushkin, as cited in Davey, 1983). Importantly, Pushkin found a closer relationship between children's attitudes and those of people in the neighbourhood, than between the children's attitudes and those of their parents. Indeed, Harris (1998) has argued that peer groups are generally more influential than parents in shaping children's values.

However, while the preceding discussion serves to highlight the plausibility of SIT as an explanation of children's acquisition of prejudice, there are a number of issues which are problematic for SIT, and/or are in need of direct research assessment. Firstly, a straightforward application of SIT to the case of children ignores the fact that they experience marked changes in both their cognitive (e.g., concrete operational thinking) and social cognitive abilities (e.g., ethnic constancy, moral reasoning, decentration, empathy) and that these acquisitions are sequential and age-related. That is, children's social cognitive abilities are preceded by their cognitive acquisitions, and both are developed during the middle childhood years (e.g., Feffer and Gourevitch, 1960; Kohlberg, 1976; Selman and Byrne, 1974). These acquisitions are potentially very important because there are good grounds for supposing that they might impact upon children's prejudice. For example, it might be speculated that a dominant-group child who is able to decentre and perceive the social environment from the perspective of a minority-group child would be less likely to develop prejudice toward members of that outgroup. Similarly, a dominant-group child whose moral judgements go beyond the external consequences of actions and the individual's need to focus on right as defined by social authority or universal principles, might also be less likely to develop ethnic prejudice. However, while there is some indirect evidence consistent with these speculations (e.g., Clark et al., 1980; Madge, 1976), the impact of children's developing social cognitive abilities on their ethnic prejudice remains to be assessed directly.

Secondly, although SIT provides a plausible account of much of the extant findings, only a handful of studies have directly tested SIT predictions with young children (e.g., Nesdale, in press-a; Nesdale and Flesser, 1999; Turner and Brown, 1978; Vaughan et al., 1981; Yee and Brown, 1992). While these studies, with the exception of Yee and Brown, have provided consistent support for SIT (see next point), few, if any, studies with children have directly assessed SIT's fundamental assumption that individuals identify with particular groups in order to achieve, maintain or enhance positive self-esteem (Tajfel and Turner, 1979). This point is of some significance, not least because it has proven to be somewhat controversial in the adult literature (see Brown, 1995; Hogg and Abrams, 1988; Rubin and Hewstone, 1998).

Thirdly, while each of the studies identified in the previous point, with the exception of Yee and Brown (1992), provided support for SIT, it is difficult to go beyond the conclusion that each provided evidence about the children's *ingroup bias* rather than their *outgroup prejudice*. As with much of the adult research, most of the research with children has used the minimal group paradigm (Tajfel et al., 1971) according to which, children who have been randomly assigned to groups, are asked to allocate rewards or points between the members of the groups. Consistent with research with adults, Turner and Brown, (1978) and Vaughan et al. (1981) found that the children allocated rewards so as to maximize the difference between the arbitrarily created groups, in favour of the ingroup. Similarly, Nesdale and Flesser (1999), but not Yee and Brown (1992), found that children who were arbitrarily assigned to a high- versus low-status group, expressed greater liking for the ingroup versus the outgroup, rather than liking for the ingroup and dislike for the outgroup (see also Aboud and Mitchell, 1977; Genesee, Tucker, and Lambert, 1978). Thus, contrary to the SIT claim that social categorization (i.e., the allocation of people into distinct groups) is sufficient to trigger intergroup discrimination, the studies with children suggest that the effect of self-categorization (i.e., defining oneself in group-based terms), at least that instigated by simulation techniques such as the minimal group paradigm, is to initiate an ingroup focus and bias, rather than dislike or rejection for the outgroup.

Fourthly, an alternative implication might be that, contrary to SIT, mere social categorization is insufficient to instigate 'real' outgroup prejudice (i.e., dislike or hatred which can give rise to verbal and physical harassment of ethnic outgroup members), at least in children. According to this view, social categorization might well instigate ingroup bias or preference in children, but full-blown ethnic prejudice requires the presence of additional precipitating conditions. It might be speculated, for example, that such conditions could include: (a) a lack of development in the child of social cognitive abilities such as decentration, moral reasoning and/or empathy; (b) the extent to which prejudice towards a particular ethnic outgroup is widely shared and expressed unequivocally by people in the child's social environment (Proshansky, 1966); (c) the degree to which there is tension, competition and conflict between the dominant and ethnic minority groups (Brown, 1995); and (d) the extent to which members of the dominant group feel that their social standing is threatened by an ethnic outgroup (e.g., Long et al., 1994; Stephan et al., 1998). Although there is considerable support for the impact of threat on prejudice, at least in relation to adults, research findings in relation to children on this and the other conditions are simply lacking.

In sum, despite not having been explicitly formulated to encompass children's prejudice, the preliminary conclusion to be drawn from the present discussion is that SIT makes a good fist of accounting for the development of prejudice in children. At the same time, the discussion also makes clear that the fit between SIT and the case of children is not perfect and that some modifications to the theory would be required to take the 'peculiarities' of children into account (see Nesdale, in press-b). In addition, further research would be needed to test specific aspects of the theory in relation to children.

Conclusions

As foreshadowed at the outset, the literature on the development of children's prejudice is marked by considerable diversity. There is variation in the methods used by researchers to measure children's prejudice, the estimates of when prejudice emerges in children, the factors that influence its emergence, and the nature of explanations which have been proposed.

Although such a conclusion might well be articulated in relation to a number of social psychological phenomena, children's prejudice is somewhat unique in that so little closure has been achieved, despite the extensive amount of research which has been undertaken. Doubtless contributing to this has been the almost perverse attachment of researchers to the ethnic preference paradigm, long after serious questions were raised concerning its validity as a measure of children's prejudice. As we have seen, however, such criticisms have not been limited to that technique – all of the most frequently used measurement techniques have serious limitations, not the least being their susceptibility to constructed responses, especially as children increase in age. One implication of this is that further advances in the area await the emergence of new approaches which overcome these limitations. Currently, the greatest promise appears to lie in the use of techniques which incorporate unobtrusive or implicit measures, perhaps in conjunction with more structured interviews.

A second and related implication is that the findings obtained with children younger than six or seven years inspire greater confidence than do those obtained with older children, especially in relation to the development of their ethnic awareness, ethnic self-identification, and ethnic preference. As it happens, although there are exceptions (e.g., Aboud, 1988), a relatively common view is that real ethnic prejudice does not actually appear in children until well into middle childhood (e.g., Goodman, 1952; Katz, 1976; Milner, 1996; Proshansky, 1966). By this time, it is considered that the process of ethnic attitude differentiation, integration, and consolidation has been progressed by the child's attainment of ethnic constancy and the gradual acquisition of the language of racism. That is, the child has acquired the cognitive and linguistic foundations upon which a full-blown intergroup attitude can be constructed (Katz, 1976; Proshansky, 1966). However, while there is separate evidence of the latter two achievements, the nature of their relationship to ethnic prejudice, as well as to each other, remains obscure.

A third implication is that the paucity of clearcut findings concerning children's ethnic prejudice during the middle childhood years makes it near impossible to draw a definitive conclusion concerning the relative efficacy of competing explanations, such as those provided by sociocognitive theory (Aboud, 1988) and social identity theory (Tajfel and Turner, 1979). At present, there is research support for both approaches.

Having said that, it is also clear from the earlier discussion that, even without modification, SIT provides a compelling account of much of the extant research findings relating to children's prejudice. More importantly, in focusing on children's social motivations as the key to the development of their intergroup attitudes, an SIT-based approach facilitates a shift in emphasis away from the long-standing orientation in much social developmental research towards the dominance of cognitive processes. Beyond that, however, an SIT-based emphasis holds considerable promise of instigating further theory development and research and, ultimately, of providing a more complete account of the development of ethnic prejudice in children. Given the importance of the problem, the significance of this achievement cannot be over-emphasized.

5   The Socialization of Tolerance

Julie Robinson, Rivka Witenberg, and Ann Sanson

Given the multicultural nature of Australian society and the level of ethnic conflict worldwide, the need for tolerance of racial and ethnic difference is blatantly clear. This chapter reviews research exploring the existence of tolerance among children and adolescents and the processes related to the development of tolerance. The area is a complex one and has been approached from a variety of theoretical and methodological perspectives, resulting in many diverging findings. We first discuss some complex definitional issues surrounding tolerance, intending to alert the reader to the differing conceptual and measurement approaches used by researchers, which contribute to the lack of agreement in findings.

We then review research concerning young children's tolerance. Despite the prevailing view that prejudice is virtually universal among young children, the evidence suggests that tolerance is not only possible but common among them. There are marked individual and contextual differences in levels of prejudice and tolerance, which appear to be related to several social and cognitive factors.

The next section contains a discussion of how tolerance for others develops in adolescence, based on research exploring attitudes towards others' political rights and their rights to different beliefs and practices from one's own. Adolescence appears to be a vital period in the development of these forms of tolerance, which are influenced by education and cognitive skills.

In the final section, we draw together the conclusions emerging from these areas of research, and return to some thorny methodological problems which need addressing in future research.

Definitional Issues

Tolerance is an ambiguous concept, open to several interpretations. Examination of various dictionary definitions of tolerance highlights this. In this chapter we focus particularly on research on two of the major ways of conceptualizing tolerance.

The first set of definitions of tolerance emphasizes forbearance, enduring or 'putting up with' others – a grudging acknowledgement of those different to oneself. For example, the Macquarie Dictionary defines tolerance as a disposition to be patient and fair towards those whose opinions and practices differ from one's own, and Vogt (1997) describes it as the individual enduring that which is disliked, threatening, or which involves negative feelings. It is notable that tolerance, thus defined, does not presume acceptance of others' opinions and practices. This definition of tolerance implies that one can be tolerant and prejudiced simultaneously. For example, a shopkeeper can hold prejudiced attitudes towards customers from a different ethnic or racial group, but be tolerant in order to maintain their custom. This possibility is rarely acknowledged in the literature, which tends to assume that tolerance and prejudice are mutually exclusive and/or are opposites of each other.

Secondly, tolerance can be defined as 'a fair and objective attitude toward those whose practices, race, religion, nationality, etc., differ from one's own' (Random House Dictionary). When specifically related to racial and ethnic differences, this 'freedom from bigotry' is expressed by the absence of prejudice. Much of the research that discusses tolerance has implicitly adopted this sort of conceptualization of tolerance, but as will be seen, there are often questions about how adequately it has assessed it. As noted above, the absence of bias in behaviour does not necessarily reflect 'a fair and objective attitude'. Further, research seldom determines whether respondents noticed the markers of racial/ethnic difference (e.g., skin colour, physical features) when making judgements. It is hard to argue that the absence of discrimination is evidence of tolerance if the person failed to recognize that differences existed.

A third view of tolerance is that it involves a conscious rejection of prejudiced attitudes and responses. That is, one's own negative stereotypes are recognized, judged against experiential knowledge or value systems, and rejected.

Finally, the strongest meaning of tolerance is the full acceptance and valuing of others while recognizing the differences between them and oneself. This is the ideal espoused in most multicultural societies – to celebrate difference. However, little research has specifically addressed this definition of tolerance.

The adoption of one definition over another has consequences for how tolerance is operationalized and also for the selection of research questions. Freedom from bigotry may always be considered 'good'. In contrast, forbearance towards value systems that conflict with one's own is likely to have moral limits. For example, is it morally appropriate to tolerate (or 'put up with') the promotion of racism by another group? Acknowledgement of these limits means that an individual can be both tolerant and intolerant at the same time.

It is clear that the definitional issues around tolerance are complex. There are both strong and weak conceptualizations of tolerance, and both pose research challenges. Most authors do not deal with these definitional issues in any depth, and tend to simply equate tolerance with lack of prejudice or absence of rejection. Very often, methods of measuring tolerance in any one study cross definitional boundaries. Research concerning the development of racial and ethnic tolerance in young children, reviewed in the following section, has tended to adopt the definition of tolerance as a lack of bias. In contrast, the research on adolescents reviewed in Part IV tends to view tolerance as forbearance. We will return to the problems caused by the lack of correspondence between conceptual and operational definitions throughout the chapter.

Development of Ethnic and Racial Tolerance in Young Children

Whether authors frame research in terms of positive attributes such as tolerance and acceptance (e.g., Carter et al., 1980), or a negative attribute, prejudice (e.g., Aboud, 1988), appears to depend primarily on their perspective. These authors review the same research literature, employ overlapping sets of measures, and often find parallel patterns of results. Because the operational definition of tolerance and acceptance is usually an absence of racial or ethnic bias, the difference between the two sets of authors is one of emphasis.

The prevailing emphasis in American and British developmental research has been on prejudice. The conclusion has been that ethnic and racial prejudice is both universal and strong among young children. This appears to have obscured evidence that an absence of ethnic and racial bias is also commonly observed among young children. This can partly be explained by the measures and statistical analyses that have been used. Here we address those methodological issues before summarizing Australian and overseas findings. We then examine some of the factors that appear to influence the development of tolerance in children.

Measurement and Statistical Issues

Two measurement issues concern data that have been interpreted as evidence of tolerance and prejudice. The first harks back to the definitional issues introduced earlier. Prejudice and tolerance are attitudes. That is, prejudice reflects an unfavourable judgement towards a particular group. Discrimination involves behaving differently, usually unfairly, toward the members of a group. There is no necessary relationship between prejudice and discrimination, just as there is no necessary relationship between other attitudes and behaviour. Discrimination can occur in the absence of prejudice (e.g., unprejudiced employees may be constrained to act in a discriminatory way by the policies in their workplaces). Conversely, discrimination may not occur in the presence of prejudice (e.g., prejudiced people may refrain from discriminating when this behaviour leads to legal sanctions).

There is therefore a logical flaw in interpreting the presence of ethnic bias in children's peer preferences or interaction patterns (i.e., discrimination) as evidence of prejudice, and, depending on which definition of tolerance is adopted (see above), a logical flaw in interpreting the absence of such discrimination as evidence of an attitude of tolerance. Despite this, almost all conclusions about tolerance and prejudice in young children have been based upon data concerning beliefs or behaviours.

Most of the instruments that have been designed to assess racial and ethnic attitudes in young children (see Nesdale, Chapter 4) actually assess either beliefs about the attributes of group members or knowledge of stereotypes, since they make no attempt to assess whether the attributes are judged to be positive, negative, or neutral. It cannot be assumed that any particular attribute (e.g., tendency to tease others) will universally be judged favourably or unfavourably. Thus, the same belief can be associated with different attitudes. Furthermore, without information about the strength of judgements or the importance of the attributes in participants' value systems, it is impossible to determine whether a particular number of positively and negatively evaluated beliefs is evidence of tolerance or prejudice. For example, it may be possible to have a positive overall attitude towards a group that one believes is characterized by five negative and two positive attributes if the latter attributes are of central importance to one's value system and the former are not.

Moreover, three very different types of behavioural measures are commonly used to assess prejudice: preferences for unknown peers or dolls (e.g., 'Here are photographs of some new children who might be coming to your class. Put the photographs on the board so that the more you like them the closer they are to you, and the less you like them the further away they are'); preferences for known peers (e.g., 'Here are photographs of the children in your class. Which of them would you most like to play with?'); and the frequency or qualitative characteristics of interactions or relationships between children who differ in racial or ethnic background (e.g., 'Here are photographs of the children in your class. Who is your best friend?') (see Robinson, 1998, for further detail). Clearly readers need to be alert to the need to critically evaluate the ways in which prejudice and tolerance have been measured.

The second methodological issue concerns how the operational definition of these measures influences results. For example, two techniques have been used to assess preferences for classmates: peer nominations (e.g., 'Who do you like the most?'), which involve a forced choice, and sociometric ratings (e.g., 'Rate all the children in your class according to how much you like them'). The latter technique leads to findings of less racial bias. Similarly, children can be asked about the extent to which classmates are friends, or how much they accept them. When acceptance is the criterion, lower levels of ethnic bias are found.

In addition, two issues concerning statistical analyses may have contributed to an overestimation of racial and ethnic bias in children's peer preferences. Firstly, researchers have almost exclusively used statistical analyses that focus on group patterns (e.g., conventional analysis of variance). This has led to a failure to attend to individual differences within groups. Whitley et al. (1984) found that while a conventional analysis suggested that race was a powerful determinant of preferences, a round robin analysis (which examines differences within groups) showed that children were responding to the characteristics of individual peers and not rating all peers of one racial group in the same way. Secondly, few studies have considered effect sizes. In an exception, Singleton and Asher (1979) found that although children preferred peers from their own racial group over those from other groups, the 'race of rater by race of peer' interaction accounted for less than 1 per cent of the variance in children's preferences. The authors concluded that there were 'rather high levels of cross-race acceptance' (1979: 940). If these authors, like most others, had failed to consider the size of the effect, they would have drawn the opposite conclusion.

Absence of Racial/Ethnic Bias Among Children

Australian Data Overseas research has commonly concluded that racial and ethnic biases are relatively strong among children from the majority group until approximately seven years of age, after which these decline. Australian data show little evidence of this pattern. Three studies of four to six-year-old children that compared peers of different ethnic and racial backgrounds and used different measures of peer preference and interaction, all failed to find evidence of ethnic bias (towards children of English, Greek, or Italian immigrants) or racial bias (towards children of Chinese, Vietnamese, or Indian immigrants) among majority-group children (Carapetis and Robinson, 1995; Gleeson, 1998; Robinson and Maine, 1998). Moreover, racial or ethnic bias was found only among a small number of minority groups and then only under very particular conditions.

Similarly, two studies of school-age Australian children show limited evidence of racial bias. Black (1987) found that most Australian school children 'don't mind' which ethnic or racial background an unknown peer is drawn from (Lebanese, Italian, Vietnamese, or Anglo-Australian) for many types of relationships in which bias has been reported in overseas research, but that a preference is expressed for some relationships. In a second study, Black-Gutman and Hickson (1996) found no evidence of racial bias in the traits that Australian children of European descent attributed to Asian Australians. Moreover, while these children ascribed fewer positive attributes to Aboriginal Australians than to other targets, this was often balanced by a smaller number of negative attributes. The balance showed no clear age-related pattern.

In summary, there is very limited evidence that either preschool or school-age Australian children, from either majority or minority backgrounds, show consistent evidence of ethnic or racial bias in their peer preferences or their attribution of traits to members of other groups. These findings cannot be attributed to an absence of prejudice in the wider community (e.g., Black-Gutman and Hickson, 1996; Sanson et al., 1998).

Overseas Research Although North American and British research on young children often finds ethnic and racial bias in trait attributions and preferences for unknown peers (or dolls), such biases are often absent in their interactions (e.g., Porter, 1971) and in the frequency (e.g., Silberman and Spice, 1950) and qualitative characteristics (Holmes, 1996) of friendships. Indeed, studies have found ethnically and racially biased preferences or attitudes and unbiased patterns of interaction (e.g., Porter, 1971) or friendships (e.g., Hraba and Grant, 1970) in the same child. In addition, young children's trait attribution to familiar peers and to the ethnic groups from which these peers are drawn are often unrelated (e.g., Holmes, 1996). It is also worthy of note that although North American and British research typically finds ethnically and racially biased beliefs and preferences, especially among children from the dominant group, there are also a number of exceptions (e.g., Holmes, 1996; van Ausdale and Feagin, 1996).

Individual, Target, and Task Differences

Many studies of beliefs and preferences for unknown peers either report that there is an own-group bias among children belonging to the majority group, but not among children from minority or lower status groups (e.g., Brand et al., 1974), or directly indicate that a sizeable minority of children from the latter groups are unbiased (Aboud and Doyle, 1995). Failure to show a bias towards the dominant group may result from misidentification with this group by members of minorities (see Nesdale, this volume). However, the pattern has also been found when the dominant group is not the target (e.g., Davey, 1983). These findings are compatible with Katz and Kofkin's (1997) hypothesis that the developmental paths for African-American and European American children's racial attitudes differ.

In addition, findings indicating that children who are prejudiced towards one outgroup may be tolerant towards others have been reported in studies of peer preferences in Britain (e.g., Kawwa, 1968), Australia (e.g., Robinson and Maine, 1998), North America (e.g., Aboud and Mitchell, 1977), and Italy (e.g., Lo Coco et al., 1998), and in studies of children's racial beliefs (e.g., Black-Gutman and Hickson, 1996).

Furthermore, whether or not bias is found in children's peer preferences depends on the relationship or activity for which peers are being chosen. For example, Black (1987) found that Australian children only expressed a preference among peers when asked about long-lasting and intimate relationships. However, even this pattern is not universal. For example, although Holmes (1996) found that race and ethnicity influenced romantic relationships but not friendships, the former could not be characterized as longer-lasting or more intimate than friendships. Indeed, one partner in the relationship was usually oblivious to his/her status.

Data Concerning Racial and Ethnic Acceptance

A relatively small number of studies explicitly assess racial and ethnic tolerance and acceptance, rather than whether or not a bias is present. In these cases, the measures have been developed specifically for this purpose. For example, Klein (1996) studied the cross-cultural tolerance of 3rd and 6th grade Canadian children using the Cross Cultural Sensitivity Scale (Pruegger and Rogers, 1993).

He reported that tolerance was widespread, with 'all subjects scoring fairly high' on the measure.

Nevertheless, many studies that aimed to measure peer preference have inadvertently measured acceptance, a favourable evaluation of the possibility of contact, by asking 'Would you like to play with these (outgroup) children?'. It appears that most majority group children in the US (e.g., Williams and Morland, 1976) and elsewhere (e.g., Morland and Hwang, 1981) accept outgroup peers as play partners.

Aboud (1988) argues that the above question is a flawed measure because it 'does not seem to show any variance' (1988: 32). She proposes that the high levels of acceptance yielded by this measure is a product of 'yea-saying', or of children's willingness to play with anyone for the sake of playing. However, levels of acceptance and rejection of peers from other groups, and levels of acceptance of own-group peers, do show variability across samples (e.g., Morland and Hwang, 1981). In addition, Aboud's latter suggestion implies that children are indeed tolerant of ethnic/racial differences, at least when choosing playmates.

Conclusion

The research cited above clearly indicates that an absence of ethnic bias in beliefs, peer preferences, interaction, and relationships, and explicit acceptance of racial and ethnic differences, are displayed by a large number of preschool and school-age children in a variety of nations. Intra and interindividual differences in bias and acceptance appear to have two main sources: differences in cognitive development and differences in socialization experiences.

Factors that Influence the Development of Tolerance in Children

Cognitive Development

For the past 25 years, cognitive theories have dominated research on the development of racial and ethnic categories and racial and ethnic attitudes and discrimination. Nesdale (Chapter 4) provides a detailed discussion and evaluation of one of the most influential theories on the latter topic, Aboud's (1988) sociocognitive theory of the development of prejudice.

A number of relationships between cognitive abilities and level of ethnic bias have been identified. For example, Doyle and Aboud (1995) found that even-handedness in the attribution of traits (attribution of unfavourable traits to one's own group and favourable traits to other racial groups), was correlated to two perceptual abilities, the extent to which persons of different races were perceived to share similarities, and the extent to which persons of the same race were perceived to differ, and to one cognitive ability, the extent to which one could take the perspective of peers from another group and accept that they may have different peer preferences to one's own.

However, there are several reasons to question the universality of such relationships. If the high levels of racial and ethnic bias observed in many studies of majority-group children under seven years of age are a direct consequence of their cognitive and perceptual limitations, it is unclear why the children do not display these biases towards peers from all other racial groups, and for all relationships. Moreover, the finding that ethnic and racial biases are small or absent among minority-group children who are under seven years of age would imply that these children do not share the cognitive or perceptual limitations that characterize majority-group children of the same age. These issues, and the relatively low variance in ethnic and racial bias accounted for by cognitive abilities, suggest that socialization experiences may also be important.

Socialization Experiences

Parents When parents show by conspicuous example that they accept persons from other racial or ethnic backgrounds, it can have a dramatic effect on the development of children's peer preferences. For example, although most British studies report an own-group bias in preferences for unknown peers among children from the majority group, the opposite pattern has been found among those children who have adopted siblings of African descent (Marsh, 1970). Similarly, while Holmes (1996) found that race was a criterion in most young children's selection of a boyfriend/girlfriend, this was not the case among children whose mother and father were from different racial backgrounds.

However, parents' racial and ethnic tolerance may have little influence on their children's attitudes if it is not expressed unambiguously in words or behaviour. For example, Aboud and Doyle (1996b) found that there was no correlation between mothers' racial attitudes and children's racial beliefs, and that children were unaware of their mothers' attitudes. Similar findings have been reported in other countries (e.g., Weigl, 1995). Despite this, parental attitudes appear to be associated with the quality and quantity of children's intergroup interactions (Patchen, 1982).

It is also likely that specific parenting practices promote or inhibit the development of tolerance. One requirement for the strong version of tolerance, as whole-hearted acceptance, is the ability to see a situation through another's eyes. While the cognitive capacity for such perspective-taking, and its emotional counterpart, empathic responses, develop in early childhood, there is wide variation in the extent to which children develop these attributes, and parenting practices appear to be implicated in this. In particular, parental use of inductive reasoning techniques (listening to the child's point of view; explaining how others are affected by the child's behaviour; explaining reasons for rules to the child; and negotiating rules and agreements where possible) appears to promote the development of these attributes (Eisenberg and Miller, 1990). Thus, although no research has directly assessed their impact on racial and ethnic tolerance, it is likely that inductive parenting practices increase the likelihood that children will adopt tolerant (and accepting) perspectives.

Peers Peers appear to influence the socialization of racial and ethnic attitudes and biases both passively and actively.

The number of peers from one's group relative to that of other groups in one's classroom, grade, and school appears to influence tolerance. Whether or not bias is seen in peer preferences (e.g., Loomis, 1943), intergroup interactions (e.g., Carapetis and Robinson, 1995) or friendships (e.g., Kawwa, 1968) appears to be influenced by whether or not one's group represents a majority, and the size of the minority relative to the size of the majority.

Longitudinal research suggests that interracial contact per se does not improve peer relations between children of different ethnic backgrounds (e.g., Singleton and Asher, 1979). However, naturally occurring benign and/or cooperative contact between children enhances the socialization of ethnic and racial tolerance. Several specific aspects of the quality of interaction may also be relevant, including the level of engagement between children (e.g., Doyle, 1982), the number of social overtures (Finkelstein and Haskins, 1983) or other-directed speech (Doyle, 1982) produced by children, and the level of conflict (Finkelstein and Haskins, 1983).

As appears to be the case for parents, whether or not children's friends hold tolerant attitudes may have little influence on the development of tolerance unless these attitudes are expressed unambiguously. Aboud and Doyle (1996b) found that there was no relationship between the racial beliefs of children and their friends, and that children were unaware of their friends' racial beliefs. In contrast, when peers make their ethnic and racial beliefs explicit, either spontaneously (van Ausdale and Feagin, 1996) or at the instigation of researchers (Aboud and Doyle, 1996a), they appear to exert considerable influence.

Most of the research relevant to peers focuses on school contexts. However, children spend considerable extracurricular time with peers, during which there may also be norms, policies, and practices that limit or enhance children's opportunities for intergroup contact, and the likelihood of positive interactions when contact does take place (Braddock et al., 1995).

Schooling School experiences influence racial and ethnic attitudes and discrimination in three ways: (a) by attempts to directly affect ethnic and racial socialization; (b) by exposing children to the attitudes of their teachers; and (c) by elements in the 'hidden curriculum'.

Explicit attempts to modify young children's racial or ethnic attitudes via school curricula have taken several main forms: reinforcement, perceptual differentiation, curriculum interventions, cooperative learning, and interracial contact. Reviews of the effectiveness of these strategies, a detailed review of seven cooperative learning techniques that meet Allport's (1954) conditions for benign contact (equal status, cooperative activities, and explicit support from relevant authorities), and a summary of 12 conditions necessary for school-based interventions to be effective in reducing prejudice or increasing tolerance, are provided by Hawley and Jackson (1995). Few meta-analyses of the effectiveness of curriculum interventions have been conducted. Those that have indicate that role playing and anti-racist teaching are both effective in reducing student prejudice, although both are more effective when directed at elementary or high-school students than at young adults (McGregor, 1993). However, the ways in which all these techniques are applied, and the policy context in which they are applied, appear to influence their outcomes. Other curriculum interventions (e.g., cultural information programmes) may have a negative effect if they focus on differences between groups.

Teachers' attitudes also appear to be related to interracial acceptance (e.g., St. John and Lewis, 1975) and interactions in the classroom (Patchen, 1982), although these effects may differ across ethnic and racial groups (e.g., Corenblum et al., 1997). A number of programmes that aim to have teachers act as models of ethnic and racial tolerance have been developed. However, there is currently little empirical evidence that these are effective (Zeichner, 1995).

In addition, the hidden curriculum (reflected in the topics included in the curriculum, pedagogical methods etc.) may also subtly perpetuate prejudice. School textbooks in the US have long been noted for either ignoring, trivializing, or demeaning the experiences of persons of minority racial and ethnic backgrounds (e.g., Oakes, 1985).

Mass media In both books (e.g., Pescosolido et al., 1997) and adult-directed television programmes (e.g., Graves, 1996) in the US, members of ethnic and racial minority groups are under-represented, and their roles, occupations and personality characteristics are limited in ways that are likely to perpetuate stereotypes. However, Greenberg (1986) has argued that the prominence of minority group athletes such as Michael Jordan, in commercials, sporting, and news programmes helps to break down ethnic stereotypes by appealing to children from a variety of backgrounds and highlighting their common interests. Unfortunately, these depictions may also perpetuate subtle stereotypes. In all mass media, persons with lighter and darker skin colours are likely to be depicted achieving success in different domains (e.g., academic and sporting, respectively), and the definition of success is usually that used by the dominant culture (Heath, 1995).

Although educational television for children on both commercial and public networks in the US frequently depicts positive intergroup interaction, only one programme, Sesame Street, has developed a curriculum specifically designed to promote racial and ethnic tolerance (Graves, 1996). The physical and cultural differences between groups that are noticed by children in everyday interactions are explicitly discussed, the value of diversity is upheld, and similarities between members of different groups are highlighted. This curriculum was developed in 1992 and its effects have not yet been subject to systematic research. Indeed, there is little empirical research on the ways in which television viewing habits impact upon the development of racial and ethnic attitudes or discrimination.

Conclusion

Empirical evidence suggests that, for at least some children, intra- and inter-individual differences in racial and ethnic attitudes and discrimination are associated with the development of particular cognitive abilities and exposure to particular socialization experiences. Although each of these factors have been discussed separately, they appear to interact in complex ways (e.g., Phinney et al., 1997), which may differ across racial and ethnic groups.

It is also instructive to reflect on the possible sources of interindividual differences in ethnic and racial attitudes and discrimination that have not been the subject of systematic research. For example, research on the contribution of young children's temperament is lacking, and that concerning personality in older children has had a very narrow focus: self-esteem and the security of ethnic identity. Research has produced highly inconsistent findings in both cases.

The Development of Tolerance as Endurance in Adolescence

Evidence about tolerance as 'putting up with' another, comes from two bodies of research: those on political tolerance and belief discrepancy. Political tolerance involves a willingness to extend rights to a range of social, racial, religious, and political groups, which are disliked (Owen and Dennis, 1987). Belief discrepancy examines tolerance of others who hold beliefs and perform practices different from one's own (e.g., Wainryb et al., 1998). Knowledge about political tolerance comes from large scale surveys conducted by political scientists and sociologists, mostly using samples of adolescents and adults (e.g., Avery, 1989) and occasionally children (Zellman and Sears, 1971). Research into belief discrepancy has been conducted by psychologists, who have primarily assessed responses to dilemmas and adopted a structural cognitive model (e.g., Enright et al., 1984). While this research does not deal directly with racial tolerance, these studies extend our knowledge about the development of tolerance more generally and the factors which influence it, knowledge which could be useful in drawing inferences about racial tolerance. Together, the evidence indicates age-related differences, with the most important changes occurring during adolescence. Research has further highlighted the positive influences of education, cognitive skill, and moral development, and the negative influence of dogmatism. The context sensitive nature of tolerance has also been observed.

Methodological Issues

These studies are not free of methodological flaws. While there is a general consensus that survey research is useful in some domains, the methodology yields less useful data in more sensitive areas such as prejudice and tolerance

(Chong, 1993) nor does it lend itself to in-depth analysis of underlying beliefs or assessment of developmental pathways (Vogt, 1997). The use of dilemmas has also been criticized for lacking relevance and ecological validity. Other weaknesses relate to social desirability or the perceived expectation of the researcher (see Nesdale, Chapter 4). Research findings on both political tolerance and belief discrepancy are reviewed below.

Political Tolerance

Avery (1989) suggests that adolescence may be the most critical period for the development of political tolerance. While few age-related differences have been observed in the primary-school years, important developmental changes occur during adolescence. This is presumably linked to the shift from concrete to formal operations, occurring predominantly in early adolescence, which allows abstract reasoning and reflection on our ideas and beliefs. Adolescence is also an age of rapid acquisition of new knowledge.

The notion that cognitive skills form a necessary basis for tolerance is not entirely new. Selznick and Steinberg (1969), who examined the origin of anti-Semitism and racism, concluded that being tolerant was related to education. They argued that biased beliefs about Jews were transmitted through the socialization process, while education induced cognitive capacities enabling the person to reject anti-Semitic and other racial beliefs. Being able to think clearly and critically and possessing necessary knowledge, it appears, allowed for the reassessment of unfounded biased beliefs such as 'Jews drink blood' or 'All Aborigines are drunks'. Thus, such skills allow for the possibility of developing more tolerant attitudes and beliefs.

More recent studies have examined the relationship between both education and cognitive factors (such as cognitive development levels and critical and reflective thinking), and one's willingness to extend civil liberties or human rights to disliked groups. For example, Bobo and Licari (1989) found that cognitive skills accounted for 33 per cent of the variance in political tolerance. The effect of education on tolerance was significant even when a person had strong negative feelings about the group membership, skin colour, or creed of other people. Similarly, Chong (1993) found that participants' level of education and whether they attended to ideas or feelings, affected whether they were prepared to extend political rights to an unfavoured group. Participants who focused on democratic rights were usually more educated and tended to be more tolerant. Those who focused on their feelings tended to be both less educated and less tolerant. The ability to think critically and reflect on our attitudes and beliefs appears to be a necessary but not sufficient condition for political tolerance. The relevance of these cognitive skills to racial tolerance is suggested by Selznick and Steinberg's (1969) study cited above.

Education not only promotes cognitive skills but is also the basis for more and better knowledge. For example, McColsky and Brill (1983) found a consistently high correlation between scores on knowledge of the law and political rights and political tolerance. However, factual knowledge by itself appears to have little impact on the development of more tolerant attitudes and beliefs (Vogt, 1997). It appears that effective reasoning and problem solving are affected by both the efficacy with which people deploy their reasoning skills and by the knowledge base they have, whatever domain is being considered. Advanced cognitive skills affect how we think, while prior knowledge influences both how we think and what we think (Witenberg, 1998). The studies reviewed above provide evidence that cognitive development, cognitive skills, and prior knowledge assist in the development of tolerance, particularly political tolerance. These factors are likely to be integral to the development of all forms of tolerance including racial tolerance.

The relationship between education and racial tolerance is also evident from surveys on White people's attitudes to Blacks collected in the US. Smith (1981) found that attitudes towards desegregation were directly correlated with the level of education among 22,000 adults who had responded to national surveys conducted between 1954 and 1977. Although there was a general increase in acceptance of desegregation, which Smith called an 'era' effect, it was the university educated group that was most in favour of desegregation, followed by those who had attended high school.

Some researchers have suggested that education does not work directly but in conjunction with the influence of parents and the mass media. While the mass media do not appear to influence political tolerance of adolescents, parents can do so by challenging and encouraging ideas that are relevant to political tolerance (Owen and Dennis, 1987). Similarly, teachers and schools can influence political tolerance by promoting democratic principles and moral values (Kohlberg, 1984). Teachers can also influence racial tolerance in adolescents by being impartial and creating a classroom climate that is non-discriminatory, particularly when working with minority students (Nielsen, 1977).

Moral development is another factor that has been considered relevant to tolerance. Are people who are 'more moral' also more tolerant? While this is a difficult question to answer conclusively, a positive correlation between cognitive moral reasoning and political tolerance has been found. For example, Avery (1989) found that those Year 9 and 11 students who scored higher in moral reasoning also showed more political tolerance towards unfavoured groups. It has also been suggested that strong moral beliefs about equality and justice may lessen intolerance while dogmatism, 'a way of not thinking', diminishes our ability to be tolerant (Vogt, 1997).

Several studies have shown that tolerance and intolerance coexist in individuals of all ages, including children and adolescents. It appears that people are selective about whom and what they will tolerate, and under what circumstances they are prepared to be tolerant. Hence, tolerance cannot be conceptualized as a global structure and should be viewed as multifaceted and context sensitive. For example, McColsky and Brill (1983) found that a very high percentage of their participants defended 'freedom of speech' as a democratic principle, but such rights were only accorded to 'acceptable' individuals or groups, and not to groups such as Nazi sympathizers. On the other hand, extending democratic rights to disliked others, but not accepting them as neighbours, sets discriminatory limits on tolerance. Such 'focused intolerance' is undoubtedly also applicable to racial tolerance.

Belief Discrepancy

Research on tolerance towards persons who have opposing beliefs confirms that adolescence is a vital period. For example, in a series of studies using dilemmas, children in primary school, adolescents, and college students were asked to judge people who had opposing views to their own on a range of social, moral, and political issues (Enright et al., 1984). Based on age differences in modal responses to the dilemmas, Enright and his co-workers concluded that tolerance underwent a developmental progression from intolerance, through tolerance as endurance, to open-minded acceptance of others with opposing beliefs. Seventh graders tended to express intolerant views towards others with opposing beliefs. Older adolescents expressed tolerant views towards others and affirmed the rights of others to hold opposing beliefs. Tolerance showed a strong, positive correlation with Piagetian cognitive stages. This finding parallels the relationship between cognitive development and political tolerance found in the studies reviewed earlier.

Other researchers have confirmed the developmental nature of tolerance towards persons holding opposing beliefs (Wainryb et al., 1998), but they have also questioned whether tolerance can be conceptualized as a global construct (Siegelman and Toebben, 1992). Enright et al. (1984) did not differentiate between different types of dissenting ideas (i.e., social, moral, and political) or consider different contexts (such as having the person with dissenting beliefs as a neighbour or visiting such a person). For example, Wainryb et al. (1998) found that although some adolescents tolerated the holding of opposing beliefs about hurtful practices, acting on these beliefs was uniformly condemned. Siegelman and Toebben too found that when content and context were accounted for, no single construct for tolerance emerged. What people were asked to tolerate, and under what circumstances, influenced their responses. This again highlights the multidimensional and context dependent nature of tolerance.

Conclusion

In summary, evidence concerning tolerance as endurance suggests that the capacity for political tolerance and tolerance towards those with opposing beliefs (and for more whole-hearted acceptance) develops in adolescence and requires particular cognitive abilities. It seems likely that these same cognitive abilities underlie other forms of tolerance, including racial/ethical tolerance. Interindividual variability appears to be linked to education, and parent and teacher variables. In addition, there is intra-individual variability in what adolescents will tolerate. Parallel evidence that adolescents tolerate some racial/ethical groups but not others (see Part III) supports the notion that similar patterns hold for racial tolerance, political tolerance, and tolerance of those with opposing beliefs.

Overall Conclusions

In this chapter we have reviewed evidence about two separate facets of tolerance. One relates to young children's beliefs and preferences, and we have seen that the evidence for ubiquitous biases in favour of same-group members is not as strong as is sometimes claimed. Much of this research was framed as research on prejudice, but viewing it from the angle of children's tolerance or acceptance of others reveals much inter-individual variability as well as variation across contexts (types of interaction and groups involved). Both socialization factors, like the family and school, and cognitive factors, seem to play some part in creating this variability.

The second area reviewed relates to older children and adolescents, and refers to forbearance towards other groups. Given the dearth of data specifically about racial groups, we have reviewed literature on tolerance towards other groups in general (e.g., those with different beliefs to oneself), and have drawn out the implications for tolerance towards other racial groups. It is clear that cognitive changes in adolescence allow more complex thinking about one's own and other groups, and give the potential for tolerance in its strongest form (recognition of differences between groups along with full acceptance of their rights). Here too, the context-dependence of tolerance and intolerance is a key finding. Social influences have received relatively little research attention but appear to be relevant. Given recent calamitous examples of ethnic groups previously tolerating each other (at least at the level of 'grudging acceptance') quickly shifting to a position of intolerance and hatred when political events intervene (e.g., Rwanda, former-Yugoslavia), the role of social factors which might explain the variability between individuals, and variability across time and contexts, appears an important focus for future research.

A final issue that bears on the interpretation of all the research reported in this chapter, as well as pointing to an important direction for future research, is the methodological issue of the match between the conceptual definitions of key constructs, and the way they have been operationalized by researchers. We began this chapter by noting the many different meanings of tolerance. We have also noted that relatively few researchers have specifically focused on racial or ethnic tolerance (in any of its meanings) in their research. Nevertheless, they have frequently interpreted findings of lack of prejudice or lack of bias as indicating tolerance or acceptance. Exactly what form of tolerance/acceptance is involved is often ambiguous. Moreover, if children do not orient to the racial/ethnic marker (skin colour or other features) of interest to the researcher, lack of evidence of bias cannot be equated with tolerance, because the children may not realize that there is a difference to be tolerated.

We would recommend that future researchers play much closer attention to definitional/conceptual issues. Firstly, they must decide what aspect of tolerance, acceptance or prejudice they are interested in, and define it carefully. Then, they must ensure that their measures do in fact tap this facet, and not another potentially related facet. Until this occurs, a mass of data will continue to accumulate which is actually quite hard to interpret. Given the importance of tolerance to the future well-being of our society, we hope future researchers will take up this challenge.

6 Prejudice and Personality: The Case of the Authoritarian and Social Dominator

Patrick C. L. Heaven

The link between prejudice and personality traits is not new to social psychology, but has a long and illustrious history extending at least to the 1930s with the formulation of the frustration-aggression hypothesis (Dollard et al., 1939). Over the years, other personality traits have also been suggested as possible precursors to prejudice and intolerance, including: low self-esteem, insecurity, and anxiety, as well as authoritarianism (see Duckitt, 1994, for a thorough review).

Rather than focus on selected traits such as self-esteem or anxiety, other scholars have sought to explain prejudice through well-established and formal personality theories. Thus, for example, Eysenck (e.g., Eysenck and Wilson, 1978) suggested that his personality dimensions E (extraversion), but more particularly P (psychoticism or toughmindedness), underpin the whole range of social and political beliefs. Eysenck argued that it is P, an inherited personality dimension, that makes people dogmatic, machiavellian, and emphatic, and which shapes their *choice* and *expression* of attitudes. The high P individual was viewed as cold, unempathic, hostile, and therefore a likely candidate to be intolerant of others, especially minority groups. Although the possibility that social and political views are shaped by the 'big five' personality dimensions has received very limited empirical support in Australia (Leeson and Heaven, in press), this line of research continues to generate some research activity elsewhere, particularly in Europe (e.g., Riemann et al., 1993; Van Hiel and Mervielde, 1996).

The present chapter will focus on two personality variables shown to have strong links with prejudice, namely, right-wing authoritarianism and social dominance orientation. Authoritarianism will be seen to have had a major impact on the nature of psychological research into prejudice. Whereas it has a well-established (and vigorously debated) body of scientific literature, social dominance orientation is a relatively new construct. It is, however, an important development and, as we shall see, closely tied to right-wing authoritarianism. A large proportion of the chapter will trace the key developments of authoritarianism, noting its eventual fall from grace and its re-emergence as right-wing authoritarianism. This will be followed by a briefer discussion of social dominance orientation (SDO). Although it has generated relatively few research studies outside the US, SDO holds considerable promise as an individual difference measure capable of predicting what are referred to as hierarchy-enhancing myths.

The Nature of Authoritarianism

The view that intergroup relations in general and prejudice in particular can be explained by resorting to personality factors received a tremendous boost in 1950 with the publication of *The Authoritarian Personality* (Adorno et al., 1950/1982). The research, begun in 1943, was sponsored by the American Jewish Committee. As the abridged edition (published in 1982) of this classic volume reminds us, research into anti-Semitism by Adorno and his colleagues blended psychoanalysis and social science, such that its impact on social psychological scholarship at the time was overwhelming. Jahoda (1954) referred to the book as 'historically relevant' and Billig went so far as to suggest that the book '...constitutes a major landmark in the history of psychology, as well as being the single most important contribution to the psychology of fascism' (1978: 36). Computerized searches show that within 15 years of publication, several hundred scientific papers and book chapters had been published on 'authoritarianism' or the 'authoritarian personality'.

The main *raison d'être* of the book was to uncover the causes of anti-Semitism, but it focused also on ethnocentrism, political and economic conservatism, and the potential for fascism. Research evidence of that period concluded that authoritarians are rigid, dogmatic, and strongly supportive of what were referred to as 'traditional values'. They were also seen as being status oriented, domineering towards minority group members, while also being submissive to high-status individuals. The research was influenced by the view that one's inner forces, that is, one's personality, is the primary determining factor of intolerance (Adorno et al., 1982). It was argued that social attitudes (prejudice, anti-Semitism, and ethnocentrism) are a function of deeply rooted personality characteristics. This characteristic was referred to as the potential for fascism and, in the authors' view, would predispose an individual to adopt prejudicial views.

A central theme of Adorno et al.'s (1982) analysis is that the parent–child relationship has a significant impact on the development and character of the child and is crucial in the formation of an authoritarian disposition. The parents of these children were described as harsh and eager to use punishment; they demanded strict obedience and acceptable behaviour of their children (Cherry and Byrne, 1977). Empirical evidence at the time seemed to support this thesis. For example, Dickens and Hobart (1959) found that parental treatment of children induced particular personality needs which the child could meet by adopting an authoritarian approach. Thus, the mothers of such children believed that strict discipline is necessary to develop a 'strong' character. Likewise, Harris et al. (1950) found that the mothers of children classified as prejudiced, exhibited authoritarian attitudes and expected obedience promptly from their children. Hart (1957) found that as mothers' levels of authoritarianism increased, so they tended to prefer using non-love parenting techniques.

   Very little (if any) credence was given to the role of cultural context or to the possibility that prejudice might reflect other determinants, such as one's group identity, cultural norms, or life's experiences. On the contrary, the main tools of investigation were the clinical interview and projective tests (Thematic Apperception Test), with the whole investigation firmly imbedded in psychoanalytic theory. The researchers explained their position thus:

> An adult's social outlook or ideology is an aspect of her or his personality and is strongly influenced by deeper (psychodynamic) aspects of personality. The adult personality is in turn shaped by personality development in childhood, which to a degree reflects the character of the family. It is recognized that the culture and institutional structure of society are important influences, but they remain contextual and rather shadowy. (Adorno et al., 1982: vi)

Adorno and colleagues (1982) viewed the authoritarian personality as a complex syndrome of behaviours, attitudes, and dispositions. This syndrome comprised nine elements that have been listed in Table 6.1. The dimensions are relatively broad ranging and include supporting the norms of the ingroup, to leader–follower distinctions, to an emphasis on sexual 'goings on'.
   No doubt, what most impressed researchers working in this area was the use of attitude scale construction in combination with projective and clinical techniques. Interviews were conducted with a wide variety of respondents and

Table 6.1 Components of F-scale authoritarianism

Conventionalism:	A desire to support the norms established by the ingroup or those in positions of authority.
Authoritarian submission:	An uncritical acceptance of the ingroup or those in positions of authority.
Authoritarian aggression:	Intolerance and rejection of those who violate conventional values.
Anti-intraception:	The perception that creative and imaginative individuals are a 'threat'.
Superstition and stereotypy:	The tendency to think rigidly and believe that much of what happens to us is 'mystically' determined.
Power and 'toughness':	Identification with the leader; an emphasis on strong-weak, leader–follower distinctions.
Destructiveness and cynicism:	A generalized hostility particularly to the weak and members of outgroups.
Projectivity:	A belief that here are wild and dangerous forces operative in the world.
Sex:	An emphasis on 'sexual goings-on'.

Source Derived from Adorno et al. (1982).

the clinical data were used to generate the attitude inventories. According to Sahakian there was a '...constant interplay of statistical analysis with the clinical technique' (1982: 248). The dimensions listed above were seen to covary in their determination of prejudice, and the authors made careful use of item discrimination to produce successive iterations of their attitude measures. The rationale of Adorno et al. (1982) was that it is possible to measure prejudice by tapping into the fascist (authoritarian) personality without reference to any specific ethnic group. In order to achieve this, they therefore developed a measure of the prejudiced personality, the fascism (F) scale. Billig (1978) has commented that very few social psychologists showed great interest in the original intent of Adorno and colleagues or of their underlying theory, but rather seized upon the F scale turning it into *the* measure of 'authoritarianism'.

Authoritarianism and Prejudice: The Empirical Evidence

The earliest evidence that F scale authoritarianism is significantly related to prejudice was demonstrated by Adorno et al. (1982) where F scale scores were found to correlate with scores on measures of ethnocentrism (ETH) and anti-Semitism (AS). As well, F scale links with prejudice received wide support from several independent researchers. Thus, for example, Hites and Kellogg (1964) reported a correlation of -.55 between scores on the F scale and a two-item measure of prejudice among 141 college students in the deep south of the US. They found that authoritarians were more likely than non-authoritarians to endorse segregation in schools and churches.

Siegman (1961) concluded that F scale authoritarianism predicts only certain types of prejudice. Israeli students completed several personality and attitudinal measures including prejudice towards Arabs and Jewish immigrants from North Africa. Of interest is the finding that both forms of prejudice were related ($\underline{r}$ = .66, $\underline{p}$ < .01), but that only prejudice towards Arabs was predicted by F scale scores. Thus, Siegman concluded that, although the basic thesis of Adorno et al. (1982) was confirmed, not all prejudice is related to authoritarian personality.

That authoritarianism may predict different types of prejudice found added support in a study by Diab (1959). He surveyed Arab students studying in the US and determined their levels of authoritarianism and attitudes toward four ethnic groups: Armenians, Kurds, Circassians, and Jews. Authoritarianism predicted prejudice toward Jews, but not toward the other groups. Diab (1959) suggested that the Arab respondents viewed the Jewish ethnic group as quite distinct from the other groups and that the predictors of attitudes differ for each cluster. He argued that social pressures under some circumstances may be so powerful as to override the ability of personality to predict social and ethnic attitudes. Thus, although the respondents may dislike Kurds, Circassians, and Armenians, they remain 'more acceptable' than Jews. As Diab put it, 'The social pressures in this context may be looked upon as the group norms regulating the attitude of ingroup members towards the outgroup' (1959: 185).

Shortly after the publication of *The Authoritarian Personality*, doubts began to emerge about the pre-eminence of personality factors as predictors of prejudice, with several influential studies championing the role of cultural factors. This was a significant development, not least because it foreshadowed later experimental work on social identity and group influences on prejudice. In an early report, Christie and Garcia (1951) selected students from California and a southern state in the US that practiced legally sanctioned segregation of Blacks. They found that students from that state were significantly more likely than the Californian students to endorse the items on both the F and ETH measures. In addition, scores on the F and ETH scales were significantly correlated for both groups. The differences in the endorsement of items between the groups led the authors to conclude that situational factors also play an important role in determining one's level of prejudice and that the influence of authoritarianism may have been overstated. Under some conditions, it was argued, group influences may be more important than personality factors in shaping prejudiced attitudes.

This sentiment received unqualified support from Pettigrew (1958) who published a well-cited study based on samples from South Africa and the southern US. He examined the correlates of prejudice among English- and Afrikaans-speaking White South African students as well as among 366 White adults resident in northern and southern communities in the US. Among both groups of students F scale scores correlated significantly with prejudice. However, it was also found that, although both groups of students and both groups of adults had similar F scale scores, Afrikaners and southern residents were significantly more prejudiced than their counterparts. Pettigrew concluded that in some cultures the pressure to conform to racist views is so powerful that it has a significant effect on personal views about race and ethnicity. In such cultures where prejudice is tolerated, if not endorsed, personality factors appear less influential than group norms in determining prejudiced attitudes, simply because individuals do not have the latitude to select attitudes that reflect their personality. He concluded: 'In areas with historically embedded traditions of racial intolerance, externalizing personality factors underlying prejudice remain important, but sociocultural factors are unusually crucial and account for the heightened racial hostility' (1958: 40).

Pettigrew's (1958) work laid the foundation for further South African research into the correlates of prejudice, although some of this yielded equivocal results. Perhaps the most prolific was Orpen (1970, 1971) who conducted many studies, albeit with small unrepresentative samples. In one study, for instance, he found among a sample of 88 White English-speaking university students that, whereas two measures of prejudice were significantly correlated (r = .50, p < .01), neither correlated significantly with a balanced F scale. This led to the conclusion that personality and prejudice are unrelated under cultural milieu that promote racial intolerance (Orpen, 1971). Just the opposite findings were obtained among 100 Afrikaans-speaking White students (Orpen, 1970), after controlling for acquiescence, F scale scores were found to correlate significantly with ethnocentrism. Importantly, these students were also found to be significantly more authoritarian and ethnocentric than those in the original study (Adorno et al., 1982). Orpen concluded in the following terms: '...Afrikaners have to a large extent internalized the prevailing authoritarian norms to the point where they form part of their basic personality structure, which in turn makes them especially receptive to the prejudiced ideas current in their culture' (1970: 120).

It is possible, of course, that Orpen's results may have been affected by sample biases of one kind or another. A noteworthy study by Duckitt (1988) among a large heterogeneous sample of White South Africans attempted to shed some light on the issues raised by the work of Pettigrew (1958) and Orpen (1970, 1971). Duckitt selected over 700 respondents for study, dividing them into English and Afrikaans speakers with different levels of education and those who had either a rural or city background. Following Pettigrew's thesis that in South Africa prejudice reflects group pressures, Duckitt reasoned that prejudice should be more strongly linked with conformity indices than with authoritarianism. This thesis was not supported. Among all subgroups of his sample, prejudice was significantly linked with scores on a balanced measure of authoritarianism, but not with scores on an approval motivation measure, except in one of nine groups. Among English speakers with low education, approval motivation and prejudice correlated $r =$ .14, $p < .05$, while authoritarianism and prejudice correlated $r = .23$, $p < .01$. Thus, Duckitt concluded that '...normative pressures may be much less important in determining prejudiced attitudes in highly prejudiced societies than has generally been assumed' (1994: 241).

In summary, studies of authoritarianism had a major impact on our understanding of the psychological factors underpinning prejudice. On the one hand, data suggested a strong link between F scale authoritarianism and prejudice but, at the same time, it became clear almost from the very onset that this link was tempered by situational and cultural factors. This raised doubts in the minds of some as to the veracity of the personality-prejudice link. It was the emergence of some serious technical concerns regarding the F scale, however, than eventually sounded the death-knell of this line of investigation.

Critical Appraisal of Authoritarianism

Mention has already been made of the significant correlations between responses to the F and ETH scales. However, what appeared to escape the authors and others who used these measures at that time was the considerable overlap in content between some of the F and ETH items, thus probably accounting for their significant and sizeable correlations (Lindgren and Harvey, 1981). Take the following examples:

F scale item:
"Homosexuals are hardly better than criminals and ought to be severely punished" (Adorno et al., 1982: 186).
ETH scale item:
"Filipinos are all right in their place, but they carry it too far when they dress lavishly and go around with white girls" and "It would be a mistake

ever to have Negroes for foremen and leaders over whites" (Adorno et al., 1982: 142).

It is difficult to conceive of the F scale item as anything but a measure of prejudice rather than personality; some F and ETH items, therefore, share content and their correlations are hardly surprising. Similar criticisms have been made about item similarity between the F scale and measures of political and economic conservatism (Hyman and Sheatsley, 1954).

Altemeyer (1981) has alerted us to other related problems. He suggests that the nine components said to comprise authoritarianism are too vague; superstition and stereotype, for instance, have little to do with each other and one can quarrel about the actual meaning of some of the factors. Another problem is the fact that some items are said to predict more than one dimension of authoritarianism. Item analysis also reveals that the average interitem correlations for the final form of the scale is about .13, unacceptably low according to Altemeyer.

A major problem of the F scale that does much to undermine its credibility is the fact that successive factor-analytic studies have tended not to uncover the nine dimensions said to form the core of authoritarianism. Altemeyer (1981: 18–26) has reviewed the studies that are available on this topic, and the main results of his analysis are summarized in Table 6.2. What is immediately clear from Table 6.2 is the lack of support for the position of Adorno and colleagues (1982). It may very well be that authoritarianism comprises the said nine dimensions; the trouble is that this is not reflected in the measuring instrument.

Table 6.2 Factor-analytic studies of the F scale

Author	Sample	Analysis	Results
Christie and Garcia (1951)	386 Berkeley students 114 'Southwest' city students	Cluster analysis on 57 students from each	7 clusters – Berkeley 8 clusters – SW city
Aumack (1955)	38 prisoners	30 F scale items plus 25 other items	14 clusters with mixed F scale and other items
Camilleri (1959)	100 UCLA students	Centroid extraction with rotation	14/27 items loaded on wrong factor
Krug (1961)	704 students	Centroid extraction with Quartimax rotation	6 factors; only 5/29 items loaded $\geq$ .40
Kerlinger and Rokeach (1966)	1,200 students	Principal axes with Promax rotation	5 factors rotated; 3 deal with aggression conventionalism, and submission

Source Derived from Altemeyer (1981)

A compounding problem is that the factor structure has been found to vary from sample to sample. As Altemeyer concluded:

> By and large, it would seem that the test measures very little which is identifiable and comprehensible ... One would think this simple fact – that the psychometric properties of the F Scale indicate that it cannot measure the construct it was intended to measure – would preclude any further discussion of the scale's validity. (1981: 25)

Another major concern expressed about the F scale and one that was identified in the early 1950s, was the problem of acquiescent response bias. As all of the items of the scale were worded in one direction (or unidirectionally), it was difficult to ascertain whether participants who received high F scale scores did so because they agreed with the *content* of the scale, or because they went for the easier option of simply agreeing (or disagreeing) with each statement regardless of content. Bass (1955) concluded that about 75 per cent of the variance of the F scale could be directly attributable to acquiescence, while Altemeyer (1981) argued that acquiescence reduces, if not eliminates, the scale's validity. Thus, some scholars set about attempting to construct 'balanced' versions of the F scale (BF scales), although this proved more difficult than first anticipated.

Several problems were identified in the process of trying to reverse items. Two closely related problems concern the problem of maintaining the original meaning of an item when the reversal is attempted *post hoc* (Christie et al., 1958: 146). They are:

1) The problem of logical opposition to the original: Is it possible to reverse an original item in such a way that the meaning of that item is not altered? Opinion differs on this and there is considerable debate about the extent to which an item undergoes a change of meaning upon reversal.

2) Psychological opposition to original items: Some reversals might be incapable of discriminating high from low authoritarians (see also Altemeyer, 1981), while others might miss what Christie et al. (1958) referred to as the 'psychological point' of the original.

What complicated the acquiescence debate further was the consideration that, just possibly, one *could* expect high authoritarians to agree with statements on the F scale regardless of content. That certainly would not be out of character for such individuals. Additionally, it was noted that simply reversing items did not necessarily work too well, as the scores between the positively and negatively worded items were more consistent for *low* authoritarians than they were for high authoritarians. Finally, Rorer (1965) further clouded the already muddled picture by claiming that the issue of acquiescent response set was a 'myth' and that it was not possible to interpret personality tests (such as the F scale) in terms of a personality trait such as acquiescence response style (1965: 150–151).

Not only has the F scale been attacked on psychometric grounds, but especially also in its guise as a measure of authoritarianism. Thus, one damning line of attack has centred on questions of validity. In one of the earliest reviews of research using this instrument, Titus and Hollander (1957) noted that F scale authoritarianism did not always predict authoritarian behaviour as one would have expected. In a study conducted in a military setting, no significant differences were noted between high- and low-authoritarian cadets with respect to whom they nominated for leadership positions. Moreover, high authoritarians were *less* likely to receive peer nominations as a military leader. The review concluded by noting that, although the F scale was found to correlate highly with some paper and pencil measures, it was less successful in predicting interpersonal behaviours.

These general conclusions received sustained support from a number of different sources. In an Australian study, Ray and Lovejoy (1983) found that scores on a balanced measure of authoritarianism (BF scale) were not related to behavioural ratings of dominance, aggression, and submissiveness. In similar work with the same BF scale, Heaven (1984) found it to predict conservatism only, but not behavioural ratings of authoritarianism.

Titus (1968) found that F scale scores were weak predictors of actual behaviours one would regard as authoritarian. Table 6.3 lists the behaviours assessed as well as their relationship with the F scale after correction for attenuation. Perry and Cunningham (1975) set out to test whether three subscales of the original F scale (conventionalism, authoritarian submission, and superstition and stereotype) predicted the authoritarian-submissive trait. A sample of Israeli students received an official-looking letter from their university requesting them to report to a room on campus to complete a questionnaire. It was predicted that those who did respond to the letter would score significantly higher on the F scale than those who did not respond. In other words, it was

Table 6.3 F scale associations with authoritarian behaviour

The F scale did not correlate with:
        Likes to push others around.
        Avoids pushing others around.
        Is inclined to be suspicious of the motives of others.
        Barely modifies his behaviour regardless of the circumstances of the situation.
        Often modifies his behaviour to fit the circumstances of the situation.

The F scale correlated significantly with:
        Tends to follow orders of superiors only after critical thought.
        Tends to follow orders of superiors without critical thought.

The following yielded equivocal findings:
        Is inclined to trust the motives of others.

Source Derived from Titus (1968)

predicted that high F scorers would show greater submissiveness. However, results showed no significant differences on the subscales between the two groups of students, calling into question the validity of these subscales.

Conclusion

Notwithstanding some major problems with the F scale, and the disputes that arose regarding its validity, there can be no doubt that the publication of *The Authoritarian Personality* was a significant achievement in the approach of psychologists to the problem of prejudice and also in the scope of its methodological approach. It certainly spurred psychologists to invest enormous amounts of energy and time into studying the personality correlates of the prejudiced individual. However, the flaws associated with the F scale which have been briefly touched upon here, seemed so insurmountable that they sounded the steady demise of this approach to explaining prejudice.

Coincidentally, it was about this time that Sherif and colleagues conducted their classic Robbers Cave study (Sherif and Sherif, 1953) and Tajfel began his experiments on group influences on prejudice (see Tajfel, 1981a, for an integrative review). These developments were to overtake and herald the demise of the work of Adorno and colleagues (1982) and take psychologists down new avenues of research into prejudice and intergroup conflict.

Right-Wing Authoritarianism

Work on F scale authoritarianism and prejudice underwent a steady decline in the late 1960s and lay in abeyance during the 1970s. In what turned out to be a landmark publication, Altemeyer (1981) set out to review research into F scale authoritarianism and explain the rationale of his approach to right-wing authoritarianism (RWA). Concluding his review of the extant literature, he noted that one is surrounded by the 'wreckage' of research into authoritarianism. As he put it:

> A major failing of the research we have just reviewed is that nearly all of the investigators who found positive results failed to determine if these results were attributable to the scale as a whole, or mainly to subsets of items with rather obvious connections to the criterion ... it is rather stupefying to realize that we end up knowing so little. For we found not only that the theory is unconfirmed ... but also that all of this research was incapable of testing the theory from the start. Why ever on earth, then, was most of it done? (1981: 80)

Altemeyer (1981) has done much to revive our interest, and faith, in authoritarianism and how we measure it. He conceives of RWA as comprising three dimensions which are said to covary within the individual. They are:

1. 'Authoritarian submission – a high degree of submission to the authorities who are perceived to be established and legitimate in the society in which one lives;

2. Authoritarian aggression – a general aggressiveness, directed against various persons, which is perceived to be sanctioned by established authorities; and

3. Conventionalism – a high degree of adherence to the social conventions which are perceived to be endorsed by society and its established authorities'. (1981: 148)

Right-wing authoritarianism does not refer to support for right of centre political or economic movements, but rather to support for the legitimate authority in any given society or community (Altemeyer, 1996). According to Altemeyer, RWA is an individual difference variable that predicts one's support for authorities and one's level of rejection of outgroups, that is, those with differing ethnicity, views, and values. He does concede that situational factors do sometimes play a major role in determining one's manifest level of RWA (witness the Milgram experiments).

Whereas Adorno et al.'s (1950/1982) work was heavily influenced by psychodynamic considerations, Altemeyer (1996) suggests that RWA may have a genetic as well as environmental influence, although the influence of the former is less well established. For instance, there is good evidence that RWA scores (as well as other measures such as traditionalism) correlate highly among monozygotic twins – in the order of .50 to .60. However, the evidence for non-identical twins is equivocal, with correlations ranging from .04 to .71 (see Altemeyer, 1996: 73–74). Thus, the genetic argument is weakened.

Evidence that RWA may be due to the effects of social learning is quite compelling, Altemeyer (1996) suggests that these forces coalesce into a personality trait during the adolescent years. Thus, as a child, the typical RWA individual has been socialized into believing that some behaviours are 'sinful' and should be avoided; that the authorities, who always have our best interests at heart, should be obeyed at all times; that 'traditional' family values are to be encouraged; and that members of outgroups are undesirable and unacceptable individuals who have lost their way. Moreover, the potential to experience a wide and varied range of opinion from all sorts of people has been kept to a minimum. In the words of Altemeyer, such individuals have been 'tied to a short leash' and 'travelling in a relatively tight circle' (1996: 80).

High-RWA people are characterized by particular forms of cognitive functioning. Altemeyer (1996) reports empirical evidence to suggest that authoritarians are particularly susceptible to shoddy analytical thinking. No doubt, because they are so used to being on a 'short leash' and obeying authorities unquestioningly, they tend to believe those who provide information they want to hear, are likely to ignore or overlook situational factors when they hear what they want to hear, and so forth. High RWAs, therefore, are attracted to fringe political movements on the right. High-RWA people, it has been demonstrated, are also more likely than low RWAs to make the fundamental attribution error (Altemeyer, 1996).

In a series of eight studies spanning about four years, Altemeyer (1981) proposed a 24-item RWA measure (subsequently updated in Altemeyer, 1996). Perhaps surprisingly, it contained a core of original F scale items, as well as some newly created ones. An important feature of this new scale (and the successive revisions) is the sizeable covariation of the positively worded and negatively worded items as well as the overall interitem correlation (.23) of the original scale.

The Validity of the RWA Scale

You may recall that one problem identified with the original F scale was its lack of construct validity. Therefore, before we examine the links between RWA and prejudice, it is important to take note of the scale's validity.

In one of his first studies, Altemeyer (1981) assessed the extent to which the RWA scale as well as the original F scale, a BF scale by Lee and Warr, Rokeach's dogmatism (D) scale, Wilson and Patterson's conservatism (C) scale, and Kohn's authoritarian-rebellion scale predicted endorsement of a number of government injustices including illegal bugging, denial of right to assemble, political harassment, and illegal drug raids (all scales cited in Altemeyer, 1981). The RWA performed consistently better than any other measure achieving the highest correlation with each of the four injustices and with the sum of the four. The RWA scale was also superior at predicting the punishment of lawbreakers and at predicting punishment to 'learners' in a bogus shocking-learning experiment. High-RWA scorers were also found to support government action aimed at severely limiting the actions of fringe-groups on both sides of the political divide.

Heaven (1984) was able to show that, compared to a BF measure, the RWA scale was better at predicting behavioural ratings of submissiveness ('accepting direction from others') and authoritarianism ('at once submissive to superiors, but domineering toward subordinates'). Peterson and colleagues found that high RWAs were more likely than low RWAs to endorse harsh and punitive measures to solve the drugs and AIDS problems (Peterson et al., 1993). Blass (1995) showed that low RWAs, but not high RWAs, attributed more responsibility to the teacher when viewing film clips of the Milgram experiment. This is as expected; high RWAs no doubt simply believed that the teacher was doing as he/she was told. Duckitt and Farre (1994) observed that, although high-RWA Whites in South Africa were found to be prejudiced toward Blacks, they did support the infringement of civil liberties by a future Black South African government, in line with our expectations of authoritarians.

Interesting cross-cultural research in the former Soviet Union and the US has verified that conventionalism is a key component of right-wing authoritarianism (McFarland et al., 1992). Predicting that authoritarianism would be allied with an endorsement of ingroup values, the researchers found that RWA correlated significantly negatively with attitudes to Russian progressivism and belief in national rights (of ethnic minorities). RWA was also found to correlate with the prevailing ideologies in each culture. Thus, among Soviets, RWA correlated significantly positively with a belief in equality and negatively with a belief in laissez-faire individualism. As expected, the direction of these correlations was reversed among a US sample.

RWA and Prejudice

Research to date shows quite consistently the significant links between RWA and prejudice in a wide variety of settings and with samples from different cultures. For example, RWA correlated significantly with prejudice toward homosexuals (Haddock et al., 1993). Among high-RWAs, it was found that prejudice was best predicted by symbolic beliefs. That is, high-RWAs, but not low-RWAs, believed that homosexuals adhered to a different set of values and belief systems than heterosexuals. Thus, the belief that homosexuals have a different belief system sets them apart from heterosexuals making them an easy target for RWAs.

It would also appear that, compared to religious fundamentalism, RWA is a much better predictor of homophobia and racial and ethnic prejudice (Wylie and Forest, 1992). Evidence also shows that, compared to low-RWAs, high-RWAs are more likely to vote for legislation that would disallow illegal migrants access to welfare, medical benefits, and educational opportunities (Quinton et al., 1996).

Research using the RWA scale has shown, as expected, that it is strongly predictive of aggressive attitudes toward nation states regarded as undesirable. For example, Doty and colleagues (Doty et al., 1997) surveyed student attitudes toward Iraq over several years. Scores on the RWA measure were found to consistently predict negative attitudes to numerous hypothetical situations, such as the levels of US force against Iraq should Iraq invade Saudi Arabia, not leave Kuwait, or not release hostages. High-RWA individuals were also in favour of more aggressive and destructive responses to Iraq than less aggressive responses such as the use of economic sanctions. The authors concluded that, in the present case, RWA has the ability to 'move' attitudes toward the stereotype of masculinity.

The psychometric properties and correlates of the RWA measure have also been assessed in South Africa. Based on data collected before South Africa's transition to majority rule, Duckitt (1993) found among White university students that high-RWA individuals were likely to endorse anti-Black sentiment, subtle racism, social distance, and not to support interracial behavioural intentions. As such, these results are not particularly surprising, but they do show that with a valid and reliable measure of authoritarianism, RWA does have significant links with prejudice even in cultures that could be described as authoritarian. This would refute some earlier suggestions (e.g., Orpen, 1971) that in some instances factors such as authoritarianism are irrelevant to explaining racism.

Finally, laboratory research has clearly shown that RWA predicts prejudice under particular conditions. Verkuyten and Hagendoorn (1998) manipulated respondents' personal and group identity. When Dutch students were thinking of themselves as unique individuals, that is, when their personal identity was salient, their prejudice toward Turkish migrants was best predicted by RWA. However, when their national identity was salient, Dutch students' prejudice was best predicted by their ingroup stereotypes and not RWA. Thus, personality factors appear to be important predictors of prejudice, but only under conditions when personal identity is salient.

In conclusion, the RWA scale has enjoyed considerable acceptance as a reliable and valid measure of right-wing authoritarianism and an indicator of prejudice. The remaining section of this chapter will focus on a new construct, social dominance orientation.

Social Dominance Orientation

Sidanius and colleagues (e.g., Pratto et al., 1994; Sidanius, 1993) have recently proposed a new individual difference variable capable of predicting prejudice. This construct, referred to as social dominance orientation (SDO), is defined as the extent 'to which one desires that one's ingroup dominate and be superior to outgroups' (Pratto et al., 1994: 742).

A casual glance might suggest considerable overlap between SDO and RWA, although a look at the items of the two measures does suggest some important qualitative differences. Consider the following sample items (Altemeyer, 1996; Pratto et al., 1994):

> SDO item:
> 'To get ahead in life, it is sometimes necessary to step on others', or 'Some people are just more deserving than others'.
> RWA item:
> 'Life imprisonment is justified for certain crimes', or 'The real keys to a "good life" are obedience, discipline, and sticking to the straight and narrow'.

Whereas Altemeyer (1981, 1996) moved authoritarianism from a psychodynamic perspective to a social learning one, SDO is grounded in social dominance theory (Sidanius, 1993). This asserts that most societies are group-based with clearly defined social hierarchies, be they along ethnic, caste, or sex lines. Those at the apex of the hierarchy (in Britain, the US, and Australia it is males and Whites) employ attitudes and behaviours whose function is to maintain the existing social order. Put differently, their attitudes to other groups reflect their desire to maintain their dominant position. Thus, for example, men tend to score higher on SDO than women, while in the US, Whites score higher than African-Americans. Likewise, White Americans are more likely to be opposed to cross-racial dating than Blacks. An additional noteworthy feature is that the links between SDO and prejudice are much stronger among Whites than they are among Blacks – evidence of behavioural assymetry (Sidanius, 1993).

Evidence is also beginning to emerge of cross-cultural differences in SDO and the results to date fit with social dominance theory. For example, recent data have demonstrated that White South African students score significantly higher than African-American, Black South African, and White Australian students (Heaven et al., in press). The differences in mean scores between the two South African groups are, no doubt, a legacy of the Apartheid years when Whites enjoyed both political and economic power.

Using a measure of SDO, successive studies (e.g., Pratto et al., 1994; Sidanius et al., 1992; Sidanius and Liu, 1992) have shown quite consistently that high-SDO individuals accept what are referred to as hierarchy-enhancing myths, that is, they accept racist and sexist ideas. Thus, SDO underpins a range of group, social class, caste, and racial inequalities and can be viewed as an important motivator that underlies ethnic and group inequalities.

In one study among US respondents, it was demonstrated that SDO was better able than measures of general conservatism to explain the significant relationships between support for the Gulf War and the beating of Rodney King by LA policemen (Sidanius and Liu, 1992). Using structural equation modelling to analyse the data, it was shown that SDO, rather than general conservatism, provided a better fit to the data and was best able to explain the observed relationships.

Although both SDO and RWA predict prejudice, these two measures are only modestly related (Pratto et al., 1994). What, then, are the major differences between RWA and SDO? Referring to SDO as the 'other authoritarian personality', Altemeyer (1998) has argued that social dominance orientation provides an essential (and missing) component of the broader personality configuration of the prejudiced individual. Whereas RWA is concerned with conventionalism and submission to authorities, SDO is more concerned with dictating and dominating others. Those high on RWA revere established authorities, while SDO individuals do not. Although both RWA and SDO are strongly related to a wide range of prejudice measures, they themselves are only moderately related, as low as .11 in some samples (Altemeyer, 1998). Thus, RWA and SDO explain unique aspects of prejudice.

Some of the differences between SDO and RWA are quite clear-cut. For instance, there are consistent and clear sex differences on SDO (men score higher), but not on RWA. RWA is associated with religious fundamentalism, whereas SDO is not. Machiavellianism tends to correlate much more strongly with SDO than RWA. Whereas RWAs do not think of themselves as prejudiced, SDO individuals accept that they are. RWAs value conformity, SDO individuals value power; SDO correlates with Eysenckian psychoticism (Eysenck and Eysenck, 1976), RWA does not; RWA correlates with traditionalism, SDO does not (Altemeyer, 1998).

Although largely untested outside the confines of North America, the utility of SDO as a reliable and robust indicator of prejudice is impressive. When used together, some studies have found that RWA and SDO are capable of explaining sizeable proportions of the variance of prejudice (in the order of 50–60 per cent), swamping the influence of other factors such as educational levels, for instance (Altemeyer, 1998).

Conclusion

Research into the links between the authoritarian personality and prejudice has made great strides over the last 15 years. From its origins 50 years ago in the shadow of the Second World War and the Holocaust, this line of investigation generated enormous interest and energy, spawning hundreds of studies into the correlates of F scale authoritarianism. At last, it seemed, psychologists had found the key to unravelling the mystery of prejudice. Following devastating critique of the original methods used and of the F scale itself, it would appear that we now have reliable and valid personality indicators of prejudice in the form of the RWA and SDO scales.

These measures are closely allied to the theoretical frameworks from which they originated and have proven useful in predicting prejudice inside and outside the laboratory. These instruments are only moderately related and much more work needs to be done to uncover their distinctiveness, particularly in non-Western domains and outside North America. For example, Feather (in press) has recently shown that Australians value egalitarianism much more than do Americans or Canadians and it may be the case that such findings impact on the links between SDO, RWA, and prejudice.

The idea that individuals' personalities can account for prejudice independent of other factors has a long history in social psychology. Right-wing authoritarianism and social dominance orientation are the latest additions to an extensive list of personality dimensions that at various times have received research attention. However, as in the past, a comprehensive analysis of how such personalities develop and whether such dimensions are stable and relatively enduring is yet to emerge.

Part III:

Social Cognition, Mood, and Attitudes

7 Stereotyping and Prejudice: A Social Cognitive Approach

Vance Locke and Lucy Johnston

Walking into a pub you are confronted by a large, burly, male bouncer at the door, who tells you, in no uncertain terms, that you can't come in. When pressed the bouncer explains that 'your type' is not permitted in here. Is the bouncer prejudiced? Are you being stereotyped?

As undergraduates studying psychology, we learn that our perceptual systems are attuned to information important for our survival. The visual system is adept at discerning movement, depth, and colour, while the auditory system is most sensitive to the frequencies at which humans typically speak. Similarly, the human mind is tuned to our social surroundings. Since perceptual and cognitive psychologists have spent the best part of the last century investigating the processes of the mind, it makes sense that social psychologists have turned to the methods and theories developed in these areas to help us understand the working of the social mind. In this chapter we will consider the application of these theories and methods to the study of stereotypes and prejudice. For example, in helping us to understand what the bouncer means by 'your type' and how this effects his judgements of and behaviour towards people at the pub. We will consider the nature of stereotypes, the impact of stereotypes on judgements of others and whether stereotypes are fixed beliefs or whether they can be changed. Importantly, we will also tackle the difficult question of whether prejudice is inevitable or whether we can control our use of stereotypes and expression of prejudice.

Calling a Stereotype a Stereotype

Accurate definitions have important ramifications for the measurement of stereotypes and prejudice. To understand the material presented in this chapter it is important to distinguish between stereotypes and prejudice. The original definition of a stereotype provided by Lippmann (1922) was drawn from the printing press in which an image, or text, is set in a rigid form which loses much of the depth and detail of the figure, but produces a likeness that captures enough of its essence to allow easy reproduction. Thus stereotypes, or 'pictures in our head' as Lippmann called them, are, in more modern psychological terms, mental representations of social groups and their members which contain enough detail to allow us to know what group members are like without ever meeting them (Stangor and Lange, 1994). Like the mental representation we hold of many other things (e.g., animals, furniture), these representations contain attributes and traits, both positive and negative, usually ascribed to the group and its members, and expectations about the behaviour of members of the group. Cognitive psychologists have been interested in mental categories for many years and have developed several tools with which to understand their content, structure, and influence. Social psychologists have recently begun to consider stereotypes as mental categories and to use tools developed in cognitive psychology to examine the impact of stereotypes on judgement and behaviour.

Prejudice captures the affective nature of the response to members of different social groups. It is the 'I don't *like* your type' reaction and its consequences. This is clearly the phenomenon that most of us feel is so important to reduce in society. Other chapters in this book will explore more fully the subtleties of prejudice in its different forms. However, for our purposes, we can conceive of prejudice as a negative evaluative tendency towards a group and its members. In other words, the 'you and your type aren't welcome here – go drink elsewhere' rejection by the pub bouncer. This is the phenomenon that recent social-cognitive research suggests stereotypes may play some part in.

The rest of this chapter will examine some of the modern approaches to the understanding of stereotypes and the relationship between stereotypes and prejudice. As we will illustrate, there are two roles stereotypes may play in prejudice. One is an explicit role as a tool used by prejudiced people to help guide their judgements and the other is an implicit role where stereotypes may influence the judgement made by any person, whether prejudiced or not, for whom the stereotype is evoked unintentionally or without awareness.

The Failure of Introspection

As Freud (1901) recognized almost a century ago, many cognitive processes are not open to conscious inspection. There is no doubt that we have conscious access to the output of our many cognitive processes – this is what occupies our stream of consciousness. So if you are interested in *what* people think, rather than *how* they think, then it is legitimate to ask them. For example, prejudice is clearly the output of some well-learnt judgemental processes. Whether you like or dislike a particular social group and its members is open to conscious inspection and it is legitimate to ask someone their feelings toward a group. Of course whether they will tell you is a different matter. But how we get these thoughts, how we dredge our long-term memories for information, and how we use mental representations such as stereotypes to make these judgements, may not be open to inspection. Nisbett and Wilson (1977) strongly argued this case in an influential review of the non-conscious processing literature. In one example, they constructed a mock retail scenario in which participants were asked to choose a pair of nylon stockings from four piles of *identical* stockings. However, the participants were not aware that all the stockings were identical and believed they were being allowed a free choice from among four different makes of stocking. In post-experimental interviews the participants suggested that quality had been the most important factor in their choice, despite the fact that the four piles contained identical stocks of the same brand of stockings. The data that Nisbett and Wilson had gathered suggested that the most important factor in participants' choice was, in fact, the positioning of the product, with most participants choosing stockings from the right-most pile. It seems that the most important factor affecting stocking choice was something that participants were unaware of, and the reasons they gave for their choices were *rationalizations* for their selection of one particular pair of stockings over other identical pairs. So perhaps the first lesson we should learn from this is a simple one: if you want to know how someone's mind works do not ask him or her!

What cognitive psychology tells us is that while people may be able to report accurately the content of their stereotypes, they are very unlikely to be able to report how stereotypes operate and how they influenced their judgements. Therefore, what you will see as we review some of the recent research examining the links between stereotypes and prejudice are many measurement methods borrowed from cognitive psychology and adapted to meet the needs of social psychologists. You will also see that social psychologists have become major contributors to the understanding of basic cognitive processes as they occur in our daily lives.

Before we review this literature, it is important to provide some context to the current theories. One of the most important implications of the social-cognitive approach is that stereotypes are seen as relatively mundane inhabitants of our mental world. Indeed, they are like any other category of knowledge. They are not necessarily bad, nor are they indicative of mental deficiency, as some early research suggested (e.g., Adorno et al., 1950). Stereotypes, like other mental representations, are shortcuts the mind uses to simplify and understand the social world.

We Don't Like Stereotypes (We Love Them)[1]

This approach should not, however, be seen as condoning the use of stereotypes. Without a doubt, stereotypes have many bad effects in society. Perhaps you missed that drink at the pub, or that job you were going for, because of your ethnic origins or gender. Being at the receiving end of a stereotype-driven judgement is not a good thing. However, from the perceiver's point of view, stereotypes *are* a good thing. They offer a simple and straightforward way of judging people and allow decisions to be made with a minimum of effort. In other words, stereotypes exist because they offer the individual a shorthand way of engaging with and understanding the world around them. The bouncer, for example, does not have to enter into a conversation with you to understand who you are. All he has to do is look at you to know you are one of 'them'.

Macrae et al., (1994) employed dual-task methods to demonstrate that stereotypes are capacity-saving devices that free us from the need to consider every piece of information we receive about someone. In one experiment, for example, they asked participants to form an impression of a target person (John) from a series of traits presented one at a time on a computer screen, while simultaneously monitoring an irrelevant passage describing the economy and geography of Indonesia.[2] When John was identified as a member of a stereotyped group, by use of a group label (e.g., skinhead) presented while the participants read the personality traits, participants not only showed superior recall of the stereotypic traits presented during the impression formation task, but also superior recall of the information about Indonesia contained in the prose passage. In other words, knowing that John was a skinhead made the impression formation task easier (we all know what skinheads are like) which freed mental resources for other tasks, such as remembering the geography of Indonesia.

This research demonstrates that stereotypes allow us to form an impression of an individual without a lot of mental effort. Of course, this has great advantages for the user. More free mental space to do all the important things that demand our attention. But while stereotypes are potentially a useful tool for the user, John the skinhead might not think so. He might have provided all this information about himself in an attempt to show that he is more than just a skinhead – but we ignore it. We use the stereotype despite the personal information (e.g., traits and attributes) provided about John, and conserve those mental resources for other duties. In other words, we benefit from the saving in information processing time and mental effort while John suffers. As Trope puts it 'the price of these information processing advantages is bias in the judgement of individual category members' (1989: 133). This position typifies the 'cognitive miser' view of the social perceiver. Whenever possible, the social perceiver is thought to strive for cognitive efficiency and expedience. We think only when we have to and we do so reluctantly. Accordingly, categorization and stereotyping are seen as necessary capacity-saving, simplifying cognitive mechanisms for the social perceiver with prejudice an unfortunate but inevitable by-product of this striving for cognitive economy.

If we are to believe this position, the outlook is very gloomy. Consider the following questions carefully: Do you know the stereotype of politicians, accountants, Germans, and the English? If you do, and there is enough empirical evidence to believe we all do (e.g., Augoustinos et al., 1994; Devine, 1989; Lepore and Brown, 1997), then why do we not all use stereotypes and express prejudice? In 1989, Patricia Devine attempted to answer this question with a model which tried to tie together what we know about the cognitive efficiency afforded to everyone by stereotypes with the fact that there are differences in people's level and expression of prejudice.

Stereotyping and Prejudice: Explicit Processes

Devine (1989) argues that, because we learn stereotypes very early (e.g., Hamilton and Sherman, 1994; Katz, 1976) and because they have functional properties (as we have seen), they are known to everybody and are frequently accessed. This is not such a stretch of the imagination. It is hard to imagine a person who does not know the major stereotypes in their society. The result of this long learning process, according to Devine, is that everybody, irrespective of his or her personal beliefs, activates stereotypes when in the presence of a group member or some symbolic representation of the group. More importantly for research, considering the role of prejudice in stereotype activation, everybody, irrespective of their personal beliefs, activates stereotypes when *judging* outgroups or outgroup members. Although everybody activates stereotypes when judging these groups, individual differences in beliefs about the accuracy of stereotypes do exist. Society may convey, to all its members, knowledge about the stereotype of each important social group. However, prejudice towards such a group will result only if one's personal beliefs about that group are congruent with the content of this stereotype. Devine believes that stereotypes and prejudice are intricately linked, but argues that the mere possession of a stereotype need not inevitably lead to prejudice.

Devine (1989) developed a specific cognitive model of the association between stereotypes and prejudice, which formalizes this dissociation between knowledge of, and beliefs about, groups. This dissociation model (Devine, 1995) draws upon the distinction, often made in cognitive psychology, between automatic and controlled processes (Hasher and Zacks, 1979; Posner and Snyder, 1975; Schneider and Shiffrin, 1977). Automatic processes have been characterized as the rapid spontaneous activation of some set of associations without conscious effort or attention, and are typically construed as resistant to intentional manipulation (e.g., Neely, 1977). Controlled processes, in contrast, are usually considered to be slow, to require maintenance through the operation of a limited capacity attentional system, and to be influenced by conscious intention (e.g., Bargh, 1989; deGroot et al., 1986; Neely, 1977).

Devine's central proposal is that, when making judgements about any social group, *all* individuals will experience the automatic activation of stereotypical trait information associated with this group, regardless of their level of personal prejudice. This reflects the fact that knowledge about this stereotype will be possessed equally by everyone, due to its long history of use, and its automatic activation cannot be influenced by personal beliefs. However, Devine argues that individual differences in levels of prejudice will serve to determine whether this stereotypical trait information remains active, or is intentionally inhibited, at a strategic level of processing. Specifically, Devine proposes that low-prejudice individuals, unlike high-prejudice individuals, will subsequently strategically inhibit the stereotypical trait information that became activated automatically when the social group was being evaluated. Thus, according to Devine's position, while immediate automatic stereotype activation is unavoidable, irrespective of personal beliefs, the operation of conscious/controlled strategies based on personal beliefs will determine whether this information remains activated to help guide judgements.

Before examining some of the research motivated by the dissociation model, keep in mind that this model suggests a major reworking of one of the founding principles of the 'cognitive miser' model: no thinking unless you have to. To be a non-prejudiced person you have to exert mental energy to consciously inhibit the stereotype which has been automatically activated. Given that a person wants to be non-prejudiced then, over many years, they should have had many instances of this activation and inhibition cycle. Despite years of practice performing this inhibition, Devine proposes that we still activate the stereotype to help us judge someone even when it is not useful. So, what does the evidence tell us? Are we slow learners?

Augoustinos et al. (1994) examined the activation of stereotypic information when participants were judging Australian Aborigines. In this study, high- and low-prejudice participants were presented with words and asked to indicate whether, in their opinion, each word accurately described Aborigines. The words were selected so that half were related to the stereotype of Aborigines and half were not; and in these sets, half were positive and half were negative in affective tone. The dependent measure was the time taken to make the yes or no response to each word. The faster the response time, the greater the activation of that word. Since the participants in this study had ample time to consider their responses, this method only assesses controlled and not automatic processes. Since the measure of activation was also the measure of the degree to which participants endorsed the descriptions of Aborigines, it is unclear what role self-presentation strategies might have played. It is plausible that participants may vary in the time it takes them to respond to certain traits because they are modifying their responses in accord with an impression management strategy. With this caveat in mind the results provide an interesting picture of the relationship between stereotypes and prejudice. Both the high- and low-prejudice groups showed greater activation of the stereotypic than non-stereotypic traits when making their judgements. In addition, there was an effect of the evaluative tone of the traits. High-prejudiced people showed greater activation of both stereotypic and non-stereotypic negative words while low-prejudice people showed greater activation of both stereotypic and non-stereotypic positive words. Since both high- and low-prejudiced people showed greater activation of stereotypic than non-stereotypic words at strategic levels of processing these findings clearly contradict the dissociation model which predicts that only high-prejudiced individuals will show enhanced activation of stereotypic words at strategic levels of processing. These findings also suggest an impact of the affective tone of the traits that remain active at strategic levels of processing (Augoustinos and Walker, 1995). In other words, the emotional tone of the information activated in our heads when we judge a person or group may be an important factor in prejudice. We will address this issue further when discussing the next two experiments.

In another test of Devine's model Locke et al., (1994) examined both the type of information activated automatically, and that which remained activated once conscious processes had been given enough time to operate. Importantly, the task was designed so that participants, high and low on a questionnaire measure of prejudice towards Aborigines, were engaged in the task of judging Aborigines. Remember, according to Devine (1989), people will automatically activate stereotypes to guide their judgements, so it seems critical that the activation of stereotypes be measured while people are in the act of judging the groups towards which they are prejudiced. To this end, each experimental trial started with a target label presented on the computer screen, indicating which category is to be judged on that trial (either 'Aborigines' or 'Yourself'). This was then followed by a coloured trait word that appeared on the screen for a brief time before being masked by letter fragments in the same colour as the word. The trait words presented to the participants contained equal numbers of words that were and were not stereotypic of Aborigines and half of each of these word sets was positive in emotional tone and half was negative. Participants were required to name the colour of the display as quickly as possible. Previous research suggests that the greater the degree to which information has been activated the longer the colour-naming latency will be for that information (e.g., MacLeod and Rutherford, 1992; Warren, 1972). Significantly, the time between the presentation of target label and the trait word, the stimulus onset asynchrony (SOA), was varied. It was either very short (240 ms) or much longer (2,000ms). Manipulating SOA allows a dissociation between information that is automatically activated (the 240ms SOA) and that which remains activated once strategic or conscious processes are able to modify the activation of this information (the 2,000ms SOA) (Neely, 1977). Put another way, automatic processes are fast and so, if the stereotype has been activated automatically, then it should be detectable within 240ms of the judgement process being initiated. In contrast, the consciously controlled inhibition process should take time to muster (longer that 240ms) but should have exerted any influence by 2,000ms. After the colour-naming response was detected, the pattern mask was replaced by the trait word, this time presented in white, and participants were required to indicate whether the word described the previously mentioned target. By separating the measure of activation from the judgement processes this method provided a measure of activation that is unlikely to be influenced by impression management strategies.

Locke et al.'s (1994) results suggest that high-prejudice participants automatically activated only stereotype-related information, but low-prejudice participants activated a range of information, both related and unrelated, positive and negative. In the controlled processing stage, neither high- nor low-prejudice participants inhibited any information, activation of traits was the same with the long SOA as with the short SOA. This pattern of results is displayed in Figure 7.1. This clearly contradicts Devine's dissociation model in which she suggests that everyone will automatically activate the stereotype of a group when asked to judge them. Instead, Locke et al. (1994) found that only high-prejudice people show a disproportionate automatic activation of stereotypic information. The failure to find any evidence of stereotype inhibition also challenges the predictions made by Devine's dissociation model. Instead, it

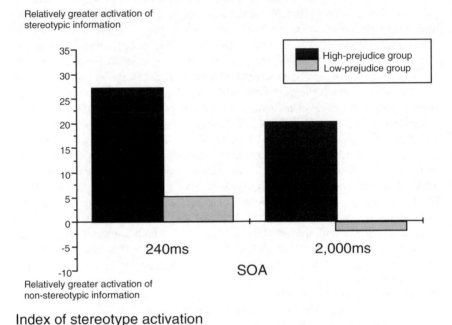

Figure 7.1 Mean stereotype activation index for the high- and low-prejudice participants at the short and long SOAs.

Note Mean activation index calculated by taking colour-naming latencies for stereotype-unrelated words from the colour-naming latencies for stereotype-related words. The resulting index is positive when there are longer colour-naming latencies for the stereotype-related traits.

would seem that the information that is automatically activated is that which is going to be used in the judgements of the target group. For high-prejudice people this means a preponderance of stereotypic information is available to help them make their judgements. Of course, the stereotype of Aborigines held by White Australians contains a predominance of negative information (Marjoribanks and Jordan, 1986). Thus, while high-prejudice participants automatically activated both the positive and negative components of the stereotype, the overall emotional tone of the entire set of information activated would, most likely, be negative. This issue was picked up in a further study by Locke and Walker (1999).

Locke and Walker (1999) report a study in which the basic experimental paradigm used by Locke et al. (1994) was adapted to examine the types of information activated when male participants, high and low on measures of prejudice towards women (as assessed by the Women in Society Questionnaire;

Lewis et al., in press), were asked to judge women. The trait words were selected to contain equal numbers that were and were not stereotypic of women. Half of each trait word set was positive and half negative in emotional tone.

Once again it was found that high-prejudice participants alone produced evidence of automatic stereotype activation when judging the target group. As with the previous experiment, both the positive and negative components of the stereotypes seemed to be disproportionately activated. Once they were able to engage strategic processes, the high-prejudice participants continued to display this heightened activation only for the negative stereotypic traits. The positive stereotypic traits were no more activated than the positive non-stereotypic traits at this strategic level of processing. In contrast, the low-prejudice participants showed no evidence of stereotype activation at either the automatic or strategic level of processing. These results are illustrated in Figure 7.2.

The fact that the activation of the positive components of the stereotype was modified by the high-prejudice participants once they had the opportunity to utilize strategic processes, is, we think, due to the fact that the stereotype of

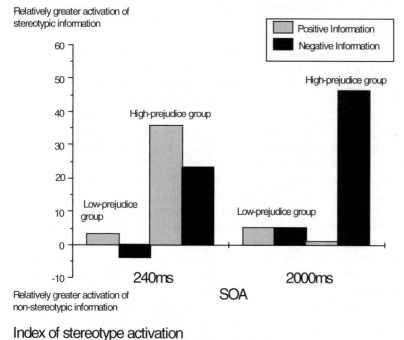

Figure 7.2 Mean stereotype activation index for the high- and low-prejudice males at the short and long SOAs when judging the positive and negative traits.

Note The resulting index is positive when there are longer colour-naming latencies for the stereotype-related traits.

women, unlike that of Aborigines, contains fairly similar proportions of positive and negative information (Williams and Best, 1982). As such, the strategic modification of the automatically activated stereotype may pare the available information to leave only that which drives those negative judgements of the target group that led to those people being classified as high-prejudice in the first place. The positive parts of the stereotype may be inhibited because they were inconsistent with the pejorative views held by the high-prejudice participants. The last two experiments produced a consistent pattern of results with high-prejudice participants producing evidence of disproportionate *automatic* stereotype activation when judging the target group. These results clearly contradict the predictions derived from Devine's dissociation model and suggest that prejudice-linked differences in the activation of stereotypic information, relative to non-stereotypic information, are apparent at an automatic level of processing.

Using slightly different methods and populations, other researchers have shown similar effects. Kawakami et al., (1998) explored the relationship between stereotype activation and prejudice toward African-Americans. Rather than using a colour-naming task, Kawakami et al. asked participants to say the trait word presented, out loud, as fast as they could. The faster participants were able to name a trait word, the greater the activation of the concept in memory (Neely, 1991). Once this task had been completed, the participants completed several paper-and-pencil measures of prejudice and were divided into high- and low-prejudice groups. Importantly, the White participants were aware the task they were performing involved measures of their attitudes towards African-Americans: 'the repeated presentation of racial category primes and stereotypic traits makes the racial focus of the task salient' (Kawakami et al., 1998: 409). Like the Locke et al. (1994) and Locke and Walker (1999) experiments, the activation of stereotypic information is being assessed while participants are making explicit judgements of the target group. The results of the word-naming task indicated that high-prejudiced individuals alone were faster to name stereotypic traits following the presentation of the 'Black' label. Since this effect was evident at both the 300ms and 2,000ms SOAs, it seems that high-prejudice people automatically activated the stereotype of African-Americans and that this activation is not consciously modified in any fashion. Further, the low-prejudice individuals showed no evidence of stereotype activation at either the automatic or conscious level of processing. Obviously, this evidence confirms the pattern of results obtained by Locke et al. (1994) and Locke and Walker (1999).

Lepore and Brown (1997) took a different approach to testing the dissociation model. They adapted the experimental techniques employed by Devine (1989) and primed White British participants, high and low on measures of prejudice towards Afro Caribbean people, with either category labels (e.g., 'Blacks', 'Afro Caribbean') or category labels and elements of the Afro Caribbean stereotype (e.g., 'unemployed', 'rude', 'dirty'). Following the priming phase, the participants were asked to rate an Afro Caribbean person on a number of scales that measured the degree to which the stereotype was being used to form an impression of the target. They found that priming with a category label (e.g., Blacks) does not induce stereotype activation in everybody. Only the high-prejudice participants rated the target more stereotypically when primed with the category labels. In contrast, when primed with elements of the stereotype as well, both high- and low-prejudice individuals showed evidence of stereotype activation. The fact that both groups used the stereotype to form impressions after being primed with the stereotypic elements demonstrates, once again, that everybody, irrespective of their levels of personal prejudice, has learnt the stereotypes of the major social groups in society and activation of these can influence subsequent judgements. However, the earlier finding shows that only high-prejudice people activate stereotypes in response to category labels. In other words, when we are required to think about a group about whom a stereotype exists, only those of us who are prejudiced towards the target group will evoke the stereotype.

So, what does all this tell us about the relationship between stereotypes and prejudice? Are we cognitive misers who spring into action and inhibit any pejorative thoughts? The evidence reviewed above suggests not. In contrast to the view that stereotypes are automatically activated in the mere presence of a member of the stereotyped group, the evidence reviewed above suggests that people are, at the very least, strategic in their laziness. In contrast to the predictions derived from the dissociation model, not everybody automatically activates the stereotype of well-known social groups. Perhaps low-prejudice people have, after years of consciously inhibiting the automatically activated stereotype, automated the inhibitory processes to the degree that stereotypic thoughts no longer come to mind (Monteith et al., 1998). This possibility remains open to further investigation. What is clearly emerging from the literature though, is that low-prejudice people do not automatically activate the stereotype of a group to help guide judgements of that group. As a result, there is little need for low-prejudice people to engage inhibitory processes. Indeed, the only hint of inhibitory processes in the research to date came from high-prejudice participants in one study (Locke and Walker, 1999).

More generally, it seems that it is only those people who are prejudiced, or, perhaps, put another way, who believe the stereotype to be accurate and for whom the negative components might be useful, that use it to judge others. Importantly, this use is automatic and therefore fast and efficient. As we have argued earlier, stereotypes are cognitive tools (Gilbert and Hixon, 1991), which offer great efficiency at little cost to the cognitive system. However, this is surely only the case for those people for whom the content of the stereotype and the valence of their judgements coincide. What use is an automatically activated stereotype if its content contradicts the feelings you have towards a group and its members? It is hardly efficient to have bodies of information we are never going to use made available to us.

Bargh (1989) distinguished between classes of automatic processing, differing in their dependence upon goal-directed processing. Specifically, Bargh notes that certain automatic processes may only be elicited when people are pursuing particular processing goals. For example, if you are driving a car along the freeway then seeing a police car in the rear-vision mirror may produce an automatic response: quickly jamming on the brakes and hoping they did not have the radar pointed your way. In contrast, seeing the same police car while you are walking along the side of the freeway is unlikely to cause you to slow your stride. It is the same stimulus in both cases, but in these different contexts it is unlikely to trigger the same automatic response. Processes are learnt in a context and, with practice, they become automated or easier and faster to perform. It would seem unlikely that the stereotype of particular groups would always be relevant. When you are in your psychology classes listening to another riveting lecture, have you activated the stereotype of all those around you? Sure, you have formed an impression of the lecturer – he or she is important to your enjoyment of the course. However, when you walked into the lecture theatre did you activate all the available stereotypes? Did you activate the stereotype of the Asian woman in the front row; the burly physical-education student near the door; the Arts student dressed like an undertaker? No? Why would you? It would only clutter your mind. In other words, cognitive economy is served by the tactical activation of information that serves to help you perform some task. This view contrasts with the cognitive miser (Fiske and Taylor, 1991) account of the social perceiver and suggests that we can been seen more as 'motivated tacticians' (Fiske, 1993).

It is perhaps easier to conceive of certain processes, such as activating stereotypes, becoming proceduralized to the point that, when a particular process is engaged in (e.g., negatively judging a member of a social group), certain processes are automatically engaged to help. Repeatedly accessing the stereotype (when it is negative in emotional tone at least), to help make a prejudiced judgement, may eventually automate stereotype activation whenever a judgement of the same group is engaged in. What we can be more certain about is that prejudiced people, but not unprejudiced people, automatically activate the stereotype of a group when explicitly engaged in the process of judging the stereotyped group.

A Guide to Staying Prejudiced

We know that stereotypes can save us from exerting extra mental effort by reducing the need to draw inferences from multiple sources of information and, instead, relying upon established mental representations. Accordingly, the stereotype used by prejudiced people must be relatively stable and resistant to change. How does the prejudiced person avoid daily changes to stereotype content when they meet a new member of the group they are prejudiced against? Take our earlier example. While most bouncers are large and threatening looking (no doubt a prerequisite for the job), there are many bouncers who are friendly and articulate. What does the prejudiced person do when the world isn't as simple as applying an existing stereotype? One answer is that people only absorb information consistent with their beliefs, which translates into a bias for processing, or encoding of, stereotype consistent information (von Hippel et al., 1995).

Locke and Walker (1999) reported an experimental attempt to address this prediction. They developed a reading-time task that assessed the time it took high- and low-prejudice participants to read sentences describing women performing stereotype-congruent (e.g., the baby cried and Mary was sympathetic) or stereotype-incongruent (e.g., the baby cried and Mary was annoyed) actions. Male participants completed the reading-time task under instructions that directed them either to evaluate, or else simply to remember, information concerning target group members. Consistent with the 'motivated tactician' view of the social perceiver outlined above, it was expected that only when the participants were actively judging the target group would stereotypes be activated and available to help guide encoding.

The results indicated that high-prejudice participants displayed shorter reading times for stereotype-congruent sentences, relative to stereotype-incongruent sentences, but only when they were instructed to make evaluative judgements of the group members' actions rather than simply remember those actions. In contrast, the low-prejudice participants showed no evidence of faster reading times for stereotypic information under either instruction condition. The high-prejudice participants' results suggest that the automatic activation of stereotypic information translates into an encoding advantage for stereotype-consistent information. This occurred only when the participants were asked to judge the target group. Differential activation of stereotypes for high- and low-prejudice people occurs only when the stereotypes are required to guide social judgements of the group. These findings suggest that prejudice-linked differences in the automatic activation of stereotypic information function to facilitate the encoding of stereotype-congruent information about members of the target group under conditions where they will be useful. When judging members of the stereotyped group the stereotype is useful for the high-prejudice participants and so they activated it to help guide their judgements. This activation helps to simplify the judgement process and makes it easier to encode and potentially remember stereotypic information.

One possible explanation for this comes from work by von Hippel et al. (1995). They employed a paradigm developed by Hastie (1984), in which participants are presented with sentences describing relatively ambiguous behaviours (i.e., Jane was watching the monster truck rally) and are asked to provide extensions for these sentences. von Hippel et al. suggest that high-prejudice participants should be more likely to supply continuations that provide explanations for the described behaviours (e.g., Jane's boyfriend is a car enthusiast) when these behaviours are incongruent with the stereotype (e.g., when the sentence describes a female performing a stereotypically male behaviour). This effect, they argue, results from the more elaborative (and time-consuming) encoding shown by high-prejudice participants for stereotype–incongruent information, relative to the fast and efficient encoding of stereotype congruent information. This elaborative processing is employed by the high-prejudice participants, von Hippel et al. argue, to try and 'explain away' the stereotype-incongruent information and maintain the integrity of the existing stereotype. Consistent with von Hippel et al.'s predictions, participants in Locke and Walker's

(1999) study who were identified as high-prejudiced using the Attitudes Towards Women Scale (Spence et al., 1973) were indeed more likely to provide continuations that were explanations of the stereotype-incongruent behaviours than were low-prejudice participants.

So not only do high-prejudice people selectively encode information consistent with the stereotype, but also they actively 'explain away' any inconsistencies. This stereotypic encoding bias may then serve to reinforce the stereotype held, and to provide additional stereotype-congruent information that can guide evaluations of the target person in the future. The end result is a self-reinforcing feedback loop that is providing the prejudiced person with constant validation of their stereotypes.

Implicit Stereotyping and Prejudice

Up to this point, we have been dealing with the influence of stereotypes on our explicit judgements of groups and their members. This is akin to asking whether people, when they are explicitly aware of someone's group memberships, use the stereotype of that group to help guide their judgements. Of course, we are usually aware of people's membership in various racial, ethnic, and gender groups. However, there are other common social circumstances where this is not the case. Imagine a friend complaining about a rude and abrupt police officer who pulled them over for speeding. You try to console them by pointing out that men in positions of power are often overbearing. They embarrass you by pointing out that it was a female police officer. Most of us can attest to similar situations – assuming that our lecturers will be male; that the nurse attending to us will be female; and that the physical education students will be superbly fit, but dumb. When we are making judgements of a person that seem to be unrelated to their group memberships, we can still be influenced by stereotypes without our knowing it. Greenwald and Banaji (1995) call this *implicit stereotyping*. A stereotype influencing our judgements without our awareness is a scary thought. Unfortunately, there is increasing evidence that it can happen.

Banaji et al., (1993) had participants complete a scrambled sentences task in which jumbled sentences containing either the traits *dependent* (stereotypic for women) or *aggressive* (stereotypic for men) had to be arranged into grammatically correct sentences. In a subsequent task, participants rated the behaviour of either a female or male target. Despite the fact that the male and female targets performed exactly the same behaviour, the female target's behaviour, but not the male's, was rated as more dependent when participants had unscrambled the sentence containing 'dependent' beforehand. Conversely, the male target's behaviour, but not the female's, was rated as more aggressive when participants had unscrambled the sentence containing 'aggressive'. Because the participants were informed that the priming and the judgement tasks were two independent and unrelated experiments, and because none of the participants expressed any suspicion that the two tasks were linked when subsequently asked, this suggests that this stereotype priming effect is the result of unconscious processes.

Some researchers have even argued that stereotypes may not just influence our judgements and feelings towards others, but may also change the way we behave. For example, Bargh et al., (1996) had participants complete a scrambled sentence test which, for half the participants, contained words related to the stereotype of the elderly (e.g., bingo, conservative). When the participants were finished, the time it took them to walk from the experimental room to the only exit (a nearby elevator) was surreptitiously timed by an experimenter posing as a participant waiting in the corridor. Those participants who had been exposed to words stereotypic of the elderly in their sentence unscrambling task took longer to complete the walk. In other words, the stereotype of elderly people had been activated, without their awareness, and this activation actually produced differences in motor behaviour.[3] Such findings suggest that stereotypes contain motor information that can be activated and can influence our behaviour (Bargh et al., 1996). Moreover, the implicit activation of the stereotype can result in the use of these motor components without our awareness.

Thankfully, this effect is not limited to negative elements of stereotypes. Dijksterhuis and van Knippenberg (1998) attempted to demonstrate this by selecting a category label that evoked the stereotype of a warm and caring group with the highest of moral and intellectual standards, and great physical attractiveness to boot. Stuck with the only group to meet these high standards, academics, Dijksterhuis and van Knippenberg had their participants complete a priming task in which they were exposed to a category label (professor) for such a brief period that they were unaware that it had been presented at all; hence participants could not respond strategically to this label. After the priming task, the participants were led to a separate area and asked to complete a quiz in which they had to answer general knowledge questions. It will come as no surprise to those of you engaged in psychology courses that participants primed with the professor label were able to answer correctly more of the questions than those participants who were not primed with the label. The priming of the concept 'professor' actually improved performance in an unrelated general knowledge quiz. Of course, there is no suggestion that priming someone with the term 'professor' miraculously imbues people with more knowledge. Rather, it is more likely that the prime facilitates behavioural patterns associated with professors, such as logical reasoning and concentration, that help in selecting the right answer from the knowledge they already possess.

The worrying prospect is that stereotypes, when brought unintentionally to mind, can influence our behaviour. As Bargh suggests, given the conditions used to implicitly prime the stereotypes above, '... it is hard to see how even motivated individuals would have the opportunity to control the immediate, nonconscious effect of the stereotype of their own behaviour' (in press: 14). This suggests that even low-prejudice people may be unable to avoid stereotype activation and use when the stereotype is implicitly activated. Remember, Lepore and Brown (1997) have shown that low-prejudice people do indeed show stereotype activation and use when they are implicitly primed with elements of the stereotype. However, the outlook may not be as bad as it seems. Macrae and

Johnston (1998) have pointed out that the environment is bound to contain cues for many different behaviours and that any useful cognitive system must, at some level, edit potentially conflicting behaviours. To demonstrate this point, they used the now familiar scrambled sentence task where the experimental group unscrambled sentences containing words related to helping (e.g., assistance, helped) and the control group unscrambled sentences relating to no particular construct. When the participants had completed this task, the experimenter informed the participants that the next phase was to be conducted by another experimenter who she would have to go and get. The experimenter then collected together her possessions and, in the process of leaving, dropped some pens from her pile of goods. The important thing was the dropped items. Half of the participants saw regular pens drop on the floor while the other half saw pens that were leaking. Consistent with previous research, the group primed with the 'helping' sentences was more likely to pick up the regular pens than the control group. However, the group primed with 'helping' sentences was not more likely than the control group to pick up the leaking pens. Other competing actions (such as trying to avoid the possibility of getting ink on our fingers) can inhibit the operation of implicitly activated concepts. In a second experiment, participants who believed they were late for the next appointment were less likely to help pick up dropped items than were participants who believed they had ample time to get to the next appointment. Macrae and Johnston point out that 'behavioral control may be initiated by unconscious processes that are triggered by the implicit registration of external cues in the immediate task environment' (1998: 414). So just as behavioural actions may be implicitly primed, so might inhibitory actions. An activated construct does not inevitably lead to construct-related behaviour.

You should also realize that there must be a natural limit to this kind of effect. Clearly implicit primes (even those satanic messages apparently embedded on your CDs) are unlikely to result in extreme acts (e.g., murder) since there are many other factors, both internal (e.g., personal values) and external (e.g., the presence of witnesses) which inhibit the performance of such acts. Motor priming effects are probably limited to simple motor operations and judgements. As Bargh et al. observed, the people they primed with the stereotype of the elderly may have walked more slowly from the experiment, but they do not rush off to 'buy condos in Florida' (1996: 240).

Before moving on, we should make it clear that the implicit stereotype activation outlined above differs from the kind of explicit process outlined in Devine's dissociation model. In the dissociation model Devine (1989) is talking about, the stereotypes come to mind automatically when we are making a judgement of a group – whether that judgement is pejorative or not. In contrast, here we are suggesting that, since everyone has stereotypes of the major groups in our society, then their influence may be equally unavoidable for all of us when we are unaware they have been activated, or unaware they may influence our behaviour. Recent evidence suggests a lack of any relationship between implicit and explicit measures of prejudice (Dovidio et al., 1996; Dovidio et al., 1997; Locke and Walker, 1999; von Hippel et al., 1995); only high-prejudiced individuals demonstrate explicit use of stereotypes but both high- and low-prejudiced individuals show the effects of implicit stereotype activation.

Stereotype Change

The research reviewed thus far has demonstrated the role, both explicit and implicit, that stereotypes play in the judgements of social groups and their members. Stereotypes are useful to individuals, allowing for simple and straightforward evaluation and decision making, as shown in our bouncer example. If stereotypes were to change with ease and rapidity their utility as simplifying mental structures, guiding and shaping information processing, would ultimately disappear. Indeed, we have cognitive mechanisms in place which perpetuate our stereotypes and make them resistant to change, such as the preferential encoding of stereotype-consistent information described earlier. Being at the receiving end of prejudice or discrimination can be both unpleasant and unfair (for example, not getting a job because of the employer's prejudice against working women). Accordingly, both social psychologists and legislators have invested much effort in reducing prejudice and discrimination in society. We know that stereotypes are involved in the production of prejudiced judgements and, as such, offer a point at which we can potentially intervene in the prejudice cycle. Reducing stereotypes may, in turn, reduce the production of prejudiced judgements.

The approach of social-cognition researchers to changing stereotypic beliefs has focused on the processing of stereotype-inconsistent information. In a typical experiment perceivers are presented with information, including stereotype-disconfirming information, about a number of members of a stereotyped group and are then asked to evaluate the group and its members on stereotype-relevant characteristics (Hewstone et al., 1992; Hewstone et al., 1994; Johnston and Hewstone, 1992; Johnston et al., 1994; Weber and Crocker, 1983). The question researchers ask is – how do perceivers respond to this disconfirming information? Are they less stereotypic in their evaluations of the group than control perceivers who have not received any stereotype-disconfirming information? What happens when you learn that the pub bouncer is an intelligent, caring individual? Do you revise your stereotype and no longer consider bouncers to be unintelligent thugs? Trait-ratings typically do reveal a reduction in perceivers' stereotype-based evaluation of the group in response to the presentation of disconfirming information. This effect is, however, moderated by the perceived typicality of the disconfirming group members.

If the disconfirming group members are considered to be typical group members and show only minor disconfirmation of the group stereotype then revision of the group stereotype occurs. If, however, the disconfirming group members are considered atypical of the group, or extremely disconfirm the group, stereotype revision of the stereotype is unlikely. In such situations, the disconfirming exemplars are considered to be exceptions or unusual members of the group and this provides a justification for not changing one's stereotype of the group. Meeting one intelligent, gentle bouncer is unlikely to result in us believing that all bouncers are in fact intelligent and non-aggressive. Rather, we simply consider this particular bouncer as an 'exception-to-the-rule'. This process is known as 'subtyping' and has been repeatedly demonstrated in experiments on stereotype change. Provided that there is some justification, or reason, for isolating the disconfirming exemplars from the group, they are subtyped and the overall group stereotype does not change (Kunda and Oleson, 1995, 1997). Evidence of the subtyping of atypical group exemplars also comes from a real-life example. A school-police liaison programme was set up in a large British city in which a police officer was assigned to certain inner-city schools. This officer spent time at the school over a two-year period involved in various activities with the pupils. It was hoped that exposure to this police officer would result in a change in the predominantly negative evaluation of the police by the teenagers. Results showed that the pupils liked the liaison officer but that this did not generalize to the police in general who were still evaluated negatively at the end of the period (Hopkins et al., 1992). The liaison officer was considered atypical of the police in general and was isolated, or subtyped, from them (Hewstone et al., 1992).

So, presenting stereotype-disconfirming information can result in a reduction of stereotype-based beliefs, provided that the disconfirming group exemplars are not too extreme or atypical of the group. The mere existence of disconfirming information is not normally, however, sufficient to exact any revision of stereotypic beliefs. The experiments described above all involved presenting perceivers with a pre-packaged set of behavioural information, including disconfirming information, which they are required to process before evaluating the group. We have already seen that prejudiced people only absorb information which is consistent with their beliefs (Locke and Walker, 1999) so when not forced by the experimental set-up to process the stereotype-inconsistent information it may simply be ignored. In everyday settings we are information seekers (Yzerbyt and Leyens, 1991) who can control the information received about members of stereotyped groups and, as such, can actively decide to accept or reject new information, especially stereotype-disconfirming information, as we see fit. In a series of studies which allowed perceivers to select what information they wished to receive about members of stereotyped groups, it was found that they chose information which confirmed their pre-existing stereotypic beliefs and did not actively seek stereotype-disconfirming information. When perceivers in this paradigm received stereotype-inconsistent information they did not revise their stereotypes of the group although perceivers who received the same information in a traditional forced processing paradigm did revise those stereotypes (Johnston, 1996; Johnston and Macrae, 1994). Consistent with the motivated tactician meta-theory, however, when the salient processing goals (e.g., to be accurate) were inconsistent with stereotype maintenance, the confirmatory bias could be overcome. Under these conditions perceivers sought both stereotypic and counter-stereotypic information and did revise their stereotypes in response to stereotype-inconsistent information (Johnston, 1996).

Stereotype change research has focused on the identification of core cognitive processes involved in the moderation of stereotypic beliefs but has been somewhat negligent in the investigation of the impact of individual differences such as prejudice level. One recent study involved presenting stereotype-inconsistent information about members of one social group to high and low endorsers of stereotypes (analogous to high- and low-prejudiced individuals) prior to their evaluating members of both the group about which they had received stereotype-disconfirming information and members of other stereotyped groups. Low endorsers of stereotypes modified their stereotype of the group about which they received disconfirming information but did not differ from low endorser controls in their evaluations of the other groups. High endorsers modified their stereotypes of all the groups relative to high endorser controls regardless of whether disconfirming information had been received about that group or not (Johnston, 1998). It was hypothesized that low endorsers were motivated to be non-stereotypic in their evaluations of others and so incorporated any disconfirming information they received into their stereotypes. On the other hand, it was hypothesized that high endorsers were motivated by situational factors such as the social norms governing stereotype use. Receiving stereotype disconfirming information was taken as a cue that stereotyping was inappropriate in this situation and hence they reduced their stereotypes of all groups; they were not sensitive to the specific disconfirming information presented. The influence of individual differences, such as prejudice level, on stereotype change needs much further research.

Conclusion

Clearly the story being told by social cognition researchers has changed over recent years. From the view that stereotypes are a necessary evil that everyone learns and activates when judging members of the stereotyped group, we have moved to a view of stereotypes as tools that prejudiced people employ, perhaps in an automatic fashion, to facilitate negative and stereotyped judgements of the groups they are prejudiced towards. There is also some evidence that we may all be open to the influence of stereotypes, regardless of whether we are prejudiced or not, when they are activated outside of our awareness. All this gives our pub-going patron little comfort. Does this person change skin colour or dress in a more conservative fashion every time friends invite him or her to the pub? We hope not. But it may help us understand what is going on in the bouncer's mind. Forearmed with this knowledge, psychologists may be better able to develop strategies to change stereotypes and reduce prejudice.

Notes

1. With apologies to 10cc.

2. This experiment was conducted in Wales where the geography of Indonesia is not as well known as it is in the southern hemisphere.

3. Since the words 'slowness' and 'weakness' were not among the stereotypic words contained in the scrambled sentence task, the effect must have been mediated by the activation of the elderly.

8 Affect, Prejudice, and Discrimination: In the Politics of 'Gut Feeling', Feeling Better is What Counts

Leith S. Baird and Julie M. Duck

Dating from the general election of March 1996, Australia witnessed a conservative transformation, not unlike those that occurred in Britain, the US, Canada, and New Zealand at earlier dates (Grant, 1997). The rise of a new political independent, Pauline Hanson, and her One Nation Party was the distinctive element. Hanson was elected on an unabashed populist rhetoric in which various minority groups including Aborigines and Asian immigrants came in for hostility and attack (see Lynch and Reavell, 1997). For instance, in her maiden speech to parliament, Hanson spoke of Aborigines as a 'new privileged class' and of the danger of Australia being 'swamped by Asians'. In subsequent public statements, she called for the repudiation of treaties with Indigenous peoples, cuts to immigration, an end to multiculturalism, and the re-introduction of national service in order to protect Australia against Asian aggression.

Despite condemnation from some sections of the community for her divisive comments, racist sentiments, and prejudices, many Australians apparently identified with what Hanson was saying: 'When she appeared on television, her views seemed to command overwhelming approval. When she arrived in country towns or walked through shopping malls her progress was cheered' (Manne, 1998: 4). Indeed, in the Queensland state election of June 1998, One Nation received almost 23 per cent of the vote. Political commentators seeking to explain the success of Hanson and her party suggested that feelings of anger, resentment, and disappointment stemming from political and economic insecurity had fuelled a search for scapegoats. Rationally, the abolition of benefits to Indigenous people and the reduction of Asian immigration would not provide the desired economic and political solutions. However, as one political scientist concluded, 'In the politics of "gut-feeling" what counts is that you feel better, whether or not the problems you face have actually been solved' (Wells, 1997: 25).

'Gut-feelings' and associated drives to reduce negative affective states have long been viewed as important factors in intergroup attitudes and behaviour and they form the basis of the classic scapegoating theory of prejudice (Allport, 1954; Miller and Bugelski, 1948; Zawadzki, 1948). According to this theory, derived from the frustration-aggression hypothesis (Dollard et al., 1939), frustration results in increased outgroup hostility via the displacement of aggression. However, since the 1970s, cognitive approaches that considered prejudice as 'a phenomenon in the minds rather than in the guts of men' (Tajfel, 1969: 190), have tended to dominate the literature on intergroup phenomena (see Hamilton and Trolier, 1986; Messick and Mackie, 1989, for reviews). Although Tajfel (1978b, 1981a) and Tajfel and Turner (1979) incorporated motivational processes (specifically, the need to maintain a positive social identity) in his theory of intergroup behaviour and social identity theory, he said little about mood or emotion. A more recent theoretical extension, self-categorization theory (Turner et al., 1987; see Reynolds and Turner, Chapter 10), is also almost exclusively concerned with cognitive processes in interaction with social context. Indeed, it is only in very recent years that there has been a resurgence of interest in the way in which generalized affective states such as emotion and mood colour our social judgements and intergroup behaviour (see Mackie and Hamilton, 1993).

In keeping with early experiments on the scapegoating theory of prejudice (e.g., Miller and Bugelski, 1948), recent studies have found that transient negative affect can increase the expression of prejudiced attitudes and discriminatory behaviour (see Bodenhausen, 1993; Esses and Zanna, 1995; Forgas and Fiedler, 1996; Stangor et al., 1991; Stroessner et al., 1992). Moreover, these studies suggest that this is so even when the mood has nothing to do with the group or its members, that is, when the mood is incidental to, rather than integral to, the intergroup context (Bodenhausen, 1993). However, contemporary accounts tend to focus on negative mood per se (rather than frustration) as a factor that accentuates the expression of stereotypes and discrimination. They also tend to emphasize the mediating role of cognitive factors such as information processing and thus reflect an effort to understand how cognitive and affective variables interact to influence intergroup behaviour (see Esses and Zanna, 1995, for similar points). For instance, in his reformulation of the frustration-aggression hypothesis, Berkowitz (1989, 1990, 1993) suggests that affect mediates between aversive occurrences and aggression toward outsiders by activating anger-related feelings, thoughts, memories, and behavioural tendencies. Likewise, Esses and her colleagues (Esses et al., 1993; Esses and Zanna, 1995) have demonstrated that negative mood can accentuate the use of negative outgroup stereotypes because negative information and negative interpretive categories are cognitively more accessible.

In this chapter, we describe some recent empirical work that examines negative mood as an antecedent of intergroup discrimination in the minimal group paradigm, an experimental paradigm that permits the investigation of intergroup behaviour uncontaminated by interpersonal attraction or the possibility of personal gain (see Tajfel et al., 1971). Specifically, we focus on the way in which incidental negative affect accentuates discriminatory behaviour via the recruitment of motivated processing of group information with the goal of mood repair. Our focus on the effects of mood on behavioural discrimination in minimal group contexts, as distinct from stereotyped appraisals, is of interest not only because this issue has received less attention in the literature, but also because the cognitive mechanisms underlying the two are not necessarily comparable (see Abele et al., 1998). In the first case, judgements can be based on knowledge structures activated from memory. In the second case, there is by definition little knowledge about the groups.

We begin by providing some theoretical background on the effects of mood on social judgements and information processing. Next, we describe the minimal group paradigm and theoretical perspectives on intergroup discrimination. Finally, we consider empirical research that examines the influence of mood on intergroup discrimination in the minimal group paradigm.

Background

The Influence of Mood on Information Processing and Social Judgements

Recently, the impact of generalized affective states on social judgements has become an important focus of research. A central theme has been the way in which affect elicited in one context can affect judgements in other contexts (Bower, 1981; Forgas, 1991; Forgas and Bower, 1988; Isen, 1984, 1987; Schwarz, 1990; Schwarz and Clore, 1988; Wyer and Srull, 1989). Findings suggest that affect may inform both the content of judgements (e.g., through memory mechanisms, selective priming, and use of mood-related information) and the extent and depth of information processing. That is, mood states influence what information is attended to and what contents will be activated from memory (informational effects) and mood states also activate motivations or goal states, which in turn influence the extent and nature of further processing (processing effects; Mackie and Hamilton, 1993). The effects on information processing are potentially of more relevance to outcomes in the minimal group paradigm where there is little knowledge about the groups to be primed or activated.

In general, findings also contrast the effects of positive and negative affect on information processing and social judgements (but see Stroessner et al., 1992, for an account of symmetrical effects based on attentional allocation). For instance, across a wide variety of contexts and settings, positive moods tend to improve memory for pleasant events and increase the chances that positive ideas will come to mind (e.g., Bower, 1981; Isen, 1984). Further, people in a positive mood tend consistently to engage in faster and more superficial, heuristic processing and to use quick and easy strategies, cognitive shortcuts and heuristics, and intuitive responses when making social judgements (e.g., Bodenhausen, 1993; Clark and Isen, 1982; Isen, 1984; Mackie and Worth,

1991; Schwarz, 1990). Presumably, good mood interferes with people's capacity to process information systematically, or people in a good mood avoid extensive processing in order to maintain their positive affective state.

Findings on the effects of negative mood – the issue of central concern here – are more variable. This is ostensibly because automatic effects of negative mood on content, priming, and processing may be checked by controlled or regulatory processes associated with a motivation for mood repair and an awareness of social norms that inhibit taking one's bad mood out on others (Esses and Zanna, 1995). For instance, according to a number of studies, unpleasant feelings promote the recall of unpleasant memories and heighten the accessibility of thoughts with a negative meaning (e.g., Bower, 1981), but mood-congruency effects are not always found (see Bower, 1991; Forgas and Bower, 1988). Although negative information may be especially accessible, in an attempt to alleviate their mood, individuals who feel bad might try not to think of or recall material that could increase or prolong their negative affect (Isen, 1984). Moreover, in the context of social judgements such as the expression of group evaluations, there may be inhibitory social norms or standards that prevent people who are in a negative mood from expressing mood-congruent opinions or evaluations even if these are accessible (Berkowitz and Troccoli, 1990; Forgas and Bower, 1988). One standard might be that people ought not to be harsh to others in the absence of a good justification. Another is that people ought not to let their negative feelings bias their judgements. In general, people in a negative mood also tend to use more systematic and deliberative processing in an attempt to monitor their environment (Achee et al., 1994; Forgas, 1991; Schwarz, 1990). However, they may use more goal-directed, motivated processing and look selectively for rewarding outcomes that alleviate the negative mood state (Clark and Isen, 1982; Forgas, 1991; Isen, 1984; Schwarz and Clore, 1983). Indeed, there is increasing evidence to suggest that people are active mood regulators who selectively use different judgemental strategies as a means of mood control (Baumgardner and Arkin, 1988; Erber and Erber, 1994; Forgas, 1995).

Forgas (1992, 1995) drew on this notion to explain the differential effects of mood on social judgements in a more integrated fashion (viz., the Affect Infusion Model or AIM). He suggested that people are selective in the way that they process information and that the choice of processing strategy used in making social judgements is influenced by factors such as personal relevance, salience, complexity, and familiarity of the target as well as by affective state. According to the AIM, good moods typically recruit either direct access of stored judgements or heuristic processing and negative moods typically recruit either substantive, deliberative processing or motivated processing in the service of mood repair or a pre-existing goal. However, other contextual factors determine which particular processing strategy is used. For instance, people in a negative mood may engage in a more targeted and motivated, as opposed to a more systematic and deliberative, processing style to the extent that the cognitive task or social judgement is personally relevant. Bodenhausen (1993) has also suggested that use of deliberative, systematic processing in negative moods may also be less likely when the cognitive task or social judgement is incidental to rather than integral to the mood.

The Influence of Mood on Intergroup Discrimination in the Minimal Group Paradigm

Because mood has pervasive effects on social information processing, it is not surprising that a growing body of research has shown effects of transient mood on stereotyping (see Mackie and Hamilton, 1993, for a review). For instance, good mood is presumed to promote more heuristic and faster processing and hence greater reliance on simple categorical information or stereotypes (e.g., Bodenhausen, 1993). By contrast, negative mood is presumed to promote more deliberative processing and hence more individuated judgements of others. But there have been few systematic accounts of the effects of mood on behavioural discrimination. In one account, Forgas and Fiedler (1996) sought to show that, in different contexts, both happy and sad moods could accentuate intergroup discrimination in the minimal group paradigm and to demonstrate the relevance of group membership as a factor that moderates the effects of mood on discrimination. Their results pertaining to the effects of negative affect on intergroup discrimination in personally relevant group contexts are of particular relevance to our own research.

In the minimal group paradigm there is no face-to-face interaction between participants, no past history, and no expected future interaction. Participants are simply assigned into groups on the basis of some arbitrary criterion and are asked, on a series of distribution matrices, to allocate points among several pairs of recipients identified only as ingroup and outgroup members (and not including themselves) (e.g., Tajfel, 1970; Tajfel et al., 1971). The matrices are designed to assess four major allocation choices: maximizing absolute gain for the ingroup member; maximizing the ingroup member's gain relative to that of the outgroup member, maximizing the joint gain of the ingroup and outgroup members, and distributing resources between the ingroup and outgroup members equally (fairness). Results of numerous experiments using the minimal group paradigm indicate that minimal categorizations may be sufficient to produce biased judgements and discriminatory behaviour against the outgroup (see Brewer, 1979; Brewer and Kramer, 1985; Tajfel, 1970, 1982b; Tajfel et al., 1971; Tajfel and Turner, 1986). Indeed, according to one review, 'intergroup discrimination under conditions of the minimal group paradigm is a stable, consistent and experimentally replicable phenomenon' (Diehl, 1990: 288). Further, results suggest that when allocating points, respondents typically choose to maximize differences in favour of the ingroup rather than merely to maximize ingroup profit per se, thus emphasizing the apparent importance of 'beating the outgroup' (Hogg and Abrams, 1988: 49).

According to social identity theory (e.g., Hogg and Abrams, 1988; Tajfel and Turner, 1979) the consistent pattern of discrimination or ingroup bias reported in the minimal group paradigm arises from the operation of two fundamental psychological processes, cognitive categorization and motivated social comparison. Social categorization leads to the cognitive accentuation of within-category similarities and intercategory differences, transforming a distribution of individuals (including the self) into distinct groups, ingroup and outgroup. When ingroup membership is internalized as part of the self-concept (i.e., is used to locate self with respect to others) perceptions and behaviour become depersonalized. That is, members display prototypical or normative ingroup behaviour and hold stereotypical perceptions of self and others. Further, the operation of self-enhancement motives guides the accentuation process so as to favour the ingroup and hence the self. Because of a basic need for a positive self-concept (the self-esteem hypothesis), group members make social comparisons that maximize the positive distinctiveness of the ingroup over the outgroup and the stronger the identification with the ingroup, the more pronounced the ingroup bias or intergroup discrimination (but see Turner, 1999b, for a recent criticism of the self-esteem hypothesis and the assumed link between identification and bias).

In a series of experiments, Forgas and Fiedler (1996) examined the effects of transient mood and group relevance on intergroup discrimination in the minimal group paradigm. Mood was manipulated through various strategies including exposure to positive, negative, or neutral videotaped material, through false feedback in which respondents' performance on a judgement task was described either as impressive and well above average, or as disappointing and well below average, or through autobiographical recall in which respondents were asked to remember and describe in detail an episode from their past when they felt either particularly happy or particularly sad. Participants were categorized as either overestimators or underestimators ostensibly on the basis of their performance on a size estimation task. In half the conditions, group relevance was emphasized via information that described the otherwise minimal categorization as a stable and significant personality characteristic. Although there was no face-to-face interaction between participants, no past history, and no expected future interaction, participants were told that:

> The tendency to overestimate or underestimate quantity is a stable and highly significant personality feature that is linked to other personal and social characteristics. It almost seems that overestimators and underestimators see the world in fundamentally different ways; in fact, they tend to be very different people on many quite unrelated attributes, suggesting that being an overestimator or an underestimator is related to basic psychological differences between people. (1996: 32)

Forgas and Fiedler (1996) reasoned that, when group membership is of low personal relevance and members have little knowledge about or involvement in their group, happy moods might increase intergroup discrimination due to the use of a faster, more heuristic judgemental style and a reliance on basic categorical information about group membership. That is, a combination of happy mood and heuristic processing might lead to a tendency to favour the ingroup in the absence of strong motivation or personal involvement. They also reasoned that when group membership is personally relevant, negative moods should increase intergroup discrimination because enhancement of the positive distinctiveness of the ingroup (and hence the self) is an obvious means of mood repair. The latter prediction is of particular importance because group memberships are likely to be relevant and involving in more naturalistic and less minimal groups, that is, in real social groups outside the laboratory.

Their results provided reliable evidence that the effect of mood on discrimination depended on group relevance. When the personal relevance of the group was low, positive mood resulted in faster, more heuristic processing and greater intergroup discrimination. In contrast, when group relevance was high (i.e., based on a stable and significant criteria), negative mood enhanced intergroup discrimination following slower, more motivated processing. Moreover, the level of discrimination on matrices where maximum discrimination could only be achieved by sacrificing maximum ingroup profit was most pronounced in the negative mood, high relevance contexts. Forgas and Fiedler concluded that the 'combination of a negative affective state, and a personally involving group membership may create a potentially dangerous motivational force for discriminatory judgments and behaviours.' (1996: 38)

A number of issues arise from Forgas and Fiedler's (1996) discussion of the effects of negative mood on intergroup discrimination. Firstly, although their results are consistent with the notion that members of a personally relevant group who were in a sad mood discriminated in order to feel better, no post-discrimination measures of mood were taken and it remains unclear whether intergroup discrimination actually facilitated mood repair. Secondly, their assumption that motivated processing in search of mood repair is necessarily associated with longer response latencies is problematic. In fact, to the extent that negative mood invokes targeted information search and efficient and directed choice or decision strategies, reduced, rather than prolonged, processing latencies might be expected (see Forgas, 1994). In a study that required people to search for and select partners, Forgas (1991) himself predicted and found that people in a negative mood selectively searched for and remembered rewarding information about potential partners, employed a global impression formation strategy, and made faster and more efficient judgement choices. This was apparently due to the directive nature of their search. Thirdly, although Forgas and Fiedler (1996) emphasize the personal relevance of group membership as an important factor moderating the effects of mood, it is possible that other social contextual factors may play a major interactive role in cueing processing strategies and thus in determining behavioural and perceptual responses. Ingroup status is one key social contextual factor that has been identified in previous research on intergroup discrimination in the minimal group paradigm (see Sachdev and Bourhis, 1987, 1991). The importance of ingroup status has also been noted in discussions of the motivational component of social identity theory, the self-esteem hypothesis – an hypothesis that Forgas and Fiedler acknowledge has parallels with their own account of motivated intergroup discrimination.

The Self-Esteem Hypothesis

Researchers concerned with the motivational component of social identity theory have argued that fluctuations in self-esteem can be both an antecedent and a consequence of intergroup discrimination. According to Abrams and Hogg (1988) and Hogg and Abrams (1990), depressed or threatened self-esteem promotes intergroup discrimination because of the need for self-esteem, and successful intergroup discrimination enhances social identity and thus elevates self-esteem. There are some similarities between this hypothesis and the notion of motivated intergroup discrimination in the service of mood repair, although negative mood states need not involve negative self-referent cognitions.

The self-esteem aspect of social identity theory has been associated with inconsistent and contradictory findings, prompting a theoretical shift away from self-esteem as an important motivational component (see Hogg and Abrams, 1993). Some research suggests that persons whose self-esteem has been artificially lowered tend to engage in more intergroup discrimination as if to improve their self-esteem (e.g., Finchilescu, 1986; Hogg and Sunderland, 1991; Wagner et al., 1986), but the evidence is not entirely consistent (see Ng, 1985). There are also findings that indicate that increased positive discrimination between ingroup and outgroup members has a beneficial effect on a person's self-esteem (Hogg et al., 1986; Lemyre and Smith, 1985; Oakes and Turner, 1980). Although others have found little support for this notion (Hogg and Turner 1985a, 1985b, 1987; Wagner et al., 1986). Indeed, Hogg and Sunderland (1991) suggested that enhanced self-esteem as a consequence of intergroup discrimination is likely only when the ingroup readily imbues positive self-regard, such as in a high-status ingroup. It is also possible that negative mood is more likely to motivate intergroup discrimination in the service of mood repair in groups that are not only personally relevant, but also of high-status relative to the outgroup target.

Empirical Studies

In a series of four experiments we examined further the links between negative affect and intergroup discrimination in the minimal group paradigm. In these experiments we sought to examine the interplay between negative mood and ingroup status as contextual factors influencing discrimination. We also aimed to provide fuller evidence for discrimination as a motivated affect-control strategy. Finally, we sought to examine the role of regulatory or controlled processes (such as inhibitory social norms or standards) that are likely to influence the expression of intergroup discrimination in negative mood contexts.

In each minimal group experiment we emphasized the personal relevance of the 'minimal' categories following the instructions used by Forgas and Fiedler (1996). That is, although there was no face-to-face interaction between participants, no past history, and no expected future interaction, participants were told that the categorization was based on a stable and highly significant personality feature that is consistently linked to other personal and social characteristics. The manipulations of status were overlaid. Specifically, participants were told not only that there were stable and significant differences between the categories or groups, but also that it was generally considered desirable to be a member of a particular group, the ingroup in high-status contexts and the outgroup in low-status contexts. Mood was induced either using videotaped material (e.g., excerpts from comedy shows or sad movies) or using autobiographical recall of positive and negative life events. To ensure that mood rather than situational self-esteem was manipulated, none of the inductions involved explicit self-referent cognitions. In each experiment we measured response latencies and mood was re-measured following the discrimination task (along with measures of task enjoyment) in an attempt to provide evidence of motivated processing and mood repair.

Experiment 1

In the first experiment, we examined the effects of ingroup status (high status, low status, no specific status information) and mood (negative, neutral, positive) on intergroup discrimination. Following Forgas and Fiedler (1996), we assumed that a negative mood state would motivate group members to attempt to improve or repair their mood by enhancing the positive distinctiveness of their ingroup (and therefore themselves). However, following Hogg and Sunderland (1991) we predicted that most discrimination would be displayed in negative mood contexts where the salient ingroup categorization readily imbued positive self-regard, that is, in high-status ingroups. Sachdev and Bourhis (1987, 1991) have argued that whereas members of low-status groups tend to internalize their relative inferiority, high-status groups provide a positive social identity for group members. Thus, members of high-status ingroups are strongly motivated to defend this rewarding identity via ingroup favouritism – a tendency that might be accentuated by transient negative affect because it serves as a method of affect-control.

As predicted, high-status group members were more discriminatory than members of low-status or no-status groups and the effects of status were moderated by mood. Specifically, high-status group members in a negative mood displayed most discrimination. In keeping with some findings in the literature (e.g., Forgas, 1991), responses in the negative mood conditions were associated with faster decision times, perhaps reflecting members' highly targeted search for, and quick convergence upon, a strategy in the context of an obvious mood repair goal. However, the effects of mood on response latency were not moderated by status. There was also some evidence of increased mood repair and greater self-reported task enjoyment in the high-status, negative-mood condition – the condition in which group members displayed most discrimination.

The results of Experiment 1 provided further evidence for the influence of transient negative mood on intergroup discrimination in the minimal group paradigm. They suggested that when members belong to a high-status group that readily imbues positive self-regard, negative mood states accentuate an existing tendency to discriminate against low-status outgroups. However, the results of Experiment 1 provided a less reliable basis for drawing conclusions about the information processing and motivational mechanisms underlying this effect. Thus, in three subsequent experiments we focused on providing evidence for intergroup discrimination as a motivated affect-control strategy. These experiments used three distinct approaches to the issue.

Experiment 2

In Experiment 2, participants were all categorized as members of a high-status ingroup and a negative mood state was induced. That is, we examined intergroup discrimination in the condition identified in Experiment 1 as the one most likely to foster discriminatory behaviour. Respondents were asked to complete the allocation task either after standard instructions for matrix completion or after instructions indicating that they should be fair, favour the outgroup (outgroup bias), or favour the ingroup (ingroup bias). We reasoned that if the combination of negative mood and high status provides a strong motivational force for ingroup bias in the service of mood repair, explicit instructions to favour the ingroup should accentuate the display of bias and facilitate mood repair. This would be due at least in part to the fact that explicit instructions to display ingroup bias would over ride any inhibitory social norms against discrimination. Moreover, responses should be made quickly because the instruction to favour the ingroup accords with an obvious motivational goal. By contrast, instructions asking members to show a countervailing response, outgroup bias, or perhaps even intergroup fairness, should be resisted, should be associated with longer decision times, and should facilitate less mood repair ostensibly because these behavioural responses conflict with the obvious response strategy.

As predicted, results provided evidence of a clear preference for ingroup bias in this negative mood, high-status context, and an obvious resistance to the display of outgroup bias. In the absence of explicit instructions, group members displayed significant ingroup bias, but this tendency was further accentuated when they received instructions to do so. Respondents who were instructed to be fair were merely less biased and respondents who were instructed to favour the ingroup did so much more readily (i.e., more intensely and more quickly) than respondents who were instructed to favour the outgroup. In fact, members who were asked to favour the outgroup found it more difficult to decide how to allocate points, took significantly longer over the task, and were less confident that their allocations were right as far as they were concerned. By contrast, group members who spontaneously used ingroup bias and particularly group members who were asked to do so, enjoyed the task more and reported more mood repair and more task enjoyment.

The results of Experiment 2 thus suggested that the spontaneous use of intergroup discrimination in negative mood, high-status contexts might reflect a highly targeted, motivated strategy aimed at mood repair. Results also indicated that in contexts where the desire to discriminate is supported by others (and thus unchecked by inhibitory social norms against the expression of discriminatory behaviour), high-status group members do not restrain their desire to discriminate against low-status, outgroup members as a means of affect-control. In these contexts group members do not deliberate – they discriminate and they enjoy associated mood repair.

Experiment 3

In Experiment 3, we examined whether the intergroup discrimination typically displayed by respondents in negative mood, high-status contexts could be attenuated by simple instructions that made them aware of their mood or that directed them to deliberate longer over their allocation decisions. Our reasoning was that self-regulatory mechanisms that sometimes intervene to determine what people experiencing unpleasant feelings will think about, say, and do to others might routinely be underplayed when a clear strategy for mood relief is available. However, awareness of one's negative mood and its likely effects on behaviour might prompt greater adherence to inhibitory social norms (see Finman and Berkowitz, 1989). More deliberative processing of group information might also heighten group members' concern with equity (see Forgas, 1994) or draw attention to their mood and its possible consequences (Finman and Berkowitz, 1989).

As in Experiment 2, respondents were all categorized as members of a high-status group and a negative mood was induced. In this experiment we used a 2 (mood awareness: aware, unaware) x 2 (decision time: extended, standard) factorial design. Half the respondents were informed that peoples' decisions on the allocation task are affected by various factors including their mood – the other half received no such information. Further, half the respondents were required to deliberate on each allocation matrix for a set, extended period of time before making their decision – the others were instructed to complete each matrix in their own time.

Results indicated significant main effects for mood awareness and decision time on intergroup discrimination. As predicted, when respondents in a negative mood, high-status context were directed to pay particular attention to their mood and the effect that it might have on their judgements, the level of intergroup discrimination was significantly attenuated. This is consistent with the suggestion of Berkowitz and Troccoli (1990) that awareness of one's negative affect activates 'higher-level' cognitive processing, including consideration of the social rules defining what is desirable in the situation. In addition, when negative mood, high-status respondents were forced to engage in longer, and presumably more systematic (versus motivated) processing, the level of interdiscrimination was also attenuated. This accords with the suggestion that more substantive processing may lead to reduced ingroup favouritism as participants become more vigilant and pay greater attention to equity considerations (Forgas and Fiedler, 1996) or become more aware of their mood (Finman and Berkowitz, 1989).

As in previous experiments, there was evidence of more mood repair and, to a lesser extent, more task enjoyment among those who discriminated most – respondents who were unaware of their mood and respondents who completed their decisions quickly and without extended deliberation. Put another way, significant main effects on mood repair indicated that the mood aware and extended time conditions were associated not only with reduced discrimination but also with reduced mood repair. Taken together, these results are encouraging in demonstrating that the motivation to discriminate felt by respondents in high-status, negative-mood contexts can be easily attenuated (at least in the laboratory). Although, the results are discouraging in suggesting that when respondents constrain their 'automatic' desire to discriminate in such contexts, they derive less emotional satisfaction from their behaviour.

Experiment 4

Although these experiments provided consistent evidence for both intergroup discrimination and associated mood repair in negative mood, high-status contexts, they failed to demonstrate unequivocally that discrimination was enacted in the service of a mood repair goal. To provide further evidence that discrimination is mediated by a motive to regulate mood, we examined the effects on discrimination of mood (negative, neutral) and perceived mood lability (fixed, labile) adapting a paradigm used by Manucia et al. (1984). Following the mood induction, but prior to the intergroup allocation task we administered a placebo drug under the pretext of a medical study on the effects of a new drug, Mnemoxine. Half of the respondents were led to believe that following ingestion of the drug their mood was temporarily fixed or resistant to change, whereas half received no such instruction. We reasoned that if participants in a negative mood are motivated to discriminate in the service of a mood repair goal, then the belief that their mood cannot be altered should attenuate this discriminatory response.

As expected, results indicated a significant interaction between mood and lability. The effect of mood on discrimination was qualified by members' perceptions of mood lability. Members in a negative mood who believed that their mood was labile showed more bias or discrimination than other participants and, notably, members in a negative mood who believed that their mood was fixed showed no more bias than members in a neutral mood. That is, when group members experiencing negative affect believed that their mood would be unresponsive to the 'positive' impact of ingroup bias, they did not discriminate. Further, results indicated that those group members who engaged in the most ingroup bias also enjoyed the greatest mood improvement following the allocation task. Members in a sad mood, who believed that their mood was labile, displayed significantly greater mood repair than members in a sad mood who believed that their mood was fixed. They also completed the task more quickly and reported more positive perceptions of the task, outcomes that are consistent with the notion of targeted processing of group information. Further analyses indicated that the effect of lability on mood repair in the negative mood conditions was no longer significant when the association between discrimination and mood repair was statistically controlled. This suggests that group members who believed that their mood was labile felt better *because* they discriminated. We concluded that for high-status group members in a negative mood, discrimination is a motivated affect-control strategy used in the service of mood relief, and mood repair is a direct effect of such discrimination.

Conclusions

Clearly, the factors underlying the success of politician Pauline Hanson and associated expressions of hostility toward Aborigines and Asian immigrants are complex and multifaceted, and accounts that reduce the Hanson phenomenon to the politics of gut-feeling and emotional scapegoating are overly simplistic. Our contention is far more modest. In this chapter we have simply argued that prejudice and discriminatory behaviour – responses that are firmly grounded in motivational and cognitive factors associated with social identity and the intergroup context – can be *accentuated* by negative affective states and the desire to feel better. More broadly, our message is that mood and feeling are important contextual factors that have tended to be downplayed in cognitive accounts of stereotyping and discrimination. It should be recognized that in any intergroup context, mood will presumably influence what information is attended to and what contents will be activated from memory, and mood will also activate motivations or goal states which in turn will influence the extent and nature of further processing (see Mackie and Hamilton, 1993). In this way, the interplay between 'the mind and the guts of men' (cf., Tajfel, 1969) may provide a fuller understanding of stereotyping and prejudice.

Specifically, our experimental research based on the minimal group paradigm suggests that the combination of a negative affective state and a high-status group membership can create a strong motivational force for discriminatory behaviour even when the negative affect is incidental to the group categorization. This is in part because discrimination against outgroups is a successful strategy of affect-control. Our research suggests that, at least in laboratory contexts, members of high-status groups who are experiencing negative affect, respond quickly with discrimination, enjoy discriminating, and experience concomitant improvement in mood. In short, they selectively process information about groups in a way that provides rewarding ingroup (and self) outcomes.

Further research on the effects of negative mood on intergroup discrimination might increase our understanding of the way cognitive and affective factors interact to produce social judgements and social behaviour.

Specifically, research needs to consider the effects of incidental negative affect in more naturalistic group contexts where the group memberships are more personally relevant, the mood potentially longer lasting, and the options for affect-control more diverse, and where specific ingroup norms regarding prejudiced attitudes and discriminatory behaviour might exist. Research should also consider possible differences in outcome according to the type of negative affect that is experienced (such as anxiety, irritation, disgust; see Bodenhausen, 1993).

Other aspects of the negative mood-discrimination link might be explored. One focus that is currently receiving attention in the literature is the role of integral affect (frustration, anger, pride, anxiety) that arises directly from thinking about members of other social groups or from the intergroup encounter (e.g., Dovidio and Gaertner, 1993; Fiske and Ruscher, 1993; Stephan and Stephan, 1985; Wilder, 1993). For instance, if one's affective experience is attributed directly to the interaction with outgroup members, it may introduce additional cognitive and motivational factors that influence how information is encoded, elaborated, and used in judgements (Stroessner et al., 1992). Our view of discrimination as a motivated affect-control strategy also needs to be balanced against evidence which suggests that the expression of prejudice can serve to create negative affect and discomfort rather than relief. This may occur when persons are more prejudiced than their personal standards allow (e.g., Devine and Monteith, 1993). Finally, despite particular concerns about the motivated nature of intergroup discrimination in negative moods (see Forgas and Fiedler, 1996), the effects of positive mood on prejudice and discrimination should not be overlooked (e.g., see Abele et al., 1998).

Like Forgas and Fiedler (1996) we would argue that still far too little is known about how feelings impact on intergroup judgements and behaviour. But, an appreciation of affect as an important contextual factor promises to enrich and extend current thinking about stereotyping and intergroup relations.

9 Prejudiced Attitudes, Group Norms, and Discriminatory Behaviour

Deborah J. Terry, Michael A. Hogg, and Leda Blackwood

In the international context, Australia has traditionally regarded itself as being one of the success stories of mass immigration. Although interracial tensions have existed, a range of different policy and legislative initiatives have controlled the expression of xenophobic, racist, and ethnocentric attitudes. Thus, it was not surprising that the election of Ms Hanson to Federal Parliament in 1996 and the emergence of the One Nation Party in Australia attracted so much media attention. A number of views have been postulated for the initial success of the One Nation Party and, indeed, for the rise in popular support for relatively extreme right-wing ideologies in other countries, such as France and Germany. One view is that the emergence of political parties that espouse such ideologies constitute active minority groups that successfully change the views of the electorate (Hogg and Hornsey, 1998). An alternative view is that parties such as the One Nation Party simply tap existing resentment in the broader community. With its pronouncements against Aboriginal people, Asians, and other minority groups, it can be argued that the One Nation Party and Ms Hanson gave voice to the sentiments of many Australians, who had previously been suppressed by a racially-tolerant legislative and social climate (see also Rapley, 1998). In such an environment, pluralistic ignorance (see Prentice and Miller, 1996) is likely to prevail – that is, people infer corresponding attitudes from the absence of the expression of such attitudes, and begin to believe that unlike them, most people do not hold ethnocentric attitudes. In other words, it can be surmised that the views expressed by members of the One Nation Party, and the large amount of media attention that the party received, generated a change in people's perceptions of the wider community norms relating to multiculturalism and racial tolerance. We would argue that by legitimizing ethnocentric attitudes through a change in the broader normative climate, a critical condition for the translation of prejudiced attitudes into discriminatory actions was met.

The analysis that increases in popular support for extreme political views and racial antipathy may reflect changes in the broader normative climate, rather than changes in underlying attitudes, is based on the distinction between prejudiced attitudes, on the one hand, and discriminatory behaviour, on the other. The link between attitudes and behaviour has, traditionally, been a central area of concern for social psychologists. However, in this research literature, it has increasingly been recognized that there is no simple attitude-behaviour relationship (see Eagly and Chaiken, 1993), and that to predict behaviour accurately it is necessary to take into account other variables. In this respect, social norms have been suggested as a potentially important construct (e.g., Cialdini and Trost, 1998; Fishbein and Ajzen, 1975). However, research to date has failed to demonstrate strong support for the role of norms in attitude-behaviour relations, a pattern of results that has led some commentators to conclude that social factors are not important in this context (e.g., Ajzen, 1991). In contrast, we have argued on the basis of social identity theory (Tajfel and Turner, 1979; Turner, 1982; see also Hogg and Abrams, 1988; Reynolds and Turner, Chapter 10) and self-categorization theory (Turner, 1985; Turner et al., 1987) that a strong theoretical case can be made for the role of group norms in attitude-behaviour research, a perspective that has received some support (Terry and Hogg, 1996; Terry, Hogg, and White, in press; Wellen, Hogg, and Terry, 1998; see also Terry, Hogg, and Duck, 1999; Terry, Hogg, and White, 1999).

The aim of the present chapter is to examine – from a social identity/self-categorization perspective – the role that group norms may play in the link between intergroup attitudes and behaviour. After outlining this perspective, the results of two studies designed to test the central prediction that people are more likely to behave in accordance with their intergroup attitudes if the attitude is normative for (i.e., it is supported by) a self-relevant reference group, are presented. This research extends our previous research into the important realm of social attitudes. In common with the vast majority of attitude research, this research focused on attitudinal objects that pertain not to social targets (such as groups of people) but to a range of other outcomes, including health-related and consumer outcomes (see e.g., Terry and Hogg, 1996; Terry, Hogg, and White, 1999). Indeed, it is not since the seminal work of LaPiere (1934) and Kutner et al., (1952) that research on attitude-behaviour consistency has focused on intergroup attitudes. Moreover, in recent research on prejudice and discrimination, the role of group influence has received relatively little theoretical and empirical interest (cf., Jetten et al., 1996).

Background

Attitudes-Behaviour Relations

Social psychology has long tried to explain why, despite popular opinion to the contrary, attitudes do not appear to have a strong impact on people's behaviour (Eagly and Chaiken, 1993; Wicker, 1969). There is some support for an explanation in terms of measurement (Ajzen and Fishbein, 1977; Jaccard et al., 1977). In this respect, it has been argued that if attitudes and behaviour are assessed at the same level of specificity, then a greater correspondence can be obtained, and indeed there is support for this view. However, even when issues of measurement are addressed, the evidence still points to a lack of strong support for the view that people's actions are guided by their attitudes. Other researchers have challenged the view that there is a simple attitude-behaviour relationship at all, arguing instead that we need to employ more complex models if we are to predict people's behaviour from their attitudes. Influential in this respect has been the theory of reasoned action (Fishbein and Ajzen, 1975), and its recent extension, the theory of planned behaviour (Ajzen, 1987, 1991; see also Terry et al., 1993, for an overview of these theories).

A central component of both the theories of reasoned action and planned behaviour is the assumption that, in addition to attitudes, social norms have an important influence on behavioural outcomes. Both theories propose that behavioural intentions are the most proximal determinant of behaviour. Intentions, in turn, are proposed to be influenced not only by the favourableness of people's evaluation of performing the behaviour – that is, their attitude towards the behaviour – but also by the subjective norm, defined as people's perception of social pressure from significant others to perform the behaviour. According to Fishbein and Ajzen (1975), attitudes and norms have additive effects on behavioural intentions, the relative strength of which will vary across different behaviours and populations. In the theory of planned behaviour, Ajzen (1987, 1991) proposed that the extent to which the individual understands that performing the behaviour is under his or her control (perceived behavioural control) would emerge as an additional predictor of intentions and actual behaviour – the latter effect being evident only in relation to behaviours that cannot be performed at will.

Two decades of research on the theories of reasoned action and planned behaviour have revealed, across a range of different behavioural contexts, support for the proposed links between intentions and actual behavior (Ajzen, 1988, 1991; Sheppard et al., 1988; Terry at al., 1993) and between attitudes and intentions (Ajzen, 1988, 1991). There is also general support for the inclusion of the notion of perceived behavioural control in the theory of planned behaviour (Ajzen, 1991). Research has, however, found only weak support for the proposed role of subjective norms. For instance, Ajzen (1991) found that the norm-intention link was non-significant in more than half of the 19 extant tests of the theory of planned behaviour (for similar results, see Godin, 1993; Hausenblaus et al., 1997). In light of consistent evidence linking intentions to attitudes and perceived behavioural control, Ajzen concluded that personal factors are more influential in the prediction of intentions than social factors.

Attitudes, Norms, and Behaviour

Terry and Hogg (1996), Terry, Hogg, and Duck (1999) and Terry, Hogg, and White (1999) questioned the conclusion that personal factors are more important in the prediction of behavioural intentions than social factors, suggesting that the lack of stronger support for the proposed role of subjective norms may reflect limitations in Fishbein and Ajzen's (1975) conceptual treatment of this construct. Specifically, Fishbein and Ajzen did not conceptualize norms in line with the wider social psychological literature on social influence – that is, as the accepted or implied rules that specify how people should behave – and conceived of norms as being additive across significant others rather than being linked to specific behaviourally-relevant reference groups. Furthermore, Terry and Hogg reviewed evidence suggesting that norms may moderate the effects of attitudes on intentions (the contingent consistency hypothesis; see e.g., Grube and Morgan, 1990), and noted that evidence of a link between normative beliefs (i.e., the perceived expectations of specific individuals and groups, a set of beliefs proposed to underlie the subjective norm) and attitudes, question the assumption made in the theories of reasoned action/planned behaviour that the normative and attitudinal components of the models are cognitively independent (Liska, 1984). Rather than playing down the role of norms and group influence, we have suggested that a reconceptualization of the normative component of these theories, in line with recent social psychological models of group influence, specifically social identity theory (Tajfel and Turner, 1979; see also Hogg and Abrams, 1988; Reynolds and Turner, Chapter 10) and self-categorization theory (Turner et al., 1987), may help to preserve a central role for norms in the study of attitude-behaviour relations.

Social identity theory is a general theory of group processes and intergroup relations, which distinguishes group phenomena from interpersonal phenomena. When people define themselves in terms of a self-inclusive social category (e.g., a sex, class, team) two processes come into play: (1) categorization, which means that differences between ingroup and outgroup and similarities among ingroup members (including self) on stereotypical dimensions are perceptually accentuated; and (2) self-enhancement which, because the self-concept is defined in terms of group membership, seeks behaviourally and perceptually to favour the ingroup. Recently, Turner et al. (1987) extended social identity theory to focus more specifically on the role of the categorization process – self-categorization theory. Derived from social identity and self-categorization theories is a model of social influence in groups – called referent informational influence (Turner, 1991) – that is underpinned by the cognitive process of self-categorization. When a social identity is salient (for example a person's ethnic identity), available, and usually shared, social comparative information is used to construct a context-specific group norm – a group prototype. It describes and prescribes beliefs, attitudes, feelings, and behaviours that optimally minimize ingroup differences and maximize intergroup differences (the principle of metacontrast). As well as underpinning the construction of a contextually-salient ingroup prototype, the process of self-categorization assimilates self to the prototype (depersonalization) and transforms self: Self-perception, beliefs, feelings, and behaviours are now defined in terms of people's cognitive representation of the defining features of the group.

On the basis of the sociocognitive processes of categorization and depersonalization, a clear case can be made for the role of group norms in attitude-behaviour relations. Self-categorization as a member of a self-inclusive and contextually-salient group membership means that the self is defined in terms of the ingroup prototype. If the prototype embodies an attitudinally-congruent group norm, then assimilation of self to the prototype underpins a process by which the person's behaviour is brought in line with his or her attitude, presumably because the fact that the attitude is normative – and hence group-defining – renders the attitude accessible. According to Fazio (1986), the critical factor for attitude-behaviour congruency is the cognitive accessibility of the attitude – highly accessible attitudes are proposed to guide behaviour through the mediating process of selective perception of the situation. We would take this analysis further, and argue that ingroup members adhere behaviourally to a normatively-supported, and hence accessible, attitude because to do so serves to reduce uncertainty about the appropriateness of a given course of action (Hogg and Mullin, 1999), at the same time as validating both their status as a group member and the self-concept. In contrast, when an attitude is not normative, attitude-behaviour correspondence should be reduced not only because the attitude is relatively inaccessible, but also because it has not been legitimized by a salient group membership. From a social identity/self-categorization perspective, the lack of evidence linking norms to intentions is not surprising, given the fact that subjective norms are not tied to a behaviourally-relevant reference group. We would argue that the norms of such a group will influence behaviour, but that the extent to which the group membership is a salient basis for self-definition also needs to be taken into account. Furthermore, the social identity/self-categorization perspective is in line with the contingent consistency hypothesis, which, as noted, states that people are more likely to behave in accordance with their attitudes if the normative climate supports the attitude. We would go one step further in arguing that norms should increase the correspondence between attitudes and behaviour to the extent that the attitude is normative – that is, the norm and attitude are congruent – for a self-inclusive ingroup, and the social identity is a salient component of a person's self-definition.

Early experimental research on attitude-behaviour relations did find some support for the contingent consistency hypothesis. Frieders et al. (1971), for instance, found evidence for greater attitude-behaviour consistency when participants were informed that two other participants in the study shared their attitude. Similarly, Schofield (1975) found that people were more likely to behave in accord with their attitudes when they received information indicating that most people in the previous sessions had been willing to perform the behaviour. These results are supportive of our reconceptualization of the role of norms in attitude-behaviour relations; however, a stronger test of the social identity/self-categorization perspective would be to link the normative information more clearly to a relevant ingroup and to take into account the salience of the group membership (either in terms of perceived group identification or as a manipulated variable). The effects of norm congruency on attitude-behaviour consistency should be strongest for people for whom the group membership is a salient basis for self-conception. In two tests of the theory of planned behaviour, Terry and Hogg (1996) found that the perceived norms of the reference group of friends and peers influenced intentions to engage in regular exercise and sun-protective behaviour, but only for those who identified strongly with the group, a pattern of results that was replicated in a study of community residents' recycling behaviour (Terry, Hogg, and White, in press). In more recent experimental research (Terry, Hogg, and White, 1999; see also Terry, Hogg, and McKimmie, in press; Wellen et al., 1998) found that participants were more likely to behave in accordance with their attitude when exposed to an attitudinally-congruent ingroup norm than when exposed to an incongruent norm, particularly if the group membership was contextually salient.

In the context of intergroup attitudes and behaviours, the analysis outlined above suggests that people should be more likely to express their ethnocentric attitudes behaviourally if such attitudes are normative for a group which is a salient basis for self-perception. Prior to outlining how group norms may help to elucidate the conditions under which people's intergroup attitudes are reflected in their behaviour, previous approaches to the study of intergroup discrimination are discussed briefly.

Previous Approaches to the Study of Intergroup Discrimination

Early research on prejudice and discrimination was based on the view that prejudiced people are those whose personalities render them vulnerable to the discriminatory views that are prevalent in a society at any given time (e.g., Adorno et al.'s 1950, concept of authoritarianism; see e.g., Heaven, 1983, Chapter 6). However, explanations for hostile intergroup attitudes and behaviour that rely on the psychological characteristics of the constituents of the group, by definition, predict stable and unchanging intergroup relations (Billig, 1976; Hogg and Abrams, 1988), and hence cannot account for the apparent sudden rises and falls in prejudice that appear over time. Instead, explanations for prejudice and discrimination need to be at the same level of abstraction as the phenomena of interest, viz., at the intergroup or collective level. In this respect, prejudiced attitudes and behaviour have been linked, theoretically, to realistic conflict (in terms of the compatibility of the groups' interests and goals; Sherif, 1966; see Platow and Hunter, Chapter 12) and to fraternal (cf., egoistic) relative deprivation (Runciman, 1966), which focuses on the perceived discrepancy between the group's fortunes and the person's expectations for the group. Despite support for both perspectives (e.g., Sherif et al., 1961; Vanneman and Pettigrew, 1972), neither the presence of incompatible goals, nor feelings of fraternalistic deprivation appear to be the minimally sufficient conditions for intergroup hostility (e.g., Brown and Abrams, 1986).

In recent years, robust support has been found for a social identity theory account of intergroup discrimination. According to social identity theory, ingroup-favouring attitudes and behaviour are motivated by the desire to achieve or maintain a positive social identity. In other words, the accentuation effects that result from the categorization process are biased in favour of the ingroup because the ingroup is self-inclusive, and hence contributes to a person's feelings of self-worth. Using the minimal group paradigm, it has been demonstrated that even when the basis for group membership is random (Billig and Tajfel, 1973; also Tajfel et al., 1971), participants favour the ingroup in the allocation of resources. In other words, categorizing people into two discrete groups, one of which is self-inclusive, appears to constitute the sufficient conditions for intergroup rivalry, a process that accounts for the presence of intergroup hostility in the absence of goal incompatibility or perceptions of relative deprivation.

Although social identity theory is widely regarded as having successfully articulated the minimally sufficient conditions for discrimination, group norms are surprisingly omitted from this analysis (see Jetten et al., 1996). This probably stems from the fact that early social identity research employed the minimal group paradigm, which was designed explicitly to study intergroup discrimination in the context of random or relatively trivial categories that were devoid of the usual characteristics of groups, including norms and face-to-face interaction (Jetten et al., 1996). However, in an early interpretation of the minimal group effect, a generic social norm for competitiveness was invoked to explain the evidence for ingroup favouritism (see also Hartstone and Augoustinos, 1995), whereas the countervailing norm in Western cultures for fairness was used to account for the fact that although reliable, the evidence for discrimination in the paradigm is typically not strong (Billig and Tajfel, 1973). This explanation is not widely accepted, given that there is no theoretical basis from which to predict the particular generic norms that will be salient in a particular context. Moreover, a generic normative explanation cannot account for the reliable effects that socio-structural variables (e.g., group status) have on responses to the minimal group task (Brown, 1995).

Although the generic normative explanation is not widely accepted, the role that specific group norms play in accounting for discrimination has received little attention. Some early research did, however, point to the importance of taking into account the socio-normative context when explaining the occurrence of prejudiced attitudes and behaviour. Siegel and Siegel (1957), for instance, found evidence of situational instability in the construct of authoritarianism – women assigned to dormitories characterized by more liberal norms showed a marked decline in their authoritarianism scores over a period of a year, a pattern of results not observed for those assigned to traditional sorority housing. In a similar vein, Minard (1952) observed that while miners adhered to the norms of racial antipathy when out of the mine, more harmonious norms prevailed in the mine (see also Pettigrew, 1958). In a minimal group study, Diehl (1988) manipulated information about the preferred strategies of outgroup members, but found evidence of intergroup bias irrespective of whether the outgroup favoured discrimination or fairness.

On the basis of social identity/self-categorization theory, specific (not generic) ingroup norms should have stronger and more direct effects on discriminatory responses than outgroup norms. According to the process of referent informational influence, when a particular social identity is a salient basis for self-definition, the self is assimilated to the context-specific group norm (group prototype). Thus, ingroup norms – because of their self-relevance – should have stronger effects on intergroup discrimination than outgroup norms. In support of this contention, Jetten et al. (1996) found that in both experimental and naturally-occurring groups, participants' allocation strategies were influenced by the nature of the ingroup norm (for fairness or discrimination). This research provides evidence for the view that specific ingroup norms do influence discrimination. However, the role that attitudes play in this regard, and, indeed, the interplay among prejudiced attitudes, norms, and discriminatory behaviour has been a neglected area of research.

Prejudiced Attitudes, Group Norms, and Intergroup Discrimination

According to the proposed analysis of the role of group norms in relation to intergroup discrimination, people should be more likely to behaviourally express ethnocentric and xenophobic attitudes if such attitudes are normative for a self-inclusive and contextually salient or important ingroup. To do so serves both to reduce people's uncertainty in terms of the appropriateness of the attitude and to engender a sense of meaning about the social world. Behaving in accordance with a normative attitude also validates the self-concept and the person's status as a group member. Thus, the cognitive activation of a group prototype not only makes an attitude that concurs with the group prototype accessible, the motivational processes that underpin group behaviour (self-enhancement, Tajfel and Turner, 1979; and uncertainty reduction, Hogg and Mullin, 1999) provide the prescriptive impetus to translate an attitude into a behavioural response.

Although this approach has received some support in relation to non-social attitudes (e.g., Terry and Hogg, 1996; see Terry, Hogg, and White, 1999), its utility in the more socially-relevant domain of intergroup attitudes has yet to be examined. Moreover, beyond an examination of the proposed moderating roles of group salience and strength of group identification, other factors that may influence the strength of the effects of ingroup norms have received little research attention. In the context of intergroup attitudes, the extent to which such attitudes are expressed in discriminatory behaviour should be increased for those people motivated to attain a positive social identity. Thus, people's beliefs about the nature of relations between their own group and relevant outgroups should moderate the impact of group norms on attitude-behaviour consistency, a perspective that specifically articulates the socio-cognitive focus of self-categorization theory with the broader macro-social emphasis. In addition to predictions that follow directly from the socio-cognitive mechanisms that underpin group-mediated influence, there are others that can be derived from the macro-social emphasis of social identity theory (Tajfel and Turner, 1979; also Ellemers, 1993; Hogg and Abrams, 1988). For dominant group members, it is proposed that an insecure social identity will accentuate the likelihood that people will behaviourally express their attitudes towards minority groups. As

Tajfel (1974) pointed out, a completely secure identity for consensually-accepted dominant groups is extremely rare – a dominant social position must not only be attained, it must be preserved. Although dominant groups are constantly striving to maintain their superior position, stronger status protection responses should be elicited when group members perceive that this position is insecure. Under conditions of instability where the status hierarchy might change or be weakened, the dominant group is likely to be threatened. Thus, for members of a dominant group, attitude-behaviour consistency should be influenced by the attitudinal congruence of the ingroup norms, particularly when they perceive that their high-status position is under threat. It is under these conditions that status protection motivations should strengthen the correspondence between a normatively-supported intergroup attitude and corresponding behavioural responses.

Empirical Research

A Laboratory Study of Intergroup Attitudes, Ingroup Norms, and Discriminatory Behaviour

To test the utility of the proposed social identity/self-categorization reconceptualization of the role of norms in intergroup attitude-behaviour relations, two studies were conducted. The first study was designed to examine the impact of ingroup norms on the behavioural tendencies and attitudes of participants with pro-multiculturalism attitudes (Blackwood et al., 1999). Normative information attributed to Australian students that was either congruent or incongruent with participants' attitudes towards multiculturalism was presented under conditions of either high or low salience of national identity. In addition, the moderating effect of the perception of economic group-status threat was examined. Based on social identity/self-categorization theory, it was proposed that the effects of the group norm would be more marked for the participants in the high-contextual-salience condition than for those in the low-contextual-salience condition. It was further proposed that the effect of group norms on participants in the high-salience condition would be most marked for those who perceived high levels of economic group-status threat.

Participants in the study were Anglo-Australian first-year psychology students from the University of Queensland who participated in the study for partial course credit. A total of 197 students (126 women, 42 men) participated in the study; however, only data from those participants (N = 168) who indicated that they were pro-multiculturalism at Time 1 and who participated in the study at both Times 1 and 2, were included in the analysis. In the pre-manipulation session (Time 1), participants completed the first questionnaire, which in addition to requesting demographic details, comprised 12 items that were designed to tap perceptions of the extent to which the national economic climate was under threat (e.g., 'Relative to the costs of living, I feel that Australian wages have declined over the last ten years'). A single-item measure of overall support for multiculturalism (on a 9-point scale) was also obtained at Time 1. This measure was used to compute the amount of attitude change across the course of the study.

One week after the pre-manipulation questionnaire was completed, participants returned for the experimental session. Participants in the high-contextual-salience condition watched a video that comprised advertisements that had been designed to elicit nationalist sentiment (e.g., advertisements developed by the Australian Tourism Commission). For participants in the low-salience condition, the video comprised a compilation of advertisements selected to match the pace and mood of the high-salience video but not to elicit national identity. Following the salience manipulation, participants were provided with either attitudinally-congruent (80 per cent of Australian students supported multiculturalism) normative information or attitudinally-incongruent (80 per cent of Australian students opposed multiculturalism) normative information. The normative information was presented in two forms: five statements from a representative sample of Australian students and summary data of students' attitudes to multiculturalism, ostensibly obtained from a recent survey of Australian students.

The participants were then introduced to the dependent variables measuring behavioural support for multiculturalism. Three items were used to assess willingness (behavioural intentions) to support multiculturalism. Embedded with similar items on environmental protection and homosexuality, participants were asked to indicate their willingness to engage in three behaviours opposing multiculturalism (responses on these items were recoded to reflect support for multiculturalism). Based on research that has suggested that prejudice may be manifested in the withholding of behavioural support (e.g., Devine, 1989), an additional item was designed to tap covert expressions of racism. It required participants to indicate the order in which they would support seven motions (including one supporting an anti-racism campaign) being placed on the agenda for the National Union of Students' Conference. The behavioural support item was scored in terms of whether the motion was placed in the top three for placement on the agenda (high support) or in the lower four (low support). To assess changes in attitude towards multiculturalism from Time 1 to Time 2, participants were again asked to respond to the item used at Time 1 to assess overall support for multiculturalism.

Initial analyses indicated that the experimental manipulations of contextual salience and norm congruency were successful. The focal analyses revealed no main or interactive effects of norm congruency or contextual group salience on behavioural support. On willingness to engage in attitudinally-congruent behaviour, there was a significant Norm x Salience interaction. This interaction is presented graphically in Figure 9.1. For participants in the high-salience condition, there was a significant effect for norm congruency. In line with predictions, participants presented with attitudinally-congruent normative information (pro-multiculturalism) displayed a greater willingness to engage in behaviour consistent with their attitudes than those presented with attitude-

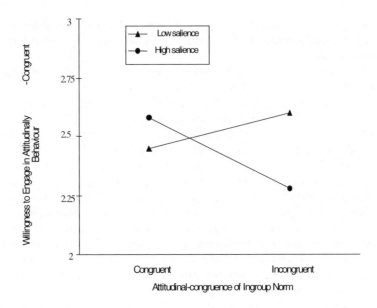

Figure 9.1 Interaction between attitudinal congruence of ingroup norm and contextual group salience on willingness to engage in attitude-congruent behaviour

incongruent norms. The willingness of participants in the low-salience condition to behave in accordance with their attitudes was unaffected by the presentation of normative information. On the attitude-change measure, there was a significant main effect of norm-congruency with participants exposed to the attitudinally-incongruent normative information (anti-multiculturalism) exhibiting a greater shift towards opposition to multiculturalism compared to those exposed to the attitudinally-congruent normative information. Although the latter effect was not dependent on the contextual salience of national identity, there was some evidence that it was most marked for those who identified strongly, in an enduring sense, as an Australian (a measure of this variable was also obtained at Time 1).

On the measure of willingness to engage in attitudinally-congruent (pro-multiculturalism) behaviour, there was a significant main effect for threat with less willingness to engage in attitudinally-congruent behaviour among those who perceived high economic group-status threat. This main effect was qualified by a significant Threat x Norm x Salience interaction. As shown in Figure 9.2, when participants perceived high levels of economic group-status threat and contextual group salience was high, there was a significant effect of group norms: willingness to engage in attitude-consistent behaviour was weaker for those exposed to an incongruent group norm than for those exposed to a congruent group norm. When high levels of group-status threat were perceived

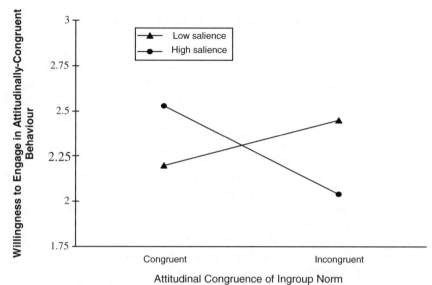

Figure 9.2 Interaction between attitudinal congruence of ingroup norm and contextual group salience on willingness to perform attitude-congruent behaviour for participants perceiving high economic group-status threat.

but contextual salience was low, the effect of congruency of norms was not significant. A similar pattern of results was obtained on the measure of (positive) change in attitude to multiculturalism from Time 1 to Time 2. Specifically, there was a significant shift in attitudes in the direction of the attitudinally-incongruent norm – that is, attitudes towards multiculturalism became less positive – among the participants who perceived high levels of economic group-status threat and for whom the national identity was contextually salient, a pattern of results not observed for those in the low-salience condition who perceived high group-status threat.

On the measure of behavioural support (support for an anti-racism campaign), there was some evidence that the effects of the attitude-incongruent (anti-multiculturalism) normative information was influenced by perceptions of economic group-status threat. High-threat participants were considerably more likely to oppose an anti-racism campaign when presented with the attitude-incongruent norm than were low-threat participants.

A Field Study of the Attitudes of White Australians towards Asian Australians

In order to examine the ecological validity of the results of the laboratory study, a survey of a randomly selected sample of residents in Queensland, Australia was conducted (Terry and Johnson, 1999). This survey examined the interplay

152   *Understanding Prejudice, Racism, and Social Conflict*

between intergroup attitudes and relevant ingroup norms in the prediction of discriminatory behavioural tendencies towards Asian Australians and stereotypic judgements of Asian Australians. It was expected that prejudiced attitudes would be most likely to be expressed in discriminatory behavioural tendencies and judgements when it was perceived that there was normative support for these views from a person's immediate reference group of friends and family.

Potential respondents were randomly selected from three electorates in Queensland, Australia – these electorates were chosen because they encompass the largest urban centre in Queensland, a rural area, and a large regional centre. Of the 1,060 questionnaires sent out, 31 per cent were returned. Preliminary analyses showed that the sample was representative of the population from which it was drawn. To assess attitudes towards Asian Australians, participants rated this group on three semantic differentials (e.g., 1, *very unfavourable*, to 9, *very favourable*). Ingroup norms were assessed with two items that required respondents to indicate whether their friends and family supported a right-wing political party that had recently emerged in the Australian political arena at least partly on an anti-Asian immigration platform. The outcome variables comprised two measures of behavioural tendencies towards Asian Australians: (a) a 5-item measure of willingness to engage in anti-Asian behaviours (e.g., signing a petition against Asian immigration); and (b) a 2-item measure of support for the new right-wing political party (One Nation Party) – for example, voting for the party in the upcoming Federal election. The third outcome measure assessed the extent to which participants perceived Asian Australians in stereotypic terms. Specifically, respondents were required to make judgements concerning the accuracy with which a number of positive traits that are stereotypically associated with Asian Australians (e.g., self-disciplined, hard-working, respectful) described both Asian Australians and White Australians. Discrepancy scores were then computed for each trait – the ratings given to Asian Australians were subtracted from those given to White Australians. A measure of negative stereotypic beliefs about Asian Australians was computed as the sum of the discrepancy scores across each of the traits (high scores were indicative of less positive stereotyping of Asian Australians).

After control of the effects of gender, age, education, and right-wing authoritarianism (Adorno et al., 1950), there was consistent evidence that discriminatory tendencies were most marked for those people who perceived an anti-Asian ingroup norm (in terms of the amount of support for the right-wing conservative party). Moreover, in line with predictions, the effects of people's attitudes were moderated by the attitudinal congruence of the perceived reference group norm. As shown in Figure 9.3, the strength of the relationship between anti-Asian attitudes and willingness to engage in anti-Asian behaviours was most marked for those whose perceived reference group norm was in accord with their attitudes (depending on the direction of initial attitude, the perceived reference group norm was recoded so that a high score indicated support for the

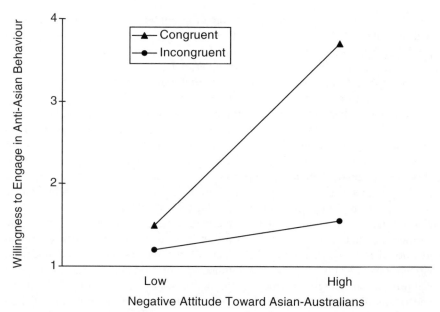

Figure 9.3 Interaction between negative attitude towards Asian-Australians and attitudinal congruence of ingroup norm on willingness to engage in anti-Asian behaviour.

person's attitudinal position). A similar result was obtained on the measures of support for the One Nation Party and stereotypic perceptions of Asian Australians.

Conclusions

Taken together, the research reviewed in the present chapter provides support for the assertion that people are more likely to behave in accordance with their intergroup attitudes if the attitude is normative for (i.e., it is supported by) a self-relevant reference group. In the laboratory study of pro-multiculturalism participants, it was found that ingroup norms for multiculturalism from a self-inclusive ingroup influenced willingness to engage in pro-multiculturalism behaviours but only when the relevant identity was contextually salient. This pattern of results was essentially mirrored on the measure of attitude change across the course of the study. The results of the laboratory study indicate that the nature of the normative environment is an important factor in determining whether people behaviourally express their intergroup attitudes, a pattern of results that was replicated in the field study of a randomly selected sample of White Australians. As noted, the role of group influence has received relatively little theoretical and empirical interest (cf., Jetten et al., 1996) in recent research on prejudice and discrimination, yet phenomena such as the relatively sudden increases in the behavioural expression of prejudice are difficult to explain without acknowledgment of the role that the broader normative climate plays in providing support for people to bring their intergroup behavioural intentions and responses in line with their intergroup attitudes.

As expected, there was evidence in the laboratory study that the effects of group norms were most marked for those who perceived high levels of group-status threat. When ethnocentric attitudes are normative of a self-inclusive and important ingroup, the extent to which such attitudes are expressed in discriminatory behaviour should be increased for those people motivated to attain a positive social identity. Thus, stronger status-protection responses should be elicited when group members perceive that this position is insecure, a prediction that was supported by the results of the laboratory study. Future research on the interplay among prejudiced attitudes, group norms, and discriminatory behaviour should seek to, more explicitly, address the predictions that can be derived from the macro-social emphasis of social identity theory by examining the effects of the factors that should underpin perceptions of status threat among dominant-group members – these include the stability of the intergroup structure, the permeability of intergroup boundaries, and perceptions of the legitimacy of their status position (Turner and Tajfel, 1979; see also Ellemers, 1993; Hogg and Abrams, 1988). When the dominant group perceives its superior position to be stable, group members should tolerate, or even promulgate, perceptions of permeability, given that such beliefs minimize the risk of collective action by low-status groups. However, under conditions of instability where the status hierarchy might change or be weakened, the dominant group is likely to be threatened, particularly if the relative status position is considered to be legitimately attained or the intergroup boundaries are perceived to be open (Hogg and Abrams, 1988; Zuckerman, 1979). Thus, for members of a dominant group, attitude-behaviour consistency should be influenced by the attitudinal congruence of the ingroup norms, particularly when they perceive that the intergroup boundaries are open or they perceive their dominant position to be legitimate, and when the social structure is perceived to be unstable.

In addition to being dependent on intergroup beliefs, intragroup factors should influence the likelihood that group norms will moderate the relationship between intergroup attitudes and behaviour. The strength of the attitude-behaviour relationship is likely to be most influenced by the attitudinal congruence of the group norm when the person's position in the group is insecure. In the course of group socialization, full acceptance as a group or organizational member has been proposed to involve judgements of prototypicality – that is, judgements concerning the extent to which the person matches the consensually agreed upon set of characteristics that exemplifies membership in the group (Moreland et al., 1993). In their effort to validate their sense of self and their status as a group member, the normative climate is likely to be a particularly powerful determinant of the attitude-behaviour consistency of new recruits to a group. So, for example, in the context of newly-acquired group membership (e.g., in a work context), the group norm in relation to a relevant outgroup is likely to strongly influence whether or not the new recruit behaves in accord with his or her attitude towards the outgroup.

In sum, the empirical results reported in the present chapter support the analysis that recent increases in the expression of xenophobic and ethnocentric attitudes and support for extreme political views that have been observed in a number of countries, including Australia, may reflect changes in the broader normative climate relating to multiculturalism and racial tolerance. In Pauline Hanson's maiden speech to the Australian parliament, she made the following statement:

> Arthur Calwell was a great Australian and Labor leader, and it is a pity there are not more men of his stature sitting in the opposition benches today. Arthur Calwell said: 'Japan, India, Burma, Ceylon and every new African nation are fiercely anti white and anti one another'. Do we want or need any of these people here? I am one red-blooded Australian who says no and who speaks for 90% of Australians. I have no hesitation in echoing the words of Arthur Calwell. (cited in Rapley, 1998)

This statement clearly supports the supposition that the views expressed by members of the One Nation Party, no doubt assisted by the large amount of media attention that the party received in the Australian Press, served to generate a change in people's perceptions of the wider community norms relating to multiculturalism and racial tolerance. We would argue that by doing so, ethnocentric attitudes were legitimized, which meant that a critical condition for the translation of prejudiced attitudes into discriminatory actions was met. We also acknowledge the fact that political parties that espouse right-wing ideologies could operate as active minority groups, and hence serve to actually change the views of the electorate (Hogg and Hornsey, 1998). Nevertheless, the theoretical analysis outlined in the present chapter, combined with the supportive experimental and field data, points to the importance of taking into account the broader normative climate in any account of the conditions under which people will behaviourally express such intergroup attitude.

Part IV:

Prejudice and Group Life

10 Prejudice as a Group Process: The Role of Social Identity

Katherine J. Reynolds and John C. Turner

It makes sense to understand prejudice as a group process. Firstly, prejudiced attitudes and actions are shared amongst large social groupings. Secondly, prejudice is directed towards others because of their membership of a particular group (e.g., race, ethnicity, nationality, gender, age, political affiliation). Thirdly, to the extent that members of a particular group are prejudiced towards members of another group, the relationship between these groups could be an important determining factor. In fact, it could be argued that prejudice is of interest to social scientists, politicians, lawmakers, and members of the community precisely because such attitudes and behaviour are shared by groups of people and stem from people's group memberships. Prejudice would not be a significant problem worthy of public interest and extensive research if it were confined to a few isolated individuals.

These points may seem fairly non-controversial but when it comes to articulating the *psychological processes* that underlie prejudice the controversy within social psychology becomes apparent (F. Allport, 1962; Asch, 1952; Turner, 1987; Turner and Oakes, 1986). Group factors related to prejudice are often neglected and researchers turn to alternative explanations, such as (a) personality or individual difference factors which are believed to predispose certain individuals to display prejudice (i.e., authoritarianism, social dominance orientation, dogmatism; see Heaven, Chapter 6 for more details), and (b) purely psychological causes that can automatically and inevitably lead to the expression of prejudice via individual cognitive or motivational processes (i.e., information processing capabilities related to attentional resources and mood; see Locke and Johnston, Chapter 7 and Baird and Duck, Chapter 8, respectively; see also Tajfel, 1969; Turner, 1999b, Turner and Giles, 1981). Here, the character of the individual person is used to explain prejudice independent of social contextual factors and *current* social forces; a problem Turner has identified as the 'prejudice' model of social antagonism (i.e., prejudice, discrimination, and social conflict; Turner, 1996; Turner et al., 1998).

There is, however, an alternative view based on social identity theory (Tajfel and Turner, 1979) and self-categorization theory (Turner et al., 1987) in which the group-based realities of prejudice, discrimination, and social conflict are recognized explicitly. These theories argue that group memberships and the societal structure that frames group relations are central to the analysis of individuals' cognition and behaviour. Understanding this relationship between society and people's psychology is referred to as interactionism (Turner and Oakes, 1986, 1997).

Based on this approach, prejudice, along with many other social psychological phenomena, are believed to be an outcome of a complex system of social relations that cannot be reduced to an analysis of individuals as isolated, asocial psychological units. Attempts to dislocate individuals' psychological functioning from social context and social forces are viewed as individualistic (i.e., they ignore group-based processes and focus on individuals *as individuals*) and reductionistic (i.e., they seeks to explain a complex system that possesses its own unique features in terms of its constituent parts).

In this chapter, social identity and self-categorization theories will be described in detail. Social identity theory (Tajfel, 1978c, Tajfel and Turner, 1979) provides an analysis of ingroup favouritism or ethnocentrism (i.e., the view that 'we are better than them'), intergroup discrimination, and social change. Self-categorization theory (Turner, 1999b; Turner et al., 1987; Turner et al., 1994) focuses on the more fundamental psychological basis for group behaviour and the distinctive outcomes that emerge from this process. Through description of self-categorization theory the aim is to address questions such as: What is the relationship between the individual and the group? How are people able to become groups and behave collectively? When do people think, feel, and act as group members? Why does one group (e.g., race) become relevant in a particular situation and not another (e.g., nationality)? What are the psychological implications of group or collective psychology? Answers to all these questions are necessary in order to appreciate fully the group-based aspects of social antagonism.

We then move on to outline the findings from two recent studies that highlight the role of group processes in explanations of prejudice. The research points to the inadequacy and limitations of the individual differences approach to prejudice (Altemeyer, 1998; Heaven, Chapter 6). We conclude that *social antagonism is a psychologically rational and valid product of the way members of certain groups perceive the social structure of intergroup relations – it arises from and reflects their subjectively-apprehended understanding of the relationships between groups in society* (Turner, 1999a; Turner et al., 1998). In the remainder of this chapter we review relevant literature in order to clarify and communicate what we mean by this statement.

Social Identity Theory

The Minimal Group Findings

In the early 1970s, a group of researchers under the direction of Henri Tajfel published a programme of research that was to have a far-reaching impact on our understanding of prejudice. At this time, in addition to various personality explanations for prejudice, the most popular intergroup explanation was realistic group conflict theory (Campbell, 1965; Sherif, 1967; see Platow and Hunter, Chapter 12). Put simply, this theory argues that when group interests are incompatible, such as when more than one group desires a limited and valued resource (e.g., an area of land – Kosovo, East Timor, or Jerusalem), then intergroup competition can lead to negative outcomes – social conflict, group hostilities, and prejudiced attitudes and behaviour. On the other hand, compatible goals, such as when success requires the input from members of different groups, can foster positive outcomes such as tolerance and fairness.

Against this background, Tajfel and colleagues set out systematically to identify the *minimal* conditions necessary for intergroup discrimination to occur. In order to establish a 'no discrimination' baseline they started by conducting a study where the seemingly most meaningless division between participants was introduced. The study was designed to minimize variables typically associated with social discrimination, such as conflicts of interest, a history of hostility, or personal interaction. Once the baseline was established other variables were to be integrated and their relative impact on the development of discrimination investigated.

In Tajfel et al.'s (1971) two studies, schoolboys were classified into distinct groups supposedly on the basis of fairly trivial criteria. In one study, they had to estimate the number of dots on a screen. In a separate study, participants had to indicate their aesthetic preference for paintings by Klee and Kandinsky. Participants were then placed in their own cubicle or room and were told that based on their responses to the initial task they were either an overestimator or underestimator or that they were a member of the Klee group or Kandinsky group.

In all cases, participants thought they had been allocated to groups based on their judgements or the choices on the first task, but allocation to groups actually was made on a random basis. The groups in these studies were 'minimal' in the sense that there was no social interaction between the groups, no shared goals, and the boys did not know who was in their group (hence the term 'minimal group paradigm' is used to refer to studies using this methodology).

Participants then had to complete a second task that involved the allocation of points that symbolized money to two other individuals (never themselves) who were identified by their group membership and code number (e.g., member no. 12 of Klee group or member no. 27 of Kandinsky group). A distribution matrix that comprised 13 pairs of numbers (see Table 10.1) was used to reveal participants' preferred distribution strategy. Participants completed a number of matrices and had to make choices between two individuals who were members of (a) the same group as the participant (i.e., both ingroup members); (b) the other group (i.e., both outgroup members); or (c) different groups (i.e., one ingroup, the other outgroup). Participants were also informed that they would receive the amount of money that the other participants anonymously allocated to them.

Table 10.1 An example of distribution matrix used in the minimal group paradigm.

Distribution matrix

member no. 12 of Klee group   11 12 13 14 15 16 17 18 19 20 21 22 23
member no. 27 of Kandinsky group   5 7 9 11 13 15 17 19 21 23 25 27 29

Please fill in below details of the column you have just chosen:

                    Amount
Reward for member no. 12 of Klee group   ____
Reward for member no. 27 of Kandinsky group   ____

Types of distribution strategies

Fairness (F):	Maximum joint profit (MJP)	Maximum ingroup profit (MIP)	Maximum difference (MD)	Favouritism (FAV)
Equal distribution of points (e.g., 17 to ingroup and 17 to outgroup)	Maximum number of points (e.g., 23 to ingroup and 29 to outgroup)	Maximum number of points to ingroup (e.g., 23 to ingroup and 29 to outgroup)	Maximize difference between groups in the ingroup's favour (e.g., 11 to ingroup and 5 to outgroup)	Composite of MIP and MD strategies

Note   There were other matrices used to assess the pattern of point distribution (for details see Tajfel et al., 1971; Tajfel 1978a).

In terms of the matrix in Table 10.1, let's assume that the Klee group is your ingroup; if you decided to allocate 17 points to the ingroup and 17 points to the outgroup this would reflect a fair strategy (F). An allocation at the right extreme would give 23 points to the ingroup and 29 points to the outgroup; this would represent maximum profit to the ingroup (MIP) and maximum joint profit (MJP). If you selected the other extreme and allocated 11 points to the ingroup and 5 points to the outgroup this would represent the maximum difference in favour of the ingroup (MD). In other words, the ingroup would not receive the most money possible but would receive more relative to the outgroup.

Tajfel et al.'s (1971) findings indicated that fairness was a widely used distribution strategy but that participants also tried to maximize ingroup profit and ingroup gain relative to outgroup gain (i.e., MIP and MD). Within this strategy, relative gain was more important than absolute gain. The matrices were also completed in relation to two individuals from the same group (i.e., both Klee group members or both Kandinsky group members). In these cases, ingroup and outgroup allocations were made on separate matrices so it was possible to give the outgroup more without giving the ingroup less and vice versa. The findings indicated that allocations to ingroup members were nearer to MJP than those for outgroup members.

It was concluded that people favoured their own group in their allocations (i.e, giving more money to their group) and discriminated against the group to which they did not belong. Therefore, there was strong evidence that mere awareness of being in one group as opposed to another could produce intergroup discrimination (Tajfel, 1978a). A finding that has gained considerable support since these studies were reported (for reviews see Brewer, 1979; Diehl, 1990; Turner, 1981).

Evidence that categorization in terms of apparently meaningless, empty, trivial, minimal groups could lead to intergroup competition and ingroup-favouring responses was a surprise. Remember these studies were meant to establish a 'no discrimination' baseline and then variables typically related to discrimination were going to be investigated in turn. However, the minimal group studies themselves revealed intergroup discrimination. The ingroup was treated consistently better than the outgroup.

An obvious implication of the minimal group studies was that they provided evidence that incompatible group interests were not always necessary or sufficient for intergroup discrimination. Furthermore, while much of the research up until this time had focused on intergroup competition and treatment of outgroup members, there was evidence in the minimal group studies that *ingroup memberships* may be a neglected feature of the analysis of intergroup relations (Tajfel and Turner, 1979). In order to explain these findings a new theory of intergroup discrimination was required.

The Search for an Explanation: Social Identity and its Implications.

In trying to explain the minimal group findings and how ingroup–outgroup memberships alone could produce ingroup favouritism, Tajfel and Turner developed social identity theory (Tajfel, 1972; Tajfel and Turner, 1979). A central issue in the social identity theory analysis of the minimal group studies relates to the question of why participants behaved in terms of the experimenters' categories. Why did participants use the meaningless division into underestimators or overestimators, or Klee and Kandinsky groups as a guide for action in their allocation of points? Tajfel argued that 'Distinction from the "other" category provided ipso facto an identity for their own group, and thus some kind of meaning to an otherwise empty situation' (1972: 39–40).

In other words, in minimal group studies participants identify with the minimal categories; they define or categorize themselves and others in terms of category information provided by the experimenter. Supposedly meaningless and trivial categories are infused with meaning by the participant through defining oneself and others in group-based terms. The group-based aspect of self-definition is termed social identity and is the 'part of the individual's self-concept which derives from his [or her] knowledge of his [or her] membership of a social group (or groups) together with the value and emotional significance attached to that membership' (Tajfel, 1978a: 63).

There has been an extended debate in social psychology about whether groups are real entities that are meaningful psychologically (see Turner, 1987, for a review). The concept of social identity suggests that the group has a psychological reality that cannot be reduced to, or explained by, individual processes. In other words, in many instances, 'we do not act as isolated individuals but as social beings who derive an important part of our identity from the human groups and social categories we belong to' (Tajfel et al., 1984: 5).

In order to represent and locate social identity, Tajfel proposed a continuum of human behaviour framed at one end by interpersonal behaviour – characterized as being based on personal relations and individual characteristics, and at the other, intergroup behaviour that was shaped by membership in social groups. In line with the work of researchers such as Sherif and Asch, the intergroup end of the continuum explicitly recognized that groups are real entities that are psychologically meaningful. Furthermore, both interpersonal and intergroup extremes were given equal status on the continuum but through placement at opposite ends they were also recognized as distinct.

In general, movement to the intergroup extreme was believed to have the following implications:

> Members of the ingroup would treat members of the outgroup as undifferentiated items in a unified social category. This will be reflected simultaneously in a clear awareness of the ingroup–outgroup dichotomy, in the attribution of members of the outgroup of certain traits assumed to be common to the group as a whole, in value judgments pertaining to those traits, in the emotional significance associated with these evaluations, and in other forms of behaviour associated with the ingroup-outgroup categorization. (Tajfel, 1978c: 45)

Turner (1982, 1984) developed aspects of this idea further by proposing 'a tentative and provisional theory of group behaviour in terms of an identity mechanism' (1984: 526). He differentiated between an individual's conceptualization of themselves – his or her self-description or self-categorization – in terms of personal identity and social identity. While personal identity relates to our individual qualities that make us unique and different from others (relevant to the particular judgement being made), social identity comprises self-descriptions that emerge from social group memberships (e.g., sex, race, nationality, political affiliation, occupation, sports-teams). The identity mechanism provided an important link between the interpersonal and intergroup ends of the continuum and elaborated a psychological basis for understanding individual and group behaviour. The interpersonal-intergroup continuum is transformed through the 'identity mechanism' into a cognitive, social psychological theory of the group.

In addition, Turner's (1984) 'self-stereotyping hypothesis' placed self-identification or self-categorization at the core of the theory. He argued that 'it is the cognitive redefinition of the self – from unique attributes and individual differences to shared social category memberships and associated stereotypes – that mediates group behaviour' (1984: 528). The 'cognitive redefinition' is the process which explains how individuals can psychologically be group members and 'reinstates the group as a psychological reality and not merely a convenient label for describing the outcome of interpersonal processes' (1984: 535).

In these terms, it can be seen that the group is not an external classification provided by outside observers, as is the case, for example, with sociological groups, but has internal psychological meaning for members. As Turner stated:

> We are concerned here with group membership as a psychological and not a formal-institutional state, with the subjective sense of togetherness, we-ness, or belongingness which indicates the formation of a psychological group. (1982: 16)

Through understanding this process of psychological group membership it is possible to explain how externally defined groups may become psychological groups.

Another important aspect of social identity theory relates to positive social identity and positive distinctiveness. Based on the general assumptions (a) that individuals strive for a positive self-concept; (b) that social groups and therefore, individuals' social identity can be evaluated in positive or negative terms; and (c) that group evaluations are based on comparisons with other relevant groups, it is argued that individuals aim to achieve or maintain a positive social identity.

A basic principle of social identity theory, then, is that to the extent that a particular group membership becomes *significant* for self-definition, perceivers will seek a positive social identity. Therefore, establishment of *positive distinctiveness* of an ingroup from a relevant outgroup is seen as one important basis for discriminatory action and can explain the minimal group studies. Participants are able to make sense of the minimal group situation by positively differentiating the ingroup from the outgroup on the only available dimensions of comparison – the resources represented by the matrices.

Put slightly differently, participants assume that they themselves are characterized in positive rather than negative ways (e.g., Eiser and van der Pligt, 1982) and they have knowledge that certain characteristics or resources are good rather than bad (i.e., it is better to have more than less money). Allocation of more money to one's own group relative to the outgroup is an indication that 'we are better than them' and enables participants to achieve or maintain a positive self-evaluation (Reynolds et al., 2000).

There have been a number of other interpretations offered for the minimal group findings. For example, that participants thought the experimenter expected discrimination and so they conformed to this expectation (i.e., there was a demand characteristic inherent in the experimental design; Gerard and Hoyt, 1974) and that there was a 'generic social norm' that suggested discrimination was the socially desirable strategy (Tajfel, 1970; Tajfel et al., 1971). This is not the place to explore each of these in detail because they are discussed extensively elsewhere (Tajfel, 1978a; Tajfel and Turner, 1979; Turner, 1978, 1983; Turner and Bourhis, 1996) and all have been found to be limited and inadequate accounts of the findings.

While much of the social identity analysis of the minimal group findings has been accepted there are also common misunderstandings (e.g., Altemeyer, 1998;

Operario and Fiske, 1998; see Turner, 1999a; Turner and Reynolds, in press, for more detail). Most notably, it is assumed that social identity theory argues that whenever there is an ingroup–outgroup dichotomy there will be evidence of ingroup favouritism and discrimination. Such a position is used to justify a pessimistic view of human nature and the inevitability of social antagonism (Turner, 1999a; Turner and Reynolds, in press). However, from the outset this position was rejected and it was argued that ingroup favouritism is not an automatic, indiscriminate outcome of ingroup and outgroup categorizations but is functionally dependent on (a) whether participants define themselves in terms of the ingroup, (b) whether the outgroup is a relevant comparison group in the context of interest, and (c) the extent to which the comparative dimension (i.e., points symbolizing money) is important and relevant to the intergroup comparison (Tajfel and Turner, 1979). These points become clearer within social identity theory's broader analysis of social conflict.

Positive Distinctiveness, Social Conflict, and Social Change

Social identity theory and its analysis of positive distinctiveness was used to explain intergroup conflict and social change. In order for groups to positively differentiate themselves from each other they must engage in social comparison. Such comparison increases awareness of groups' relative position – low or high status – in relation to some valued dimension. The way in which low subjective status or a threat of lower status are interpreted by group members could serve to undermine positive social identity and lead to a range of reactions amongst low- and high-status group members.

Social identity theory argues that the perceived stability and legitimacy of status differences and the perceived permeability of group boundaries (the ease with which group members can become members of one group compared to another) interact to determine the strategies that are available to achieve and/or maintain a positive social identity and positive differentiation for the ingroup. Three main mechanisms are social mobility, social creativity, and social competition, and in this order these strategies represent least to most potential for social antagonism. Members of both high- and low-status groups can engage in each strategy to afford and/or maintain positive distinctiveness and the strategies are not mutually exclusive (see Branscombe and Ellemers, 1998, for an analysis of how these strategies relate to coping with discrimination).

Members of groups with low prestige can embrace a personal *social mobility* solution by attempts to pass from a low- to a high-status group. For example, in an organization women can adopt the norms, values, and attributes that characterize working men; homosexuals can deny publicly their sexual preference and 'pass' as heterosexual; Aborigines and new migrants can assimilate and practice the customs of the dominant group. Such upward individual social movement does necessitate psychological disassociation with the low-status group and its members. The norms, values, and beliefs characteristic of the low-status group are rejected, leading to a reduction in commitment to that group. In addition, social mobility requires that the boundaries between the low- and high-status groups are permeable; it has to be believed that it is possible to become a member of the preferred group.

Members of high-status groups can also engage in social mobility with the same psychological implications (e.g., reduced commitment to the high-status group). For example, it is possible that during times of apartheid in South Africa some White South Africans perceived intergroup relations between Blacks and Whites as stable but illegitimate and they therefore rejected the values and beliefs of the White minority. At least in the short term the social mobility approach does not generate social change. The relative positions of the low- and high-status groups remain constant. Potential change in the actual intergroup relationship is unlikely because of blurring of the group boundaries and limited attachment by group members to their group. Without committed and active group members there will be limited impetus to address perceived inequity in the social system (e.g., Kelly and Breinlinger, 1995)

Social creativity is another strategy in which positive social identity is attained without there necessarily being changes in the actual social position of the low- and high-status groups. Positive group identity can be achieved by redefining the comparative situation. Group members can (a) compare themselves to the opposing group on some new dimension (e.g., Whites may be smart but Aborigines are spiritual), (b) change the meaning of the dimension of comparison such that a negative attribute is defined as positive (e.g., Black is beautiful), or (c) alter the comparative frame of reference so that there is a downward comparison where an inferior outgroup serves as the basis for comparison (e.g., migrants).

Social creativity can be used by members of high-status groups to assert, justify, and perpetuate their high status and positive distinctiveness. For example, in a system that is unstable and illegitimate, it is possible through social creativity to reframe and reintroduce an illegitimate position as being legitimate. In general, commitment to, and identification with, one's group can remain strong and intergroup discrimination and conflict may be reduced because social creativity affords a form of positive self-definition without radical change to the status-quo.

Negative intergroup prejudice and conflict are most likely to occur when group members engage in *social competition*. That is, when members of subordinate and dominant groups compete on dimensions which both groups value. In order to engage in social competition there must be a collective perception that the social system is insecure (illegitimate and/or unstable) and therefore that a potential for change exists. As a result, the level of identification and commitment low-status members feel for their group increases and it is possible to engage in collective action in order to achieve more of the mutually valued resource or outcome (e.g., protests, lobbying institutions, building alliances; see Reynolds et al., in press; Wright et al., 1990).

But what about the high-status group? If high-status group members believe their superiority on some dimension is legitimate, but also that it is unstable, that the group is threatened by the activities of the low-status outgroup, then a highly ethnocentric and discriminatory stance could prevail. Threats to the status quo increase the insecurity of the high-status group and could impinge on its positive social identity. Perceived instability of the status hierarchy increases high-status group members' motivation to discriminate between their own and other groups (e.g., Ellemers et al., 1992; Ellemers et al., 1988; Turner and Brown, 1978).

The social identity theory of intergroup relations, then, also recognizes that status differences may exist without much ethnocentrism and discrimination (Tajfel and Turner, 1979). Consensual inferiority or superiority, where low- or high-status groups accept their position on a particular dimension, depends on the nature of social system. The fact that consensual systems are possible further reinforces the point that social identity processes do not mean that ethnocentrism and intergroup discrimination are *inevitable*. It is not simply the case that ingroup identification is going to generate the conditions for intergroup discrimination. The social creativity strategy indicates that it is possible to identify with a particular ingroup and engage in intergroup differentiation without this leading to social antagonism (see Turner, 1999b for a more detailed discussion). In fact, it is precisely because ethnocentrism and intergroup discrimination are not universal that social identity theory is so important; it is directed towards understanding how group members react psychologically to threats to positive distinctiveness and the conditions under which group members accept or reject their inferiority or superiority.

In summary, social identity theory argues that people categorize themselves in terms of social identities, they evaluate their groups through processes of intergroup comparison, and they seek to achieve positively valued distinctiveness for their group. These judgements and evaluations – and the amount of prejudice and discrimination they involve – are always constrained by shared beliefs and theories concerning the stability and legitimacy of status differences between groups (e.g., Ellemers, 1993; Tajfel and Turner, 1979).

Self-Categorization Theory

The Process that Underlies Psychological Group Membership

Social identity theory has proved to be a fruitful theory of intergroup behaviour. While positive self-evaluations and motivational variables are central to social identity theory, self-categorization theory explains 'variations in how people define and categorize themselves and the effects of such variations' (Turner, 1991: 155; Turner et al., 1987). Through the identity mechanism and the self-stereotyping hypothesis (Turner, 1982, 1984) variations in self-identity became fundamental to the analysis of the reality of the group. It was necessary to explain, and understand more fully, personal, as well as social identity and the relationship between them. Self-categorization theory was directed at these tasks.

In self-categorization theory, the concepts of personal and social identity are represented in a hierarchy of potential self-categorizations. For illustrative purposes, three levels are identified: the superordinate (self as a human being), intermediate (self as a group member), and subordinate (self as an individual person). The superordinate level is more inclusive than the intermediate and the intermediate more so than the subordinate (Rosch, 1978).

Social identity is represented at the intermediate level. It is argued that when a person's social identity becomes salient the process of *depersonalization* associated with defining oneself as a group member leads to heightened perceptions of similarity and *interchangeability* between the individual and like-minded others – ingroup members. Impressions of oneself and others are no longer made on an individual basis but are related to self-definition as a group member in terms of the ingroup stereotype. It is the process of depersonalization and self-stereotyping as a group member that makes it possible to act collectively and forms the basis of *collective psychology*.

Self-definition in group-based terms (as with all perception) involves comparison. Social identity depends on ingroup–outgroup comparison; there must be a relevant contrasting outgroup in the context of interest. Personal identity operates at the subordinate level where there is no salient contrasting outgroup and comparisons are made within the ingroup. Thus, personal identity is also a comparative process where on the dimension of comparison the differences between oneself and other ingroup members are emphasized (Reynolds and Oakes, 1999; Turner et al., 1994; Turner and Onorato, 1999).

People can categorize themselves, then, as an individual in contrast to other individuals in terms of their personal identity, or they can categorize themselves as a group in contrast to other groups in terms of social identity. However, given that we have so many possible identities what is it that determines whether one or the other will become relevant and meaningful in a particular situation? The type of identity (its content) and level of identity (subordinate, intermediate, superordinate etc.) that becomes psychologically operative or salient in a given situation has been of core interest to self-categorization theorists.

The Issue of Salience

In self-categorization theory it is argued that all perception involves categorization and that categorization itself is a process used to give stimuli context-dependent meaning. Three interrelated factors – perceiver readiness, comparative fit, and normative fit – are used to define the selective, meaningful, and relational properties of categorization; they explain which categorization becomes salient in a given situation.

Perceiver readiness refers to individuals' 'readiness' to categorize a particular social situation in a certain way and is related to their knowledge and theories about the social world and their expectations, motives, values, and goals (Oakes et al., 1994). However, regardless of how 'ready' a perceiver is to judge a situation in a particular way there must be evidence in the situation that sustains such a categorization.

The principles of comparative fit and normative fit are also used to explain category salience. The meta-contrast principle is the basis of comparative fit (Turner, 1985). This principle states that in a particular context, stimuli will be categorized as the same when the average differences perceived between them (intraclass differences) are less than the differences between them and other stimuli (interclass differences). In relation to social identity and group-based perception this means that there is an accentuation of perceptual similarities within the group and the accentuation of perceptual differences between groups.

Stimuli are grouped or categorized through a context-specific assessment of similarity and difference, but there is a content as well as a structural dimension to categorization. In order to separate stimuli into different categories there must be normative fit (Oakes, 1987). The way in which similarities and differences are established must 'fit' with perceivers' understanding of those categories and the relationship between them; the categorization needs to make sense in terms of 'our normative beliefs and theories about the substantive social meaning of the social category' (Turner et al., 1994: 455).

Through use of an example it might be easier to grasp the concepts of comparative fit and normative fit and the dynamic context-dependent nature of category salience. Imagine that there are three other people and yourself involved in a discussion. As the discussion progresses only one of the three people agrees with you. The other two agree with each other but disagree with you and your like-minded colleague. Here, there are categorical divisions, there are similarities and differences between people. Comparative fit relates to the way stimuli (in this case yourself and the others involved in the discussion) are grouped together. It is argued that you and your like-minded colleague will consider yourselves to be members of the same group when the average differences perceived between the two of you (intraclass differences) are perceived to be *less* than the differences between the two of you and the other people involved in the discussion (interclass differences).

It could be that you and the three other people were discussing Aboriginal land rights and that the two groups that developed comprised members of different races (e.g., Anglo Australians and Aborigines). If it was the group of Anglo Australians that were more hesitant and unsure about the benefits of changes to land rights and the Aborigines who were committed to such changes then there is likely to be *normative fit*. The pattern of similarities and differences (Anglo Australians and Aborigines) is consistent with normative expectations about the position of these social groups and the relationship between them (of course some people may have different normative expectations and expectations can change).

Based on the interaction between comparative and normative fit it is likely that impressions of yourself, your supporter, and the others would be made in terms of race-category membership; one group stereotyped in terms of being Aborigines and the other as Anglo Australians. However, it is unlikely that this group of people would be differentiated in terms of their race unless you (the perceiver) had specific theories and beliefs about the social meaning of these particular groups and your expectations about the groups' relative views on the dimension of comparison – attitudes to land rights – were confirmed. For example, if the Anglo Australians were pro-Aboriginal land rights and the Aboriginal Australians were against such a move, then another categorization, say Labor versus Conservative voters, may be more meaningful.

In line with this analysis, if you and the others were discussing another issue, different ingroup and outgroup alliances may develop and impressions of the ingroup and the outgroup would vary (for example, Males versus Females, Arts versus Science students) (Hogg and Turner, 1987; Reynolds and Oakes, 1999). Furthermore, if a group of people who had a more extreme view entered the discussion then the original ingroup and outgroup members may be seen as more similar to one another and different from the interlopers (Haslam and Turner, 1992). It is the case, therefore, that the type of categorization and its associated meaning is an outcome of an interaction between the perceiver and the situation; it is context-dependent. Category salience is a dynamic outcome of categorization-in-context.

In summary, we are both individuals and group members and these poles of human experience influence the psychology of the person. Given that groups and individuals exist objectively, both personal (individual) and social (group) categorizations are necessary to reflect and represent social life (Oakes et al., 1994; Tajfel and Turner, 1979). Based on self-categorization theory, the type of impressions formed of others is relative to how the self is perceived in a particular situation. Through the process of depersonalization, when identification shifts from 'me' and 'I' to 'we' and 'us', the self is defined less in terms of differing individual persons and more as an interchangeable representative of a particular social category. The social meaning of these categorizations depends on the interaction between the relative accessibility of a particular self-category (perceiver readiness) and the fit (comparative and normative) between certain categories and the realities of the situation.

Social Identity and Social Influence

In terms of the themes of this chapter, an important outcome of depersonalization is *social influence*. The social influence process provides the 'missing link' between collective and individual psychology; it is central to the interplay between group relations in a social system and an individual's attitudes and actions in a particular situation (Turner, 1991). When social identity is salient it makes sense to anticipate that members of the same group who are in the same social location should agree about aspects of that situation. In other words, those judged to be similar to oneself – ingroup members – become a source of information about social life. Furthermore, agreement with others ensures that our judgements are 'objective' and correct and not the outcome of distortions or personal biases.

Sharing of ingroup memberships provides opportunities for agreement and disagreement and *mutual influence* (Turner, 1991; Turner and Oakes, 1989). It has been demonstrated that social identity leads members of the same group to (a) expect to agree about a particular stimulus entity and (b) strive to reach agreement (Haslam et al., 1998). Naturally, it may be the case that we find ourselves in disagreement with other ingroup members. But, because of the expectation for agreement this gives rise to uncertainty and attempts to bring expectations in line with reality by (a) changing our views in line with ingroup opinion, (b) attempts to influence other ingroup members to adopt a different stance, (c) recategorization of ingroup members as being outgroup, and (d) clarification of the stimulus situation (i.e., ensuring that reference is being made to the same thing; David and Turner, 1996, 1999; McGarty et al., 1994; Turner, 1991). Each of these strategies indicates the importance of ingroup memberships in both shaping and reflecting our theories, beliefs, and values about reality.

The self-categorization perspective argues that the level and content of the self changes and that broader social attitudes and norms that derive from the dynamics of intergroup interaction within society shape the psychology of the person. In this way, intergroup relations become *self* through social identity processes and associated outcomes such as social influence (Turner, 1991, 1999a; Turner et al., 1994). Consequently, the nature of intergroup relations shapes attitudes, opinions, beliefs, and ideologies; they influence individuals' understanding and explanation of social reality.

An Alternative Analysis of Prejudice

We have presented an analysis thus far that portrays group-based impressions and related social actions as the outcomes of self-categorization of oneself and others in ingroup–outgroup terms. The way we categorize our own group and other groups depends on social comparison and reflects the interaction between group members' collective understanding (their theories, beliefs, and ideologies) about the social structure and the subjectively-perceived relationship between groups in the context of interest. Such an analysis has implications for how we understand social antagonism. For example, a group is likely to discriminate against minorities if they interpret their group's position in the social structure as legitimate (their theories, ideologies, and beliefs will endorse and reflect this position) and where in a particular social comparative context their status is challenged and under threat.

To help clarify these points, we can look to recent events in Australia that involved the One Nation Party. One Nation's policy platform is believed by many to be racist; it is seen to advocate an immigration policy where decisions are based on an applicant's race and to be discriminatory towards Aborigines. Many university students and others have publicly disagreed with the way supporters of this political party portrayed Aborigines and Asian immigrants. They responded collectively through social protest and, at times, displayed acts of aggression and discrimination towards One Nation supporters. Furthermore, the actions of each of these groups can be understood as attempts to influence others and the political process with the aim of changing the nature of intergroup relations (e.g., One Nation wanted a shift in resources away from Aborigines and recent immigrants, to farmers and poor families; those in opposition to such moves desired institutional recognition of Aboriginal rights and compensation for infringement of such rights).

In the traditional view of prejudice, One Nation supporters are viewed as prejudiced and racist and the students are not. In addition, the attitudes and behaviour of members of both of these groups are believed to arise from *different psychological processes*. One Nation supporters' position is believed to be an outcome of defective judgement (e.g., an information processing problem) and deficient personality (e.g., authoritarianism) whereas the students' attitudes and beliefs (which are much more aligned with those of the social scientists who conduct prejudice research; see Oakes and Haslam, Chapter 11) are judged to be rational and reasonable and to provide a bench mark from which to assess others' views.

However, in this chapter it has been argued that *both* groups are engaged in the *same psychology*; that their respective perspectives stem from the *same* categorization process in interaction with intergroup relations and social structural factors (see also Oakes and Haslam, Chapter 11). Members of these groups are oriented to the social debate from different locations in the social structure and therefore have different beliefs, values, interpretations, and preferred outcomes regarding intergroup relations. In these terms, rather than being a product of asocial attitudes and actions, intergroup phenomena can be understood as an outcome of normal and adaptive cognitive processes that enable self-categorization of oneself and others in group-based terms (Turner, 1999a; see also Tajfel, 1969). It can be viewed as a product of collective psychology and the realities of intergroup relations.

The debate surrounding One Nation can be interpreted as an example of genuine political and social conflict. Groups have developed collective stereotypes based on their beliefs and values and are engaged in collective action to advance one political platform over another. There is nothing psychologically wrong with groups' attempts to influence the political debate and bring about social change. While there may be some political advantages in portraying those with whom there is disagreement as ignorant, irrational, or defective, such an analysis raises serious issues if it is accepted as an account of psychological functioning. If certain disagreements between groups are reduced to defective psychology then what does this mean for the positive, functional aspects of social disagreements, constructive debate, and human social progress?

Under certain conditions, relativities in perspective fuel attempts at political and social change to intergroup relations which can result in various modes of conflict (from public debate to aggression). In other situations, the interaction between social reality and social categorization can lead to cooperation and tolerance, for example, where ingroup and outgroup members are perceived to share the same superordinate ingroup (Oakes et al., 1999; Sherif, 1967; Turner et al., 1987). While there is no doubt that some strategies that groups use to persuade, influence, and succeed may be preferred over others, it is limited to reduce all disagreement to defective (individual) psychological processes. The more difficult task, which social identity and self-categorization theorists (and others) have pursued, is to recognize and understand collective psychology, examine group relations within a particular social structure and identify the conditions that motivate groups to engage in particular forms of conflict or cooperation.

Attempts to modify the intergroup structure, then, are mediated by group processes, collective beliefs and action, and social influence. These factors shape individuals' attitudes, beliefs, and opinions; their interpretations of social reality (Oakes et al., 1994; Sherif, 1967; Turner, 1999a). In this way, collective psychology functions to influence individual psychology. Consequently, in order to explain 'prejudice', an analysis of both collective and individual psychology is necessary. However, rather than an individualistic and reductionist interpretation where the causes of prejudice are dissociated from their social context, it needs to be recognized *explicitly* in theory and research that collective and individual psychology reflect a complex interaction between the individual and the social system (Turner, 1999a; Turner et al., 1998).

The Role of Personality and Group Factors in Explaining Prejudice: Recent Empirical Investigations

At present there is a resurgence of interest in personality explanations of prejudice (Altemeyer, 1998) where it is believed that there are personality types that more or less directly predict negative intergroup attitudes. The most prominent and ambitious attempt to understand the psychology of prejudice in these terms has involved the construct of *authoritarianism* (Adorno et al., 1950; Altemeyer, 1981, 1988, cf., Pettigrew, 1958; see Heaven, Chapter 6). However, there are many problems with the 'authoritarian personality' explanation of prejudice. As highlighted in the Introduction, the personality approach reflects an individualistic analysis of psychological functioning. The focus is on the fairly stable character of the individual person *as an individual* and neglects the group-based, social identity processes that are related to intergroup discrimination, prejudice, and social conflict.

Typically, authoritarianism is believed to stem from parents who mould their child's attitudes and behaviour through rewards and punishment, direct teaching, and modelling (although, the role of extended family, peers, and the media is also recognized; see Robinson, Witenberg, and Sanson Chapter 5). There are two main problems with this social learning interpretation: Firstly, it has difficulty accounting for evidence that prejudice can increase and decrease in a uniform way amongst groups of people in reasonably short time frames (Sherif, 1967). While there is some recognition that levels of authoritarianism can vary as a function of experiences across the life span or in response to a critical social event (e.g., Altemeyer, 1988), the psychological process necessary to explain such flexibility is rarely addressed. Secondly, there is limited analysis of the source of parents' and influential others' own beliefs, values, and ideologies and the conditions under which their own views may be moderated or attenuated.

In line with self-categorization theory, in order to account for the dynamic nature of prejudice it is necessary to explain how opinions, attitudes, beliefs, and behaviour become shared and are mediated by social variables. The personality explanation of prejudice is limited because the influence group memberships and social structure can have on a person's *immediate* attitudes and action are neglected. Furthermore, as can be seen from the distinction between personal identity and social identity, there is a psychological discontinuity between people acting as individuals and people acting as group members. Based on self-categorization theory it is argued that intergroup behaviour is made possible by depersonalization; a mechanism whose very function is to enable action as *other than* an individual person. Its function is to attenuate, eliminate, and overwhelm individual differences. Given this discontinuity, it is not possible to extrapolate directly from individual processes (i.e., personality) to shared collective intergroup behaviour (Turner, 1999a; Turner and Giles, 1981) such as social antagonism.

Along these lines, Verkuyten and Hagendoorn (1998) recently examined the determinants of prejudice as a function of different levels of self-categorization. In their first experiment an assessment was made of participants' ingroup stereotypes (those related to Dutch treatment of minorities) and their individual differences in authoritarian attitudes (ten items from Altemeyer's Right-Wing Authoritarianism, RWA, scale). Participants' identification was then manipulated by making salient either their personal identity as an individual or their social identity (being Dutch). Levels of prejudice towards people with Turkish origin (the minority group with the lowest prestige in the Netherlands) were assessed through a social distance measure of prejudice (Bogardus, 1925).

Participants in the personal and social identity conditions did not differ in their level of endorsement of ingroup stereotypes, authoritarianism, or prejudice. However, in line with predictions, there were differences between the personal and social identity conditions regarding the pattern of correlations between prejudice, stereotype endorsement, and authoritarianism. In the personal identity condition, prejudice was significantly correlated with authoritarianism but not with ingroup stereotypes. Conversely, in the social identity condition, prejudice was correlated with ingroup stereotypes but not with authoritarianism. The more participants perceived the Dutch as favouring gender equality, hospitality, and tolerance, the lower their level of prejudice. Verkuyten and Hagendoorn (1998) extended and replicated these findings in a second experiment.

On the basis of these results it was argued that the determinants of prejudice are related to the *level* of the perceiver's self-categorization. Salient identity impacts on the criterion for judgement such that personal standards are relevant in the personal identity condition, whereas when social identity is salient, collective standards specific to the particular identity become psychologically meaningful. In other words, depending on self-categorization, either individual- or group-related factors influenced outgroup evaluation.

In line with self-categorization theory predictions and Verkuyten and Hagendoorn's (1998) studies, we conducted a study where participants completed the RWA scale, an identification manipulation designed to make either personal or social identity as Australians (compared to Americans) salient, and then the Modern Racism Scale (MRS) (McConahay, Hardee, and Batts, 1981). The MRS was used to assess levels of prejudice towards Aboriginal Australians, so the scale was worded to make sense in an Australian context. Example questions are 'Aborigines are getting too demanding in their push for land rights' and 'Aborigines have more influence upon government policy than they ought to have'. A control condition was also included where participants completed the scales under normal testing conditions.

Consistent with Verkuyten and Hagendoorn's (1998) main findings, the relationship between RWA and MRS did vary significantly in our personal identity and national identity condition (see Reynolds et al., in press). In the national identity condition, authoritarianism was less predictive of prejudice towards Indigenous Australians than in the personal identity condition ($\underline{r}$s: .39 and .67, respectively and these values differed significantly from each other). These research findings suggest that (a) personality characteristics such as authoritarianism may not always be predictive of prejudice and (b) social identity salience is important in understanding prejudice (see also Haslam and Wilson, 2000).

Yet despite the fact that our results are in line with predictions and previous work, they could also be open to misinterpretation. More specifically, it is important to note that self-categorization theory does not simply predict that social identity salience will reduce the extent to which authoritarianism is predictive of prejudice. The direction and strength of the correlation should depend on whether (a) the salient identity is related to authoritarian and prejudiced beliefs; and (b) within a particular sample of participants, there are similar or different attitudinal and behavioural standards relevant to expressions of authoritarianism and prejudice.

In other words, where social identity salience reflects a reasonably common position amongst participants in relation to authoritarianism and prejudice then there should be high consensus among group members and a reduced correlation between these two variables. However, stronger correlations would be predicted when social identity salience increases awareness about tensions and differences among sub-groups within the sample, or if there is limited consensus (or opportunities to reach consensus) regarding how a particular social identity relates to authoritarianism and prejudice. In these conditions, there could be an increase in the dispersion of scores such that the correlation increases.

To investigate these ideas, a second experiment was conducted. In addition to there being a personal identity, national identity, and control condition, age identity (e.g., younger people compared to older people) and gender identity (e.g., males compared to females) were manipulated. The inclusion of age and gender was based on an examination of the 30 items that comprise the RWA scale. This analysis suggested that items of the RWA scale may be sensitive to the different norms, values, and ideologies of various groups in society. For example, a number of items specifically refer to beliefs about the role of youth in society (e.g., 'It would be best for everyone if the proper authorities censored magazines and movies to keep trashy material away from the youth'). Also, several items require comparisons to be made between males and females and relate to attitudes towards feminism (e.g., 'The sooner we get rid of the traditional family structure, where the father is the head of the family and the children are taught to obey authority automatically, the better').

In fact the RWA scale could be interpreted as a measure of widespread societal values and ideologies rather than an assessment of an individual's personality (Billig, 1976; Duckitt, 1989; Reynolds et al., in press). It highlights a series of core tensions that exist between groups in society (i.e, whether you are for or against freedom for young people or pro- or anti-feminism) and these could play a role when participants complete the scale items under normal testing conditions.

In relation to this point, based on self-categorization theory, it was anticipated that because our sample of participants included males and females from a range of age groups, when gender identity and age identity were made salient, differences in attitudes could lead to a stronger relationship between RWA and MRS. In these conditions, social identity salience should increase awareness of the intergroup differences and participants should respond more in line with the social meaning of these group-based differences. However, consistent with the findings of Experiment 1, in the national identity condition authoritarianism should be less predictive of prejudice. Here *shared* norms and values about the nature of authoritarianism and prejudice amongst our Australian participants should frame responses.

In line with predictions, there were strong positive correlations between authoritarianism and prejudice when gender identity and age identity were salient (rs: gender = .89, age = .71). Importantly, a weaker correlation emerged where Australian social identity was made salient (r = .-.01), that is, in the condition where responses were anticipated to be less differentiated and more consensual. In line with previous findings, the correlation was stronger in the personal than the national identity condition (r = .28) but this difference was not significant.

Such results demonstrate that it is not simply the case that social identity salience *reduces* the extent to which authoritarianism is predictive of prejudice. The relationship between authoritarianism and prejudice varied significantly depending on whether the social identity salience process was one that consensualized or differentiated participants' beliefs and values about authoritarianism and prejudice. Such findings support the conclusion that a range of group-based beliefs and values may influence responses on authoritarianism and prejudice measures.

Overall, there is more work to be done to expand on the specific nature of the findings of these experiments. But there is no doubt that the results provide evidence that authoritarianism may be limited in its capacity to predict prejudice across contexts and levels of identity. The relationship between authoritarianism and prejudice varied significantly depending on the salient self-categorization of the participant. On the basis of such evidence, it is difficult to conclude as Altemeyer does in relation to right-wing authoritarians, that prejudices are 'largely matters of personality' (1988: 60). In these experiments, personality did not influence prejudice in a consistent, stable way. The experimental work supports the view that in order to understand prejudice, it is necessary to recognize the psychology of individuals *as group members* and the impact of broader intergroup relationships and people's collective understanding of those relationships.

Conclusion

In this chapter we have outlined a social identity and self-categorization analysis of social antagonism and contrasted this, in particular, with the individual differences or personality approach. This latter analysis suggests that the best way to understand prejudice is to examine individuals' underlying personality structure and identify those factors which lead certain people to be more prejudiced than others. Inherent in such an approach is the assumption that personality is relatively stable and able to predict prejudice across time and situations (cf., Reynolds and Oakes, 1999; Turner and Onorato, 1999).

In contrast, based on social identity and self-categorization theories, it is argued that prejudice cannot simply be explained through an analysis of individuals' psychology *as individuals*. Groups are real and have psychological significance for members. Consequently, individuals' collective psychology *as group members* in interplay with the realities of intergroup relations are important in trying to understand both social antagonism and individual psychology.

Groups within society differ in their values, goals, and beliefs and at times these various interpretations of social reality lead to 'prejudice' and social conflict. The level of outgroup denigration and hostility is constrained by shared beliefs concerning the security (legitimacy and/or stability) of the status differences between groups (e.g., Ellemers, 1993; Tajfel and Turner, 1979). Social antagonism is most evident when groups' perceive their ambitions as legitimate but they are thwarted, or their position is threatened, by the activities of other groups.

In conclusion, the essential message of this chapter is that 'prejudice' is not an outcome of irrationality, deficiency, and pathology *it can be understood as a psychologically rational and valid product of the way members of certain groups perceive the social structure of intergroup relations – it arises from and reflects their subjectively-apprehended understanding of the relationships between groups in society* (Turner, 1999a; Turner et al., 1998). In our view, progress in understanding 'prejudice' requires recognition that it is a group process that originates in the psychology of the group, intergroup relations, and the reality of human social conflict.

Note

We would like to thank Alex Haslam and Michelle Ryan for their comments on an earlier version of this chapter.

11 Distortion V. Meaning: Categorization on Trial for Inciting Intergroup Hatred

Penelope J. Oakes and S. Alexander Haslam

Every field of intellectual endeavour has its canon, its hardcore reading list of contributions that just about everyone in the area would define as seminal, whether they agree with their message or not. The canon of the social psychology of prejudice would, without doubt, include Tajfel's *Cognitive Aspects of Prejudice* (1969), widely cited as a watershed, a defining moment from which the field has never looked back.

That paper did two crucial and related things. Firstly, it went on the offensive against the 'blood and guts' (as Tajfel put it) irrational individualism of previous analyses of prejudice, arguing that prejudice reflected intergroup antagonism arising from rational attempts to understand social reality. Secondly, as part of this rational analysis, the paper cemented the role of *categorization* as the essential cognitive basis of intergroup attitudes and actions (see also Allport, 1954; Lippmann, 1922). Since 1969, there has been widespread agreement that if we understand the role of categorization in social thinking we will be closer to providing a coherent account of the social psychology of prejudice. Categorization is seen as the first step, the crucial process responsible for dividing people into ingroups and outgroups, 'us' and 'them'. When this is followed by evaluative discriminations that define 'us' as better than 'them' we have what many recognize as prejudice (e.g., see Brewer and Brown, 1998; Duckitt, 1994; Hamilton and Trolier, 1986; Taylor, 1981).

Does this mean that categorizing in itself can be held at least partly responsible for prejudice? Are we prejudiced *because* we categorize? In the spirit of the classic schoolyard taunt, 'You started it!', should we blame categorization for laying the foundations of the images and attitudes that fuel prejudice? And, given that categorization is regarded as an essential universal of human thinking (Bruner, 1957), do we therefore accept some level of prejudice as inevitable? It is vitally important that we get the answers to these questions right, because if categorization really is not the problem, we may be wasting our time on scapegoats while the real culprits flourish.

This chapter addresses these issues in the context of current differences of opinion within social psychology about the nature of categorization and its role in the genesis of prejudice. We invite readers to consider the case of *Distortion versus Meaning*. Categorization stands before the court of social psychology charged with conspiracy to pervert the course of tolerance and harmony and inciting intergroup hatred. The prosecution will allege that 'categorization, per se, propels the individual down the road to bias', (Wilder, 1986: 292), that 'the road to ... discrimination begins with the simple act of categorization' (Bodenhausen and Macrae, 1998: 7), and that 'the mere division of people into groups' creates 'discrimination in favour of ingroup members and against outgroup members' (Stephan, 1985: 613). Witnesses for the prosecution will contend that evidence of perceptual accentuation, outgroup homogeneity effects, construal influenced by category content, and ingroup bias, demonstrates an inherent propensity for categorization to bias social perception and action. Appearing for the defence, we will argue that categorization does not bias or distort, but is in fact the principal guarantee of meaningful and appropriate social perception. We do not deny that categorization has been identified at the scene of crimes such as bigotry and intolerance, but we contend that it bears no special relationship to these phenomena. Indeed, we present evidence that it is also implicated in cooperation, altruism, understanding, and appreciation in both interpersonal and intergroup relations. We ask that the jury do not allow their *political* evaluation of some of categorization's outcomes to colour their judgement of the process itself. We submit that categorization has been misunderstood and wrongly accused, and that we cannot hope to develop a truly powerful analysis of prejudice and racism until its name has been cleared.

The Basic Evidence

We begin by outlining the basic facts in this case, findings accepted by both sides as evidence of categorization at work. What is at issue, of course, is the interpretation of this evidence, but we shall come to that later. Categorization is known to be responsible for the perceptual accentuation of similarity within, and difference between, categories, and the assimilation of impressions of individuals to preconceived assumptions about what category members are like. It is also implicated in the genesis of ingroup bias, the tendency for individuals to favour, in various ways, groups to which they belong (ingroups) over groups to which they do not belong (outgroups). The accumulated evidence of these effects is extensive – we shall simply summarize the main points and refer to some classic demonstrations (for further review and discussion see Brewer and Brown, 1998; Fiske, 1998; Hamilton, 1981; Oakes, 1996; Oakes et al., 1999).

In a seminal study, Tajfel and Wilkes (1963) presented participants with a series of eight lines differing from each other in length by a constant ratio. In one 'classified' condition the four shorter lines were labeled 'A' and the four longer 'B', while in an 'unclassified' condition no labels were presented and in a 'random' condition there was no predictable relationship between the length of line and the label attached to it. It was found that when reporting the length of the lines, participants in the classified group, and these participants alone, accentuated the distinction between the two classes of lines by exaggerating the difference between the shortest of the longer four and the longest of the shorter four. On average, participants judged this difference to be more than twice what it actually was. There was also some evidence to suggest that participants in the classified condition minimized differences between lines within each of the two classes. The following principle emerged from this study:

> When a classification is correlated with a continuous dimension there will be a tendency to exaggerate the difference on *that* dimension between items which fall into distinct classes, and to minimize these differences within each of the classes. (Tajfel, 1969: 83)

Numerous studies explored the potential for extrapolation of Tajfel and Wilkes' findings to the social domain (e.g., see Doise, 1978; Doise et al., 1978; Krueger and Rothbart, 1990; McGarty and Penny, 1988; McGarty and Turner, 1992; Tajfel et al., 1964; Taylor et al., 1978; Walker and Antaki, 1986; Wilder 1978). This work is widely cited as demonstrating that categorized individuals are seen as more similar within and different between groups than those who are not categorized (but see McGarty, in press, for critical discussion of the robustness of this effect). For example, Allen and Wilder (1979) divided participants into two groups, in fact randomly, but allegedly on the basis of preferences for paintings. Participants then completed a questionnaire assessing their beliefs on a range of topics including art, politics, and college life. They completed this once with their own views, then again as if they were either another ingroup member or an outgroup member. Responses revealed that participants assumed within-group similarity and between-group difference of opinion on both relevant (i.e., art) and ostensibly irrelevant (e.g., politics) dimensions.

One development of this basic accentuation finding that has particular relevance for understanding prejudice is the *outgroup homogeneity effect*. This refers to the apparent tendency for within-group accentuation of similarity to apply to outgroups rather more than it does to ingroups – '*they* all look alike to me', a common catch-cry of the 'prejudiced' perceiver (e.g., Linville, 1982; Linville and Jones, 1980; Park and Rothbart, 1982; Wilder, 1984; for review see Haslam et al., 1996). One example of this phenomenon is provided by Park and Rothbart (1982). They asked male and female participants to estimate the proportions of males and females who would endorse each of 54 attitudinal and behavioural items which varied in their relevance to sex stereotypes. As predicted, opposite-sex estimates were more sex-stereotypical than same-sex estimates: for example, men's estimates of the proportion of women endorsing stereotypic items was higher than women's estimates of the same proportion.

In addition to findings of categorical accentuation effects, there is much accumulated evidence that the encoding, retrieval, and interpretation of stimulus information is affected by category content (see Kunda and Thagard, 1996 for review). The classic example comes from Duncan (1976) who manipulated the race (Black/White) of both the perpetrator and the victim of an 'ambiguous shove'. The White participants tended to see the shove as fooling around when perpetrated by a White actor, but as violent behaviour when perpetrated by a Black actor, particularly when the victim was White (see also Allport and Postman, 1947; Sagar and Schofield, 1980). Interpretation of the Black actor's behaviour was guided by category content that defined Blacks as 'impulsive and given to crimes and violence' (Duncan, 1976: 591).

When we use categorization to segment the social world, we include ourselves amongst the stimuli to which it is applied. That is, we often divide individuals into 'ingroup members', those with whom we perceive ourselves to share relevant characteristics (e.g., fellow Australians, fellow Republicans, men) and 'outgroup members', those from whom we perceive ourselves to be different on the relevant dimensions (Americans, Monarchists, women). Evidence suggests that, under some conditions, simply dividing people into an ingroup and an outgroup can produce evaluative biases which favour the ingroup (and the self) at the expense of the outgroup.

The first evidence of this came from a seminal study by Tajfel and colleagues (1971). They divided schoolboys into 'minimal' groups – group membership was anonymous (meaning that best friends were as likely to be in the outgroup as the ingroup), there was no social interaction within or between groups, no interdependence, no history of hostility, no link between group membership and individual self-interest. The boys were then asked to distribute rewards between two anonymous others, an ingroup member and an outgroup member. The results are well known. This trivial, in fact random, division into groups was sufficient to provoke ingroup-favouring responses in the allocation of rewards, even at the expense of absolute ingroup gain (see Turner, 1981; Turner and Bourhis, 1996 for further review and discussion).

Doise and colleagues (1972) demonstrated that this ingroup favouritism in the distribution of rewards extended to stereotypic representations. In a *minimal* group procedure participants were asked to describe the two groups on a number of evaluative dimensions. As anticipated, it was found that stereotypic representations of the outgroup were less favourable than those of the ingroup (see also Brewer and Silver, 1978; Howard and Rothbart, 1980). Thus, the discriminatory distribution strategies were backed up and perhaps justified by prejudicial images of the two groups – 'we are good, they are bad'.

The Case for the Prosecution

Building the case against categorization as prime suspect in the crime of prejudice rests on interpretation of the effects outlined above as evidence of *distortion*. It is argued that (a) perception is distorted such that the reality of individual differences and personal uniqueness is misrepresented as group-based similarity and difference, and (b) motives associated with self-evaluation are distorted such that the ingroup is indiscriminately favoured at the expense of the outgroup at all times.

From the outset, the accentuation effects of categorization were interpreted as a distortion of perception. Tajfel himself argued that stimuli were being perceived as more similar and different than they *really were*, than they would appear to be if the perceiver made more effort or took 'a closer look' (see Tajfel, 1972). Tajfel suggested that the accentuation effects might account for some features of the social stereotypes seen to underlie outgroup derogation. If, for example, a perceiver believed that having Black or White skin was *correlated* with certain personal characteristics (e.g., laziness, intelligence) in the way that length was correlated with the A/B label in Tajfel and Wilkes' (1963) classified condition, then in terms of those characteristics they would see members of one racial category as both very similar to each other and very different from members of the other category. This would set the stage for distinct and exaggerated stereotypes of each group to emerge, representing Blacks as lazy and Whites as industrious, Blacks as stupid and Whites as intelligent.

The fact that this distortion appears to be asymmetrically applied, affecting images of outgroups rather more than those of ingroups, fits well with the case against categorization. Explanation of the outgroup homogeneity effect has relied, to a significant extent, on the idea that we homogenize outgroups more because we are less familiar with them (e.g., Linville et al., 1989). In other words, when we *know* groups we recognize their actual variability; perceived homogeneity is a distortion that requires the support of ignorance (see also Judd and Park, 1993). Park and Rothbart suggest that 'the principle of outgroup homogeneity' (1982: 1051) combines with the 'principle' of ingroup favouritism to provide fertile ground for the development of inaccurate, negative images of outgroups and intergroup conflict.

The effects of category content on the construal of social information, such as in the Duncan study noted above, have also been interpreted as evidence that categorization compromises accuracy. Wilder (1986: 294) claims that such effects demonstrate the influence of 'categorical blinders' that restrict perceivers' perspectives on new information. This often produces confirmation of pre-existing category-based expectations, sometimes even when disconfirming, inconsistent evidence is available and particularly when the available evidence is ambiguous (e.g., Darley and Gross, 1983; Kunda and Sherman-Williams, 1993; cf., Borgida et al., 1981). Juxtaposed with the long-standing assumption that social category content tends to constitute an inaccurate misrepresentation of the characteristics of group members (Fishman, 1956; Judd and Park, 1993) it is not surprising that this sort of construal through categorization has been defined as a distortion of the 'true attributes' of individuals. Again, it is assumed that these true attributes would be apparent to a motivated perceiver prepared to take 'a closer look' (e.g., Fiske and Neuberg, 1990).

The findings of ingroup favouritism in the minimal group paradigm are tendered as evidence that categorization in and of itself can provoke the evaluative discriminations between groups that are so defining of prejudice. Thus, Wilder concludes that intergroup discrimination can be 'a direct product of the categorization process' (1981: 228), and this conclusion has been drawn by many commentators on the minimal group studies (e.g., Altemeyer, 1994;

Hamilton and Trolier, 1986; Messick and Mackie, 1989; Operario and Fiske, 1998; Stephan, 1985). Drawing on aspects of the social identity theory interpretation of minimal intergroup discrimination (Tajfel and Turner, 1979), motives for positive self-evaluation are seen as the driving force behind this effect. Because the ingroup includes the self, acting to affirm the superiority (on whatever basis) of the ingroup affirms the superiority of the self. This process is thought to be so powerful that virtually any basis for categorization will be seized upon as an opportunity for ingroup favouritism. For instance, Perdue and colleagues (1990) demonstrated that simply using collective pronouns, such as *we*, *us*, and *ours* or *they*, *them*, and *theirs* is sufficient to engender ingroup bias. They unobtrusively paired nonsense syllables with terms such as *we* and found that these were rated as more pleasant than those associated with terms such as *they*. There is, moreover, recent evidence that the categories underlying such bias and discrimination can be activated without conscious awareness, their damaging effects following automatically unless the perceiver is able and motivated to apply a circuit breaker (see Blair and Banaji, 1996; Bodenhausen and Macrae, 1998; Devine, 1989).

In summary, it is alleged that categorization can be held responsible for prejudice on two grounds. It distorts reality – when we perceive through the medium of social categories we do not see what is really there. Our impressions of people are derailed by exaggerated judgements of similarity and difference and the interference of preconceptions about what category members will be like. This perception of individuals as instances of categories 'rather than as individuals to be judged on their own merits' (Stephan and Rosenfield, 1982: 116) is the first culpable step towards the injustice of prejudice and discrimination. Secondly, as well as distorting sensory intake in this way, categorization automatically entrains our basic need for a positive sense of self, such that we indiscriminately favour ingroups to the detriment of outgroups. Once we have identified an individual as 'one of them' rather than 'one of us', unfair allocation of rewards and general derogation and mistreatment are likely to follow.

The Motive: Cognitive Economy

Establishing motive is often a deciding factor for the prosecution, and those who accuse categorization have argued that the driving force behind its use is the inherently limited processing capacity of the perceiver – 'for reasons of cognitive economy, we categorize others as members of particular groups' (Fiske and Neuberg, 1990: 14); 'we categorize people into groups as a means of reducing the amount of information we must contend with' (Hamilton and Trolier, 1986: 128). Were it not for these limits on capacity, people would be able to treat each stimulus they encounter, including each person, as a unique event, and the 'unfortunate' (Fiske and Neuberg, 1990: 14) distorting effects of treating them as category members could be avoided.

So pressing is this need to conserve capacity, it is argued, the information processing system is *automatically* geared to achievement of cognitive economy with scant regard for the human and social consequences. Work initiated by Devine (1989) has argued that the automatic activation of categories is so powerful it can produce 'prejudice-related discrepancies' (Monteith, 1993: 469) in which category content that the perceiver does not actually endorse or believe in is activated by highly salient cues (such as skin colour). Thus, perceivers become the victims of 'spontaneous, unintentional stereotype use', applying beliefs which are not their own but are foisted upon them by the prevailing culture. Similarly, Bodenhausen and Macrae suggest that the effects of automatic categorization are 'typically not consciously intended by perceivers; rather, they arise spontaneously because of basic properties of the information processing system' (1998: 20). Categorization is therefore the root cause of 'unwanted thoughts' (Macrae et al., 1998) which might lead individuals to act in ways counter to their real beliefs. They may, for example, appear prejudiced when they believe they are not.

The prosecution appears to be offering the option of plea bargaining here. Categorization is guilty, no doubt about that, but the defence might like to consider a plea of diminished responsibility due to limited information processing capacity (cf., Fiske, 1989). People really don't mean to perceive others as group members or to act as group members, they certainly don't *mean* to be prejudiced, but categorization makes them do it, and 'social categorization is a necessary, if unfortunate, byproduct' (Fiske and Neuberg, 1990: 14) of our limited capacity. The effects of categorization are, it seems, not only accidental but inevitable (though see Operario and Fiske, 1998, for a discussion of the way in which power can both limit and exacerbate this dynamic). Might the court, therefore, extend leniency whilst feeling confident that the culprit is now exposed and its activities placed under constant surveillance.

The Case for the Defence

The defence does not wish to plea bargain. We aim to establish our client's essential innocence in this matter through a rebuttal of the fundamental prosecution argument that categorization distorts reality and subverts self-evaluation. We do not deny the evidence of accentuation and construal effects or ingroup favouritism in the minimal group paradigm. However, we contend that these phenomena reflect rational strategies of impression formation and action in a social world defined by *groups and intergroup relations* as much as by individuals and interpersonal relations, and that categorization works in both these spheres (the group and the personal) to produce meaning by defining stimuli in context-dependent, self-relative terms. If categorization 'causes' prejudice it also and in equal measure 'causes' close relationships between friends; spontaneous respect and liking for members of some groups; reductions in conflict and prejudice through defining superordinate, shared identity; and the cooperative subordination of individuals to teams, work groups, families, nations, and so forth. In all these instances it provides the basis for self-definition and associated relations with others, from which flows rational, intentional social action in pursuit of both individual and collective values and goals.

Our understanding of the role of categorization in social thinking is formalized within *self-categorization theory* (SCT) (Turner, 1985; Turner et al., 1994), three basic assumptions of which we reiterate here. Firstly, whereas the work discussed above tends to treat group-based perception as 'categorized' and individual impression formation as relatively unmediated and direct (e.g., Brewer, 1988; Fiske and Neuberg, 1990), SCT argues that all person perception – including self-perception – is the outcome of a process of categorization, a process which operates at varying *levels of abstraction*. The difference between individuated and group-based impression formation is that the latter is more abstract, more inclusive, than the former, defining differences between and similarities within *groups* of people. Categorization at the individual level, on the other hand, defines interpersonal differences and intra-individual consistency, and there can be social categorization both more and less abstract than these two intergroup and interpersonal levels. Thus, a perceiver might focus on the distinct and fairly stable personalities of Tom, Dick, and Harry (interpersonal differentiation), or they might stereotype them as Australian (Tom and Dick) and American (Harry) at the intergroup level, or appreciate their commonalities with all human beings (in contrast to dogs, perhaps), or consider Tom in terms of an intrapersonal categorization which compares Tom before he graduated, to Tom after graduation. These different bases of social judgement can produce highly variable impressions (e.g., post-graduation Tom is very serious compared to student Tom; as an Australian in contrast with Americans, Tom is happy-go-lucky), and SCT argues that this is because they all emerge from the *comparative* process of categorization.

Secondly, SCT places a strong emphasis on categorization as a *context-specific* comparative process geared to resolution of the stimulus field in a way that is most meaningful to the perceiver. This contrasts with the widespread assumption that categorization is the activation of cognitive structure through matches with isolated stimulus cues (e.g., Blair and Banaji, 1996: 1143; see Oakes, in press). In this latter view, 'attributes' are rather concrete, absolute aspects of stimulus reality which are also represented in categories. When the relevant attributes appear in a stimulus (e.g., extreme nationalism) they trigger the relevant category (e.g., American). In SCT, on the other hand, there is no assumption of a fixed relationship between certain attributes and certain categories. Rather, categories emerge through use as the perceiver makes sense of the whole stimulus field, not just isolated stimuli. To take an example from some of our recent work on stereotype change (Oakes et al., 1999), what does the category 'a student at a Catholic University' mean, what attributes are associated with it? We found that this depends on the *comparative context* in which that category is used. When students at the Australian National University were asked to describe students at the Australian Catholic University they defined them as religious, conservative, and conventional – no participants suggested that Catholic students were 'progressive'. However, in another condition of the study ANU students expected to describe members of the extreme right-wing fundamentalist Call to Australia (Fred Nile) Party as well as Catholic students. Here, 25 per cent of them included 'progressive' in their stereotype of the Catholic students, and the ascription of 'religious' dropped from over 60 per cent to 44 per cent.

The point is that being Catholic compared to Fred Nile, really does mean something different from being Catholic compared to generally non-religious ANU students. Similarly, being American compared to Iraqis during the Gulf War meant something different from being American in contexts where that conflict was not made salient (Haslam et al., 1992; see also Diab, 1963). We understand that our best friend may attack us in a Faculty meeting where the survival of her Zoology Department requires sacrifices from Psychology, but such hostility over a dinner together as friends would be interpreted entirely differently. We know that meaning varies with context, and SCT argues that categorization works to capture the context-specific configuration of similarity and difference in order to allow an *appropriate* interpretation of action in that context.

Formally, the hypothesis is that categorization is determined by an interaction between category-stimulus *fit* and *perceiver readiness* (Oakes, 1987; Oakes et al., 1994; cf., Bruner, 1957). In essence, to the extent that we see our friend's opposition to us in Faculty as shared by all members of the Zoology Department, aimed at all members of Psychology (comparative fit), consistent with Zoology's fight for survival (normative fit), and we are motivated both to defend Psychology and to maintain the friendship (aspects of readiness), we are likely to interpret it as group-based rather than personal (for relevant evidence of the role of fit in variation between interpersonal and intergroup categorization, see Hogg and Turner, 1987; Oakes et al., 1991; Reynolds and Oakes, 1999, 2000; van Knippenberg et al., 1994; Yzerbyt et al., 1998). We may later comment to our colleagues that 'zoologists are aggressive and self-interested' (after all, we have our own group-related interests as a psychologist to defend!), even though we know that these are not qualities we would usually attribute to our friend (in fact, at the interpersonal level of categorization we might feel that we are rather more aggressive than she is). However, to perceive her as aggressive and self-interested *as a zoologist* is not, we contend, distortion. It is an appropriate, meaningful, accurate representation of the *intergroup* relationship (not the interpersonal one).

This brings us to our third point. SCT follows Tajfel in emphasizing a qualitative discontinuity between interpersonal and intergroup contexts. The difference between categorization at the interpersonal and intergroup levels, as a cognitive process, is inalienably related to an assumed difference between interpersonal and intergroup *social reality* (see Oakes, 1996; Oakes and Turner, 1990; Turner and Oakes, 1986, 1997). Life – social life, families, work, political processes, cultural activity, and so forth – proceeds through the coordinated actions of groups as well as the private or idiosyncratic acts of individuals. The irreducibility of group phenomena to the individual means that there are group-level instances of behaviour and group-level characteristics of persons to which perception must give us access if it is to do its job of representing reality.

In summary, we propose that categorization is at work in all social perception, that its operation is designed to maximize its ability to represent context-specific meaning, and that part of the meaning it is required to capture involves the distinction between interpersonal and intergroup contexts. Drawing these points together, we submit that the phenomena identified above as perceptual *distortions* are in fact evidence of categorization's effectiveness in achieving these goals.

Accentuation Effects

We would claim accentuation effects as prima facie evidence of categorization's contribution to accurate, contextually appropriate perception (see Haslam and Turner, 1992, 1995; Oakes et al., 1994, chapter 6; see also Eiser, 1996). Haslam's work has demonstrated that patterns of assimilation and contrast reflect the categorization process doing its job of representing *relations between stimuli across the context as a whole*. This job, we have argued, is essential for contextually accurate perception. To elaborate, assume that you think of yourself as a moderate environmentalist and you meet, at a party, a member of a group which advocates the exclusive use of solar power, an end to all mining, and extremely punitive environmental levies on polluting industries. Is this person similar to you or different from you? Do you agree with them or argue against them? Scenario 1: this is a Greenpeace party and the vast majority of guests are moderates like yourself, who pretty much feel that paying one's Greenpeace dues is doing what one should for the environment. In this context the other person stands out as an 'extremist' and will likely be contrasted from you, defined as 'outgroup', dissimilar, and your sense of fellowship with other Greenpeace members will be enhanced by this extremist's presence. Scenario Two: the gathering is a Liberal (i.e., Conservative) Party policy launch. Also present is the Environment Minister who has just approved uranium mining in a National Park, with many of his advisers in tow. In this instance you are far more likely to assimilate the 'extremist', find common ground, perceive him as 'ingroup' and similar to you (see Haslam and Turner, 1992; see also David and Turner 1999). Neither of you has changed their actual position, but the *meaning* of those views has changed across the two contexts.

Both of these scenarios can be contrasted with a context in which you and your new acquaintance meet as individuals, no-one else present, and each express your views. What the 'accentuation-as-distortion' view is claiming is that this individualized, interpersonal assessment of your views is 'accurate', and whatever you perceive to be the 'distance' between your positions in this context is the correct one. If you disagree and dislike each other in this context, then that's the way it is and anything else is 'accentuated' and false. Our view is that (a) following SCT, judgements in an interpersonal context are as much an outcome of categorization, and therefore 'accentuated', as group-related judgements are (see Reynolds, 1996; Reynolds and Oakes, 1999), and (b) whether a given 'distance' is similarity or difference is a matter of context-dependent categorical judgement (Turner and Oakes, 1989) – you really are more similar to the 'extremist', in terms of contextually relevant goals and values, at the Liberal launch than at the Greenpeace party. The 'accentuation' effects of categorization allow us to experience given relationships as similarity or difference, agreement or disagreement, identity or differentiation, according to context. If categorization did not work in this way social relations would be impossibly static and constrained. In fact, we are able to define people who were enemies in one context as allies in another, without change in either of our positions. This is not distortion. It is social perception responsive to the dynamics of social reality.

But what about the outgroup homogeneity (OGH) effect mentioned above? Recall that this apparently indicated an asymmetrical, ignorance-based, *context-independent* tendency to homogenize judgements of outgroups whilst maintaining interpersonal differentiation within ingroups. Work by Bernd Simon and colleagues (e.g., Simon 1992, 1993; Simon and Brown, 1987) and by self-categorization researchers (e.g., Haslam et al., 1995; Haslam et al., 1996; Oakes et al., 1995) has now produced extensive evidence inconsistent with a generalized OGH 'effect'. This work demonstrates that perceived group homogeneity – both ingroup and outgroup – is *always* related to context (Haslam and Oakes, 1995; Simon, 1995). It is a predictable outcome of the categorization process as driven by the comparative, normative, and motivational principles specified in SCT and social identity theory (see Haslam et al., 1996; Oakes et al., 1994, and Simon, 1992 for detailed discussion). Where a salient intergroup relationship defines the comparative context, both ingroups and outgroups are perceived as homogeneous. The apparent OGH 'effect' occurs when ingroup judgements are in fact made in an interpersonal context (for example, where Australians are simply asked to consider 'Australians' which produces interpersonal differentiation within the group) while outgroup judgements are, by definition, always intergroup (Australians consider 'Americans' which produces comparison between the national groups, intergroup differentiation, intragroup homogeneity). Again, the view of accentuation effects as distortions of a sovereign individuated, interpersonal social reality can be challenged – homogenization of both ingroups and outgroups occurs in a predictable manner which indicates that social perception is sensitive to the comparative and normative realities of the social context, and individuals' goals within that context.

Category-Based Construal

We turn now to the effects of category content on the construal of stimulus information. As with accentuation, the characterization of construal effects as bias appears to require some unconstrued form of social perception as an accurate standard against which the outcomes of ingroup–outgroup categorization can be defined as 'biased'. Again, this sets up a false distinction between categorized and uncategorized perceptual experience. It also denies the role and indeed the rights of the social perceiver him or herself, asserting that the perspective of the researcher defines *psychological* validity – where perceivers make judgements with which the experimenter disagrees, it is assumed that they reflect bias and distortion (see Mackie, 1973; Oakes and Reynolds, 1997; Turner and Oakes, 1997).

To elaborate, let's look back at the Duncan (1976) study outlined earlier. We need to ask who has the right to define the 'correct' interpretation of the explicitly *ambiguous* shove his participants witnessed. The distortion theorists appear to claim that it is the experimenter and the social-scientific community, people who are not placed in any sort of relationship with the stimulus individuals, and who evidently reject the stereotype of Blacks as violent. The White participants in the study, on the other hand, were asked to engage with and make sense of the scenario. Their potentially differing relationships to the White and to the Black protagonists – respectively, intragroup and intergroup (especially when the victim was White) – evidently did affect their own salient identity and therefore the motives, values, and background theories that they brought to bear in interpreting events. At least some of the White participants experienced the encounter as one involving 'a Black person and a White person' (rather than two individuals or two students, or whatever) and the meaning that those categories had for them included an expectation of conflict and hostility. The Black actor's 'ambiguous shove' was interpreted with reference to that expectation, that 'theory' about what the Black/White distinction is all about, while the same action from a White actor was interpreted with reference to different expectations and theories. Note that in this interpretation *both* judgements, of the Black and the White protagonist, require categorization – the conclusion that the White actor was 'fooling around' was a product of participants defining him as 'ingroup', similar to themselves, just as the perception of the Black actor as 'violent' followed from his categorization as 'outgroup' and different (see Reynolds and Oakes, 1999). We would, of course, expect a rather different pattern of attributions if the study was conducted with Black participants (see Hunter et al., 1991).

So, what are we really doing when we reject, as bias and distortion, the differences in interpretation observed in Duncan's study? There is no independent evidence that categorization was operating in the judgements of Black actors but not in those of White actors. There is, therefore, no evidence that categorization was distinctively responsible for the impressions defined as 'biased' (the Black shove was violent) but not the ones treated as uncontroversial (the White shove was 'playing around'). It seems, then, that we are making value judgements about the *end products* of the categorization process rather than presenting evidence of the nature of the process itself. In essence, the 'bias' interpretation expresses an objection to the existence of the racial distinction and the associated values of those on (at least) one side of it. We want to say that race shouldn't matter, and that Blacks should certainly not be stereotyped as violent. But might we not (depending on relevant political values) be prone to exactly the same pattern of judgements if we were to interpret an 'ambiguous shove' perpetrated by a Serb on an ethnic Albanian, versus two Albanians shoving each other? Or (if the Faculty row became really heated) a zoologist shoving a psychologist versus the psychologist doing the shoving? The point is that we have group identities, and those identities come with values, goals, and expectations which play a crucial role in mediating social perception such that we understand and can function in reality from the perspective of (and in defence of) those values. The way in which values mediate social perception is most definitely a social-psychological issue, but the validity of those values and associated acts is a matter of *politics*, not psychology.

We have discussed these issues at length in the context of the question of stereotype accuracy (Oakes et al., 1994; Oakes and Reynolds, 1997) and of the general validity of social perception (Turner and Oakes, 1997). Our aim is not to defend political or social *relativism*, the idea that all views and values are of equal validity – this is the fatal stumbling block for some social-constructionist analyses (e.g., Wetherell and Potter, 1992) with which we disagree in fundamental ways. While social constructionism does usefully emphasize the fact that perceivers 'take an active role in defining situations rather than responding automatically to stimuli', it makes the mistake of suggesting that these constructions are 'autistic products, divorced from "reality"' (Mackie, 1973: 441). In fact, as Mackie insists, 'the situation is "out there" even if its meaning is not' (1973: 441; see also Augoustinos and Walker, 1998). From a similarly 'realist' perspective, our point is that we must recognize the inherent, inescapable *relativity* of meaning in human social perception. The categorization process is heavily implicated in this, as it produces the variable, context-dependent identities from which perceptual relativity flows. However, it cannot, in our view, be indicted as producing bias and distortion through this process. If it does so, then all human perception, all human life, is bias because we are not computers or omniscient, all-seeing beings and there is no neutral, disinterested thought – 'perception and thought … are actively involved in representing and understanding the world *from the point of view of the participating perceiver*' (Turner and Oakes, 1997: 367, emphasis added). As active constituents in the political ebb and flow of social life, we have every right to reject and protest 'the point of view of the participating perceiver' in Duncan's study, to take all legitimate steps available to eliminate the values his findings expose. But to condemn categorization as the culprit in this case is to misconstrue the nature of human psychology, with potentially tragic consequences (see below).

Ingroup Favouritism

Finally, we return to ingroup favouritism in the minimal group paradigm. We shall discuss this very briefly here as the explanation of intergroup discrimination is also dealt with in this volume by Reynolds and Turner. Tajfel (1972; see Tajfel and Turner, 1979) argued that it was the need to create meaning in an otherwise empty situation, particularly meaning for the self – identity – that led participants to act in terms of the minimal categories. Insofar as their identities did become engaged with the minimal groups (and this did not always happen; Turner, 1975) ingroup favouritism could be seen as positive self-evaluation. This interpretation catalyzed the development of social identity theory, Tajfel and Turner's more general analysis of intergroup relations, within which the complex social-psychological and social-structural mediators of ingroup favouritism are detailed.

It is a basic tenet of experimental social psychology that one should never generalize directly from experiments to reality. Experimental findings need to be understood through the theory which places them in the context of other relevant work (Turner, 1981). No reading of social identity theory could lead one to the conclusion that categorization in itself provokes intergroup discrimination – that particular unwise generalization from experimental data has retarded our understanding of prejudice for long enough and should be consigned forthwith to the dustbin of history (Turner, 1999a).

What categorization can do, as elaborated in self-categorization theory, is define identity, including group-based identity. What that identity then implies, the attitudes and behaviour it encourages, will emerge through the interaction of a range of factors (see Ellemers, 1993; Ellemers et al., 1999), and intergroup discrimination is only one of many possibilities. Indeed, exactly the same process of categorical self-definition can, under appropriate conditions, reduce intergroup hostility (e.g., Brewer and Miller, 1984; Gaertner et al., 1989; Hewstone and Brown, 1986) and produce cooperation (De Cremer and Van Vugt, 1999; Morrison, 1997), a sense of justice and fairness (Tyler and Dawes, 1993) and the potential for extreme heroism and self-sacrifice. How, then, can categorization, per se, be to blame for intergroup discrimination?

The Summing Up

The task facing you, the jury, is to decide whether we are prejudiced *because* we categorize, and therefore whether or not categorization should be found guilty on the charges of conspiracy to pervert the course of tolerance and harmony and inciting intergroup hatred. Arguments for both the prosecution and defence have been presented and must be evaluated on their merits. However, in summing up for the defence we wish to make some final comments on the consequences of the verdict, because the implications for the elimination of racism and bigotry are very serious.

In a scholarly consideration of stereotype accuracy in 1973, sociologist Marlene Mackie suggested that the 'moral preferences' of social scientists had distorted their approach to the issue. She argued that commitment to an egalitarian ideology, with which any evidence of real differences between minority groups would be inconsistent, worked to 'discourage a *test* of ethnic stereotype accuracy' (1973: 432), and to encourage strongly worded statements about the patent inaccuracy of such beliefs. At the same time, however, social science was delighted to report and even promulgate extremely negative 'stereotypes' of groups such as mental hospital administrators and bureaucrats, groups towards which its practitioners did not 'feel protective' (1973: 443). Apparently, group-based generalizations constructed by sociologists were acceptable, but 'folk categories [were] defective constructs' (1973: 439). This selective rejection of the end products of categorization was, Mackie argued, severely retarding scientific analysis of the process, and betrayed a rather paternalistic attitude towards the 'primitive' thought processes of 'the people' in contrast to the alleged sophistication of scientists (see 1973: 439).

In our view, this problem still besets the social psychology of prejudice and racism. There seems to be an almost insuperable reluctance to recognize intergroup conflict as an intended outcome of human agency. Categorization has become the favoured psychological scapegoat for beliefs and behaviours we do not want to acknowledge. Categorization itself has an honourable purpose – conserving cognitive capacity – but intergroup conflict emerges as an unfortunate side-effect of the 'distortions' of perception and motivation that categorization produces. A recent revision of this approach suggests that prejudice and discrimination do sometimes happen 'by design' rather than unintentionally – powerful people (but not the powerless; cf., Reynolds et al., in press) can deliberately use categorization and negative stereotypes to rationalize the inequality from which they profit (Operario and Fiske, 1998). Again, then, those towards whom we do not 'feel protective' are required to face the music, to take responsibility for their values and actions, but the masses are excused 'because their thoughtways are primitive' and they are 'mistaken in their evaluation of others' (Mackie, 1973: 439). Believing this, we attempt to disabuse them. We try to change the parameters and modus operandi of their categorization processes (e.g., Hewstone and Brown, 1986; Gaertner et al., 1989). We try to correct their psychological mistakes by exposing them to the 'truth' through carefully controlled intergroup contact and a bombardment of carefully constructed 'information' (e.g., Donovan and Leivers, 1993) and 'facts' (ATSIC, 1998).

We seriously question the efficacy of these tactics because we reject the characterization of social thought that informs them. People who express beliefs with which we disagree are not, by definition, 'mistaken', the victims of relatively substandard information processing. Indeed, they are likely to be just as committed to the validity of their views as we are (Oakes and Reynolds, 1997). Why, then, should we expect our 'information' to change their minds while we remain so implacably immune to the persuasive power of theirs? Moreover, as Duckitt eloquently insists in this volume, psychological interventions will be ineffective, even dangerous, in social contexts where the reality of group differences and inequalities contradict the rhetoric of homogeneity and fairness on a daily basis (see also Haslam et al., 1999; Reicher, 1986).

The real answer to racism is, of course, political action aimed at the creation of 'societies characterized by social stability and social justice' (Duckitt, Chapter 15). There can be no guarantee that the political process will produce such humanitarian outcomes, but it at least has the potential to do so (see Haslam, in press; Oakes et al., 1994). Meanwhile, the responsibility of social psychology is to ensure that it does not subvert or impede the political process with bad theory (Haslam, 2001), and that it contributes positively through relevant investigation and analysis. In our view, holding categorization responsible for prejudice is bad theory and the interventions that theory suggests will not aid the political process. On the other hand, social psychology has contributed much to our understanding of collective mobilization and action, social influence and political persuasion, and the workings of power. If we harness these skills in the service of our resistance to racism, we might get somewhere.

In conclusion, we submit that this has been something of a show trial. The defendant – categorization – has been hauled before the court as a result of ideological pressures to identify a psychological culprit, a mechanism through which the mind might create abhorrent ideas and values without really meaning to. A guilty verdict might be comforting in the short term, allowing us to hold on to our 'moral sense of humanity's essential oneness' (Mackie, 1973: 444) and to continue wearing our rose coloured spectacles. But wrongful conviction always means the same thing – the real culprit is still out there threatening the community. We ask, therefore, that categorization be found not guilty on all counts, and that we turn our attention to hunting down the real culprits – social inequality, exploitation, and the power to influence enjoyed by those who profit from the denial of universal human dignity.

12 Realistic Intergroup Conflict: Prejudice, Power, and Protest

Michael J. Platow and John A. Hunter

In this chapter, we will review an approach to the social psychological study of prejudice and discrimination that has, at its roots, a basis in real, material conflicts of interest between various societal groups. This realistic intergroup conflict approach (Campbell, 1965) has, as its starting point, the assumption of the reality of group life and a variety of forms of material competition between groups for needed or desired resources (Sherif, 1966). In this manner, the approach differs from some other explanations outlined in this book by adopting a non-reductionistic approach to prejudice. Prejudice, in the current view, is neither an outcome of intrapsychic properties (e.g., Baumeister et al., 1996; Solomon et al., 1991) or differences in personality between individuals (e.g., Altemeyer, 1998), nor is it an outcome of relations between individuals *as individuals* (i.e., interpersonal relationships; e.g., Rabbie et al., 1989). It is, instead, an approach that considers the ongoing dynamics between groups as wholes, or between individuals *as group members* in their quests to satisfy group-based needs and desires. In this manner, the social-psychological analysis of realistic intergroup conflict dovetails with analyses in other social sciences (Haralambos, 1980; Levine and Campbell, 1972; McGarry and O'Leary, 1995).

Of course, as with any of the ideas presented in the individual chapters of this book, we are under no illusions that the realistic intergroup conflict analysis of prejudice and discrimination represents the final and complete explanation (see also Tajfel, 1982a). At the same time, however, we will endeavour to take a stand that will at times be extreme, and push our ideas for the sake of pedagogical and theoretical clarity.

In organizing this chapter, we will begin with a relatively detailed description of one of the earliest, and certainly the most famous, social-psychological studies of realistic intergroup conflict (Sherif et al., 1961). This research, which comprises a series of three field experiments, demonstrates in a rather simple and straightforward manner many of the concepts that are central to realistic intergroup conflict analysis of prejudice and discrimination. We will also consider some replications of this field research, detailed laboratory research, as well as criticisms of this approach that highlight boundary conditions of its assumptions. We will conclude the chapter with an analysis of distributive and procedural fairness on the one hand, and social protest on the other. In doing so, we will consider how the application of fairness rules both can and *can not* lead to a reduction in intergroup conflict, and how a reduction in intergroup conflict in and of itself may not always be a desired outcome.

Prejudice

The most well-known and influential social-psychological proponent of the realistic-intergroup conflict perspective on prejudice and discrimination is Muzafer Sherif. Highly critical of other theories and methods used to investigate intergroup relations, Sherif pointed out that psychology had become 'myopic' in its attempts to study human social behaviour (Sherif, 1966: 8). To recognize oneself as a social category member and to behave in accordance with this membership, he argued, had distinct psychological consequences. For Sherif, it was a mistake to extrapolate psychological processes from the level of the individual to the level of the group (cf., Asch, 1952; Lewin, 1952; Mead, 1934). Sherif argued that groups have their own reality, and that this reality is determined, in part, from material conditions, people's identification with the group, roles within the group, reciprocal interactions with other group members, and a shared set of norms and beliefs that guide group-based attitudes and behaviours.

Sherif and his colleagues acknowledged that many of these factors would affect and, in turn, be affected by the relations between groups (e.g., Sherif, 1966; Sherif et al., 1961; Sherif and Sherif, 1953). The primary determinant, however, of intergroup attitudes and behaviours was the material interests of the groups involved. Where the interests of two groups coincided, it was predicted that the relations between the groups would be relatively amicable and harmonious. Where the interests of two groups conflicted, it was predicted that relations between the groups would be relatively antagonistic and hostile. In this manner, intergroup attitudes, perceptions and images are the result of 'particular relationships between groups, not their original cause' (Sherif, 1966: 25; see also Oakes et al., 1994; Oakes, Haslam, and Reynolds, 1999). This was demonstrated in the now classic 'Boys' Camp' field experiments.

Conflict and Cooperation at Boys' Camps: Field Experiments

In the late 1940s and early 1950s, Sherif led a group of American social psychologists in conducting three field experiments with groups of previously unacquainted 11- and 12-year-old boys (Sherif et al., 1961; Sherif and Sherif, 1953; Sherif et al., 1955). The settings were ostensible summer camps. Although their parents knew about the experiments, the boys themselves did not. In this research, Sherif and his associates wanted to examine the role of intragroup and intergroup relations on a variety of group processes including the development and elimination of stereotypes, prejudice, and discrimination. They wanted to examine these processes in the absence of possible alternative explanations such as personality, pre-existing differences between the boys, and previous exposure to prejudice. Toward this end, the researchers recruited boys who were, by all accounts in that historical time and location, normal. A battery of psychological tests showed no signs of psychological abnormality (e.g., none were judged to be neurotic, excessively frustrated, or failing at school). And the boys were all from White, middle-class families and, hence, had not been subject to many of the depravations, frustrations, and prejudices that accompany impoverished and minority groups in the US (and elsewhere, of course). Moreover, the boys were from the same geographical region and were matched for physical characteristics, abilities, and pubescence, thus reducing pre-existing differences between the boys.

In fulfilling these criteria, potential participants were observed as they interacted with peers in school rooms, playgrounds, and gym classes. The school reports, medical records, and psychological characteristics of likely candidates were also assessed. Interviews were then held with parents, teachers, and other school officials. Those deemed suitable finally had to pass a doctor's medical examination.

The actual procedures of the three field experiments differed from each other in important ways, however, they did share the basic three-part structure of (1) intragroup interaction, (2) intergroup competitive interaction, and (3) intergroup noncompetitive interaction. These three stages equate to ingroup formation, the development of intergroup prejudice and discrimination, and the reduction of intergroup prejudice and discrimination. In reviewing the three field experiments, we will speak of them as a single unit because the procedures and results share many common features.

Stage 1 – Intragroup Interaction   In the first stage of the research, the previously unacquainted boys were brought together into small groups. In the first two studies, these groups were specifically created so that a priori spontaneous friendships between boys that may have developed were broken by placing the friends into separate groups. In one of the studies, the boys did not even know another group existed until a later stage.

As well as undertaking normal camp activities, such as hiking, swimming, and canoeing, participants were (surreptitiously) presented with a series of tasks that could not be completed without the help of the other members of the group. These tasks included tent pitching, carrying canoes, cooking from bulk ingredients, and building rope bridges. As these tasks and activities were undertaken, clear signs of group formation appeared. Each group developed its own particular flags, emblems, jargon, particular ways of undertaking tasks, jokes, and favourite swimming holes. Special names were chosen for their groups, such as the 'Bull Dogs' and 'Red Devils'. These names and other symbols identifying their groups were stencilled onto caps and tee-shirts. Norms regulating behaviours such as being tough, helping other ingroup members, swimming nude, and cursing emerged. Clear status hierarchies, with the emergence of leaders and followers, also developed. One of the important consequences of this process was that the friendship choices that crossed group boundaries in the first two studies prior to group formation reversed after ingroup interaction, so that the boys were now choosing as their friends the members of their ingroup.

Stage 2 – Intergroup Competitive Interaction During this second stage of the experiments, the researchers introduced a series of competitive games between the two groups of boys. There was nothing particularly unordinary about these. The groups competed in baseball games, tug-of-war, and skit competitions. Recall that in two of the experiments, the boys already knew of the other group against whom they would compete. However, for the third experiment, the existence of the other group was revealed only at this stage. Here, an important finding for the realistic conflict approach to intergroup relations emerged. Even before the competitions began, merely hearing of the presence of another group produced ingroup-favouring attitudes in the form of expressed concerns over their material resources. 'They better not be in our swimming hole' said one boy (Sherif et al., 1961: 94). This is an important observation, which we will discuss more fully below; but for now, it is important to observe that intergroup hostilities began emerging prior to intergroup competition.

Laid on top of what may be a typical sporting spirit for competitive games were the material rewards offered to boys of the winning team. Each boy of the winning team would receive a pocketknife, a highly valued commodity. In addition, the team as a whole would be awarded a trophy. Losers, however, would receive nothing. In this manner, the experimenters established a context of intergroup competition for limited and valued resources. As such, the groups moved from a situation in which they were relatively independent of each other to one in which their own material outcomes were determined, in part, by the behaviours and actions of the other group.

The intergroup competitions had strong effects on the expressed attitudes and behaviours of the boys. Friendship choices were nearly purely within boys' own groups; and when asked 'to help the administration find out what they thought of their new acquaintances and how they were enjoying camp' (Sherif et al., 1961: 136), the boys rated their own group as brave, tough, and friendly but the other as sneaky, stinkers, and smart alecks. Judgements of their own and the other group's performance on different tasks were also ingroup favouring. For example, after a competition to collect beans scattered on the ground, the boys were shown jars of beans through opaque medium and asked to estimate the number each group collected. Despite being shown the same number of beans each time, the boys judged their own group's performance to be better than the other's by overestimating the number of beans their own group collected relative to the other. Finally, these attitudes and differential judgements manifested themselves in overt behaviours, such as not speaking to outgroup members and raiding the outgroup's cabin. Unquestionably, the intergroup competition lead to prejudiced attitudes and discriminatory behaviours. In Sherif's words, the boys would appear 'wicked, disturbed, and vicious' (1966: 85) to an observer naive to the complex and extensive selection procedure.

Stage 3 – Intergroup Non-Competitive Interaction   In the final stage of the experiments, the researchers brought the two groups of boys together under conditions of non-competition. The goal here was to consider the conditions under which the prejudiced attitudes and discriminatory behaviours could be eliminated. One strategy was to appeal to moral values by having a religious minister preach to each group of boys the importance of tolerance, forgiveness, and cooperation. Although responding well to the religious appeal, as soon as the boys left, they resumed their intergroup hostilities. Another strategy was to bring the two groups of boys together for mutually pleasurable experiences, including watching a movie, lighting firecrackers, and sharing a meal. Such a strategy of equal contact is not unreasonable. In situations outside of experimental contexts, such as public classrooms, policy makers often strive to reduce ethnic and racial prejudices by bringing children from different backgrounds together for some mutually pleasurable experiences. The view is that by bringing the groups together, the individuals can obtain accurate and favourable information, and see that the members of the other group are just people like themselves in a situation where everyone is in a positive mood and is not experiencing frustrations or lack of desired outcomes. However, Sherif's camp studies taught us an important lesson nearly half a century ago: this strategy is not likely to work. When the boys from the two groups came into contact, they heckled each other and, during their meal, threw more than insults; they threw food too!

A feature that reduced the intergroup prejudices was one that the experimenters instituted in their third study. Here, the experimenters created a situation where the two groups had to work together to achieve a mutually desired outcome. That is, rather than creating a situation of intergroup competition for resources that only one group could obtain, the experimenters created a situation of intergroup cooperation for resources that could only be obtained by both groups *or* neither group.

For example, after a long day's outing the experimenters arranged for the food truck to (apparently) breakdown. The boys were hungry and so obviously wanted the food. To do this they first had to get the truck started. This, the boys decided, would be done by having a tug-of-war with the truck (the tug-of-war rope had been left in plain sight of both groups). Success would of course have been impossible without the cooperation of everyone pulling on the rope. After a few attempts the truck (which was in perfect working order) sprang into life. Several instances of friendly interactions between boys from the two groups ensued in the immediate wake of this episode. The intergroup antagonism did not, however, disappear immediately. It was only after a series of cooperative encounters for *superordinate goal* – such as mending the water supply, cooking, exchanging camping equipment – that the widespread nature of the intergroup hostility truly diminished.

By the end of this cooperative phase, and hence the experiment, many of the boys saw the outgroup members in a different light. Name calling and physical confrontations disappeared. Once antagonistic groups freely intermingled during meals, play, and around the campfire. These observations were confirmed quantitatively through the assessment of friendship choices (which now tended to cross group barriers), sociometric indices (which revealed that leaders who refused to support intergroup cooperation became less influential), and the endorsement of outgroup stereotypes (which became more positive). The most potent illustration of the extent to which intergroup attitudes had become positive was evinced on the trip home after the camp had been completed. Here, groups of boys who had at one time either avoided or abused one another (i.e., verbally and physically), chose not only to share the same bus on the long trip home, but also some of the prizes they had won during the experiment.

Implications and Replications

The implications of the results of these boys' camp studies are very clear and straight forward. Intergroup competition for limited and valued resources leads to negative outgroup attitudes and positive ingroup attitudes. These prejudices are eliminated by the introduction of sustained intergroup cooperation for a superordinate goal. But does intergroup competition inevitably lead to hostilities? And is intergroup cooperation the only way to reduce them? There have been at least three other studies reported in which this basic field experiment was replicated to try to answer these questions.

The first replication was done by Diab (1970) in Lebanon. In this study, Diab maintained many of the procedures that Sherif and his colleagues used originally: The 11-year-old boys were tested for the absence of psychological disorders, they were all strangers to each other, their home life was relatively normal. In this instance, however, the hostilities between the two groups became so strong that after intergroup competition some boys were physically stabbed with knives by other boys, and the police had to remove them from the camp (see Rabbie, 1982). Diab never got the opportunity to complete the third phase to test the intergroup cooperation hypothesis, but intergroup competition clearly lead to prejudiced attitudes and hostile intergroup behaviour.

In a second replication, Ageev (cited in Andreeva, 1984) obtained further support for Sherif's main findings in the former Soviet Union. In this field experiment, implemented in the context of a Pioneer youth camp, competitive sporting activities heightened the display of ingroup favouring attitudes. When the structure of intergroup relations was changed so that the competing groups then had to cooperate on agricultural activities, there was a substantial decrease in ingroup-favouring attitudes.

A final replication was done by Tyerman and Spencer (1983) in the United Kingdom. These researchers intentionally varied the basic paradigm, however, to consider the parameters of the effects. In this case, the boys in the competing groups were all Boy Scouts who had a long history of intergroup competitions in the context of a variety of other scouting activities. Also, there was no direct contact between the boys during the competitive stage, nor were the rewards as tangible as those in Sherif's studies (cf., Jackson, 1993). In this study, although 'fairly mild stereotypes' were reported (Tyerman and Spencer, 1983: 528), the intergroup competitions did *not* create negative outgroup attitudes; none of the hostile effects of intergroup competition observed by Sherif et al. and Diab were observed. Moreover, these researchers, unlike Sherif and his associates, were able to increase intergroup cooperation by means of sermons emphasizing common group membership. Overall, this study is extremely important, if only to tell us that competition between groups of any sort will not necessarily lead to the production of prejudice and discrimination. Here, the members of the competing groups were also members of a superordinate group of Boy Scouts. This, in itself, may have been sufficient to stifle the development of prejudiced attitudes (e.g., Gaertner et al., 1993; Mummendey and Wenzel, 1999). On top of this, however, there was a norm among the Scouts for fair play, kindness, and friendliness. Thus, in the context of these very strong norms as well as the shared superordinate group membership, it should come as no surprise that the negative prejudices did not arise following intergroup competition.

Laboratory Replications

Following the large-scale field experiments of Sherif and his associates, social psychologists wanted to gain greater confidence in many of the processes revealed in these original experiments. Like all field studies, those of Sherif et al. had the very positive feature of providing rich information in naturalistic situations. However, these rich settings have the drawback of not allowing for finer grained analyses of psychological processes. For this reason, social psychologists began studying realistic intergroup conflict in laboratory situations.

In one research programme, carried out over several years, and conducted under the auspices of a management training scheme, over 1,000 executives were brought into the laboratory for a series of group-based tasks (Blake and Mouton, 1961, 1962; see Blake and Mouton, 1986 for an extensive review). As in the Boys' Camp studies, the first phase of this research was an ingroup formation phase. After this phase, intergroup competition was introduced. In this case, each group was presented with a problem-solving task, much of the type that managers and administrators might encounter in their normal positions. The groups were told that the quality of the final decision would be determined in some manner by the experimenters, and that there would be, indeed, a group whose decision was better than the other's, and hence, one group would be a winner and the other a loser. In this manner, Blake and Mouton created a situation of intergroup competition.

Prior to determining the outcome of the competition, group members were asked to judge their own decision and the decision of the other group. As expected, groups reliably judged their own product more favourably than their competitor's product. Essentially, under this realistic intergroup conflict, the groups were saying 'The fruits of our labour are of a higher standard than the fruits of theirs.' Moreover, independent judges brought in to evaluate the reports who were previously acknowledged to be fair and competent were now seen to be unfair and incompetent by the losing group. In those circumstances where ingroup members were given the opportunity to discuss their respective solutions with members of the outgroup, there was a tendency to attack and undermine rather than to exchange objective information. Indeed, sometimes the intergroup hostility was so pronounced that particular experiments had to be stopped (like Diab's, 1970 field experiment). Similarly, when ingroup representatives were involved in negotiations with the outgroup, outgroup capitulation led to the ingroup representative being treated like a hero. When, however, the ingroup representative capitulated to the outgroup, he was then treated like a traitor and was shunned.

Questioning the Processes

But is the intergroup competition necessary? Recall that the boys in the Boys' Camp studies began showing signs of ingroup favouritism even before competition occurred. This lead Ferguson and Kelley (1964) to replicate some features of Blake and Mouton's earlier work, but this time with the complete absence of intergroup competition. In this new experiment, groups were simply asked to work independently, but in sight of each other, to complete some decision-making tasks. When asked to evaluate their own decisions and the decisions of other groups, again there was an ingroup favouritism in the ratings. This basic pattern of ingroup favouritism even in a no-competition condition was replicated by Rabbie and Wilkens (1971) with a sample of Dutch teenagers.

Other authors (e.g., Dion, 1979; Fisher, 1990) have also noted the presence of a variety of factors operating in conjunction with one another, making it almost impossible to ascertain what actually causes the effects. This view has been convincingly developed by Rabbie (1982), who identified a number of variables present in the Boys' Camp studies and its field and laboratory replications, including interdependence of fate, categorization, actual or anticipated intragroup interaction, actual or anticipated intergroup interaction, actual or anticipated loss during competitive interactions, and the experience of aversive intergroup interactions. Any of these variables, either alone or in combination with others, could easily have accounted for the observed patterns of prejudice. Indeed, laboratory data indicate that as interdependence of fate (e.g., Rabbie et al.,1989, cf., Turner and Bourhis, 1996), categorization (e.g., Tajfel et al., 1971), actual or anticipated intragroup interaction (e.g., Rabbie and de Brey, 1971), actual or anticipated intergroup interaction (e.g., Kahn and Ryen, 1972), actual or anticipated loss during competitive interactions (e.g., Branscombe and Wann, 1994), and the experience of aversive intergroup interactions (e.g., Konecni, 1979) may all fuel the display of various forms of intergroup discrimination.

The influence of these variables on intergroup hostility, of course, cannot be ignored. However, over and above such effects, there remains a large body of experimental evidence demonstrating that groups engaged in objective competition for limited and valued resources display higher levels of intergroup discrimination than those engaged in cooperation or are independent of one another (e.g., Bettencourt et al., 1992; Johnson et al., 1984; Judd and Park,

1988; Rabbie et al., 1974; Ryen and Kahn, 1975; Taylor and Moriarty, 1987; Wilder and Shapiro, 1989; Worchel et al., 1977). These findings have been confirmed in a series of recent field and survey studies which show that a realistic conflict of interests between groups is an important predictor of prejudiced intergroup attitudes amongst factory workers (Brown et al., 1986; Brown and Williams, 1984), religious groups (Strutch and Schwartz, 1989), racial groups (Bobo, 1983; Duckitt and Mphuthing, 1998), political groups (Kelly, 1988), immigrant groups (Stephan et al., 1998), and minority groups (Bobo and Hutchings, 1996).

Intergroup Behaviour and Mixed-Motive Interdependence

Realistic intergroup conflict analyses of prejudice are premised on the assumption that there exists a fundamental material conflict between groups over one or more valued resources. Because of this, a material, outcome-based analysis of social contexts becomes particularly useful in understanding intergroup conflict. Social interdependence theory (Kelley and Thibaut, 1978; Rusbult and van Lange, 1996; cf., Colman, 1982) is one framework that outlines, in a formal manner, material features of social contexts. It does this by considering the outcomes that accrue to groups (and individuals) as a function of the behaviours in which they engage. In this framework, outcomes can be anything that individuals and groups value. Often, these are relatively concrete things such as goods, services, and money, but they can also be relatively symbolic things such as status, information, and love (Foa and Foa, 1980).

As the name of social interdependence theory implies, outcome-based analyses allow us to study the nature of *interdependence* between groups. Two or more groups are interdependent when the decisions and behaviours of each affect the nature and magnitude of the outcomes received by themselves *and* the other groups (Beggan et al., 1991; Morrison, 1999). For example, in the Boys' Camp studies, when the boys were playing tug-of-war, they were in an interdependent situation because the harder one group pulled, the more the other group had to pull or the more they lost. Similarly, the groups of boys were interdependent in the overall series of competitions because ultimately one team would do better than the other, and only one team would obtain the final outcomes (i.e., the pocket knives and trophy). These competitive situations are characterized by negative interdependence. Of course, the boys were also interdependent when they cooperated for a superordinate goal. In this latter case, the positive outcomes (e.g., food from the food truck) accrued to both groups simultaneously (if they cooperated) or to neither group (if at least one group failed to cooperate). These cooperative situations are characterized by positive interdependence.

By specifically crafting social situations using the tools of social interdependence theory, social psychologists have been able to create a variety of laboratory situations in which they varied the nature of the positive and negative interdependence between groups to observe their subsequent behaviours. For example, Ruscher et al. (1991) created a negatively interdependent intergroup situation in the laboratory. By doing this, they observed that group members stereotyped outgroup members more than when the groups were negatively interdependent than independent (but see Reynolds and Oakes, 2000).

One of the most commonly studied social interdependence situations is one that is neither purely negatively interdependent nor purely positively interdependent. It is a situation that is referred to as mixed-motive in nature, because groups can pursue cooperative behaviour *or* competitive behaviour. In this case, groups can choose the path they want to pursue. An example of this type of situation is displayed in Figure 12.1. This figure, referred to generally as an outcome matrix, represents a hypothetical situation in which there are two groups, each of which can pursue one of two behaviours. In this outcome matrix, the numbers in each of the boxes (called cells) represent outcomes of

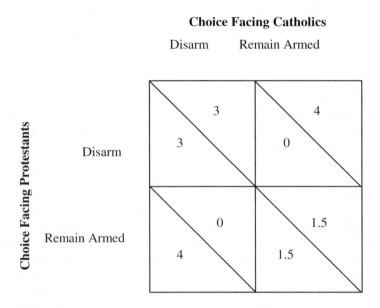

Choice Facing Catholics

Disarm   Remain Armed

Figure 12.1 An example of a mixed-motive outcome matrix used to study intergroup cooperation and competition.

Note The labels are for illustrative purposes only. Values in each cell that are below the diagonal line represent outcomes for Protestants and values above the diagonal represent outcomes for Catholics.

some sort, with bigger numbers meaning better things. For the sake of example, we have represented the two groups as Protestants and Catholics in Northern Ireland. These *are* real groups engaged in real conflict over material outcomes, and strongly negative intergroup attitudes and behaviours occur (Hunter et al., 1991; Hunter et al., 1996). In the figure, we have depicted a situation where the paramilitary of each group has the choice of remaining armed and continuing the conflict or disarming. Although the absolute value of the numbers that we placed in the figure may not match exactly the real life values, their ordinal values certainly capture some of the important material features of the conflict.

So, what would happen in this example if the Protestants remained armed but the Catholics disarmed? The matrix cell that represents the intersection of these joint decisions shows clearly that the outcomes to the Protestants would be very high (+4), but the outcomes to the Catholics would be low (0). This is because the Protestants will have the strong upper hand over the Catholics. In essence, the the Protestants would be engaging in a competitive behaviour while the Catholics would be engaging in a cooperative behaviour. Notice, however, that in this example the opposite pattern occurs if the Protestants disarm (engage in cooperation) but the Catholics remain armed (engage in competition). If both groups compete and remain armed, their outcomes are low (+1.5) because they would still be at war, but at least higher than if one were dominated by the other. And if both cooperate and disarm, their outcomes are relatively high (+3) because there would now be peace, but the outcomes are not as high as the situation where one is the clear victor over the other. So, what to do? It would be nice if both sides cooperated and disarmed together so that both could get +3. But can each side trust the other to disarm? Often intergroup trust is very low (e.g., Moy and Ng, 1996). So the more conservative option is to remain in competition by remaining armed and at war; at least this way, each side will at least get +1.5 rather than 0. Alas, here is the twist. If both sides choose conflict, they both have reason for regret, because if they both cooperated and disarmed, they would have double the outcomes (+3) than if they remained at war (+1.5).

What happens when laboratory groups are presented with this type of interdependence situation? An early intergroup study using this situation was conducted by Wilson et al., (1965). Here, four male and female university students were brought into a laboratory and the experimenter randomly created two groups of two people. The students then made two different types of choices using an outcome matrix similar to that in Figure 12.1 (but with different labels to those in the example above). Firstly, the two individuals in each group made intergroup choices; secondly, each individual within each group made intragroup choices. The results were very clear. The intergroup choices were more than twice as competitive as the intragroup choices.

Rabbie et al. (1982) also conducted a series of intergroup studies using this type of outcome matrix. Like the earlier study by Wilson et al. (1965), Rabbie et al. found that groups were more competitive than individuals. However, when comparing groups of size two (as in the Wilson et al. study) to those of size three, the former displayed the most competitive behaviour. Triads' level of competition were much closer (although still higher) to those of individuals. These are important findings because they indicate that high levels of competition between groups are not necessary outcomes (see Rabbie, 1998, for a review).

Finally, Schopler and Insko and their colleagues have conducted well over 20 separate experiments testing a variety of hypotheses regarding the greater levels of competition between groups than individuals (e.g., Insko et al., 1992; Schopler and Insko, 1992, 1999; Schopler et al., 1993). Their general conclusion is that groups are motivated both by fear of exploitation from the outgroup and by greed to gain as much as possible for themselves. One of their more recent studies has shown, however, that when groups are forced to focus on their long-term gains in this mixed-motive situation, they will engage in more cooperation. This process of focusing on long-term gains, of course, remains in line with their greed explanation, one that highlights the role of material outcomes guiding intergroup relations.

Overall, the laboratory analysis of intergroup relations from a social interdependence perspective has shown that groups are very likely to pursue competitive interactions with each other even when they have the opportunity to be cooperative. Of course, it is not the case that groups will invariably be competitive, as the research by Rabbie et al. (1982) has shown. Nevertheless, even when there is not a purely negatively interdependent relationship between the groups, certain social and psychological factors lead group members to compete with other groups. Recall our discussion of the Boys' Camp study when negative outgroup attitudes were expressed even before the intergroup competition phase of the experiment began, as well as the findings of Ferguson and Kelley (1964). These type of data have lead some authors to criticize the realistic intergroup conflict approach to prejudice; we will consider some of these criticisms in the next section.

Criticisms of the Realistic Intergroup Conflict Approach to Prejudice

The conceptual advances – beyond personality (Altemeyer, 1998) and interpersonal (Rabbie et al., 1989) analyses – offered by the realistic intergroup conflict approach to prejudice, together with its strong empirical base, ensure it a central role in accounts of intergroup behaviour (Brewer and Brown, 1998; Brown, 1995; Tajfel and Turner, 1979, 1986). Nevertheless, the approach has been criticized on a variety of grounds (e.g., Billig, 1976; Taylor and Moghaddem, 1994; Turner, 1981). Of particular importance to the current review is a substantial body of evidence indicating that compatible and incompatible goal relationships are not the sole arbitrators of intergroup relations. Indeed, many studies now highlight the contribution of other social-psychological variables to both cooperative and competitive intergroup behaviour. With respect to the former, for example, a series of studies conducted by Worchel and his colleagues (Worchel et al., 1977; Worchel et al., 1978; Worchel and Norvell, 1980) have revealed that if the intergroup encounter fails to achieve the desired superordinate goal, blame is then attributed to the outgroup and intergroup hostility is consequently exacerbated. A similar point is made in research conducted by Deschamps and Brown (1983) and Brown and Wade (1987) who highlight the crucial role of group identification in reducing intergroup hostility. These studies have revealed that the blurring of group boundaries (i.e., where the relative contribution of each distinctive group fails to be acknowledged) can sometimes impede intergroup cooperation. Research by Wilder (1984) adds further weight to the idea that additional social-psychological variables are important in the fostering of intergroup harmony through cooperation. In his work, Wilder shows that it was only cooperative interactions with people considered to be typical of their respective groups that led to more positive evaluations of outgroup members.

An additional body of evidence suggests that, although intergroup competition may be a sufficient cause of intergroup prejudice, it may not actually be necessary or in fact inevitably lead to the emergence of intergroup prejudice. There are at least three areas of study pertinent to this issue. The first area pertains to perceptions and expectations of intergroup competition. For example, in a study of attitudes towards a religious group in Israel, Strutch and Schwartz (1989) found a stronger association between perceived conflict of interests and aggression for those who were highly rather than marginally identified with their religious ingroup. Other studies indicate that when group cohesion and identification are absent, the expectation of intergroup competition per se may fail to enhance intergroup discrimination (e.g., Brewer and Silver, 1978; Brown, 1984; see Brewer and Brown, 1998; Rabbie, 1982, for reviews). A second area of study pertains to patterns of prejudice displayed by members of disadvantaged groups. Because such groups generally tend to have relatively low access to material resources, a realistic intergroup conflict approach may predict relatively high levels of intergroup prejudice (Levine and Campbell, 1972). This, however, is not often the case, as the members of such groups often display behaviours favouring members of the advantaged outgroup over their disadvantaged ingroup (Gopaul-McNicol, 1995; Hunter et al., 1997; cf., Ellemers, 1993).

The third area, as we have mentioned previously, derives from the Boys' Camp study itself, when 'as soon as the [groups] discovered each other's presence ... they eagerly challenged each other to competitive sports, each confident in their own victory' (Sherif and Sherif, 1969: 239). The boys were effectively indicating that conflicting category interests were not actually necessary for the manifestation of intergroup antagonism. The most potent body of evidence indicating that negative outcome interdependence between groups is not a necessary precondition for the emergence of intergroup discrimination comes from research in the minimal group paradigm (e.g., Billig and Tajfel, 1973; Tajfel et al., 1971; Platow et al., 1990). In this paradigm, individuals are randomly assigned into one of two mutually exclusive groups, in the complete absence of such things as negative interdependence, prior or expected future ingroup and outgroup interactions, and differences in philosophical and political beliefs. The consistent finding is that ingroup members are more favourably evaluated and are provided with greater material rewards than outgroup members (see Reynolds and Turner, Chapter 10; Reynolds et al., 2000; and Tajfel and Turner, 1986, for a fuller explanation of these findings).

These findings have a number of important implications for understanding prejudice from a realistic intergroup conflict perspective. The first is that a conflict of group interests will not necessarily stimulate high levels of intergroup discrimination. The second is that intergroup discrimination will emerge even when its appearance is likely to impede group interests. And the third is that a conflict of interests between groups is not necessary for the emergence of intergroup discrimination.

Power and Protest

Up to this point, we have reviewed research that shows that (1) material competition between groups often leads to prejudiced attitudes and discriminatory behaviours, (2) that, when placed in a context in which they can either cooperate or compete, groups tend to be more competitive than individuals, and (3) prejudice can be reduced by changing the structure of interdependence, so that groups must cooperate for a superordinate goal in order to achieve their desired ends. Although these processes are tempered by the complexities of real intergroup life – some of which social psychologists have a handle on and some which we have yet to understand fully – the basic processes outlined and identified by Sherif and his colleagues remain true. So the solution for policy makers and for peace makers sounds clear: encourage previously competing groups to cooperate, and prejudice will be reduced. This is certainly true and, if anything, is the most simple message that we can present to readers of this chapter. Indeed, several researchers have demonstrated how ethnic and racial prejudices can be reduced in classroom settings by having kids from the different groups cooperate with each other rather than compete (Johnson and Johnson, 1984; Miller and Brewer, 1986; Walker and Crogan, 1998).

This message, however, unfortunately obscures many of the factors that lead to realistic conflict in the first place. An analysis of realistic intergroup conflict considers not only the importance of real conflict, but conflict over real outcomes, be they concrete or symbolic. As we mentioned in the critiques of the realistic intergroup conflict approach to prejudice, societal groups often vary in their relative power, status, and general ability to achieve needed and desired outcomes. On the one hand, powerful groups often develop rules and ideologies that legitimate the existing differential distribution of resources (Cohen, 1986; Walster and Walster, 1975); indeed, one author has argued that 'there can be no minimal and sufficient cause [of discrimination] apart from one which is embedded in, and mediated by, the social arrangement of power' (Ng, 1982: 202; see also Sachdev and Bourhis, 1985). On the other hand, there are times when powerless groups question these rules and ideologies (King, 1963; Klandermans, 1997; Tajfel and Turner, 1986). When this happens, intergroup conflict often arises (cf., Mummendey and Wenzel, 1999).

Rules of Fairness

The power that individuals and groups maintain over the distribution of valued resources is obtained in several forms (Ng, 1980). Firstly, power can come simply from the ability to leave the situation at any time (Kelley and Thibaut, 1978). This means that the individual or group of individuals can obtain their desired resources in another situation. When this happens, these individuals or groups have the ability to act in a more cavalier manner, if they choose, without fear of negative consequences for their actions. If negative consequences result, they can just leave. When resources are not attainable in other situations – because they actually do not exist, because individuals and groups *think* they do not exist, or because getting to the new situation is effectively impossible – individuals and groups have relatively low power (Rusbult and Martz, 1995). In this latter situation, people must be more cautious in their behaviours, often appeasing those with power by behaving in a manner consistent with the power-holders' wishes (Ng, 1982).

Power also comes from the absolute control over the distribution of valued resources (Blau, 1964; French and Raven, 1960). Leaders, politicians, managers, and teachers often have complete or primary control over the distribution of valued resources to individuals and groups (Tyler, 1984, 1994; Tyler and Folger, 1980). Of course, there are formal and informal societal rules governing how the resources ought to be distributed (Törnblom and Foa, 1983). For example, some resources should be distributed equally between individuals or groups. Other resources ought to be distributed as a function of some sort of contribution, so that if some individuals or groups have made a greater contribution to society, then they should receive more of the resources. Finally, some resources ought to be given primarily to those individuals and groups who need them; others who already have these resources, and hence do not need more, should not get more.

These three *distributive justice rules* are referred to respectively as *equality*, *equity*, and *need-based* rules. There is a large body of literature demonstrating that, in general, these rules are followed in one form or another in interpersonal relations (Deutsch, 1985; Steensma and Vermunt, 1991). However, it is interesting to note that which rule is chosen often reflects individuals' own personal self interests (Grover, 1991; Messick and Sentis, 1985). So, for example, if Mary works six hours and Sue works four hours, then Mary might prefer an equity rule, allowing her to receive more resources than Sue (e.g., $6 for Mary and $4 for Sue). However, Sue might prefer an equality rule because this will allow her to receive more than she would have with an equity rule (e.g., $5 for Mary and $5 for Sue).

Azzi (1992, 1993) has shown that a similar pattern of preferences occurs at the group level. For example, when allocating political power between a majority group and a minority group, majority-group members tend to prefer an equity-type rule that gives them relatively more than the minority. In contrast, however, minority-group members tend to prefer an equality rule, giving them more power than they would have in an equitable distribution.

Moreover, in intergroup relations, these rules are often only weakly applied, if applied at all (Opotow, 1990). As we mentioned earlier in our discussion of the minimal group paradigm, when allocating resources, group members, on average, tend to give more of a particular resource to members of their own group than to members of another group, even if relative contributions and need are all equal (Tajfel et al., 1971; Platow, Harley et al., 1997). In addition, there are times when group members actually like a fellow ingroup member more when he or she violates the normative justice rules and favours an ingroup over an outgroup member rather than showing intergroup fairness (Platow et al., 1995; Platow et al., 1997; Platow et al., 1998). What is interesting in these instances is that the normative unfairness is often perceived to be fair. That is, when ingroup members are clearly violating broader societal rules of fairness, but are doing so in a manner that benefits an ingroup member over an outgroup member, (in)group members report that this is, in fact, relatively fair. This is a very important finding because it highlights the social contextual nature of distributive justice rules. It underscores the previous point that groups in power create rules not only that maintain that power, but rules that allow them to continue to obtain the lion's share of resources in the name of fairness.

Protest

When group members believe that the extant distribution of valued resources *unjustly* favours a group other than their own, they may challenge the rationalizations for these distributions (Lalonde and Silverman, 1994; Taylor et al., 1987). They may re-label what is said to be fair as unfair, and try to achieve an alternative form of distribution (cf., Bar-Tal, 1990; Billig, 1991a). This may take the form of intergroup protest. But intergroup protest is, at its core, intergroup conflict. And as we know, intergroup conflict, especially with its base in the distribution of valued resources, can lead to prejudiced attitudes and behaviours. Here, alas, is the paradox of this chapter.

The lesson of the psychological analysis of realistic intergroup conflict is that creating a context in which groups successfully cooperate will lead to the reduction of prejudice. But given that realistic intergroup conflict has as its foundation conflict over real outcomes, this psychological lesson must be taken (and given) with care. It is all too easy for members of groups who already have the lion's share of the resources and who define the nature of distributive justice to say 'let's let bygones be bygones'. If this means, however, that a disadvantaged group fails to achieve its desired resources, then it remains disadvantaged. Sometimes it is necessary for groups to protest, to strike, to favour their own group, to attempt to influence through civil disobedience (Alinsky, 1971; Haslam, 2001; Reicher, 1991; Sherif and Sherif, 1969). These represent real attempts to achieve real resources for their group.

A recent paper by Huo et al. (1996) highlights these issues. They surveyed public-sector employees in the US and identified people who reported pride in either their work organization, their ethnic group, or both. Participants were asked to recall a conflict with their work supervisor of a different ethnic background. Acceptance of the supervisor's decision and the perceived fairness of the ultimate outcome were successfully predicted by the nature of the interaction with the supervisor (i.e., whether the supervisor was honest and polite) and the absolute favourableness of the outcome to respondents. However, this occurred only among participants who reported pride in their organization; among participants reporting pride solely in their ethnic group, only the absolute favourableness of the outcome predicted their acceptance of the supervisor's decision and its perceived fairness. A similar pattern of results was observed in the political arena by Smith and Tyler (1996). The twist of this research for a realistic intergroup conflict analysis of prejudice comes from Huo et al.'s conclusion that:

> ... identification with the superordinate group [the organization] can redirect people's focus away from outcomes to interpersonal, relational concerns ... [allowing] authorities to *worry less about providing desired outcomes to group members* and to concentrate more on achieving the greater good and maintaining social stability. (1996: 44–45, emphasis added)

The call for focusing on the greater good is nice, but it is one that explicitly asks for a disregard of the material benefits to specific groups. The authors recognize that there are differences in the distribution of material resources between groups, and that such differences can lead to social conflict. Their suggestion, however, is a political one, not a psychological or scientific one. Indeed, groups not receiving material resources will recognize their relative deprivation (Tyler and Lind, 1992: 162) and will engage in social protest (Kelly, 1993; Tyler and Smith, 1998; Walker and Pettigrew, 1984); this has been shown among Indians in aparthied South Africa (de la Rey and Raju, 1996), the unemployed (Walker and Mann, 1987), and women (Grant and Brown, 1995), just to name a few. So, again, we must take the lessons of the realistic intergroup conflict approach to prejudice with care. Because it has as its foundation real conflicts between groups over real material resources, the path to prejudice reduction is necessarily lined with political and value-based decisions beyond the scope of the analysis itself.

Conclusion

The realistic intergroup conflict analysis remains a strong framework for understanding intergroup prejudices. On the basis of the data reviewed above, we can confidently conclude that the structure of interdependence between groups is a crucial determinate of intergroup attitudes and behaviour. In this manner, the realistic intergroup conflict approach has important metatheoretical implications; it tells us that intergroup cooperation and hostility are a consequence of factors largely *external* rather than internal to individuals. Positive and negative intergroup attitudes are produced by coinciding and conflictual group-based relationships. They are not a function of intrapsychic properties, personality types, or perceptions based on interpersonal interactions. As a consequence, a realistic intergroup conflict approach helps advance our understanding of intergroup conflict by highlighting the need to conceptualize and assess intergroup relations in the context and level at which they occur, and not merely as some epiphenomenon of intrapsychic and interpersonal psychological processes. In doing this, the approach overcomes some of the major limitations inherent in individualistic approaches to the study of intergroup relations (see Brown, 1988; Hogg and Abrams, 1988). Unlike these individualistic approaches, the realistic intergroup conflict approach can more plausibly explain both the widespread nature of negative intergroup relations and the rapid emergence and dissipation of hostile intergroup attitudes by reference to fluctuations in the political and economic circumstances of the groups concerned (e.g., Haslam et al., 1992).

We think it only appropriate to conclude this chapter by asking you to reflect on the rhetorical question Sherif posed over 30 years ago when he was developing his social-psychological analysis of realistic intergroup conflict. At a time when intrapsychic and personality approaches to prejudice are making a come-back (e.g., Altemeyer, 1998; Baumeister, et al., 1996; Solomon, et al., 1991), we ought to remind ourselves that:

> … on the number of wars engaged in by the major powers from 1850 to 1941 … Britain heads the list with twenty wars – more than the Japanese (with nine), the Germans (with eight) or the United States (with seven). In the years following World War II, we heard explanations of Germany's warlike tendencies on the basis of the authoritarian character … In this connection it seems reasonable to ask … Doesn't having an empire with far flung interests to be protected and expanded have anything to do with the frequency of war? (Sherif, 1966: 14)

Of course, it does not stop there. As the 20th century drew to a close, the Serbian Ministry of Information informed us of its policies with regard to Kosovo by observing that 'the question of Kosovo is not only [one] of *territory* or the number of Serbian or Albanian population: it is an inalienable *national treasury*…' (1998, emphasis added). Not surprisingly, the Kosovar Institute of History, Prishtina sees, by contrast, a history of 'expulsions of Albanians and *colonization* of Kosovo' (Institute of History, Prishtina, 1997, emphasis added). In both instances, the debate highlights resources, both concrete (i.e., land) and symbolic (i.e., 'national treasury'). And we all know about the prejudice and loss of human life on both sides.

So we ask, doesn't real intergroup conflict over material and valued resources have anything to do with prejudice? It does.

Part V:

The Language and Rhetoric of Racism

13 The Language of Prejudice and Racism

Amanda LeCouteur and Martha Augoustinos

This chapter discusses the recent development of discourse analysis in social psychology and the contributions it has made to understanding contemporary prejudice and racism. Discursive psychology is critical of individualistic and social cognitive accounts that conceptualize prejudice and racism primarily as internal psychological states that are located in individuals and groups. Rather, discursive psychology views racism as both interactive and communicative, and as located within the dominant institutional practices and discourses of a society. As we will see, discursive psychology introduces a very different approach to the study of traditional social psychological constructs such as social categorization and stereotyping. Unlike as is the case in social cognition (Fiske and Taylor, 1991), social categories and social stereotypes are not regarded by discursive psychologists as fixed and preformed cognitive structures that are located in people's heads. Categorization and stereotyping are not viewed as internal cognitive processes but, rather, as discursive practices that are flexibly articulated within specific social contexts in order to construct particular versions or accounts of reality. In the discursive approach, categorization and stereotyping are things we do in talk in order to accomplish social actions such as blaming, accusing, excusing, persuading, justifying, etc.

Discourse analysts recommend the fine-grained analysis of the language that is used to talk about 'race' and intergroup relations more generally. Most Western countries have witnessed a resurgence of debates and controversies concerning issues of race, racism, multiculturalism, nationalism, and immigration. Discursive psychology is concerned with the detail of what is actually said, argued, and discussed in such debates. This involves analysing not only everyday talk and conversation, but also formal institutional and public talk such as is found in political speeches, parliamentary debates, and newspaper articles. This chapter will review the extensive research that has already been conducted on the language of racism in countries such as The Netherlands (van Dijk, 1984, 1985, 1987, 1993), Britain (Reeves, 1983), New Zealand (Nairn and McCreanor, 1991; Wetherell and Potter, 1992), and Australia (Augoustinos, Tuffin, and Rapley, 1999). As we will see, these studies tell a remarkably similar story: that the language of contemporary racism is flexible, ambivalent, and contradictory. We hope to demonstrate that discursive psychology's contribution to understanding racism offers a unique and critical positioning compared to the more traditional approaches that have so far been presented in this book. Before doing so, we need to outline the basic theoretical and philosophical assumptions of discursive approaches, and show how these differ from traditional psychological approaches.

Discourse Analysis

Discourse analysis describes a number of social psychological approaches that are predominantly concerned with analysing the socially constitutive nature of language. Most contemporary psychology and, in particular, social psychology, adheres to the notion of internal mental representation – the basic philosophical presupposition being that there is a cognitive life-world to be explored and delineated. Social psychology has been concerned, predominantly, with examining the cognitive 'contents' of the mind; making use of notions such as attitudes, stereotypes, and representations, and has focused on how such cognitions are generated by cognitive mechanisms and processes. From this perspective, cognition is conceptualized as prior to language. Language is viewed primarily as a communicative medium through which cognition finds expression. Most social psychology also subscribes to a realist epistemology: that there is a knowable domain of facts about human experience and consciousness that can be discovered through the application of reason and rationality (science) or through hermeneutic interpretative methods. The emergence of the social-constructionist movement in psychology (Gergen, 1985) challenged this realist epistemology and cognitivism as a dominant paradigm in the discipline. This challenge can be attributed to the increasing interest in the role and function of language as a socially constitutive force in consciousness and experience. This 'turn to language', which was part of a larger intellectual tradition in the humanities and social sciences during the 1980s, emphasized the role played by language in creating and reproducing meaning in everyday social interaction and practice. The latter work of Wittgenstein (1953) is an important philosophical precursor to this view of language. Wittgenstein emphasized the interactive and conventional nature of language. As a social practice, language has no fixed meaning outside the context in which it is used. Our perception of the world is shaped by the language we use to describe it: objects, activities, and categories derive their epistemological status from the definitions we create for them. Within this view, thought and language are no longer separated. 'When we think in language, there are not "meanings" going through our mind in addition to verbal expressions. The language itself is the vehicle of thought' (Collier et al., 1991: 277).

Perhaps the most important and influential book to apply these radical ideas to social psychology is Potter and Wetherell's (1987) *Discourse and Social Psychology: Beyond Attitudes and Behaviour.* What was important about this book was that it engaged with, and directly challenged, the taken-for-granted business of social psychology: attitudes, beliefs, stereotyping, social categorization, and representations. Potter and Wetherell (1987) combine the theoretical and empirical foundations of speech act theory, ethnomethodology, and semiology to arrive at their own approach to the analysis of discourse. Based on Austin's (1962) speech act theory, a central emphasis running through their approach is that people use language 'to do things' to achieve certain ends. Words are not simply abstract tools used to state or describe things; they are also used to make certain things happen. People use language to justify, explain, blame, excuse, persuade, and present themselves in the best possible light. Thus, language is functional. As in ethnomethodology, the focus is on the ordinary, everyday use of talk that has practical consequences for participants: how people use language to understand and make sense of everyday life. Language is viewed as reflexive and contextual, as constructing the very nature of objects and events as they are talked about. The emphasis is on the constructive nature and role of language. Furthermore, words do more than just name things; there are complex relations of meaning which are taken for granted in the words and language that we use. Semiologists have studied the culturally constructed meanings with which words are imbued, emphasizing that meaning is often realized by the words which are both present and absent (the word 'river', for example, gets part of its meaning from being not 'creek', not 'stream', not 'lake', and so on).

Attitudes or Interpretative Repertoires?

A pervasive theme in Potter and Wetherell's work is the variability of people's talk. What people say depends on the particular context in which they are speaking and the function(s) that the talk may serve. In the ebb and flow of everyday life, the context within which talk occurs and its accompanying function continually shift and change. As people are engaged in conversation with others, they construct and negotiate meanings, or the very 'reality' that they are talking about. In contrast to most traditional approaches in social psychology and in social cognition research that look for stability, consistency, and order in people's attitudes and accounts, then, Potter and Wetherell stress the inherent variability of what people say. In fact, from a discourse-analytic perspective, people are expected to demonstrate considerable variability and inconsistency, as content is seen to reflect contextual changes and functional purposes of the immediate moment. Moving from a traditional realist view, which treats language as descriptive or reflective of a stable and presupposed world 'out there', discourse analysis does not attempt 'to recover events, beliefs and cognitive processes from participants' discourse, or treat language as an indicator or signpost to some other state of affairs but look[s] at the analytically prior question of how discourse or accounts of these things are manufactured' (Potter and Wetherell, 1987: 35).

   Potter and Wetherell argue that through traditional quantitative and qualitative methods of research, the great variability that inheres in people's 'attitudes' and accounts has been suppressed. The use of aggregating quantitative methods and of gross categories to code qualitative data conceals variability, and works to construct an oversimplified picture of people's attitudes and feelings. The statistical use of mean results in questionnaire data says little about the inconsistent, ambivalent or context-dependent views to which people may subscribe. As Billig (1991b) and his colleagues (Billig et al., 1988) have documented, many social psychological theories have assumed an inherent human motivation for cognitive balance and consistency. There has been surprisingly little interest in theorizing the ambivalent and 'dilemmatic' nature of people's thoughts and opinions.

More importantly, Potter and Wetherell challenge the epistemological status of the 'attitude' concept itself. The theoretical notion of an attitude, and the assumption that it can be encapsulated by the way a person responds to a questionnaire scale, assumes the existence of internal cognitive entities that are relatively enduring. Their discursive approach suggests that people may make different evaluations depending on the specific context at hand. The view that something like an attitude can be identified and located assumes that there exists an internal cognitive world. In this view, language simply reflects this internal mental world. Potter and Wetherell argue that such cognitive assumptions are problematic. They prefer to suspend and refrain from cognitivist assumptions by analysing what people have to say about particular issues, paying attention to the variability in their language and the functions that this variability serves. Their approach to the functional and contextual nature of discourse is summarized thus:

> We do not intend to use the discourse as a pathway to entities or phenomena lying beyond the text. Discourse analysis does not take for granted that accounts reflect underlying attitudes or dispositions and therefore we do not expect that an individual's discourse will be consistent and coherent. Rather the focus is on the discourse *itself*: how it is organized and what it is doing. Orderliness in discourse will be viewed as a product of the orderly *functions* to which discourse is put. (Potter and Wetherell, 1987: 4; original emphasis)

In place of the attitude concept and, indeed, of the concept of representation, Potter and Wetherell put forward the notion of 'interpretative repertoires'. These are defined as sets of metaphors, arguments, and terms that are used recurrently in people's discourse to describe events and actions. In this chapter we will be illustrating the implications of this discursive approach for the analysis of prejudice and racism, contrasting it to social and cognitive approaches such as those represented by other chapters in this book: attitude theory, social cognition, social identity theory, and self-categorization.

Social Categories in Discourse

A concept central to most of the theoretical approaches to prejudice and racism discussed in this book is categorization. The use and application of social categories is assumed to be a pervasive cognitive tendency that serves either to simplify an overly complex world (social cognition; Fiske and Taylor, 1991), or to render it more intelligible (social identity and self-categorization theories; Oakes et al., 1994). Traditional approaches view categorization as highly functional and, indeed, as necessarily adaptive if we are to function effectively (Fiske, 1998). For example, social-cognitive models argue that social categorization and stereotyping are cognitively essential because they protect us from cognitive overload (Macrae et al., 1994). This is the central idea behind the 'cognitive-miser' model that dominated social cognition research in the 1980s. In contrast, self-categorization theory argues that categorization and stereotyping are cognitive processes that do not simplify perception but enrich and elaborate upon it by bringing social interests and background theories of particular social groups to the fore (Leyens et al., 1994; Oakes et al., 1994). Social categorization and stereotyping are cognitively useful because they help us to make sense of the world and our own place within it. However, both traditions also document some of the associated cognitive consequences of categorization and stereotyping; consequences such as objectification, distortion, bias, and prejudice, all of which have been lamented by social psychologists. Discursive psychology introduces an entirely different approach to the study of categorization. Although discursive psychology does not deny that people use social categories to talk about the world (clearly they do, and in very interesting and strategic ways), it does challenge the view that social categories are rigid internal entities that are applied inflexibly. Furthermore, categories are not treated as cognitive phenomena that are located in people's heads – as preformed static structures that are organized around prototypical representations of the category. Rather, discursive psychology emphasizes that people constitute categories discursively in order to do certain things:

> Instead of seeing categorization as a natural phenomenon – something which just happens, automatically – it is regarded as a complex and subtle social accomplishment ... this ... emphasizes the action orientation of categorization in discourse. It asks how categories are flexibly articulated in the course of certain sorts of talk and writing to accomplish particular goals, such as blamings or justifications. (Potter and Wetherell, 1987: 116)

Although many social cognitive researchers regard stereotypes as distorted and biased descriptions of social groups, the social categories to which they refer are regarded as reflecting real and valid group entities in the social world. Categories such as man/woman, Black/White, younger/older, rich/poor, are treated as uncontested and nonproblematic social objects which are perceived directly through identifiable physical and social features. Although social identity and self-categorization theories are more inclined to emphasize the socially constructed nature of these categories, they too tend to treat social categories 'as static features of a predefined macro-sociological landscape' (Wetherell and Potter, 1992: 74).

In contrast, discursive psychology is interested in 'how categories become constructed in different social contexts and how the method of construction creates a subjectivity for oneself and for those defined as Other' (Wetherell and Potter, 1992: 74) Categorization is not simply a cognitive, internal process based on direct and veridical perception, but a 'discursive action' which is 'actively constructed in discourse for rhetorical ends' (1992: 77). Edwards describes categorization as '*something we do, in talk,* in order to accomplish social actions (persuasions, blamings, denial, refutations, accusations, etc.)' (1991: 94; original emphasis). Moreover, some constructions are so familiar, pervasive, and common-sensical that they 'give an effect of realism' or 'fact'. People therefore come to regard some constructions not as versions of reality, but as direct representations of reality itself. Edwards argues that the experiential basis of categories is what makes them appear to be direct, perceptual, and objective descriptions of reality. In this way, experiential realism operates as a rhetorical device in making claims about reality.

From a discursive perspective, the social categories used in talk are expected to be variable, flexible, shifting, and even contradictory, depending on their varied functional and contextual uses. Categorization may be inevitable, but there is nothing inevitable about the particular categories, or the content of those categories, that are relied upon in any instance. To demonstrate how the constitutional boundaries of seemingly mundane categories are variously constructed and strategically deployed in everyday life, we need to examine the specific detail of how categories are used in everyday talk (Sacks, 1992). For example, Augoustinos (in press) specifically focused on the social category 'Australian Aboriginal', and the contexts in which this category was deployed by university students, in discussions of race relations in Australia. She found that participants used the category 'Aboriginal' without qualification when discussing the current social problems of Australia's Indigenous people (see below for further details). However, when issues such as land rights, Aboriginal self-determination and identity were discussed, students problematized the social category 'Aboriginal' by: (a) placing constraints on the definitional boundaries of the category, and (b) questioning the legitimacy of some who claim an Aboriginal identity. What this contextual selectivity demonstrates is the important rhetorical and ideological work that is being accomplished by the use of particular categorizations in different contexts.

One specific way in which participants placed limits on the legitimacy of the category 'Aboriginal' or, alternatively, on the legitimacy of an Aboriginal identity, was in the deployment of a unifying superordinate category and identity, 'Australian'. For example, in discussing race relations, students expressed the view that differences between people should be minimized and commonalities be highlighted:

> M: [. . .] I don't know necessarily think that the way to resolve it is for what you were saying, 'you have your land, I'll have my land, let's live separately'. I don't think that's the way to really resolve it. I think I I tend to agree with you that we live in Australia, let's live together
> A: Yep
> M: And be Australians and umm work and work out a good way that we can all live together.

Repertoires of togetherness, the sharing of an Australian national identity, and the rhetoric of commonality all feature in the above extract. In the first turn, the politics of separate (racial) development is challenged and offered as an inferior option to the argument of 'one country–one people' – a view supported by A in the second turn (Yep). M continues with the suggestion that people 'be Australians' and 'live together'. The primacy afforded to a collective Australian national identity works to emphasize the commonality of people living in the same country, while also undermining the legitimacy of any differences that might disrupt this superordinate political goal. This suggestion also works to undermine the political and moral legitimacy of minority groups striving to have their varied social identities recognized and affirmed. In this way, existing differences in culture, sociopolitical history, and ethnicity can be subsumed (or even negated) by appealing to the nationalist moral imperative that all people living within the nation state adopt a superordinate national identity.

The moral necessity and importance of self-categorizing as Australian, and the discourse of a unifying national collective identity, have been a central platform of the recently formed Australian political party, 'One Nation'. Indeed the name of this party, 'One Nation', itself embodies the nationalist sentiment expressed by the talk in the previous extract. The controversial and contentious views of the party's figurehead, Pauline Hanson, have ensured that 'race' and 'identity' have resurfaced as prominent issues in Australia (see Rapley, 1998). Among its many racist policy statements was One Nation's strong contestation of the legitimacy of the social category 'Aboriginal'. For example, a One Nation candidate standing for the October 1998 national election argued that only people who had undergone traditional Aboriginal initiation rites should be regarded as Aboriginal. Mr Ted Hagger was quoted as saying 'If a person wants to become an Aboriginal they should go through the ceremony and be an Aboriginal and live in an Aboriginal situation and not have the best of both worlds'. Asked what he meant by 'Aboriginal situation', he said 'Well hunter-gatherers and people who live out there, say Lajamanu or in the Tanami desert'. Furthermore, Mr Hagger, who has a part-Aboriginal son-in-law, said he was 'darker' than his son-in-law, whom he said should be called a 'part-coloured person or whatever *but not an Aboriginal*' (*The Advertiser*, July 27, 1998, emphasis added).

This strategy of questioning the legitimacy of categorizing individuals of mixed descent, who lead urban, non-traditional lifestyles, as 'Aboriginal' was also evident in Augoustinos' (in press) analysis of student talk on race. For example, one student said:

> B: Part of the problem is we don't really have any true Aboriginals any more, they're all half-caste or quarter caste . . . that's where you get problems because they've got this conflict. I am Aboriginal but I have a white parent or I come from a slightly white background and then you get this confli… confusion.

What we see in the talk is the invocation of the category *'true Aboriginals'* to constrain and problematize the use of a more general category 'Aboriginals': a category that was used quite freely and unproblematically in other contexts by this particular speaker. Implicitly, what is also being problematized is the legitimacy of an Aboriginal identity by those of mixed descent: an issue that has received considerable political attention in Australia.

Another study examining the construction of membership categories as a crucial rhetorical move in debates about racially sensitive issues focused on political talk in an ongoing debate about Indigenous land rights in Australia. LeCouteur, Rapley, and Augoustinos (2001) argued that, in addresses by Australia's political leaders, constructions of groups central to the debate about Native Title – 'Aborigines' and 'farmers' – functioned strategically to normatively bind particular activity entitlements to category membership. In specific instances of political talk, 'farmers', for example, were portrayed as (sentimentalized) hardworking 'battlers' in the 'bush' who contribute to the nation's wealth. In this way, 'farmers' were constructed as having a legitimate entitlement to have their wishes respected by government. In contrast, 'Aborigines' who were constructed as non-contributory, passive, dependent, and as possessing only an 'affinity' to land, did not. By virtue of this management of the protagonists' identities, the respective moral entitlements of the groups were clearly established. What such discursive analyses demonstrate is that, rather than being routine, non-problematic, 'objective' group entities, social categories can be seen to be contingently-shaped, strategic constructions serving local ideological and rhetorical ends (see also Reicher and Hopkins, 1996a, 1996b).

The Discourse of Racism

Wetherell and Potter's (1992) discursive analysis of racial prejudice in New Zealand emphasizes how talk is organized rhetorically in order that attributions of racism may be avoided or denied. Indeed, all of their Pakeha ('White' majority) respondents were proficient in the use of a range of liberal and egalitarian principles such as freedom, fairness, and equal opportunity to argue for illiberal outcomes: arguments and rhetoric which justified and sustained the existing inequitable social relations in New Zealand. Wetherell and Potter identified ten common 'rhetorically self-sufficient' or clinching arguments that respondents used in their discourse to this effect. These arguments can be summarized as follows:

1. Resources should be used productively and in a cost-effective manner.
2. Nobody should be compelled.
3. Everybody should be treated equally.
4. You cannot turn the clock backwards.
5. Present generations cannot be blamed for the mistakes of past generations.
6. Injustices should be righted.
7. Everybody can succeed if they try hard enough.
8. Minority opinion should not carry more weight than majority opinion.
9. We have to live in the twentieth century.
10. You have to be practical.   (Wetherell and Potter, 1992: 177)

Although these 'rhetorically self-sufficient' arguments were used extensively in Pakeha discourse, Wetherell and Potter (1992) emphasized that they were employed in flexible and often contradictory ways. They stressed that these maxims should not be viewed as cognitive templates or schemas that structured and organized Pakeha discourse, but rather as 'tools' or 'resources' which were combined in variable ways by the respondents to do certain things, most notable of which was to avoid a 'racist' identity and to justify existing Maori-Pakeha relations. Like Billig et al. (1988), Wetherell and Potter argue for the fragmentary, dilemmatic, and contradictory nature of people's views, an approach that is considerably different from the social psychological concept of 'attitude' as an enduring, stable and consistent cognitive entity.

Summarizing a number of his own studies in the area (McCreanor, 1993a, 1993b; Nairn and McCreanor, 1990, 1991), McCreanor listed a series of common themes or patterns of ideas and language that were evident in Pakeha 'commonsense versions' of Maori/Pakeha relations:

1. *Maori culture*. Maori culture as fundamentally inferior to Pakeha culture.
2. *Good Maori/Bad Maori*. Maori fall into two groups; those who fit into society and those who do not.
3. *Stirrers*. If Maori agitators ('stirrers') would stop stirring up trouble where none actually exists, race relations would be harmonious.
4. *Maori violence*. Maori men seek out and enjoy violence.
5. *Maori inheritance*. There are few 'real' Maori left.
6. *Sensitivity*. Maori have become over-sensitive about their culture and this has led to racial tension.
7. *Ignorance*. Where Pakeha do offend Maori, they do so out of ignorance rather than intent.
8. *Privilege*. Maori have special privileges which are unfair and racist.
9. *Rights*. Equal rights for all is a democratic cornerstone; privilege is anathema.
10. *One people*. All people in New Zealand are New Zealanders, Kiwis, etc., and should be treated the same.   (McCreanor, 1993b: 60)

The theme of 'one people' (#10) coincides with a repertoire of 'togetherness' that was identified by Wetherell and Potter (1988) in Pakeha talk. Along with repertoires of 'cultural fostering' (which advocates the development of Maori culture as compensation for what is viewed as a *deficiency* within Maori) and 'pragmatic realism' (which presents Maori cultural practices as unrealistic and impractical in the modern world), this 'togetherness' repertoire was shown by Wetherell and Potter to be drawn on by speakers to articulate forms of talk that could not easily be described as oppressive or racist. Yet, according to the researchers, by virtue of the flexible and strategic deployment of such repertoires, 'the potentially disruptive force of Maori protest and anti-racism is safely contained' (1988: 182).

Other common linguistic resources and arguments in everyday (majority Pakeha) talk, and in political and media texts, that function to undermine the position of Maori have been reported. In an analysis of media discourse, Abel (1996), for example, reported on the use of a distinction between 'tame' and 'wild' Maori. 'Tame' Maori were constructed as those who worked within the system and supported the status quo; 'wild' Maori were those who demonstrated against it, thus making 'unreasonable' demands in an 'inappropriate' manner. Similarly, in her analysis of Pakeha accounts of a Maori protest, Praat (1998) identified arguments that both undermined and upheld Maori rights to sovereignty, land, justice, and equity. For example, she demonstrated how appeals to equality of treatment could be used in one context to argue for the removal of a Maori tent 'city' that formed part of an occupation of public land and, in another context, to justify lack of action on the part of civic 'authorities'.

Arguments and repertoires that problematized Indigenous Australians in similar ways to those identified in much of the New Zealand research were identified by Augoustinos and collegues (Augoustinos, Tuffin, and Rapley, 1999; Augoustinos, Tuffin, and Sale, 1999) in their analysis of everyday talk about race relations in Australia. The most pervasive feature of the talk was the negative construction and problematization of Aboriginality and Aboriginal people. This negativity did not manifest itself in what most would regard as traditional prejudiced talk (i.e., old-fashioned racism), but rather as a delicate, flexibly managed, and locally contingent discussion of the contemporary 'plight' of Aboriginal people. Given the over-representation of Aboriginal people among the poor, the unemployed, the ill and the imprisoned in Australian society, that discussions focused on such 'problems' is not surprising. What is surprising, however, was the degree to which these problems and social inequities were accounted for by the use of discursive resources which legitimated and rationalized the current 'plight' of Aboriginal people. One such discursive repertoire drawn upon by participants to account for the contemporary social problems faced by Indigenous people was an imperialist narrative of Australia's colonial past. Participants organized their talk in terms of a *cultural* hierarchy. Aboriginal problems were represented largely in Social-Darwinist terms as problems of 'fit' and of 'adaptation' to a superior culture that was introduced by the British in the course of 'settlement'. Aboriginal people's failure to fit into, or 'gel' with, the dominant culture was viewed as preventing them from improving their status through upward social mobility. In this way, Aboriginal people were constructed as culturally inferior, as failing to survive in a superior culture and, thus, as being accountable for their own social and economic disadvantage. The extract below is one example that demonstrates how Indigenous people were constructed as 'primitive' and technologically inferior in contrast to the invading British.

> A: I think too and also when you look at history you look back at the fact that the Aborigines were very very primitive *(Mmm)* and they confronted our culture that was superiorly [sic] more advanced, the wheel had been invented and whatnot but the Aborigines hadn't seemed to to advance past that very primitive stage and whatnot *(Mmm)*. Umm, they had sort of had no modern technologies as such as the British had. Like the British had gun powder and alcohol and these things, ahh, I think that was another big problem.

While acknowledging the existence and undesirability of racism and prejudice in Australian society, participants distanced themselves from accusations of overt racism by employing 'neutral' accounting, a distanced footing, and by attributing (culturally understandable) racism primarily to older generations. Several rhetorical strategies were identified that worked to diminish the legitimacy of the view that Aboriginal people can be seen as victims of racism. These included arguments that Aboriginal people were perpetrators of racism themselves, oversensitive to racial prejudice, and used claims of discrimination as excuses whenever things did not go their way. These arguments were deployed in combination with discursive moves and rhetorical strategies that enhanced the self-presentation of speakers as balanced, neutral, and fair. For example:

> A: I think that is another point about discrimination umm whenever something doesn't go the group's way they cry discrimination (*Mmm*). Umm with the Aborigines if they don't get something its discrimination for females it's the same, with other minority groups it's all the same (*umm*). And I think that discrimination is now an excuse people are using to or a crutch that if something doesn't go their way it's sort of like a child throwing a tantrum, they cry discrimination. I know it *does* exist and it *shouldn't* but I think that it's been taken vastly advantaged of (*Mmm*).

Here, A argues that minority group (Aborigines, females) self-interest determines when claims of discrimination will be mobilized. This suggestion works to undermine the genuineness of discrimination claims. In this account such claims are constructed as empty rhetoric ('excuses'), used to bolster a selfish, political agenda. The developmental metaphor of the child 'throwing a tantrum' positions Aboriginal responses to discrimination as an over-reaction, lacking in maturity, and emotional balance. By implication, of course, other (White, male, majority group) members are balanced, mature, and realistic. Note how A heads off any imputations that her/his views are biased or unreasonable by acknowledging the existence and undesirability of discrimination ('I know it does exist and it shouldn't'). What we see is evidence that participants are clearly attending to the necessity of managing their self-presentation in interactive contexts by presenting themselves as neutral and balanced (Antaki et al., 1996).

Finally, participants in this study also drew upon a nationalistic discourse that stressed the need for all people living within the nation state to identify collectively as 'Australian'. The sharing of a superordinate Australian national identity again emerged as a rhetorical device to undermine the legitimacy of subcultural identities such as 'Aboriginal' (see previous section). Such identities were constructed as divisive and as threatening national unity. This nationalist discourse was similar to the 'togetherness' and 'one people' repertoires identified by Wetherell and Potter (1992) and McCreanor (1993b, 1993c), respectively, in the talk of majority group members in New Zealand.

Other discourse-based analyses of contemporary racism have been carried out by van Dijk, focusing on texts and talk from several European countries and

North America (van Dijk, 1984, 1985, 1987, 1991, 1992, 1993). Unlike the noncognitive discursive analyses we have presented thus far, van Dijk's analyses have a cognitive foundation in that he assumes that the structural properties of discourse can be explained by the 'underlying' cognitions of language users – that is, in terms of memory processes and other mental representations of events, values, and knowledge.

Leaving to one side the fundamental epistemological difference between the two discursive approaches, it is possible to detect some points of similarity when focusing at the analytic level of the structures and strategies of text and talk that both approaches are primarily concerned to illuminate. In his focus on the role of 'elite' discourse – political, corporate, academic, educational, and media talk and text – van Dijk (1993) reported a general pattern of positive self-presentation and negative other-presentation that accords with Wetherell and Potter's (1988, 1992; Potter and Wetherell, 1987) findings concerning the ways in which talk is strategically organized to deny racism. van Dijk identified positive self-presentation on the part of the elites in terms of their use of such discursive formulations as civil-rights slogans, nationalistic rhetoric, populist appeals (claims to be listening to the 'voice of the people'), and their presentation of restrictive measures as if they were in the best interests of minorities. Minorities were portrayed in such elite discourse in ways that problematized and marginalized them as 'Other'; they were associated with illegality, deviance, passivity, and a lack of cultural adaptation.

Similar negative constructions of racial and ethnic minorities were found by van Dijk (1984, 1987) in his examination of everyday talk among White people. Such negative talk about minorities tended to be accompanied by disclaimers (formulaic constructions such as *I have nothing against migrants but . . .*) and the explicit avowal of liberal principles; both moves in the general strategy of positive ingroup presentation. Both rhetorical devices – of disclaiming, and of 'practical considerations' overriding ideals – have been identified as constitutive of racism in everyday talk by Potter and Wetherell (1987; Wetherell and Potter, 1988). van Dijk (1992, 1993) has also identified a number of other forms in terms of which denials of racism can be expressed. These include the following argumentative structures:

- *theorizing a split between action and intention* (a negative consequence is argued to be the result of the best intentions). For example, one may admit having engaged in an action that has been interpreted as negative, but deny the cognitive counterpart: 'I didn't mean it that way';
- *justification* (a negative consequence is argued to be justified, for example, by blaming the victim; or to be excusable in some way, for example, as the result of provocation);
- *reversal* (attacking anti-racists as racist);
- *moral blackmail* (anti-racism involves censorship),
- *consensus construction* ('We/This country are not racist because there are laws against it');
- *mitigation, downtoning, and use of euphemisms* (these are modes of denial that are achieved rhetorically). For example, 'I didn't insult him, I was

giving my honest opinion'; or describing White majority group members, not as racist, but as 'worried' about the impact of immigrants.

A range of similar argument forms and rhetorical modes was discussed by Reeves (1983) in his examination of British political discourse about issues of immigration and race relations. He summarized these strategies as follows:

• *Personalized, dispositional, and agential* arguments that single out (negative) personality/behaviour characteristics of immigrants to justify actions/policies. For example, Blacks are privileged in relation to Whites; they are oversensitive; they are inferior to Whites. For example, 'Either we have got to bring their standards nearer to our standards or we have got to let them drag our standards down to theirs, or we have got to have control of immigration' (Reeves, 1983: 216).

• *Abstracted social process* arguments that involve accounts of the processes that occur as a result of immigration. For example, 'Where people of different cultures and races meet, there are bound to be tensions' (1983: 220).

• *Populist* arguments in which the popularity or widespread acceptance of a measure/belief is used as justification. For example, 'The public obviously want a Bill of this type' (1983: 226).

• *Economic* arguments in which shortages of resources are proclaimed to justify limiting immigration. For example, 'We should absorb no more than our resources, economic and social can take in' (1983: 230).

• *Pro bono publico* arguments which involve the assertion that a measure will benefit all or most members of the public. For example, 'We desire no second-class citizens, we desire no race discrimination, we desire no dilapidated areas housing different communities from the majority' (1983: 233).

• *Reciprocity* arguments which justify legislation in terms of balance or exchange. For example, 'I said that we are trying honestly to deal with a situation which was not of our own making and that if accusations of racialism or discrimination could be made against anyone, it was not against us' (1983: 237).

• *Means-oriented* arguments that concentrate on ways of achieving a goal that has already been taken for granted. The focus is not on deciding whether a particular goal should be pursued, rather, there may be a focus on the fact that proper procedures were followed, or on the effects of a particular decision. Arguments are not about providing reasons for the acceptance of the decision; these values are taken for granted.

Four rhetorical 'modes' involving (a) techniques of quantification, (b) analogy, (c) ambiguity, and (d) use of quotation were also identified by Reeves as strategic means of 'deracializing' discourse. Techniques of quantification involve devices such as stressing the magnitude of immigration, typically by the use of absolute numbers of immigrants who 'come in' to a country each year rather than in terms of percentages of the total population. The use of vague and indeterminate terms denoting quantity, such as 'many' or 'a large proportion' represents another use of the rhetoric of quantification. The device of *analogy* can be used to transform an object into one possessing metaphorical connections. For example, the comparison of migration to 'flooding' or 'invasion' allows the speaker to invoke a range of unstated negative properties, in ways that will be easy to deny, if subsequently challenged. The use of *ambiguity* or indeterminacy functions in the same way. For example, referring to immigration in a particular context using vague terms such as 'the problem', allows the speaker to avoid specifying the precise nature and cause of this 'problem'. The strategic use of *quotation* refers to the quoting of assertions of another speaker to support a case. The use of forms such as 'they say …' or 'he said …' functions to insulate the speaker from accusation. Each of these features of the rhetorical organization of talk about race have been reported in Australian samples of political (LeCouteur et al., 2001) and everyday talk (Augoustinos, Tuffin, and Rapley, 1999; Augoustinos, Tuffin, and Sale, 1999).

The discursive repertoires and rhetorical devices that we have reported here as common to texts and talk about race relations should be seen as resources that can be drawn upon, combined and elaborated in complex and flexible ways in the articulation of accounts that suit the varying needs of particular local situations. However, the similarity of these patterns across a number of national boundaries also points to the power and robustness of these discursive practices in their function of justifying and legitimating majority oppression of minority groups. The ideological effectiveness of the flexible articulation and strategic deployment of these discursive resources is painfully clear in continuing contemporary discussions about issues of ethnicity, immigration, and race.

Modern Racism

The 'appropriation' and use of liberal and egalitarian principles to argue for 'racist' and discriminatory practices is, of course, a central feature of contemporary theories of modern racism (Katz and Hass, 1988; Kinder and Sears, 1981, 1985; McConahay, 1986). As previous chapters have indicated, these theories argue that, unlike 'old-fashioned' racism, which is predominantly characterized by White supremacist beliefs, contemporary racism is more subtle and insidious (Pettigrew and Meertens, 1995). Although extreme negative affect toward minority groups has been tempered by egalitarian values, this negative affect (conscious or unconscious) has not been entirely eradicated and persists in the psyche of majority group members. The contradiction between negative affect and liberal values is argued to produce considerable psychological ambivalence so that individuals struggle between their emotions and their beliefs (Gaertner and Dovidio, 1986). Moreover, the modern racist denies that he or she is prejudiced; any conscious and obvious negative feelings and attitudes are justified by 'matter-of-fact' observations that minority groups transgress central values such as hard work, thrift, and self-reliance.

Although theories of modern racism bear elements of similarity to the findings of discursive work on the conflicted and contradictory nature of contemporary race discourse, there are, nevertheless, important differences between traditional and discursive approaches. Theories of modern racism do make reference to wider social, historical, and ideological factors that have influenced and shaped the content and form of racism and prejudice over the years. However, these theories, and the questionnaire research methods that have been used to investigate variants of racism, primarily position racism as an individual and psychological 'problem'. The ambivalence and contradictions that are manifest both in questionnaire responses and in people's talk are located 'within the emotional and cognitive domain of the individual' (Wetherell and Potter, 1992: 197). In contrast, the discourse analytic approach

> locates the conflicts and dilemmas within the argumentative and rhetorical resources available in a 'liberal' and 'egalitarian' society . . . The conflict is not between a feeling and a value, between psychological drives and socially acceptable expressions or between emotions and politics, but between competing frameworks for articulating social, political and ethical questions. These conflicts and dilemmas could be said to be realized in a 'psychological' form when the members of society begin to discuss, debate, explain, justify and develop accounts in the course of social interaction and everyday life. (1992: 197)

From this perspective, racism or prejudice ceases to be an individual or psychological state and becomes, rather, a structural feature of a society which is 'organized around the oppression of one group and the dominance of another group' (Wetherell and Potter, 1992: 198). Individuals utilize whatever ideological resources a society makes available in order to justify and legitimate racist outcomes, but this is always viewed primarily within the context of oppressive structural arrangements which need continually to be justified and legitimated for their maintenance and reproduction.

By locating prejudice primarily within the individual rather than in broader social/cultural domains, social psychological theories have colluded in conceptualizing prejudice as an individual pathology. In doing so, the categories of the 'prejudiced individual' and the 'tolerant individual' have been constructed and reified as entities with clear definitional boundaries. In the words of Wetherell and Potter, 'Prejudice remains a personal pathology, a failure of inner-directed empathy and intellect, rather than a social pathology, shaped by power relations and the conflicting vested interests of groups' (1992: 208). Prejudiced individuals are seen to be irrational and illogical, requiring some kind of attitudinal and moral 'rehabilitation'. Prejudice is viewed primarily as a 'state of mind' which requires change through education and training. Politically, this has the effect of deflecting attention from the political necessity of societal and structural change.

Conclusion

In concluding, we will attempt to address some of the implications of discursive analyses of racism, and to consider what this approach has to offer, at a broad social or cultural level, in terms of its application to the countering of racism.

Discursive psychology has introduced a unique social psychological perspective on the study of contemporary prejudice and racism. Discursive research in Western countries such as Australia, New Zealand, Britain, the Netherlands, and North America suggests that contemporary racism is a complex blend of both egalitarian and illiberal principles that functions to legitimate and justify discriminatory practices and the existence of inequalities between social groups. Discourses are used flexibly and inconsistently depending on the rhetorical purposes to which they are put. A central and important feature of discursive work is the empirical demonstration of the ways in which people construct and use social categories in talk and the ideological effects and consequences that flow from such uses and constructions. This is quite different from the traditional social cognitive approach which treats categories as discrete cognitive entities that reflect fixed social objects existing 'out there' in the real world. It is an approach that emphasizes the contextual and functional ways in which categories are constructed in talk for rhetorical purposes. Categorization is not viewed as a cognitive process that is automatically triggered but as a strategic and situated discursive practice (Edwards, 1991).

As Potter and Wetherell have argued, 'Discourse analysis has radical implications for our understanding and interpretation of findings derived from traditional methods' (1987: 176). We are not advocating, in this chapter, that traditional cognitivist approaches within social psychology should be replaced by discursive alternatives. However, we do see certain crucial advantages to the discursive focus on language-based, interpretative interaction. The value of approaching racism as an interactional, language-based practice rather than as a set of more-or-less coherent and consistent cognitive attitudes that are held by different individuals relates, in our view, to the potential for change that inheres in the former approach. As Potter and Wetherell pointed out when discursive work of this kind on racism was still relatively novel: '... in the fight against racism, it is important to know how it is organized in everyday anecdote, argument and account' (1987: 65).

The importance of a focus on the ways in which realities are constructed and warranted around issues of race and ethnicity in both elite, institutional, and everyday, informal talk and texts lies in its potential to challenge, to undermine, and to *unmake* racist and discriminative realities. By examining and coming to understand the complex linguistic performances that constitute racist explanations at the level of social policy, in education, in corporate and media discourse, and at the level of ordinary, everyday talk, we place ourselves in a strategic position to promote informed critical responses that, ultimately, can serve to transform taken-for-granted racist realities.

14 'How to do X without Doing Y': Accomplishing Discrimination without 'Being Racist' – 'Doing Equity'

Mark Rapley

Race and Racism in Twentieth-century Political Rhetoric

> Work consisted once of plundering travelling caravans, and today it consists of plundering indebted farmers, industrialists, middle-class people, etc. The forms did change, all right, but the principle remained the same. We do not call it work, but robbery.
>
> Adolf Hitler, 'Warum sind wir Antisemitismus', Speech delivered in Munich, August 13th, 1920. (reproduced in Goldhagen, 1996: 281)

In his 1920 address *Why are we Antisemites*, the then obscure political agitator, Adolf Hitler, devoted his entire speech to a discussion of the danger to the German *Volk* represented by the Jews – a 'race' he described as 'parasites on the national community'. His analysis of the necessary response by the Aryan *Volk* to the threat of blood mixing and national degeneration posed by Jews was simple and explicit: 'the heaviest bolt is not heavy enough and the securest prison is not secure enough that a few million could not in the end open it. Only one bolt cannot be opened – and that is death' (reproduced in Goldhagen, 1996: 425). Goldhagen[1] has argued, in his masterly study of the Holocaust, that the annihilation of European Jewry was the inevitable product of the virulent Anti-semitism of German society – in a cultural context of institutionalized, race-based, social stratification, prejudice, and violence.

Importantly, Goldhagen argues persuasively that the apparently effortless transmutation of ordinary Germans into 'Hitler's willing executioners' would not have been possible without the temporally sustained prior existence of a systematic and, fundamentally, discursive construction of the social category, *'der Jude'*, in political rhetoric, the mass media, the academy, and in everyday talk - in what he terms 'society's conversation' (Goldhagen, 1996: 33–34). The 'parasitical' Jews, constructed as a social category in 'society's conversation' were, as such, to be feared, hated and ultimately – as befits the category of 'parasites' – to be exterminated.

While the social conversation of Hitler's Germany was, like South Africa under apartheid, explicitly based on categories of race (for example, Aryan, Untermensch, Jude) and, as such, was not only clearly describable as 'racist' by outsiders, but was also self-avowedly so, issues of race have continued to be a pervasive feature of twentieth-century politics. Racial categorizations have continued to drive political phenomena in the latter half of the century. From the contested desegregation of the southern states of the US in the 1960s, through the success of neo-fascist groupings such as that led by LePen in France since the middle 1970s, to the 'ethnic cleansing' of Rwanda and the ongoing Balkan wars, all have derived much of their motive political force – and often murderous expression – from the social categorization of some persons, by prominent political leaders among others, as belonging to a different, and lesser, racial group (see Ignatieff, 1995, 1997).

In contrast to comparatively distant historical examples, such as Hitler's Germany, and the contributions to society's conversation of such self-avowed ethnic extremists as LePen, Zhirinovsky, and Milosevic, Billig (1991b) and a number of other writers have suggested that a sensitivity or delicacy has developed, at least in the middle classes of Western cultures, about overtly 'racist' talk. From a somewhat different ideological position to that informing Billig's work – and from a lay, as opposed to an academic, perspective – Paul Sheehan also suggests the contemporary delicacy of race talk. In his recent bestseller *Among the Barbarians: The Dividing of Australia*, he argues that 'racist' has become a loaded term employed by those he terms the 'Thought Police' (for example 'postmodern' academics, Labour politicians and other members of the elite 'multiculturalism industry') to silence their opponents (Sheehan, 1998).

In making this claim, without apparently appreciating the irony, Sheehan points to one of the central theoretical and methodological principles of post-crisis (postmodern?) discursive social psychology. This is the claim that all categories in use – including such categories as 'work' or 'racist' – do not index preformed, *a priori*, natural entities in the social scientific world (as mainstream social psychology has assumed) but are, rather, discursive resources upon which members draw in the performance of action in a social world (Antaki, 1994; Edwards, 1997; Potter, 1996; Potter and Wetherell, 1987). As Hitler discursively reconstructs the predicates of the category 'work' to respecify Jewish 'work' as 'robbery', in order to effect the social production of Jewry as the embodiment of criminality, paving the way for the specification (and later implementation) of death as the only appropriate 'punishment'; so too Sheehan, in engaging in the contestation of the permissible uses of the categories 'racism' and 'racist' seeks to accomplish a redefinition of the nature of Australian society's conversation about what bigotry, prejudice, and discrimination, *as action-performative social objects*, may be.

Conceiving of society's conversation as not 'just' talk, but rather of 'talk' as social action, and of social categories as contestable, fluid, and locally contingent (Antaki et al., 1996; Edwards, 1997; Edwards and Potter, 1992; Potter, 1996, 1998) means that the stance of discursive psychology towards the investigation of social phenomena such as 'racism' and 'prejudice' is rather different to that implied by the title of this book. 'Understanding the Psychology of Prejudice and Racism' suggests, by implication, that, like rocks and trees (cf., Edwards et al., 1995), there are such social scientific or psychological *things* as 'prejudice' and 'racism' in the world, things which are amenable to scientific study, measurement, and understanding, and about which sensible and definitive statements can be made. It is one of the purposes of this chapter to call this perspective into question. In so doing, the chapter will illustrate the manner in which discursive psychological work can inform our understanding of the way in which racism and prejudice are produced in talk-in-interaction, both as solid 'things' and also as rhetorically potent devices for the discursive management of categories of persons and personhood, and the entitlements which accompany such category memberships.

A discursive approach then, as Edwards (1997, in press) points out, is deeply suspicious of theoretical positions which suggest that it is possible to discover what racism (be it 'old fashioned' or 'modern' (McConahay, 1986) 'really' is, which 'personality types' may be particularly prone to racism, or which postulate mentalistic explanations of racism (whatever 'it' is) as a consequence of automatic cognitive processes. As I hope is evident from the brief discussion above, attributions of 'race' and 'racism' are not value-free, empirical scientific statements about observable states of affairs in the natural world. Such categorizations appear rather to be inseparable from the management of moral accountability. For Hitler the (discursively constructed) predicates of their 'race' index, the culpability of the Jews for international larceny; for Sheehan the (similarly discursively constructed) extravagant attributions of 'racism' by 'the thought police' index, their culpability in stifling 'free speech'. Indeed, mainstream psychology has itself recently been called to (moral) account by Reicher et al. (1997) precisely by virtue of the explanation of racism the discipline offers.

While no longer celebrating the 'racist' basis of Nazism as Nobel Laureates in the discipline once did (see Billig, 1978), psychology continues to construct prejudicial utterances and actions of persons – based on the 'racial' characteristics of others – as being a consequence of automatic, unconscious (natural, biological, genetic?) cognitive processes, with these utterances and actions being more likely perhaps if one is (unfortunately, blamelessly, unalterably) born with a certain 'personality type'. The adoption and promulgation of these theoretical positions by psychology, Reicher et al. (1997) argue, does important work in managing the moral accountability of persons who may be described as racist, or who produce racially prejudicial utterances and actions.

The rhetorical work done by these accounts is, of course, to exculpate actors from moral responsibility for their actions. These psychological models are morally loaded. We should, on the evidence of mainstream psychology, feel rather sorry for Adolf Hitler. He was most probably born with an unfortunate personality (a genetic endowment about which he could do little) and, in later life, was nothing but the victim of an unconscious, automatic, and adaptive cognitive miserliness which drove him (and the rest of the presumably similarly afflicted German nation) to categorize the Jews as 'parasites'. The social significance of the cultural and discursive construction of the social category 'Jews' as 'parasites' (as opposed to, say, 'worthy German citizens') is, in the 'standard' (or mainstream) psychological account, glossed as an irrelevance. The standard account has little time for the *meaning* of such social categories, in essence treating all category descriptors as semantically and semiotically equivalent.

The destruction of six million Jewish men, women, and children is rendered morally neutral by explanations of racist actions as the ineluctable results of 'automatic', 'unconscious', 'cognitive' processes in the account offered by work in the social cognitive tradition. Indeed, the explanatory account offered by mainstream social psychological theorizing, which offers caveats about the impossibility of extrapolating from individual processes to prejudicial behaviour (see Reynolds and Turner, Chapter 10), only serves to cement the proposition that the perpetrators of both historical and contemporary racially-motivated massacres can not, in all fairness, be held personally, morally, accountable for their actions. That perpetrators are held to be subject to a 'qualitative change in the content of the self – depersonalization' (see Reynolds and Turner, Chapter 10) would seem to suggest that, as deindividuated moral actors, they too may be understood as being 'victims', but of automatic cognitive processes. Racial prejudice – and indeed, racial violence – is brought off as occurring within a moral vacuum; as unfortunate, but inevitable, aspects of human cognitive architecture.

A Discursive Psychological Approach

In contrast to mainstream social psychological approaches, discursive psychology treats talk-in-interaction not as a transparent medium for 'telementation' (Taylor and Cameron, 1987), or the representation and transmission of thoughts between minds, but rather as the site where categories such as 'race' – and also 'thoughts', 'minds' and 'attitudes' – are locally constructed and made relevant in the conduct of social action. Discursive psychology is then anti-cognitivist or, alternatively, non-mentalistic, in approach. What is rejected here is not so much the view that it makes sense to talk of such things as minds and beliefs, but rather the traditional approach in psychology to these matters. Thus discursive psychology views opinions, beliefs, and attitudes (be they describable as 'racist' or otherwise) not as *a priori* phenomena which it is the task of psychology to map and explain, but rather as resources which members can draw upon in talk, or which can – and often do – constitute talk's business, in order to achieve locally relevant rhetorical and social action.

This view of language, of language 'talking the world into being', differs sharply from the view of mainstream psychology. In truth mainstream psychology can barely be said to have theorized language use at all; in practice the telementational fallacy – to which mainstream psychology subscribes – treats talk's relation to things like 'cognitions' and 'attitudes' as being the same as the relation of copper wire to electricity. The medium of 'transmission' is treated as being of little, if any relevance: it is the 'mind stuff' that is supposedly unproblematically transmitted that is the focus of interest. If one is primarily interested in what electrons do when they hit a cathode ray tube, the fact that copper – as opposed, say, to titanium – wire got them there may be entirely irrelevant. Mainstream psychology takes the view that talk, like the type of flex used, is similarly unimportant: what matters is the final distribution of 'attitudes' on the screen. That it is not readily apparent how such things as 'attitudes' or 'thoughts' can be describable (let alone 'transmitted') without the use of (particular) words does not seem to have troubled the mainstream literature. That 'thoughts', 'attitudes' and 'beliefs' are constituted in and by the medium of their expression, and in and for interactional purposes, demonstrates how very misleading the view of language as telementation is, and suggests that close attention to the very particular words that are used to talk such 'objects' into existence is warranted. As Billig notes, in a borrowing from Wittgenstein: 'when I think in language, there aren't meanings going through my mind in addition to the verbal expressions: the language itself is the vehicle of thought' (Billig, 1997: 45). As such, as Wetherell (1999) points out, rather than talk giving privileged access to some 'real' interiorized mental processes: 'a pragmatic [discursive] approach assumes that what is said is organized by the local pragmatics of the situation and is revealing instead about that situation and local norms for self-description"]' (1999:9).

Furthermore, as Edwards (in press) cogently points out, in everyday talk members are pervasively attentive to topics which are also the business of academic psychology – what he describes as 'mind-world mapping', that is the project of presenting self as reporting on a 'real' world, from the perspective of an interiorized subjectivity. Additionally, members' talk is pervasively attentive to precisely the issue of moral accountability that is dismissed – or not recognized as relevant – by 'standard' psychological theorizing. Members' talk demonstrates a fine-tuned attention to the fact that that the implications of ongoing talk for individual accountability are monitored by interlocutors – as the talk is produced – and also a pervasive attentiveness to the possibility that they as speakers will be called to account (Antaki, 1994; Edwards and Potter, 1992; Sacks, 1992, 1995). Thus, whereas self-categorization theory, for example, suggests that speakers may on occasions be 'depersonalized', inspection of actual members' talk (a precaution experimental social psychology routinely fails to take) about any and all issues, not merely of 'delicate' issues such as 'race', shows only too clearly that ordinary people are routinely aware that, in everyday interaction, they will be held individually, *personally*, accountable for their utterances.

A further difficulty engendered by mainstream psychology's disengagement from social action as it is produced in everyday life, is that language in use is not, as it turns out, immediately amenable to the task to which psychology has historically pressed it. Discursive psychological work has pointed out that it is not immediately apparent how descriptions of 'mental states' by psychologists are demonstrably, empirically, superior to those of ordinary members. It is, further, unclear what 'objective' criteria might be put in place to facilitate such a judgement. Analytically, as Antaki (1994) notes, we have an *ideological* choice to make: do we privilege the categories, accounts, and descriptions that members deploy as they prosecute social action or do we privilege our own? Consequential upon this fundamental difficulty is a range of other problems with the *implicit* theoretical and epistemological claims underpinning the research practices of mainstream psychology. Mainstream work, for example, *assumes* that the categories, accounts, and descriptions of 'stimuli' offered by experimenters are ones which resonate with their partcipants and which capture 'the relevant thing' (Edwards, 1999) about whatever it is that is at issue. It is assumed that if participants are asked about their attitudes towards 'Aborigines' they have already, in their heads, a pre-packaged set of such 'attitudes' which they can display on demand. It is assumed that participants are, and only are, whatever demographic category (male, female, working class, university educated' Australian, Vietnamese) the researcher wishes to use as an independent variable. It is assumed that they respond *as such* and as nothing else. While these assumptions are absolutely fundamental to the prosecution of the research agenda of standard psychology, such epistemological claims are not routinely made in the traditional literature per se and for good reason: empirical work on the sorts of research practices that produce such data (e.g., Houtkoop-Steenstra, 2000; Rapley and Antaki, 1998) suggests that they are unsustainable.

From the perspective of discursive psychology the methodological choice is clear. Rather than produce researcher-designed attitude scales *a priori*, or persuade another (hopefully homogenous) social 'group' to submit to an interview about 'Aborigines' or 'Asians', discursive work seeks out 'attitudes towards Aborigines' at the times and in the places where such social objects matter (or rather are made to matter, as such) to, by and for ordinary persons. Thus, the inspection of naturally-occurring members' talk offers us the opportunity to study, empirically, the way the mind-world relationship, the nature of persons and their positions within it, issues of 'race' and 'racism' are confected, constructed, and contested in actual social practices. The imposition of our own, analytically prior, categorizations (for example; schemas, causal attributions, self-categorizations-as-automatic-cognitive-processes, racist talk) is avoided. As workers in the ethnomethodological tradition have argued, unless such categorizations are demonstrably made relevant, by the speakers in the talk under consideration, not only is the ascription of *a priori* analytic categories unwarranted, but it may also be characterized as guesswork (e.g., Antaki, 1994; Schegloff, 1997).

Discursive Psychology and Race Talk

As has been noted above, the discursive perspective deliberately avoids treating language and category usage as in some sense diagnostic of the enduring psychological characteristics or dispositions of persons. In the context of racial or prejudicial descriptions it does not attempt: 'to apply a litmus test to see if people really are prejudiced, whether openly or behind the camouflage of their talk … Prejudice or any other mental state or interpersonal disposition [is] something that might be attended to in various ways, in talk itself' (Edwards, in press: 1–2). Thus, what a discursive approach seeks to do is to illuminate the way in which such ostensibly academic and psychological matters as, for example, racism-as-a-characteristic-of-persons or the attribution of pervasive dispositional prejudice to others, are constructed and contested in everyday members talk-in-interaction. A discursive approach does not therefore aspire – as does perhaps some of mainstream psychology – to make definitive statements about what 'real' racism *is*, be it 'old-fashioned', 'modern' (or even post-modern), preferring instead to examine the manner in which members of a given culture bring off 'doing being racist' as a social action or, alternatively, orient in their talk to shared social knowledge of what 'being racist' might consist of (Wetherell and Potter, 1992). By virtue of such analysis it is possible to suggest what 'being racist' may mean – as such a possible state of affairs is attended to by members – in Australian society's conversation in the late 1990s.

Goldhagen (1996) draws our attention to the importance of political leaders in shaping society's conversation. Unlike early twentieth-century Germany, however, in the late 1990s the ability of political leaders to intervene in society's conversation is greatly enhanced. From the limited access of the public political meeting, the distribution of pamphlets or news-sheets, and the radio address of the 1930s, the range of sites for political intervention in the conversational production of social groups, by ordinary people, has greatly broadened at the end of the century. Political talk about 'race' in contemporary Australia, as in other parts of the world, is pervasive – particularly in the electronic media. Indeed it is to talk-back radio and television that political leaders turn when an intervention in public discourse is deemed politically urgent or expedient: Australian Prime Minister John Howard's use of a televized 'Address to the Nation' on Wik (some of which analysed later in this chapter) is a case in point. A range of work in social psychology has begun to examine the structure and management of such political talk, in particular, the way in which personal and social identities are crafted to accomplish persuasion (e.g., Dickerson, 1997; Rapley, 1998; Reicher and Hopkins, 1996a, 1996b), and the manner in which the definitions of social categories – of both persons and activities – that politicians construct as being at issue are locally tailored to achieve specific rhetorical ends (e.g., Leudar and Antaki, 1998; LeCouteur et al., 2001).

Following the example of Harvey Sacks (1995), this work has drawn attention to the manner in which apparently transparent and uncontentious categories – which are routinely taken for granted in standard psychological work – are contingently shaped and strategically deployed to accomplish very specific local purposes. Sacks' (1995) canonical analysis, *Hotrodder as a Revolutionary Category*, and a range of work in what has now come to be known as 'membership category analysis' (Hester and Eglin, 1997; Jayyusi, 1984) has shown how both the predicates (actions, predispositions, beliefs) which may be bound to a given category are contestable and fluid, and also that, in the construction of categories in talk, *entitlements* to activities can be *normatively bound* to these categories. That is, not only are category memberships not 'fact[s] of nature' (Potter, 1996), but rather category memberships are social entitlements which must be claimed in interaction.

Furthermore, what is at stake in the contestation of category memberships is that the predicates established for a category may entail the normative entitlement (or otherwise) of incumbents to the performance of actions in the world. If then, to use an example from recent Australian race talk, the category-bound predicates of 'Aboriginality' are constructed as passivity, victimhood, and unreasonableness, the consequential entitlements of incumbency in the social category 'Aborigine' cannot readily be normatively bound to entitlement to activities such as negotiation with government (LeCouteur et al., 2001).

The key discursive psychological point at issue here is that *all* categories, their predicates and entitlements, however mundane, are not given *a priori*, but rather are fluid and negotiable, and their negotiation is the business-in-hand of social interaction. The management of *apparently* straightforward and unproblematic categories is displayed in Adolf Hitler's two-part construction of the nature of 'Jewish work' in the quote heading this chapter. But note also that Hitler simultaneously pays attention to his own *moral accountability* as a speaker in the production of the utterance. In the first part, Hitler constructs (an historically continuous) version of Jewish (as opposed to, say, German) 'work' as being made up of activities not usually grouped in everyday talk (even in 1920's and 1930's Germany) under the rubric of the category. He specifies the activities constituting the category of Jewish 'work', not as actions that may be expected routinely to fall into the category of 'work' (labouring, building, or manufacturing) but rather as: 'plundering travelling caravans … plundering indebted farmers, industrialists, middle-class people' (reproduced in Goldhagen, 1996: 281).

The second part of the construction turns on Hitler producing a version of himself – attentive to his moral accountability as a speaker – as a politician who is open, frank, and forthright. He is a 'straight talker'; he deals in facts and will tell it like it is. Thus, having respecified what the category of 'work' consists in, he recasts the moral nature of these activities for *both* local ideological, *and also*, simultaneously, for self-presentational ends. He bluntly states that: 'we do not call this work, but robbery' (reproduced in Goldhagen, 1996: 281). The second part here trades on the production of Jewish culpability as an *historical fact*. Here, we see Hitler attending to producing a version of the Jews as not being merely his *opinion* but as an experientially grounded part of the historical record. As is evident, this utterance is – like all utterances – thus attentive to both the on-the-spot flexibility and indexicality of social categories ('work') and also to the normative members' practice of producing utterances which are demonstrably attentive to the moral status of the speaker (honest and forthright). Intriguingly, in the context of the thesis of the modernity of 'modern' racism, it is possible to read Hitler himself as denying 'prejudice' in the 1920s: here at least he produces a version of self as an 'objective' racist.

Traditional psychological approaches are, of course, used to viewing social categories (such as 'Jews', 'work' or 'robbery', perhaps) as directly apprehended perceptual 'objects' whose psychological significance is read off their external physical and social features (e.g., Fiske and Taylor, 1991; Oakes et al., 1994). Yet Hitler demonstrates that 'work' is an entirely flexible category of actions in the world, and furthermore one which may be – indeed is – shaped locally for strategic, ideological, and political purposes. The meaning of the category 'work' here is precisely *not* readable from its semantic or lexical features, but rather derives its meaning only from its pragmatic use. As is immediately apparent, traditional social psychological approaches, which implicitly construct the meaning of utterances as being derived from a consensual social reliance on agreed dictionary definitions, are unable to deal with the very local and situated construction of the meaning of category terms.

As with the contestation of the social and semantic meaning of categories such as 'work' and 'race' in Hitler's Germany, Australian society's conversation has been dominated, since the election of the conservative Howard government in 1996, by political debates about race, about entitlements to land, to negotiation, and to consultation. The analysis of these debates throws into sharp relief some of the key differences between 'traditional' and discursive psychology. Analysis of the naturally-occurring public discourse of Australia's political leaders offers an analytic route to the description of contemporary 'racism' and its management – and the 'understandings' of, for example, Indigenous Australians, which Australia's political leaders wish to introduce into society's conversation – which is unavailable by means of traditional approaches. While dominant social psychological theorizing may offer a plausible explanation of experimental phenomena, it is less well-equipped to take on the task of accounting for racism, and the interactional deployment of social categories to solicit support for what may be describable as 'racist' measures, as naturally occurring, 'real-world' phenomena.

What a discursive approach can offer, then, is considerably more than an enumeration of the proportions of people who agree (or at least say they do) with items on attitude scales which claim to measure 'racism' (see Walker, Chapter 2). Rather than relying on such abstracted, academic, and endlessly arguable versions of what 'really' constitutes 'racism', a discursive approach can sample the production of 'racism' as an everyday phenomenon as it is produced by members in talk-in-interaction. As such, a discursive approach is in practice better grounded in *empirical* data than are standardized psychological measures of racial attitudes, beliefs, and opinions. Further, because the focus is on the way in which categories such as 'racist' are produced in action, and attention to the indexicality and contingency of meaning is a key analytic principle, discursive approaches allow for a rich understanding of the flexibility of taken-for-granted social categories (such as 'work') at the same time as a rigorously empirically grounded analysis of the social production of category memberships and their consequential entitlements (Wetherell, 1998).

A small body of work now exists which attends to the management of racism – or rather the management of possible accusations of racism – by politicians in their talk (e.g., LeCouteur et al., 2001; Obeng, 1997; Rapley, 1998). As we have seen, while Hitler's early speeches paid considerable attention to establishing his credentials *as* a virulent, racist, anti-semite, more recently it has been observed that the rhetorical task in contemporary political talk which seeks to influence a broad (as opposed to a minority or splinter) constituency is precisely the opposite (Billig, 1991b; Obeng, 1997; Rapley, 1998; Reeves, 1983). This chapter uses the naturally occurring talk of two Australian politicians, Prime Minister John Howard and Pauline Hanson, from parliamentary and televized political contexts, to explore the issue of race, racism, and the management of the ascription of racism, from a discursive perspective. The purpose of the analysis is emphatically *not* to point an accusatory finger at these politicians but rather, through an analysis of their talk, to describe what they – as political leaders and, perhaps, as opinion-formers – orient to as constituting 'race', 'racism' or 'racist'.

To recapitulate Edwards' (in press) observation, the purpose of the analysis is not to diagnose 'real' racism or to expose 'real' 'racists' by examining utterances as if they were 'symptoms'. Rather, the task is to identify from the speakers' talk that which is constructed *there, in that talk*, as being potentially describable by an audience as 'racist', and hence as requiring a defence against the possible accusation of racism. This chapter thus draws upon a range of work in discursive psychology to examine, in real-world talk-in-interaction, the way in which an inspection of the talk of political leaders can demonstrate not only the local discursive production of 'race' and 'racism', but also the rhetorical devices and strategies employed, as morally accountable actors, to bring off their talk as showing their *absence* of racial prejudice.

The analytic materials employed here are speeches to the Australian federal parliament made by Pauline Hanson on September 10th and 31st, 1996 and the Address to the Nation on the Wik debate delivered by John Howard on ABC Television in October, 1997. All three texts are in the public domain, and are available from a range of online sources. The texts have not been edited, but line numbers have been added to facilitate reference to key points. All punctuation and paragraph structures are as in the originals.

Producing a Version of 'Racism' by Managing its Absence: 'Doing Equity'

Contemporary political leaders in liberal societies, such as Hanson and Howard are, it is suggested, faced by a 'social taboo against expressing *unjustified* negative views against out-groups' (Billig, 1991b: 134, emphasis added). Such a taboo may be made 'visible' in the subtle management of utterances – or hearably oriented-to concern in talk – to guard against appearing overtly 'racist' (Wetherell and Potter, 1992). Whereas in 1920's Germany Hitler could title a speech 'Why are we Antisemites?' in the 'Western' democracies of the 1990s, political leaders who may wish to express negative views against outgroups have to take great care to construct these views as 'justified' or warranted, or alternatively – and perhaps preferably – as not 'negative' at all.

Such a reluctance to produce explicitly negative, or possibly 'racist', utterances has been observed in research with right-wing political groups such as the British Young Conservatives (Billig, 1991b) and the (self-proclaimedly) fascist British National Front (Billig, 1978). Politicians who wish to promote policies which will disadvantage one social group, which may be identifiable as a 'racial group' (for instance Aboriginal Australians; Albanian Kosovars) are thus likely, Billig argues, to identify 'non-racial criteria for racial discrimination and non-racial reasons for criticising other races' (1991b: 134). Thus, in his study of the British National Front, Billig argues that 'those who argue against Black interests or against non-White immigration typically *deny* that they are prejudiced' (1991b: 123, emphasis added). Similarly, Reeves (1983) describes the tendency of politicians to avoid the use of overt and explicit racial categories, by employing a strategy which he terms 'discoursive deracialization'.

Allied to this policy, Obeng has suggested that: 'indirectness is an integral part of any political discourse' (1997: 80). This denial of racism, the use of indirectness and the 'non-racial' production of racial prejudice, then, would seem to be what 'modern racism' is held to be in the international literature. Australian data, however, suggest that the notion of a homogenous, measurable, 'modern racism' is problematic. The explicit disavowal or denial of overt racism in which modern racism is held, at least in part, to consist is, in the texts examined here, notable precisely for its absence. In practice, conservative Australian politicians draw upon very locally nuanced, culturally pervasive tropes of egalitarianism, mateship, and the notion of a 'fair go' not to deny racism directly but rather, at the same time as making 'racial' categories locally relevant, to accomplish a version of self as representing 'equity'. But to say that the deployment of these discursive devices in talk is what 'modern racism' *is* (as traditionalist social psychologists may wish to, perhaps as a precursor to the design of a questionnaire to measure 'it') is to miss the point of the discursive critique: there is no such 'thing' as modern, postmodern (or even antique) racism *per se*. What counts as 'racism' is always, inextricably, of its immediate time and its local place. But let us now turn to look more closely at the ways in which 'race' and 'racism' get locally produced, as such, in talk.

Pauline Hanson's Maiden Speech

Pauline Hanson, interestingly, offers a challenge to Billig's (1991b), Reeves' (1983), and Obeng's (1997) claims about the contemporary pervasiveness of subtlety, indirectness, and discretion in political talk. Billig in particular has noted that 'on the New Right the denial [of racism] is often accompanied by the claim that it is the anti-racists who are the real racists' (1981: 124). Widely branded by media commentators and political opponents as obviously, incontrovertibly, racist, on the basis of this speech, at the same time as she invokes *explicitly* racial categories, Pauline Hanson also works to discount the notion that she is reasonably describable as racist.

'Doing equity' is offered here as understandable as a defensive rhetorical device to fend off possible attributions of being motivated by racial concerns, whilst at the same time promoting actions which may be – indeed are, oriented to by the speaker – as being describable by overhearers as 'racist'. 'Doing equity' is then perhaps tentatively identifiable as being a larger scale variant of the device 'How to do X without doing Y', which form of indirection Schegloff

(1989) identifies as being the key analytic theme of Sacks' early work (Edwards, 1997: 94). Such devices attend to the moral accountability of speakers, and to local norms of preference organization. Thus, one way to 'avoid giving help' without the dispreferred production of 'refusal' is, Schegloff suggests, to treat the circumstances as a joke. 'Doing equity' then may offer a way to do 'promoting (racially) discriminatory positions' without 'being racist'.

Extract 1 (below) shows clearly the difficulty of invoking homogenous, reified, constructs such as 'modern racism'. In the very opening moments of her address (lines 9–10), Hanson shows how the explicit naming of specific racial groups (this is hardly 'indirectness' or 'discoursive deracialization') may be found in the same utterance as a much more prototypical 'modern racist' claim that it is the so-called 'anti-racists' who are the 'real' racists. The extract shows how, at the same time as deploying explicit 'old fashioned' racial categories (the speech also suggested that Australia was 'in danger of being swamped by Asians'), the supposedly modern 'camouflage' of a concern with 'equity' can be invoked (in the claimed inequitable distribution of 'benefits') as a (non-racial) reason for the promotion of a racial political agenda.

Extract 1. (From 'Australia Wake Up!' Pauline Hanson's maiden speech to the Australian Parliament)

6 My view on issues is based on commonsense, and my experience as a mother of four
7 children, as a sole parent, and as a businesswoman running a fish and chip shop.
8 I won the seat of Oxley largely on an issue that has resulted in me being called a
9 racist. That issue related to my comment that Aboriginals received more benefits than
10 non-Aboriginals. We now have a situation where a type of reverse racism is applied to
11 mainstream Australians by those who promote political correctness and those who
12 control the various taxpayer funded 'industries' that flourish in our society servicing
13 Aboriginals, multiculturalists and a host of other minority groups.

Note also that, having invoked 'common sense' as the basis for her views, Hanson directly alludes to socially shared *common knowledge* of the criteria currently employed in Australian society to infer racism in raising the fact that she – by virtue of her utterances – has been 'called a racist'. But such an 'admission' is made precisely for the purpose of redefining, and contesting, the parameters and predicates of the category 'racism'. In the same way as Hitler constructs a version of Jewish activities in order to preface the re-casting of 'work' as 'robbery', so too Hanson prefaces her recasting of what 'racism' consists in – prejudice against mainstream (White?) Australians by the politically correct – by constructing a version of her activities as consisting in the (self-evidently harmless) making of mere common sense 'comments' on clear cut inequities perpetrated at the ordinary taxpayers' expense.

Extract 2 (lines 44–45) illustrates the further deployment of an emphasis on 'doing equity' and 'fairness'. As in the first extract, Hanson clearly alludes to a concern with egalitarianism, usually glossed in the Australian vernacular as the principle of offering people 'a fair go', as being a fundamental aspect of the character of the 'ordinary Australian', a suitably vague category (Potter, 1996), of which she is offering herself as prototype. This extract is perhaps a clearer example of the deployment of 'typical' 'New Right'/'Modern Racist' rhetoric (Billig, 1991b). But again, it is not clear that an understanding of 'modern racism' as, at least in part, indexed by the *absence of explicit racial category names* can sustain a close inspection of the talk here.

Extract 2. (From 'Australia Wake Up!' Pauline Hanson's maiden speech to the Australian Parliament)

42 This nation is being divided into black and white, and the present system encourages
43 this. I am fed up with being told, 'This is our land'. Well, where the hell do I go? I
44 was born here, and so were my parents and children. I will work beside anyone and
45 they will be my equal but I draw the line when told I must pay and continue paying for
46 something that happened over 200 years ago. Like most Australians, I worked for my
47 land; no-one gave it to me.

Hanson is 'fed up with being told "this is our land"'. Those doing the 'telling' are, in the Australian context, clearly understandable *specifically* as the Aboriginal peoples. Yet while Aborigines are not named here as such, 'black and white' (line 42) are clearly hearable as indexing 'racial' categories. The talk constructs Aboriginal people and 'most Australians' as a dichotomous, or contrast, pair. Furthermore, the predicates of the two category memberships are explicitly spelt out. 'Most Australians' *work* for their land with and beside others as *equals*. Aborigines do not, and simply expect (continuing) handouts on the (spurious) basis of ancient history. Although again, on the surface, it appears that Hanson is claiming standard 'modern racist' or 'non-racial' grounds for her concerns (explicitly, at least, her concern is with fairness, reasonableness, and equity) it is evident that – having indexed an apparently innocuous group of 'land claimants' who have a 200-year-old grievance as a contrast category of persons – the claim here is, in fact, that Aborigines – *as Aborigines* – are being unfairly preferred.

It is thus apparent that Hanson not only blends what may be termed 'modern' and 'old-fashioned' racist tropes, but also provides a working account of what she constructs 'racism' as 'being', commonsensically, for 'most Australians'. 'Racism', as Extract 3 again shows, is to be understood as the absence of equal treatment of 'all Australians'.

Extract 3. (From "Australia Wake Up!" Pauline Hanson's maiden speech to the Australian Parliament)

201 I consider myself just an ordinary Australian who wants to keep this great country
202 strong and independent, and my greatest desire is to see all Australians treat each
203 others as equals

In a later address to Federal Parliament, Hanson seeks to turn the accusation of racism back on those who have accused *her* of being racist by once more 'doing equity'. In so doing she is also attentive to the necessity of constructing a version of 'racism' as consisting in the existence of a government ministry which is named for the population groups for whom it directs policy. These population groups, it should be noted, are also describable as 'ethnic' or 'cultural' – as opposed to 'racial' – groups; as 'the prior owners of Australia'; as 'disadvantaged Australians' or a range of other categories of persons which are not, in and of themselves, necessarily normatively implicative of the category of 'race' in members' talk. Not only is the category 'Aboriginal and Torres Strait Islanders' constructed here *as inevitably* a *racial* rather than, say, a national, geographical or cultural category, but the category 'race' is made strategically salient in order both to re-emphasize Hanson's personal reasonableness and commitment to impartiality in the equal treatment of 'all Australians' (and by extension – in line 3 – the reasonableness of the 'Australian people'); and also to cement the notion that a specific racial group is unfairly privileged, with the connivance of the politically correct, at the expense of members of the contrast pair – 'ordinary' Australians like her – who are committed to a fair go.

Extract 4: Hansard: Pauline Hanson. Speech to Australian Federal Parliament 31 October 1996

1 Ms HANSON (Oxley) (5.49 p.m.) – 'I make no apology for my absence from the
2 House yesterday. Prior arrangements had been made. I am appalled that the
3 government and the opposition moved a motion which was clearly directed at me and 4
   indirectly at the Australian people.'
5 The motion stated:
6 'That this House reaffirms its commitment to the right of all Australians to enjoy
7 equal rights and be treated with equal respect regardless of race, colour, creed or
8 origin'. 'This is exactly what I am fighting for. How can the House possibly move this
9 motion and still have a separate portfolio for Aboriginal and Torres Strait Islanders
10 which is clearly based on race?'

How can a speaker, particularly one alluding to the iconic Australian discourse of 'a fair go' (Extract 2, lines 44–45); whose 'greatest desire is to see all Australians treat each other as equals' (Extract 3, lines 202–203); who is on the record as 'fighting for' the 'right of all Australians to enjoy equal rights' (Extract 4, lines 5–7), be credibly attacked as 'discriminatory', as 'prejudiced', as a 'racist'? The position Hanson seeks to construct herself as representing in these Extracts is one of common sense, straight talk, and impartiality. Such a position, constructed strategically as an *inoculation against* (Potter, 1996) the charge of racism, can then act as a negative image, illuminating that which is constructed here as understandable as 'racism', by staking out a moral claim to represent its antithesis. Nowhere does Hanson, in Billig's (1991b) terms, 'deny' she is 'racist'. The device is more subtle than that. 'Racism' is not to be understood as prejudicial negative views of particular persons on the basis of the colour of their skin or of their 'race'. The version of 'racism' which Pauline Hanson wishes to introduce into society's conversation is, rather, to be understood as not giving Aussie battlers a 'fair go'; as an absence of a 'colour-blind' equity in the distribution of national resources; as the existence of ministries directly concerned with the affairs of specific population groups; as all Australians being prevented from treating each other as 'equals'. Such an account may seem to be a reasonable member's working up of what the academy has come to call 'modern racism'.

But such a version of racism also constructs the explicit invocation of 'racial' category names (Aboriginals, Asians) *as* racial category names as indexical of the 'reasonableness', 'fairness', and 'non-racist' nature of the views promoted. It is only the 'politically correct' who are squeamish about these matters. 'Doing equity' thus not only simultaneously attends to the normative social convention of being concerned with equity and fairness (a particularly heightened trope in the Australian discursive context) but also, paradoxically, turns upon a construction of racially 'negative' views as not mindless bigotry, but rather, as with Hitler's 'forthrightness' about the Jews, as merely being the expression of frank, down-to-earth, 'common sense'. Explicitly calling Aborigines 'Aborigines' is not 'being racist' it is, rather, 'being honest'.

'Doing equity' is thus not only a defensive rhetorical device to fend off attributions of 'racism', it is also simultaneously a strategic, action-performative, discursive move in the production of self as morally accountable politician; as unafraid to call a spade a spade; as 'just an ordinary Australian' who wants everyone to be equals. It is a political position for which there is considerable jockeying in Australian political talk.

John Howard and the Wik Address

The contested entitlement of Indigenous Australians to land title, and the consequences of the legal challenge to *terra nullius* in the Mabo and Wik cases, have dominated the 'race debate' in Australia, and indeed have been central to the emergence of Pauline Hanson's National-Socialist inspired One Nation Party (see Rapley, 1998). The emergence of One Nation posed immense political problems for John Howard's Liberal Party/National Party Coalition government and the Wik decision, which upheld the coexistence of Aboriginal and pastoral leaseholders' titles on Crown land, represented a major challenge to the interests of the Coalition's core constituency.

The legislative solution to the 'problem' of Wik offered by Howard, his so-called 10-point plan, promised the abolition (or 'bucketloads of extinguishment' as it was less delicately put by the Deputy Prime Minister Tim Fischer) of the title rights of Indigenous people on pastoral leaseholds. Such a legislative response was described as 'savage, mean and racist' by former Prime Minister, Paul Keating; and as issuing from a government made up of 'racist scum' by Noel Pearson, a leading Aboriginal lawyer.

In a highly charged political environment, in which he had already been publicly accused of being 'racist', Howard's intervention of choice into society's conversation about the land rights of Aboriginal people was a televised Address to the Nation. It is a text which again illustrates the way in which contemporary Australian political talk deploys 'doing equity' as defence against 'being racist', whilst at the same time strategically manipulating the predicates and entitlements of *explicitly-named* racial categories in such a manner as to bring off 'prejudicial and negative views' without appearing to do so.

The existence of a social taboo against (Billig, 1991b), or 'modern racist' delicacy about, nakedly racist or discriminatory rhetoric, is then, in the Australian context at least, far from being unproblematic. As has been seen in the Hanson material, the normative expectation of delicacy is contingently shaped – and flouted – to suit local, contingent, circumstances. However, in the case of representatives of mainstream – as opposed to minority – political positions, it may be that requirements of 'indirectness' are more onerous. That is, the requirements for such speakers to insulate their positions from charges of defectiveness on account of their partiality, in particular, of the charge of racist bias may be more evident in their talk. As such, our analytic attention may be focused on the ways these 'establishment' speakers manage the disavowal of a particular, partisan, stake and present themselves as fair and impartial.

In the Address to the Nation, Howard opens his oration with a specification of the difficulty of the debate. Yet this difficulty is introduced as in the context of the prior claim that a 'fair and decent' outcome (an 'equitable' balance?) is being struck. Having opened the speech with a claim to be motivated by a concern with fairness and equity, Howard glosses the accusations of 'racism' which are already on the record, rather like Pauline Hanson's insignificant 'comment', as nothing more than an entirely reasonable sounding 'debate' and 'difference[s] of opinion'. Even-handed, impartial, reasoned equanimity is set out, in the very opening moments of the talk, as characterizing the tone of the 'race' debate – and, hence, of Howard's contribution to, and position in, the debate.

Extract 5: Howard: Address to the Nation (line numbers added)

1	Good evening. Tonight I would like to talk to you about striking a fair
2	and decent balance in this very difficult debate about Wik, or Native
3	Title. You all know there has been a lot of debate and a lot of
4	differences of opinion but I think we all agree on one thing and that is
5	the sooner we get this debate over and get the whole issue behind us
6	the better for all of us.

With such a discursive frame established at the outset of the speech episode, Howard moves to set up what he constructs as the nub of the issue: the competing positions and rights of the two parties to the dispute over Wik. Having claimed a confected consensus on the requirement for resolution (Extract 5, lines 4–5), he continues to develop the grounds of consensual agreement (Extract 6, lines 7 and 14) by the citation of areas which he offers as being of common accord. With the suggestion that 'we probably also agree on some other things' he offers – as *instances* of the broader consensus he constructs as obtaining between himself and his audience – the identities of the groups he goes on later to define as the interested parties to the 'difficult' debate.

Extract 6: Howard: Address to the Nation (line numbers added)

7	I think we probably also agree on some other things – for example,
8	the Aboriginal and Torres Strait Islander people of Australia have
9	been very badly treated in the past and we must continue our efforts
10	to improve their health, their housing, their employment and their
11	educational opportunities. And in doing that we should always
12	remember that the Aboriginal people of Australia have a very special

13   affinity with their land.
14   I think we would also agree on how important the rural and mining
15   industries are to the future of our country. Between them they
16   contribute 63 per cent of Australia's export income and that helps
17   generate a lot of wealth, which in turn enables us to help the less
18   fortunate within our community.

Howard attends to his own stake in Wik and its resolution by presenting it as *absent*: the urgent need for the 10-point plan to become law is what *we all* agree on, not what he, John Howard, proposes. Again, like Hanson, he works to promote the impartiality, the inclusiveness, and the non-racial nature of his position by reference to the 'facts' that the explicitly named category – 'Aboriginal and Torres Strait Islanders' – have 'been very badly treated in the past' and that they 'have a very special affinity with their land'. Howard's emphasis on equity, on finding a 'fair and decent balance' (Extract 5, lines 1–2), and his explicit acknowledgment of the bad treatment of Aborigines, work to undermine the credibility of the accusation that he is promoting a 'racist' response to the Wik judgment. As in Pauline Hanson's maiden speech, claims of a concern with fairness and equity – 'doing equity' – offers a discursive device for the promotion of racially discriminatory legislation without 'being racist'.

Howard's address as a whole is structured to present the native-title issue as a simple conflict of interest between two main groups: the Aboriginal people of Australia and a group he constructs as Australia's 'farmers'. Introducing an understanding of the issue in these terms into society's conversation is the central rhetorical project of the address. Securing the agreement of the Australian public with the 'fairness' of the 10-point plan is then reliant upon the entire speech episode being constructed in such a way as to 'do equity': and to produce such an outcome Howard discursively constructs the relevant categories of protagonists (Aborigines, farmers, and himself) in such a manner as also to normatively bind moral entitlements to them. We have seen that at the opening of the address he constructs his role as no more than the morally neutral activity of helping to 'strike a fair and decent balance'.

Producing himself as merely 'problem solving' in a dispute between two others, does some work in fending off charges that the 10-point plan is partisan, one-sided, and racist. But to promote the extinguishment of Aboriginal land rights as 'fair' Howard attends to the entitlements bound to the categories of disputants he constructs. The Aborigines, who are to lose their land rights, are discursively produced as a social category which is representative of obstruction, unproductiveness, and dependency: a group who, in losing their land, are in practice not losing anything. In what amounts to a recapitulation of the argument of the lawyer Richard Windemeyer (1842) (see also Hall, 1998; Reynolds, 1998), that as a matter of natural justice (fairness?) moral title to land belongs to those who bestow labour ('work'?) upon it, farmers, the beneficiaries of the 10-point plan, are constructed by Howard as positive, productive, and engaged in socially beneficial activity as the key predicates of their category incumbency.

Although Howard suggests that Aboriginal Australians 'have been very badly treated in the past', the clear implication of this construction is that in the present they are not treated so badly. As Pauline Hanson constructed, 200 years of what is also describable as 'dispossession' and 'genocide' as a 'something that happened over 200 years ago' (Rapley, 1998: 335), Howard's description is similarly vague and non-specific. Aboriginal Australians are passive recipients of 'treatment' (good or bad) handed out by unspecified others. Aboriginal people require *others* to improve *their* health, housing, employment and education. As a social category 'Aboriginality' is normatively bound to passivity; to waiting for others to act on problems, problems which do not include dispossession of their land. In contrast, 'farmers' – a nonce category that serves to homogenize and romanticize 'the rural and mining industries' – are constructed as valuable and active contributory parts of the *future* of Australia. The binding of entitlement to land to the category of 'farmers' is cemented in Howard's highly emotive construction of this social category:

Extract 7: Howard: Address to the Nation (line numbers added)

19   Australia's farmers, of course, have always occupied a very special
20   place in our heart. They often endure the heartbreak of drought, the
21   disappointment of bad international prices after a hard worked season
22   and, quite frankly, I find it impossible to imagine the Australia I love
23   without a strong and vibrant farming sector.

Howard offers (lines 19–20) a version of a collective Australian consciousness as historically grounded, matter-of-fact, shared social reality. 'Farmers, of course, have always' held 'a very special place' in [the] heart of all Australians. Farmers, not Aborigines, 'endure…heartbreak (and) disappointment' following 'hard-worked' seasons. 'A strong and vibrant farming sector' represents 'the Australia I love', an Australia without which it is 'frankly…impossible' (line 22) to imagine.

Aboriginal Australians, having a mere 'affinity' to land rather than working it 'hard', by implication do not know 'heartbreak' and 'disappointment'. Howard's version of the two parties to the Wik debate obscures the problems that Indigenous Australians may have 'endured' over 200 years of European colonization. Australia – at least the Australia Howard loves – is it seems, imaginable without Aboriginal people. As did Pauline Hanson in her maiden speech ('I worked for my land, no one gave it to me' – Rapley, 1998: 335), Howard deploys romanticized representations of farmers in his (rhetorically disavowed) advocacy for the interests of this group. Like Hanson, he constructs threats to the welfare of hard-working 'battlers' – a 'strong and vibrant farming sector' – as threats to the nation as a whole.

The contrast pairing of the two groups' relationship both to the land and also to 'work' serves to erase the legitimacy of the distinct cultural and spiritual meaning of land to Indigenous people. Such a romanticized, Eurocentric construction of 'work' as warrant for entitlement – uncomfortably reminiscent of Hitler's use of 'work' to discredit the citizenship claims of European Jewry – in accomplishing relative inequality of connectedness to land, cements an unequal legitimacy of title.

By his careful management of these social identities, in the context of claims to equity and fairness, the moral claims that are normatively bound to the two categories are clearly established. Because of their productive use of the land, their endurance of suffering and their huge contribution to the 'less fortunate', it is only fair that farmers should have their wishes respected by the government. Aborigines, in contrast, who only have an 'affinity' to land and are passively dependent on the goodwill of others, have no such entitlement. Rather, a public concern with equity and fairness demands that we should – if 'we' are to 'do equity' – be attentive to 'improving' them.

Concluding Comments

This chapter has sought to lay out both the intellectual position and the analytic approach of discursive psychology towards racism, and in so doing to problematize many of the notions that mainstream psychological approaches take for granted. The chapter has shown, I hope, not only that discursive psychology offers a purchase on 'racism' which is outside the scope of traditional social psychological methods, but also an account which is resolutely grounded in 'race' and 'racism' as 'real' people produce and deal in these matters *as* matters of everyday practical concern. As such, the strong analytic claim here is that a discursive approach can point to data which are simply not available to traditional approaches: furthermore, most of the intractable problems of experimental social psychology simply disappear. For example, the problem of 'generalizing' the findings of questionnaire studies of 'modern racism' completed by university undergraduates to any other group in society – the bane of the traditional approach – is simply a non-issue. Whether a given measure of racism 'reliably' and 'validly' operationalizes a version of the construct again ceases to be a matter requiring any consideration. As we have seen, versions of 'race' and 'racism' are visibly and hearably operationalized in talk all the time, and variably. But here the richness and variability of the manner in which members 'do racism' – or their on-the-spot-for-local-purposes operationalization of the notion – is an analytic resource, not the source of thorny problems with values of Cronbach's alpha.

'Race' and 'racism' are thus, from a discursive perspective, not the sort of social scientific *things* about which psychology – or any other discipline come to that – can make final and definitive statements. As such it is not likely to be possible to 'understand the psychology of prejudice and racism' with the sort of scientific precision implied by the title of this collection. The sorts of social actions that are held to constitute membership in the category of those describable as 'doing racism' or 'being racist' are not only variable from time to time and place to place, but the parameters of these categories are routinely contested in everyday as well as political talk. Of course, this is only what may be expected of a notion such as 'racism' which is much more a *moral* than a *scientific* category, even as positivist research understands it. As such, the discursive perspective is troubled neither by fluctuations in the range of socially understood and sanctioned ways of 'being racist', nor by the varying moral value normatively bound to 'being racist' in the last 60 years (with 'racism' ranging both within specific societies, and also between them, from representing an unqualified good to being the epitome of evil). Of course, if we choose to understand 'racism' from the perspective of mainstream cognitive social psychology, as being merely an automatic expression of unconscious cognitive processes this poses an explanatory difficulty. How can cognitive structures change so quickly in response to social and cultural change? By what means is cognitive architecture altered by an election result? How does the cognitive apparatus that produces 'racism' come to 'know' that South Africa is no longer a society based upon apartheid? How does an automatic cognitive apparatus work out that when it has to 'depersonalize' its 'owner' in the company of Pauline Hanson's One Nation supporters that it must produce, on its owner's behalf, a different set of utterances to those it needs to produce at an Australian Labor Party meeting? And who – or what – is morally accountable for these utterances? 'It wasn't me your honour, I was the depersonalized victim of an unconscious categorization process' is not a defence to a charge of racial vilification I would rely on in court.

In truth, an homunculus still lurks at the heart of cognitively-based social psychological accounts of phenomena like 'prejudice' and 'racism' (see Augoustinos and Walker, 1995; Fiske and Taylor, 1991; Turner, 1982; Turner et al., 1987, 1991; Turner and Oakes, 1997). These approaches offer, in practice, little to advance our understanding of the (re)production of prejudicial social action, but rather merely present a recapitulation of the 'ghost in the machine' (Ryle, 1949). Even were this not so, current developments in a range of societies' conversations about the morality of ethnic cleansing and racism across the world demonstrate a worrying deviation from, and must call into question the relevance of, the notions of 'progress' implicit in the epistemological claims of positivist social science. One only needs to compare the Yugoslav Republic of Marshall Tito to that of President Milosevic or, closer to home, the Australia of Paul Keating to that of John Howard to get the point.

Notes

I would like to thank Charles Antaki, Martha Augoustinos, Derek Edwards, Amanda LeCouteur, Ivan Leudar, Iain Walker and Margaret Wetherell for their extremely helpful discussions of the issues treated here. If I have inadvertently failed to cite my inevitable incorporation of their ideas they will, I hope, see imitation as the sincerest form of flattery.

1. For a range of critical reactions to Goldhagen's thesis see the Review Symposium introduced by Radtke (1998).

Part VI:

Future Directions

15 Reducing Prejudice: An Historical and Multi-Level Approach

John Duckitt

Prejudice has been a distinctively twentieth-century concept in several interesting respects. Firstly, the idea of prejudice as a social scientific concept and a social problem simply did not exist prior to the twentieth century. During the nineteenth century and even the early decades of the twentieth, negative and derogatory racial attitudes were seen as basically natural responses by advanced Western peoples to backward colonial peoples. It was only in the aftermath of the First World War that the concept of prejudice became widely adopted to express what had only then come to be seen as profoundly unfair and irrational negative attitudes to culturally different peoples and national minorities. Secondly, once the concept had been established, prejudice rapidly came to be viewed as one of the dominant social issues and problems of the time: a problem that still remains largely unresolved as we enter the new millennium.

Prejudice and Policy: Historical Shifts

Nevertheless, although prejudice remains a major social problem, there have been substantial advances in knowledge and understanding during the twentieth century. The development of theory, however, has not occurred in linear and incremental fashion; nor has it been entirely driven by the logic of theoretical development or data from research findings. As I have previously suggested, distinct historical stages can be identified, with each dominated by a particular theoretical orientation to the concept and explanation of prejudice (Duckitt, 1994). These dominant theoretical orientations have directly reflected social and historical circumstances that made particular questions about the nature and causation of prejudice salient for social scientists at the time. Each new conceptual and explanatory paradigm powerfully determined the kind of research issues that were investigated during each period.

These prejudice paradigms were also expressed in the kind of social policy approaches to prejudice that were dominant in each period. This is summarized in Table 15.1, which shows the social and historical problem giving rise to a particular concept of, and theoretical orientation to, prejudice in the first two

Table 15.1 Twentieth-century shifts in dominant theoretical and social policy approaches to prejudice

Social and historical issue	Concept of prejudice and dominant theoretical approach	Dominant social policy orientation to prejudice and discrimination
Up to the 1920s: White domination and colonial rule of 'backward peoples'	Prejudice as a natural response to the deficiencies of 'backward' peoples: Race theories	Domination, discrimination, and segregation are natural
The 1920s and 1930s: The legitimacy of White domination and pervasive prejudice challenged	Prejudice as irrational and unjustified reaction to people who are different: Psychoanalytic and frustration theories	Assimilation as a gradual process as minorities and colonial peoples become Westernized and 'uplifted'
The 1940s and 1950s: Nazi racial ideology and the holocaust	Prejudice rooted in anti-democratic ideology and pathological needs within authoritarian personalities	Democratic and anti-authoritarian social structures and values will erode intolerance and prejudice
The 1960s: The problem of institutionalized racism in the American South	Sociocultural explanations: Prejudice rooted in the social norms of discriminatory social structures	Desegregation and anti-discriminatory laws will lead to intergroup contact which will erode prejudice
The 1970s: The problem of informal racism and discrimination in the North	Prejudice as an expression of dominant group interests in maintaining intergroup inequality	Reducing intergroup inequality through affirmative action and minority empowerment
The 1980s and 1990s: The stubborn persistence of stereotyping, prejudice, and discrimination	Prejudice as an expression of universal cognitive-motivational processes: social categorization and social identity	Multicultural policies to provide minorities with esteem and foster positive non-threatened identities and tolerance for all groups

columns, and then in a third column, the social policy orientations to prejudice and discrimination that were dominant during each period. Each 'policy era' is briefly described below.

Segregation and Discrimination

During the nineteenth century and early decades of the twentieth, racist attitudes were largely viewed as natural responses of 'advanced' Western peoples to 'inferior' or 'backward' colonial peoples or 'racially different' minorities. These attitudes had their logical social policy expressions in the political domination of these 'backward' peoples, their segregation (formal or informal), and discrimination against them. After the First World War, however, as Western colonial rule was increasingly challenged, a dramatic reversal occurred in the way in which racist attitudes were conceptualized (Samelson, 1978). The idea of the inferiority of other 'races' came to be rejected by social scientists, and racist attitudes were reinterpreted as prejudice – that is, as unjustified, unfair, and irrational negative intergroup attitudes.

Assimilation and Upliftment

During the 1920s and early 1930s, social scientists focused primarily on measuring and documenting prejudiced attitudes. Then, during the 1930s, the first attempts to explain prejudice were made, with the dominant approach being the psychoanalytically derived frustration-displacement theory (Dollard et al., 1939). This approach saw prejudice as an unconscious defence through which social stress and frustrations were displaced through the scapegoating of outgroups and minorities. The most likely targets for prejudice and scapegoating were those that differed (socio-economically, culturally, ethnically) from the dominant majority. This paradigm therefore seemed to neatly explain both the irrationality of prejudice and its pervasiveness.

This concept and explanation of prejudice had its logical expression in the social policy of assimilation (Simpson and Yinger, 1985). Through assimilation, minorities and colonial peoples would become increasingly similar to the dominant Western majority peoples, thus 'civilizing' and 'uplifting' them socially and economically into the dominant group. As a result, prejudice and discrimination against them should gradually erode.

Liberal Democracy and Political Tolerance

After the Second World War the dominant concept and explanation of prejudice shifted, driven largely by the need to explain Nazi racial ideology and its catastrophic culmination in the holocaust. The new paradigm saw prejudice and racism as intimately related to fascist and right-wing ideology and values, which were themselves viewed as expressions of pathological needs within authoritarian personalities (Adorno et al., 1950). Prejudice and racism were therefore intimately associated with political intolerance (cf., also Martin and Westie, 1959; Rokeach et al., 1960). The social policy implication of this approach was that both racial and political tolerance would grow with the spread of liberal democratic values and institutions. Thus, the defeat of authoritarianism in all its variants, and the replacement of authoritarian values and ideologies with liberal democratic values, and a belief in political equality would result in the progressive erosion of political and racial intolerance. In America, for example, the fundamental contradiction between democratic equality and racial discrimination was powerfully argued in Myrdal's (1944) classic: *The American Dilemma*.

Desegregation and Integration

At the end of the 1950s, a new paradigm shift occurred as the campaign for civil rights in the American South exploded into public awareness. The focus now became that of explaining how ordinary 'good citizens' holding strong democratic and even anti-authoritarian values could be racist and support discrimination. The explanatory paradigm that emerged saw racial prejudice as rooted in social structures in which segregation and discrimination had been legally institutionalized and become social norms, which were taught to individuals during socialization and maintained by conformity pressures (Pettigrew, 1958).

The nature of the social policies required to reduce prejudice flowed logically from these assumptions. Institutionalized barriers to contact, segregation, and discriminatory practices must be legally abolished. Schools and workplaces must be desegregated. The guiding principle underlying this was the 'contact hypothesis': that racial segregation and unfamiliarity would perpetuate racial prejudice and hostility, while intergroup contact under the right conditions would reduce it (Allport, 1954). This was essentially the social science argument submitted to the American Supreme Court in the Brown versus Board of Education of Topeka case, which resulted in the first major ruling on school desegregation in 1954.

Affirmative Action and Minority Empowerment

As Fairchild and Gurin (1978) have noted, the optimistic assumption that racial integration would eliminate racism in American society rapidly faded in the late 1960s and 1970s. As the institutionalized segregation and old-fashioned racism of the South disappeared, it was simply replaced by informal discrimination and segregation, and the subtle 'modern' racism of the North. The paradigm that emerged saw racism and discrimination not just as a problem of the South, but as rooted in the power relations between White and Black in American society as a whole.

This new paradigm of the 1970s therefore viewed racial prejudice as expressing the interests of the dominant White group, which were served by the maintenance of racial inequality and keeping Blacks as a disadvantaged, powerless, and impoverished underclass (Blauner, 1972; Bonacich, 1972; Carmichael and Hamilton, 1967). With this shift in the dominant understanding of racial prejudice in America, came a shift in the social policies seen as most needed to reduce prejudice. To eliminate racism, the social, economic, and political inequalities between Black and White would have to be changed; most notably through affirmative action and the political empowerment of Blacks in American society (Crosby and Clayton, 1990). Affirmative action and Black empowerment would also help to create more favourable contact conditions by reducing intergroup status and power differentials.

The impacts of affirmative action in America have been controversial, and are discussed in more detail later. While undeniable advances occurred in Black empowerment and the growth of a Black middle class; racism, and discrimination remained major social problems (e.g., Carmines and Merriman, 1993; Hawley, 1995). Moreover, many affirmative action programmes were abandoned or seriously weakened by the conservative American administrations during the 1980s. During this period, however, a new shift occurred in the way in which prejudice was conceptualized and explained, which led to an emphasis on new and different policies to reduce prejudice.

Multiculturalism

By the late 1970s, the stubborn persistence of American racism and discrimination, albeit in subtle and modern, rather than crude and traditional forms, had been powerfully documented (Kinder and Sears, 1981; McConahay and Hough, 1976). It began to seem that more fundamental and perhaps universal human processes might underlie prejudice. This was reinforced by research findings from the minimal intergroup paradigm (Brewer, 1979; Tajfel and Turner, 1979; Turner and Giles, 1981; see Reynolds and Turner, Chapter 10) indicating that discrimination and ingroup favouritism resulted from simply classifying individuals into completely arbitrary minimal groups. The new paradigm which emerged in the 1980s therefore saw group identities, intergroup competition, bias, discrimination, and ultimately even outgroup prejudice as arising out of the normal, natural, and universal cognitive process of social categorization, which triggered a motivated need to positively differentiate one's group from others (Brewer, 1979).

This new paradigm seemed to have important implications for reducing prejudice. The dominant policies thus far, such as affirmative action and desegregation, and their rationale in terms of the contact hypothesis, had fundamentally involved assimilationist assumptions. Thus, the implicit or explicit assumption had been that equal status, cooperative, and rewarding contact would encourage acquaintanceship and friendship between individuals from different groups by reducing or eliminating group divisions and enabling individuals to discover common interests, values, and identities. Racial and colour differences would therefore become increasingly unimportant, and as society became colour blind, racism would disappear.

Researchers, however, increasingly came to question these assimilationist assumptions (Saharso, 1989; Schofield, 1986). Their findings indicated that assimilationist and colour blind policies could be extremely disadvantageous to minorities by reinforcing an intolerant attitude to cultural and group differences and so maintaining covert prejudice and discrimination against them. These concerns meshed with the new paradigm for explaining prejudice, which in contrast to the traditional assimilationist approach, emphasized the inevitability of group differentiation and the importance, particularly for minorities, of maintaining positively valued and differentiated group identities (cf., Hewstone and Brown, 1986).

Multicultural policies emerged logically from this new paradigm. These policies rested on a view of cultural and social diversity as inevitable and valuable in their own right, and had the explicit objectives of accepting, recognizing, and supporting subcultural and minority identities and tolerance for them (Berry, 1984). During the past two decades, multiculturalism has increasingly become the dominant approach to prejudice reduction (Berry, 1984; Fowers and Richardson, 1996; Torney-Purta, 1995). However, it has not proved uncontroversial, and concerns have been expressed about the way in which multiculturalism has been interpreted and implemented (cf., Brewer, 1997). These will be discussed later and it will be suggested that a more flexible and balanced interpretation of multiculturalism may well emerge as the next policy paradigm.

Implications of the Historical Analysis

Overall, therefore, this analysis suggests that systematic shifts in the dominant policies advocated by social scientists for reducing prejudice occurred in response to changes in the way in which prejudice was being conceptualized and explained. In each case, the new policies can be seen as arising directly and logically out of the assumptions of the new conceptual and explanatory paradigm.

I have earlier suggested that these different theoretical and conceptual paradigms provided complementary rather than conflicting explanations of prejudice. This has several implications. One is that the policies are themselves complementary, and can be combined into a coherent and integrated policy framework for reducing prejudice. A second implication is that these paradigms have tended to be located at different and complementary levels of analysis. This suggests that truly comprehensive intervention policies should also encompass multiple levels, and that an overview of possible interventions might be usefully organized in terms of a multilevel framework.

A Multilevel Framework for Prejudice Reduction

Each shift in the way prejudice has been understood historically seems to concern a different causal process, with each causal process located at a different level of analysis (Duckitt, 1994). Four such basic causal processes at four distinct levels of analyses emerged from the earlier analysis. Firstly, a universal perceptual-cognitive process of categorization builds in a basic human potentiality for prejudice. Secondly, this potentiality may be elaborated into overt prejudice by certain intergroup dynamics of contact and interaction between groups. Thirdly, these social and intergroup dynamics generate social influence processes and intergroup contact conditions that create and reinforce prejudice in individuals. And fourthly, certain individual difference dimensions determine individuals' susceptibility to prejudice.

Actions to reduce prejudice should therefore operate at each of these four levels. Firstly, at the perceptual-categorization level there should be changes in the salience of particular social categorizations that maintain prejudice. Secondly, there should be interventions to change individual susceptibility to adopt and hold prejudiced attitudes. Thirdly, there should be change in the kind of interpersonal influences and contacts from which people acquire and learn prejudice. And fourthly, there should be change in the kind of social conditions and intergroup relations that generate prejudice in social groups and societies. This multilevel framework, which is summarized in Table 15.2, expands on and develops a simpler tripartite framework proposed earlier (Duckitt, 1994).

The Cognitive Level: Changing Social Categorization

At the first and most fundamental level, that of the perceptual-cognitive processes underlying prejudice, social categorization, and its outcome in ingroup identification and favouritism seem to be universal human processes that build in a basic human potentiality for prejudice. While neither of these

Table 15.2 Interventions to reduce prejudice at four causal levels

Perceptual-cognitive	Individual	Interpersonal	Societal-intergroup
Changing social categorization:	Changing the individual's susceptibility to prejudice:	1. Changing social influence: i Mass persuasion	Changing social conditions: 1. Conflict reduction
1. Decategorization	1. Prejudiced attitude	ii Support norms of tolerance	2. Liberal democracy
2. Recategorization	2. Personality	iii Media images of minorities	3. Desegregation-integration
3. Subcategorization	3. Worldview	iv Educational curricula	4. Anti-discrimination laws
4. Cross-cutting categorization	4. Social attitudes or ideological beliefs	2. Creating favourable: intergroup contact:	5. Minority empowerment and intergroup equality
	5. Intercultural ignorance	i Cooperative education	6. Integrative multiculturalism
	6. Cognitive sophistication	ii Managing workplace contact	7. Social justice and stability

processes seems readily modifiable, the kind of categorizations that are salient for people can be changed. In the past two decades a good deal of research has examined how making different categorizations of the social world salient will affect group identifications and intergroup attitudes. This research has typically been concerned with the kinds of categorizations made during interpersonal contact with outgroup members, but it clearly has implications for situations not involving such direct personal contact as well. Four kinds of salient categorizations that influence intergroup bias have been investigated: decategorization, recategorization, subcategorization, and cross-cutting categorization.

According to the decategorization approach, favourable contact with outgroup members will be most effective in ameliorating attitudes to them if the contact is personalized and not category based (Brewer and Miller, 1984). When this is the case, people should respond to each other as individuals and not as members of an undifferentiated outgroup, and this should provide opportunities to disconfirm stereotypes and discover similarities and shared values. In support of this, several laboratory studies using arbitrarily created groups have found that intergroup bias was reduced when group members were instructed to interact in a manner that should facilitate decategorization and personalization (Bettencourt et al., 1992; Miller et al., 1985).

The recategorization or superordinate identity model, like the decategorization approach, also suggests that intergroup bias will be most difficult to reduce when intergroup distinctions remain highly salient. However, it suggests that intergroup distinctions should be eliminated in a different way: by making a common superordinate identification salient. Thus, the members of both original groups acquire a new shared common group identity, which either replaces the original identities (Dovidio et al., 1998; Gaertner et al., 1989) or co-exists with them (Brewer and Sneider, 1990). Experimental tests of this approach have created two artificial groups that are later brought together either under conditions that lead the participants to categorize themselves as being part of one larger group (recategorization), or that maintain the original two groups (categorization), or as personalized individuals (decategorization) (Dovidio et al., 1998; Gaertner et al., 1989). These experiments have found least intergroup bias in the recategorization condition and most in the categorization condition.

A third approach, termed the subcategorization approach, was suggested by Hewstone and Brown (1986) and grew out of a critique of both decategoriztion and recategorization approaches, and is in a sense their direct antithesis. They suggested that favourable contact experiences between members of different groups under personalized conditions might produce more positive feelings to particular outgroup individuals but would not necessarily generalize to their group as a social entity. Only when the contrasting subgroup memberships were salient in the situation would generalization occur. In support of this, prior experimental studies had indeed shown that favourable experiences with a single individual from an outgroup did not influence the evaluation of the outgroup, unless the outgroup person was seen as typical of the group (e.g., Wilder, 1986).

Brewer and Miller (1988), however, have criticized this argument. They suggest that in spite of the laboratory findings, frequent exposure to outgroup members under personalized conditions in naturalistic contexts would help to break down stereotypes by indicating how diverse and heterogeneous the outgroup actually was. In addition, there is evidence that positive contact experiences with even atypical outgroup members can generalize and produce a more favourable view of the outgroup as a whole, at least under certain conditions (Werth and Lord, 1992).

Moreover, a problem for the subcategorization approach is how to prevent salient group categorizations from stimulating intergroup competitiveness and bias. Hewstone and Brown (1986) have suggested this would not occur if contact situations were structured so that the members of the different groups had complementary rather than similar roles in achieving a common objective. In support of this, Deschamps and Brown (1983) have found that when two groups were given separate and complementary roles in working on a task, intergroup attitudes ended up more positive than when separate roles were not assigned.

Finally, there is a fourth kind of salient categorization that seems to have important implications for prejudice and prejudice reduction. Cross-cutting categorizations means that individuals who belong to different groups on one categorization dimension may find themselves belonging to the same group on a second categorization dimension. A number of experimental studies have shown that individuals do evaluate others more favourably when they share at least one category membership with them (Brown and Turner, 1979; Deschamps and Doise, 1978; Migdal et al., 1998). Anthropological evidence also indicates that cross-cutting group loyalties of this kind seems to be important in reducing internal conflict and maintaining social cohesion in tribal societies (Levine and Campbell, 1972; Ross, 1993).

Overall, therefore, there is experimental evidence indicating that each of the four kinds of categorization helps to reduce prejudice. The first three of these approaches, decategorization, recategorization, and subcategorization, are generally seen as representing alternative models of prejudice reduction, with subcategorization being seen as a directly competing approach to the other two (Brewer and Miller, 1996; Brown, 1995). However, this may be an oversimplification. In naturalistic settings outside the laboratory, all three may complement each other in quite essential ways to reduce prejudice. Thus, if intergroup prejudice is to be reduced in any social setting, it may be important for opposing group members to decategorize at least on certain occasions and experience personalized contact with varied outgroup persons so that friendship and acquaintanceship can develop more readily. Making recategorization salient, in perhaps different situations, would have a similar effect, but also add to this by having the opposing group members discovering a common, shared identity and with it common interests and goals. However, while decategorization and recategorization may generate positive feelings to, and evaluations of, individual members of other subcategories, generalizing these evaluations from these individuals to their subgroups, may be facilitated by also having contact with those same or similar persons on occasions when the different subcategory memberships are salient.

Thus, it might be that it is precisely when people in intergroup situations are using all three kinds of categorization at different times and in different situations that intergroup prejudice is minimized. This would be particularly likely in societies characterized by multiple cross-cutting categorizations. Conversely, it might be when a particular intergroup comparison is almost always salient over different times and situations, and neither decategorization, recategorization, or cross-cutting categorizations occur significantly, that the potential for prejudice is most strong. This means that to reduce prejudice most effectively, policies should be designed to promote not just one of these four forms of categorization but the episodic co-occurrence of subcategorization with frequent decategorization and recategorization, and multiple cross cutting categorizations. To this the proviso might be added, that subcategorization should ideally occur in situations where different groups cooperate rather than compete, and occupy complementary rather than similar roles.

The Individual Level: Changing Susceptibility to Prejudice

Interventions to change prejudice in individuals may seem unambitious since they will usually target only a limited number of persons. In contrast, interventions that change societies may have widespread effects. This may be why individual level interventions have not merited much serious discussion in the social scientific literature. However, there are several reasons why this may underestimate their importance. Firstly, trying to change individuals in a specific social context such as a school or workplace may be much easier than effecting broad societal change. Secondly, many societal changes may affect prejudice precisely by changing the individuals in those societies in ways that make them less susceptible to prejudice. And finally, if individual level interventions in localized settings are shown to be effective, it might be quite practical to then apply them throughout a society: for example, by incorporating them into the educational system.

Individual level interventions have also generally not been based on clear, compelling theories of the psychological bases of prejudice in individuals. Most such interventions have taken the form of small group workshops with rather vague psychotherapeutically or didactically based rationales. For example, Bagley et al. (1979) have described group counselling interventions designed to reduce racism through increasing self-esteem, which were effective in multiracial British schools. However, since research has not shown any direct link between self-esteem and racism (cf., the review by Duckitt, 1994: 168–174), it seems unlikely that changing self-esteem was the mechanism reducing racism in this case.

To be fair, it should be noted that explaining the psychological bases of prejudice in individuals has been a neglected and poorly understood issue for most of the latter half of the twentieth century. However, there have been important recent advances (Altemeyer, 1998; Duckitt, in press; Pratto et al., 1994) that make possible a more systematic and theoretically based approach to individual level prejudice reduction interventions and the mechanisms through which they may work.

Individual level interventions seem to be broadly of two kinds: firstly, those that attempt to directly change individuals' prejudiced attitudes, and secondly, those that attempt to change some attribute of individuals that makes them receptive to prejudiced beliefs. A variety of intervention programmes have been used that try to directly modify prejudiced attitudes and stereotypes. Some are broadly cognitive, focusing on information, knowledge, awareness, and understanding about the target prejudice. Others rely more on affective changes toward outgroup members, precipitated by experiences shared with them in mixed workshop settings. Louw-Potgieter et al. (1991) describe such a 'stereotype reduction workshop', which was used with apparent success to change workers' interracial attitudes in South Africa at the time of the transition to majority rule. A more aggressive approach has been taken by racism awareness training, which was popular in the 1970s in the US. Racism awareness training, reflecting the dominant paradigm of the period, propagated the militant message that racism was an inevitable consequence of White-dominated power structures and societies (Katz, 1978; Leicester, 1989).

Important research by Devine and her colleagues (Devine, 1989; Devine and Monteith, 1993) suggests that change in racial attitudes may not occur directly. Instead, individuals seem to learn and internalize new values or standards of non-prejudice that motivate them to suppress their previously acquired stereotypes or negative attitudes. It seems plausible that workshop type intervention programmes may effect change in precisely this way.

Interventions that do not attack prejudiced attitudes directly, can reduce prejudice by changing a number of attributes of individuals that influence their susceptibility to prejudice. The most important of these are individuals' ideological beliefs, and the psychological bases of these ideological beliefs in personality and worldview.

Two relatively orthogonal social attitude or ideological belief dimensions have been shown to influence prejudice independently and powerfully; right-wing authoritarianism (Altemeyer, 1981, 1988) and social dominance orientation (Pratto et al., 1994), that is, a generalized belief in social inequality and the right of powerful groups to dominate weaker ones. While these dimensions have often been referred to as measures of personality, probably originating from the term 'authoritarian personality' used by Adorno et al. (1950), their items clearly assess social attitudes or ideological beliefs (cf., Duckitt, in press; Feldman and Stenner, 1997; Goertzel, 1987). Each of these ideological belief dimensions, however, are powerfully influenced by a particular personality dimension (social conformity for authoritarianism, and tough mindedness for social dominance) and a particular worldview (belief in a dangerous, threatening world for authoritarianism, and belief in a competitive jungle world for social dominance) (Duckitt, in press). Prejudice could thus be reduced by changing these ideological orientations, or their psychological bases in personality and worldview.

Altemeyer (1988) has tested several interventions to reduce authoritarian attitudes. For example, he found that persons with authoritarian attitudes were more susceptible to directives from legitimate authority figures to adopt less prejudiced attitudes. In the case of changing social dominance, Rokeach (1973) has developed a value confrontation technique, which he found to be effective in shifting values in a pro-equality direction. Finally, it would seem that any programmes which taught the value of democracy and civil liberties could potentially reduce authoritarian and social dominance ideological orientations (Sullivan and Transue, 1999).

No interventions have been reported attempting to change the personality bases of authoritarian and social dominance ideological orientations, that is, social conformity and toughmindedness respectively. However, shifts in childhood socialization practices seem to have been occurring in many Western countries over the twentieth century towards less strict, harsh, and punitive socialization. Since cross-cultural data suggests that this should decrease social conformity (Duckitt, in press; Ross, 1993), these trends may have influenced the decreases in authoritarian social attitudes that have occurred in those societies (Altemeyer, 1996; Lederer, 1993; Meloen, 1993).

Broader social changes may also have impacted on individuals by changing either of the two worldviews that underlie the two ideological orientations. Thus, social stability and prosperity since the Second World War in most Western countries may have reduced individuals' view of the world as a dangerous and threatening place, and so also have contributed to the overall declines in authoritarianism in these countries over that period (Altemeyer, 1996; Lederer, 1993; Meloen, 1993). Therapy or counselling based interventions (e.g., Bagley et al., 1979) or broader social changes that enhanced individuals' experience and view of others as altruistic, trustworthy, and cooperative would weaken the view of the world as a competitive jungle and therefore the social dominance ideological orientation.

There are two other attributes of individuals that affect prejudice and could conceivably be changed; intercultural ignorance and cognitive sophistication. Intercultural training has been used to develop knowledge and awareness of other groups' subjective cultures. In contrast to many individually based interventions that focus on emphasizing similarities with the outgroup, here the emphasis is on differences. The goal is to develop an empathic understanding for the way in which the outgroup understands the world, and so to avoid misunderstandings, reduce stereotyping, and improve intergroup attitudes. The culture assimilator, for example, is an attributional training technique that uses a series of vignettes describing incidents of intercultural misunderstanding through which individuals gradually learn to interpret and understand events from the perspective of the target cultural group (Smith and Bond, 1993; van den Heuvel and Meertens, 1989).

There is a good deal of evidence that formal education reduces both prejudice and authoritarianism (Altemeyer, 1988, 1996; Duckitt, 1992) almost certainly through increasing individuals' cognitive sophistication (Duckitt, 1994: 182–185). Thus, not all education reduces prejudice. 'Liberal' education, which exposes individuals to a diversity of ideas and perspectives, does reduce both prejudice and authoritarianism. On the other hand, conservative approaches to education, which aim primarily at the preservation and inculcation of traditional norms and beliefs, such as the 'Christian National Education' common in pre-transition South Africa, or the approach in Israel that Inbar et al. (1984) term conservative-achievement oriented education, do not.

In conclusion, it is clear that a variety of interventions to reduce individuals' levels of prejudice or susceptibility to prejudice are possible and have been used. Most attempts to evaluate the success of short-term intervention programmes have reported significant changes in prejudice (Altemeyer, 1988; Bagley et al., 1979; Louw-Potgieter et al., 1991). However, it is quite possible that most of the participants in these programmes may have been quite positively disposed to changing their attitudes in the beginning. Evaluations of culture assimilator training, for example, have reported significant attitude change in persons who were positive about attending the training, but none in people who were not (van den Heuvel and Meertens, 1989). The findings of Devine and her colleagues (Devine, 1989; Devine and Monteith, 1993), indicating that prejudice reduction in individuals tends to occur through the internalization of new personal values of non-prejudice, also suggests that an initial positive orientation to change may be an important determinant of how much change occurs.

Thus, the major problem with short-term individual level interventions may be that those people who are most prejudiced, and for whom change would be most important, seem least likely to be affected by such interventions. The most important ways of changing individuals' susceptibility to prejudice may therefore reside in longer-term processes such as liberal education, exposure to new environments that might change worldviews and ideological orientations, and exposure to environments in which new norms, laws, and structural conditions motivate individuals to be more positively disposed to learning new standards of non-prejudice.

Interpersonal Level: Contact Experiences and Social Influence

At the interpersonal level, the kind of contact experiences individuals have with outgroup members and their exposure to social influence from others will have important impacts in creating and maintaining prejudice or reducing it. Inevitably these contact experiences and exposure to influence will reflect the broader social structure. However, this will not occur mechanically. These influences can be structured in ways that may ameliorate the impact of even 'apartheid' type social structures, or conversely weaken the effects of a broader social structure conducive to tolerance.

Social influence Social influence interventions aim to change individuals' exposure to information and normative pressures so as to reduce discriminatory behaviour and prejudiced attitudes. Four such interventions have been empirically investigated: mass persuasion campaigns, support for norms of tolerance and non-discrimination, changing media images of target groups, and changing the content of educational curricula.

Research on the effectiveness of mass persuasion campaigns designed to reduce prejudice has been scattered and unsystematic, and it is difficult to draw firm conclusions. Simple exhortation, such as a single anti-racist sermon, does not seem effective (Crawford, 1974). Attempts to parody racist attitudes using cartoons may even strengthen prejudice in highly prejudiced persons (Lazarsfeld and Stanton, 1949). But films and television programmes with implicit anti-racist messages can have very substantial effects in changing attitudes, though the long-term effects have not been well researched (Middleton, 1960). Simpson and Yinger (1985) review a good deal of research and conclude that mass persuasion may be most effective with persons who are less prejudiced and least effective with those who are most prejudiced.

There are some disturbing indications that hate literature may be more effective than anti-prejudice communications in changing attitudes. For example, a series of studies by Altemeyer (1996) found that reasonably liberal Canadian students were not influenced by truthful accounts of the holocaust, but were significantly influenced by denials that the holocaust had occurred. 'Hate' propaganda messages were also effective in significantly reducing acceptance of homosexuals and eliminating support for feminist professors.

Exposure to norms of non-prejudice may be critically important in reducing prejudice. This is suggested by the research already noted by Devine and her colleagues (Devine, 1989; Devine and Monteith, 1993) indicating that individuals typically reduce prejudice by internalizing values of non-prejudice, which then suppress prejudiced affects and stereotypes learned earlier in socialization. It is possible that exposure to such norms may be particularly effective during adolescence or early adulthood. Thus, establishing and supporting norms of non-discrimination and non-prejudice in specific social settings, as well as in society as a whole, seems particularly important. Moreover, unlike mass persuasion campaigns or individual level, short-term interventions, which seem unlikely to be effective with highly prejudiced persons, Altemeyer (1996) has shown that highly prejudiced authoritarian persons will show greater compliance with social norms, even if they do not agree with them.

In order to establish and maintain norms of non-prejudice, organizations or institutions must openly and explicitly adopt, emphasize, and publicly enforce non-discriminatory policies in all aspects of their functioning. To be successful in schools, multicultural policies must be designed into all aspects of the school (Banks, 1995; Leicester, 1989; Torney-Purta, 1995). Business organizations similarly must make unambiguous commitments to equal opportunity and diversity, adopt measures that actively demonstrate the unacceptability of racism or discrimination in any guise, ensure that all facilities and activities are fully integrated, that target groups are adequately represented at supervisory and executive levels, and adopt training programmes to change prejudiced attitudes directly (cf., Louw-Potgieter et al., 1991).

The mass media are an important source of social influence and the representation of outgroup and minority persons in the media will inevitably influence attitudes to them. A number of ways in which prejudice can be supported or reinforced by the media have been noted, particularly through ignoring target group persons, portraying them in negative ways or low-status roles, or as a 'problem' in some way or other (Bagley et al., 1979; Duckitt, 1994: 135–136; Foster-Carter, 1984; Heath, 1995; Milner, 1983). Eliminating such portrayals will be crucial for prejudice reduction. Stephan (1987) has suggested that this would require that the media represent target group persons frequently, positively, and in individuating ways.

Finally, the kind of information individuals are exposed to about target groups should influence attitudes to them. The most important interventions in this respect have been the design of multicultural educational curricula, which explicitly set out to teach about the history, accomplishments, and culture of target groups, and emphasize the value of social and cultural diversity (Banks, 1995; Torney-Purta, 1995). Teaching about the historical background and social circumstances of disadvantaged groups should, as Glock et al. (1975) point out, counter the pernicious tendency to make dispositional rather than situational and historical attributions for their social disadvantages. Staub (1989) has also suggested that teaching about the nature of prejudice and intergroup hostility and how to alleviate them should also be included in multicultural curricula.

Intergroup contact experiences   Allport (1954) originally specified four essential conditions under which interpersonal contact between members of different groups would reduce prejudice between them: that the groups be of equal status within the contact situation, that they share common goals, that they cooperate with each other, and that group authorities support the contact. A recent review by Pettigrew (1998) has shown clear empirical support for these four conditions, and noted important new evidence for a fifth: that the contact situation have the potential for the growth of friendship between group members.

As in the case of social influence, the kind of interpersonal contact between group members in any situation will be powerfully determined by the broader social structuring of intergroup relations in the entire society. Nevertheless, there remains a good deal of scope to ameliorate the impact of even negatively structured societies by managing intergroup contact at important sites, such as the workplace and the educational system. Empirical evaluations of the impact of school desegregation in the US have indicated mixed effects, but it seems that Allport's four conditions were rarely satisfied (Cook, 1985). It has been argued that desegregation and contact are necessary and not sufficient conditions for prejudice reduction; that is, they create a situation with the potential for improving intergroup relations (Brewer, 1997).

How contact is actually structured in desegregated schools therefore seems to be critical in influencing intergroup attitudes. Intergroup contact within the traditional classroom structure typically seems not to improve intergroup attitudes and may worsen them when majority and minority children differ in social status or academic achievement level, or when academic tracking is used (Sharan and Rich, 1984). On the other hand, a number of cooperative learning strategies have been developed, in which children in mixed ethnic groups cooperate with each other (Sharan, 1990; Slavin, 1990, 1995). Evaluations of cooperative learning consistently indicate positive outcomes for intergroup relations, as well as improvements in self-esteem and academic attainment, particularly for initially low-performing children. The evidence for the effectiveness of cooperative learning has now become virtually overwhelming, and it is surprising that so little has been done to implement it more widely.

The general prescription for managing intergroup contact in work situations is essentially similar (cf., Jackson and Ruderman, 1996; Pettigrew and Martin, 1989). Complete integration of all facilities and activities is essential, but not sufficient. Institutional support is required in the form of totally unambiguous commitments by the organization to equal opportunity, non-discrimination, and the unacceptability of any kind of racism or prejudice. For equal status contact, affirmative action and selection for diversity may be necessary to ensure reasonably equal representation of target groups at supervisory and management levels. Superordinate goals can be generated through building greater organizational commitment. Situations of potential intergroup competition should be eliminated, and work roles and activities restructured to maximize activities that involve cooperative activity between members of the different groups.

Overall, social influence and interpersonal contact interventions seem to have greater potential for reducing prejudice than interventions at the individual level. Individual level interventions seem likely to be most effective for persons who are already favourably disposed to change, and least effective with persons who are most prejudiced. Interpersonal influence and contact interventions, on the other hand, will usually capitalize on the tendency for authoritarian persons to be more socially conforming (Altemeyer, 1988).

The Societal-Intergroup Level: Changing Social Conditions

Social structure and intergroup relations inevitably influence prejudice powerfully, largely by structuring the kinds of social influence and interpersonal contact experienced by members of these societies. Social structure also sets the parameters within which interventions at lower levels may have effects. The more rigidly segregated and conflictual intergroup relations are in a given society, the less scope there will be for change from interventions at the interpersonal and individual level. In situations where intergroup attitudes and relations have deteriorated to the point of open conflict, the first step in prejudice reduction must be to reduce levels of overt intergroup conflict through peace-making and conflict resolution.

A second step in such a process may be designing a constitutional framework within which the conflicting groups can co-exist. Liberal democracy is based on the core values of legal and political equality and political tolerance. However, democracy cannot guarantee intergroup tolerance, though it should create a conducive framework. Much evidence indicates that democracies have lower levels of conflict, less male gender dominance, and higher levels of political tolerance than authoritarian societies (Meloen, in press; Sullivan and Transue, 1999). In his classic, *The American Dilemma*, Myrdal (1944) argued that the core value of equality in American society provided a powerful moral lever for the improving race relations.

There are, however, situations in which constitutional systems need to be more complex than simple democracy. These are situations in which the political system is polarized around salient ethnic or cultural differences with either an escalating level of conflict or the relative size of the groups creating a system of ethnically based majority group domination. Such situations can be defused by designing democratic constitutions and political systems that penalize parties that exploit ethnic differences and mobilize on ethnic lines, and reward parties that gain broad-based support over different ethnic groups. Horowitz (1985) has illustrated how constitutional and political systems can be designed in severely divided societies to channel political processes and tensions away from dangerous ethnic cleavages.

When groups are initially segregated, desegregation is a first step to the creation of conditions in which prejudice might be reduced. As the experience in the US has shown (Longshore and Prager, 1985), and as the contact hypothesis predicts, desegregation alone will not reduce prejudice, and in adverse conditions may well worsen it. To reduce prejudice, desegregation needs to be accompanied by a series of other measures. One such measure consists of thorough-going and strictly enforced anti-discriminatory legislation to create equality of opportunity for minorities, to force changes in customary patterns of discriminatory behaviour among majority members, and to establish basic social and institutional supports for new norms of non-discrimination. As a substantial research literature on cognitive dissonance and attitude change indicates, behavioural compliance with such laws and norms should itself tend to improve attitudes to these minorities (Zimbardo and Leippe, 1991).

Equality of opportunity and non-discrimination will not ensure optimal intergroup contact conditions when minorities have been politically subordinated and economically disadvantaged. Patterns of economic disadvantage will frequently become self-perpetuating cycles. Breaking such entrenched patterns and redressing social and economic inequities between groups, requires deliberate and concerted action to empower minorities and establish true equality of opportunity. Most commonly this has involved affirmative action programmes; such as those designed to advance women and racial minorities occupationally and educationally in the US.

Evaluations indicate that affirmative action in the US has produced marked gains in terms of educational and occupational attainments for minorities and women (Blanchard and Crosby, 1988; Crosby and Clayton, 1990). The best predictors of the success of individual programmes in organizations appear to be the degree of commitment at the top and the receptiveness of key personnel to the programme (Hitt and Keats, 1984). However, these policies have elicited considerable opposition from the American public and have been seen as unfair. There has also been a steady retreat from their implementation, particularly by the conservative American administrations during the 1980s (Carmines and Merriman, 1993). Empirical evidence also indicates that affirmative action programmes can reinforce prejudice through generating negative expectancies of minorities (Maio and Esses, 1998).

Resistance to affirmative action has been shown to correlate substantially with symbolic or modern racism (Carmines and Merriman, 1993), and has often been simply dismissed as an expression of racism (cf., Kinder and Sears, 1981). Others suggest this is oversimplified, as significant numbers of minority scholars have opposed the policy as detrimental to their own group (Maio and Esses, 1998). A major issue fuelling resistance appears to be the perception that these programmes violate basic principles of procedural justice and conflict with equality of opportunity. Resistance also tends to be associated with high levels of ignorance about the nature of affirmative action and the specific policies being opposed (Twiss et al., 1988).

In a thoughtful review, Crosby and Clayton (1990) suggested two important conditions for affirmative action programmes in order to lessen resistance to them and to avoid them generating negative expectancies about minorities. Firstly, they suggest that it is critical that the policies are designed to be fair and are seen to be fair. Simple preferential quota schemes should be avoided and programmes designed that can be shown to be consistent with true equality of opportunity. Secondly, policies must always be accompanied by programmes of institutional education that clarify what the policies do to redress disadvantages fairly and show practically the benefits of diversity for the institution. Developing and implementing such policies seems to be a particularly critical challenge in the US since the future of race relations there may depend more than anything else on substantial progress in reducing massive interracial socio-economic inequalities.

To be most effective, interventions at the societal level should ideally be integrated into a coherent social policy towards minorities. The traditional approach was that of assimilation, or the 'melting pot'. However, as evidence has accumulated showing how damaging assimilationist policies can be to minorities (Saharso, 1989; Schofield, 1995; Tyack, 1995), multiculturalism, which views diversity as inevitable and valuable in its own right and aims at accepting and maintaining subgroup identities, has been increasingly recommended (Fowers and Richardson, 1996).

Nevertheless, multiculturalism has also been criticized. Brewer (1997), for example, has suggested that problems can arise from implementations of multiculturalism that politically reify and legally institutionalize group distinctions as an entrenched basis for resource allocation. Such reified group boundaries can easily become magnified and 'fault lines for conflict and separatism' (1997: 208). These risks might be minimized by a more integrative multiculturalism in which strong subgroup identities coexist with a strong shared superordinate identity (cf., Berry, 1984). It is important that such a superordinate identity not merely be the majority groups identity but a genuine 'cultura franca' (van Oudenhoven and Willemsen, 1989) reflecting the shared heritage of all groups in the society. Sharing an important superordinate identity or values, may provide an important basis for multicultural tolerance. Nevertheless, social circumstances differ, and newly established societies with dangerous ethnic cleavages may need to place more emphasis on building a strong superordinate identity than well-established older societies.

Finally, there are two societal characteristics, which are rarely discussed in the literature, but nevertheless appear to be important determinants of truly tolerant societies. Firstly, societies need to be safe, secure, and stable, and second, characterized by social justice and a cooperative and egalitarian ethos. Many studies have shown that the perception of the social world as a dangerous, threatening, and uncertain place is strongly associated with authoritarianism and prejudice (Altemeyer, 1998; Duckitt, in press; Feldman and Stenner, 1997). Recent research also indicates that the view of the social world as a competitive, inegalitarian jungle, in which the strong succeed and dominate while the weak fail, is a powerful determinant of a social dominance ideological orientation and prejudiced attitudes (Duckitt, in press). Conversely, the perception of the social world as egalitarian, fair, cooperative, and altruistic is strongly associated with tolerance and non-prejudice. Thus, creating safe, secure, and stable societies and societies that are characterized by social justice and egalitarianism will build in the social conditions most conducive to tolerance and non-prejudice.

Overall, interventions at the social structural level are potentially the most powerful ways of reducing prejudice. Typically, such interventions require political action, either from existing political and governmental authorities, or from individuals and social movements working for change. The ultimate challenge for reducing prejudice and discrimination in societies may thus involve helping to create and facilitate political processes to generate such changes.

Conclusions: Developing Appropriate Intervention Policies

While there is a considerable social science literature on what kind of interventions can be used to reduce prejudice, very little attention has been given to the issue of how to develop policies appropriate for particular conditions (for interesting exceptions, see Amir and Ben-Arie, 1989; Simpson and Yinger, 1985). However, several general guidelines are suggested by the history of twentieth-century attempts to reduce intergroup prejudice. In societies in which intergroup relations are characterized by segregation and serious polarization or conflict, it is intervention at the societal level, and specifically conflict resolution and mediation, that are necessary to create conditions in which further interventions are possible. The order in which the societal interventions are listed in Table 15.2 can be seen as representing a sequence of interventions appropriate in progressively less unfavourable situations. Thus, in the most unfavourable situation, intervention typically begins with conflict resolution, followed by the establishment of democratic constitutions tailored to defuse ethnic differences, desegregation, anti-discrimination laws, minority empowerment to reduce intergroup inequality, establishing multicultural policies, and finally, creating societies characterized by social stability and social justice.

In social conditions that are very unfavourable, interventions at the interpersonal or individual levels may be very difficult, sometimes dangerous, and often ineffective, until structural conditions are addressed. Thus, in such situations the action required is fundamentally political, and other interventions would be at best secondary.

When social conditions are broadly favourable, but much intergroup prejudice remains, interventions at the interpersonal and individual levels will be most appropriate and most effective. This seems largely the situation in countries like the US, with one important exception: the massive socio-economic deprivation of African-Americans in the urban ghettos. William Cross (1995) has documented how the sharp decrease in industrial employment in the 1970s generated a self-perpetuating cycle of inner city ghetto poverty and an oppositional youth culture characterized by low academic achievement and high rates of delinquency, violence, and crime. Such massive intergroup inequalities create a basis in 'social reality' for stereotyping and discrimination. When prejudice is based on such social realities, interventions at the individual and interpersonal levels will merely transform crude, old fashioned forms of prejudice into more subtle 'modern' or 'symbolic' forms, and result in pervasive ambivalence in apparently non-prejudiced persons. The challenge facing the reduction of prejudice and racism in the US, and other countries such as Australia and New Zealand, where minority status is powerfully correlated with socio-economic deprivation, lies first and most fundamentally in social interventions to reduce poverty and break entrenched cycles of deprivation and despair.

16 Studying Psychology Studying Racism

Stephen Reicher

The Reason for Study

Racism in Action

Onissim Burawoy, my mother's father, was very proud of his three birthdays – one more than the Queen, he used to say. The first two are explained by the fact that he was born in pre-revolutionary Russia which was still ruled by the old Julian calendar. When the Bolsheviks came to power and adopted the modern Gregorian calendar instead, his birthday shifted by the thirteen days difference between the two systems. The third birthday is somewhat more relevant to the theme of this book, since it tells us something about the nature of racism.

When Onissim was still quite young, the family moved to Germany, partly in order to escape the anti-semitic pogroms that were sweeping Russia. With hindsight, there is a tragic irony to this, since my grandfather grew to see the rise of Hitler and the birth of the Nazi state. By that point he was trained as an engineer. In the early 1930s his work took him back to Russia where he was involved in the installation of giant turbines which were so important to Stalin's industrialization program. Nonetheless, after the Nazis came to power, the Soviets sought to bar his access. The Nazis resented being dictated to by Stalin's regime. So, despite the fact that they were removing rights to citizenship from Jewish people at this period, the German authorities fought for my grandfather's right to a passport that would give him entry to Russia. When he went to get the passport, the Nazi official asked him for all his details. As my grandfather gave these details, the official repeated them and wrote them down. But as he gave his birth date the official repeated it incorrectly. 'No', said Onissim, trying to get things right. The passport officer cut my grandfather short: 'look', he said, 'either your birthday is March 5th or else you have no birthday and no passport'. And that is how my grandfather came to have a third birthday – one more than the Queen.

At one level there is something rather comic about this little Hitler refusing to be corrected by a Jew and insisting on giving him a false birthday. After all, my grandfather got the passport and soon afterwards used it to escape the Nazis and come to Britain. At another level, however, it indicates an absolute power to define all aspects of another person's reality – however trivial or absurd –

simply because of the allocation of that person to a particular racial category. It thereby indicates an absolute removal of choice from members of that category. By making them subject to the whim of others they are denied the right of agency which is central to being human. In short, it constitutes the dehumanizing of those who are defined as a racial outgroup.

There is much to recommend a definition of racist action in terms of the removal of the fundamental human capacity to create their own reality from members of a racial group. First of all, as Norman Geras argues in his polemic against the relativist philosopher Richard Rorty (Geras, 1996), the ability to link phenomena like racist action to the denial of some aspect of human nature provides a universal criterion for opposing them. Racist action is wrong in all places, at all times, and in all cultures. Opposition to racist action is founded on a far more solid bedrock than simply saying 'we don't like that sort of thing round here'. Secondly, by talking of denial of choice it is possible to describe a diverse and even contradictory range of behaviours as racist and equally to appreciate that, in different circumstances, the same behaviour may or may not be racist. Thus, racist action may equally be manifested in denying the right of the racial minority to participate in the dominant group culture or in forcing them to abandon their culture in favour of that of the dominant group. Ghettoization and assimilationism are both racist when they subsume the choices of the minority to the preferences of the majority. Conversely, facilitating the choice of minority group members to celebrate their own culture or else to adopt new cultures are far from racist acts. Thirdly, by characterizing racist action in terms of action we focus on the phenomena which led us to undertake our studies in the first place. The reason why the psychology of intergroup relations acquired such prominence in the period since the Second World War is not because the Nazis thought badly of Jewish people, but because they slaughtered six million Jews. The reason why we are concerned with issues of race and racism concerning Black people is because of the acts of discrimination which ensure that on virtually every statistic Black people are worse off while (in Britain at least) racist attacks and murders are on the increase (e.g., Bhat et al., 1988). As Iain Walker shows in his chapter, it is equally true that the reason we are concerned with racism against Aboriginal Australians is because discrimination leaves them poorer, less healthy, and with much diminished life-expectancy.

None of this is to deny that terms such as 'racism' and 'racist action' may be defined differently or indeed that it may be used in different ways and to different ends by people in their everyday lives. Mark Rapley is quite right to point out that, given the powerful moral distaste associated with things that are characterized as racist, it becomes particularly important to avoid the charge oneself and that such a charge becomes a particularly powerful way of discrediting one's opponents. Hence, the everyday usage of terms such as 'racism' and 'racist' is a powerful way of managing our social lives and the study of such usage becomes an important topic in its own right. However, I am not convinced that the analysis of how terms constitute a resource for participants is necessarily in contradiction to my use of such terms as an analytic resource. Indeed, as I shall argue further on, I believe that any attempt to understand how people are denied choice through being placed in racial groups will necessarily fail unless we include the role of language in making (and not just describing) our social world.

Equally, this stress on racist action as the actual denial of choice does not mean that I consider thoughts and feelings and expressions of dislike to be irrelevant. Not at all. But we are interested in them to the extent that they are associated with other acts of subordination – and, as I shall also argue presently, the two are not always associated. The link must be a matter of investigation rather than of presupposition. Part of my argument will be that failure to investigate this link will undermine our ability to understand why and when racism occurs. Another part will be that such a failure will draw our attention away from the structural factors which enable some groups to translate hostility into dominance while for others hostility remains just that. The danger is that by reducing racism to purely psychological categories we are in danger of missing crucial targets in the fight against racial inequality.

Psychology in Racism and Racism in Psychology

My previous point can be reframed in more general terms: the way we conceptualize the phenomena of prejudice and of racism and the way we explain them may have consequences for the phenomena themselves. In more or less explicit forms, this is a point that has been made in a large number of the chapters of this book. On the one hand, it has been suggested that we must focus on the psychology of the individual rather than always pointing to social factors, for otherwise we let people off the hook and allow them to avoid responsibility for their individual beliefs and actions. We allow the bigot and the knife-wielding thug to say 'it's not me, mate, society is to blame'. On the other hand, several authors have argued that, by restricting our analysis to individual psychology, we ignore ideological and structural determinants which lie at the heart of inequality and oppression. We therefore misdirect the fight against oppression. We become akin to the accomplice who watches a criminal flee down the street. Then, as the pursuers come after, we point in the opposite direction and exclaim 'he went that way'.

More seriously, there are times when psychology might seem to suggest that no crime has been committed or, even if there has, there is little point in pursuing the culprit. To illustrate the point, consider the case of David Irving, a self-styled historian who claims that the Nazis never organized a systematic slaughter of Jewish people. Irving was trying to sue Deborah Lipstadt for calling him a holocaust denier. He lost his case and was branded a racist, an anti-semite, and a liar by the trial judge. As just one of many examples of his views the following ditty composed by Irving for his baby daughter was read out in court: 'I am a baby Aryan, Not Jewish or Sectarian, I have no plans to marry an Ape or Rastafarian'. On the day of the verdict (April 11th, 2000) Irving was interviewed on several evening television programmes. He was asked whether he was a racist and, at least twice, he was confronted with the evidence of his poem. Both times Irving denied the charge and then qualified his response. He claimed to be no more racist than 95 per cent of the British population and then explained that 'perhaps there is part of the microchip in all of us which programs us to dislike people who look different'. If hatred of other races is wired into human nature, then we can hardly be held responsible for it and it makes no sense to charge or punish an individual who expresses such hatred. Of course, the fact that something has unfortunate consequences does not make it wrong. It does, however, mean that we should be very wary of claims that there is something about human psychology that makes prejudice and racism inevitable. We need to be especially careful that our theories serve to explain social phenomena rather than reflect widespread beliefs within our society. That is, we need to expose all our assumptions to a ruthless interrogation in order to make sure that we too have not taken for granted what is taken for granted within a world that is still stratified by race (cf., Hopkins et al., 1997).

Most seriously, however, there are times when psychology itself has been in the position of the criminal. Psychologists have explicitly taken racist positions, they have justified the notion of racial difference, and they have even used these ideas to agitate for racial discrimination. In the introduction, Augoustinos and Reynolds point out that such ideas have always attracted opposition from other psychologists and have nearly always been in the minority. However, this does not diminish their seriousness, blunt their consequences, or even lessen the suspicion with which psychological accounts of prejudice and racism are viewed by those outside psychology. The most notorious example of all is probably the misuse of IQ testing to suggest that a whole series of groups, most notably Black people, were inherently inferior. This was used to promote American legislation – the Johnson-Lodge Immigration Act of 1924 – which limited entry to those seen as inferior (Kamin, 1977). One observer drew a very clear lesson from this. He writes 'By refusing immigration on principle to elements in poor health, by simply excluding certain races from naturalization, (America) professes in slow beginnings a view which is particular to the folkish state concept'. The author was to take the logic of a state based on race to its infernal conclusion. The quote is from Hitler's *Mein Kampf* (1969: 400).

There is another even more direct link between psychology, American legislation, and the Nazi regime. As well as trying to stop people getting in, psychologists such as Terman, Goddard, and Yerkes (alongside biologists, anthropologists, and others in the 'Eugenics' movement) turned their attention to inferior people within the country who, if they were allowed to breed, would lead 'the passing of the great race' (to quote from the title of Madison Grant's infamous text). Terman warned that 'if we would preserve our state for a class of people worthy to possess it, we must prevent, as far as possible, the propagation of mental degenerates … curtailing the increasing spawn of degeneracy' (quoted in Kamin, 1977: 21). To put it more bluntly, degenerates should be sterilized. Such ideas were formalized in a 'Model Eugenic Sterilization Law' which called for the compulsory sterilization of the mentally retarded, insane, criminal, epileptic, inebriate, diseased, blind, deaf, deformed, and economically dependent people. Versions of this legislation were enacted in a number of American states – most notably California. It was because such clear models were available that the Nazis were able to pass their own law on 'preventing hereditarily ill progeny' on July 14th 1933 – so soon after coming to power. As Kuhl (1994) shows, American eugenicists were proud of their impact on such legislation in Nazi Germany.

On the surface, these eugenic arguments might seem curiously even-handed since they fall equally on the poor and the 'degenerate' of all races. But of course, since certain races were seen (and treated) as more degenerate than others, the legislation was bound to have a strong racial bias. Moreover, since the whole point of eugenics was to keep the greatness of one's race from passing, it inevitably led to calls for the prevention of racial interbreeding. As Muller-Hill (1988) shows, there was an inseparable link between measures aimed at 'degenerates' and those aimed at Jews in Nazi Germany. Indeed, on 6th May 1933, even before the law on 'preventing hereditarily ill progeny' was passed, the Nazi Minister of Justice was considering how to formulate legislative procedures which would prevent marriages of mixed race and seeking academic advice on how to proceed. This came to fruition in the Nuremberg laws of 1935 which criminalized both marriages and sexual relations between 'Jews and citizens of German or related blood' (Muller-Hill, 1988: 33).

However, the contribution of academics (including psychologists) to the Nazi holocaust did not stop with the passing of legislation. After a decision was made on the compulsory sterilization of Black children in 1937 subject to examination by 'experts', 385 individuals were taken to Profesor von Verschuer's university institute in Frankfurt and then to the university clinic where they were all sterilized. The psychiatrist, Dr. Robert Ritter, was far more productive. In a report of 31st January 1944, he mentions having clarified 23,822 gypsy cases. Of these, he concluded that some 90 per cent, being 'of mixed blood' should be subjected to sterilization and internment in camps. Of the 20,943 gypsies registered in Auschwitz, only 3,461 were transferred to other camps. The rest died by starvation, disease, or gas (Muller-Hill, 1988).

Lest we try and rest comfortable in the reassuring belief that all this evidence simply shows how far we have moved since the 'bad old days', it is worth stressing that so-called 'race-science' is not entirely a thing of the past. Augoustinos and Reynolds point to some of the most notorious examples: the work of Jensen, of Rushton and of Murray and Herrnstein. Rushton provides a particularly elaborate account of Black inferiority. For him, Black people are less evolved and this is reflected in many respects including their reproductive strategies. That is, unlike more advanced peoples, they aim to reproduce more and care less for their young. Rushton contends that this leads to Black males having larger genitalia. Yet, as Kamin (1992) shows in an article with the wonderful title 'on the length of Black penises and the depth of White racism', his sources are dubious in many senses of the word. One is a certain Dr. Jacobus, a doctor in the French colonial army during the 19th century – and that is misquoted. The other is an article in the pornographic magazine *Forum* which gets its basic arithmetic wrong. The notion of the Black man with the big penis is a staple of racist jokes. Were the consequences not so serious, it could be said that research on race and penis size is also a racist joke. To quote Kamin: 'it is certainly the case that within the institution of American Psychology we still have not yet summoned up the courage, honesty and sheer nerve to call intolerably racist research by its proper name' (1992: 53). After Kamin wrote these words, Rushton was allowed to publish his argument in 'The Psychologist', house journal of the British Psychological Society. It appears that Kamin's words do not only apply to America.

The Importance of Giving the Right Answer and Asking the Right Questions

My reason for laying such stress on these sombre examples, even while acknowledging that they represent a minority position, is not to try and make us feel guilty, but rather to make us aware of the stakes involved in our studies. There is often an assumption that science in general, and psychology in particular, is always on the side of progress. Sometimes the progress is faster, sometimes slower and, at worst, we find we are going nowhere. However, if we are moving anywhere it is always towards greater enlightenment. To put it slightly differently, our work on racism and on prejudice is always part of the solution. Well that simply isn't true. We can just as easily – and often have been – part of the problem. What is more, we can sometimes find that we have been part of the problem while seeking to be part of the solution. Our studies may have reproduced (and hence reinforced) some aspect of racist common sense (such as the inevitability of seeing people in racial terms and disliking them for their racial difference) even as we are trying to understand racism as a means to eradicating it. Yet, far from discouraging us from undertaking such studies, these dangers only add to the importance and the fascination of working in this area.

The phenomena of racism and prejudice are of virtually unparalleled importance in our society, and racism is – in part at least – constituted out of psychological accounts. As a result, this is an area in which our academic arguments actually matter. Sometimes they can matter for ill. Walter Gross, one of the main propagandists of Nazi race policy, saluted the role of foreign eugenicists in silencing opposition: 'their word', he claimed, 'was able to balance the opinion of a hundred chatterers' (cited in Kuhl, 1994: 92). But they can equally matter for good. When viewed in this perspective, seemingly dry and abstruse debates about whether prejudice results from personality type or group relations, whether human beings are cognitive misers or motivated tacticians, and whether categorization in itself is the basis for discrimination come alive. As the authors themselves show, much hangs on the answer, for if we get it right we may contribute to the fight against racism and if we get it wrong, we may become something to be fought against. If nothing else, then, this book provides a powerful reason for studying psychology. It shows that our discipline is far more than an abstract intellectual exercise and, if it indicates the potential power of our ideas, it thereby also underlines our responsibilities. In the area of racism, perhaps more than any other, it is incumbent upon us to scrutinize our concepts and models with special care, to pay particularly close attention to the ways in which they relate to phenomena in the real world … and here we have to confront a fundamental problem with the nature of psychological enquiry.

In a chapter written over 30 years ago, Herbert Blumer (1969) writes about a remarkable tendency within the social sciences to reduce the entire scientific process to one phase of it – hypothesis testing – and then to adopt a parochial stance concerning the manner in which hypotheses are tested. That is, research means experiments designed to answer very specific questions. His point is not to decry experiments. They are clearly a vital instrument in our tool box. His point is rather that the best answers in the world are of little use if one is asking the wrong questions. That is to say that we may conduct the cleverest studies and devise the cleverest theories to explain what is going on in those studies, others may then conduct further studies in response to ours and so a whole research field may grow up, however, it may have little or nothing to do with the external phenomena it purports to explain. To take one example from my own work, there has been much research which looks at the role of anonymity in producing extreme behaviour, especially extreme behaviour towards outgroups (Reicher et al., 1995; Zimbardo, 1970). Such deindividuation research purports to account for the excesses of crowds. There is one basic problem however – if you ever go and examine a crowd on the streets you will find that participants are often very well known and very visible to each other. So much for anonymity. Examples like these lead Blumer to drawing a strong conclusion: 'it can be expressed as a simple injunction: Respect the nature of the empirical world and organize a methodological stance to reflect that respect' (1969: 60).

In the remainder of this chapter, I want to take Blumer's injunction seriously and to look closely at the empirical world of racism and prejudice. More particularly, I want to revisit the basic constructs which we presume to model and address in our laboratories. It is very tempting to misuse the privilege of writing the last chapter by trying to have the last word – to judge each author and then deliver my own verdict without allowing others the chance to answer back. However, albeit with considerable difficulty I shall forego that temptation. Rather, by drawing attention to some aspects of the phenomena we are trying to explain, I hope to put readers in a better position to deliver their own judgements about the various perspectives to which they have been exposed.

The Object of Study

From 'Race' to Racialization

Before you can have racism or racial prejudice you have to have race. After all, how can one dislike, hate, and oppress a people if there is no people there to be disliked, hated, or oppressed. This point is so obvious that, in discussing racism and prejudice we generally presuppose the existence of racial groups. Thus far in this chapter I have done exactly this and so have many others in their chapters. I have talked of 'race' and 'races' and racial groups as if they were objective entities that self-evidently are 'out there' in the 'real world'. The danger is that, as long as we keep our focus on the consequences of categorization, we fail to ask how people came to be divided according to the said categories in the first place. It therefore becomes all the more important to shift our focus: we need to complement the study of race with a study of racialization (cf., Miles, 1989; Omi and Winant, 1989).

The need to question the race concept has already been touched on elsewhere in this book. Thus, in the introductory chapter, Augoustinos and Reynolds quote Richards (1997) as arguing that the unscientific nature of the race concept renders the entire argument about race differences senseless. Equally, in her later chapter with LeCouteur, Augoustinos promotes the discursive position according to which we should abandon the notion of race (or indeed any other social category) as a non-problematic social object and instead look at the way in which categories are actively constructed for rhetorical ends. However, in both cases it is stated that 'race' has no validity as an objective description of the world but the argument is not expanded. The argument is sufficiently important and goes so much against received common sense (after all, doesn't the evidence of our own eyes tell us that people are divided into White and Black?) that it merits being spelled out. What is more, the discourse analyst goes directly from the premise that race is a constructed rather than a natural category to the conclusion that we should focus entirely on the construction of racial categories in talk. However, that cuts off the possibility of an analysis of the relationship between the organization of categories in talk and other dimensions of social organization: the ways in which people are institutionally divided, allocated to different social positions, segregated in space, and so on. As I shall shortly argue, racialization certainly involves language, but it involves more besides.

So, given the evidence of our eyes, what does it mean to say that 'race' is socially constructed? Certainly there are differences in skin colour and in many other dimensions besides. However, these differences are on a continuum and racial categories involve imposing boundaries that break up that continuum and imply that people over here are 'Black' or 'negroid' or whatever, while people over there are 'White' or 'caucasian' or whatever else. The point is that the decision where to place those boundaries is, in biological terms, entirely arbitrary. There are no racial categories in nature. Nothing has decreed that we should divide people into negroids, mongoloid, and caucasians or indeed into any other racial taxonomy. Such decisions are social conventions which are made by human beings (Miles, 1989; Rose et al., 1984).

The arbitrariness with which people are allocated to racial categories is well illustrated by a story which may or may not be apocryphal. A journalist is supposed once to have asked Papa Doc Duvalier, the Haitian leader, how many people in his country were White. '99 per cent', Duvalier replied. The journalist was taken aback and asked the leader how he defined 'White'. Duvalier responded by asking the journalist how he defined 'Black'. 'Anyone with Black blood', said the journalist. That is exactly how I define White' said Duvalier. Since human populations are so intermixed nearly all of us could be allocated to virtually any so-called 'racial group' depending on which criterion was used. For instance Fryer (1984) answers the question of what happened to the 10,000 or so people of African descent who were in Britain at the start of the nineteenth century. They did not disappear, they intermarried. It would be a rash person who sought to claim with absolute certainty that there were no African ancestors in their family.

The arbitrariness with which racial categories are defined is well illustrated by a historical example. As Francis Jacob states in his foreword to a UNESCO collection on 'Racism, Science, and Pseudo-Science': 'the concept of race ... can mean virtually anything: depending on the author one reads, there may be four human races, or fifteen, or twenty-eight or even forty three' (UNESCO, 1983: 9). In his magisterial study of the revolt against slavery in San Domingo, C.L.R. James (1989) showed how the colonial society of the time was divided into 128 categories of race depending on how many of one's great great great great great grandparents were of African origin. This might seem absurd to us today. It might seem even more absurd that there was a strict hierarchy such that those who were one-sixteenth Black could lord over those who were one-eighth Black but were in turn lorded over by those who were a mere one-thirty-second Black. However the system seems strange only because it is not ours. It is no more or less absurd than simply splitting people into White and Black – and, it might be added, no more or less pernicious in its usages.

If racial categories are not inevitable, it obviously follows that neither racism nor racial prejudice can be inevitable. However, to argue that race must be understood as a social rather than a biological entity does not make it any the less real. Indeed, as I stressed from the outset, race and racism are all too real for those whose opportunities and capabilities are restricted by them. The question, however, is how they came to be real? How is it that people come to be seen in terms of race not only by individuals but by legislation and by the procedures of both official and unofficial agencies? How is it that social practices come to be stratified by race in so many ways – whether it be in terms of who gets into the country, who gets what sort of jobs, who gets to live where, and so on? The answer cannot be given in the abstract but must involve an historical analysis of particular cases.

For instance, if one wants to understand the increasing racialization of British society over the second half of the twentieth century one would have to include the following factors: (a) the rise of scientific racism in the period of the slave trade and its consolidation as a justification of imperial expansion; (b) the establishment of Black servicemen in Britain during the Second World War; (c) the need for labour in order to complete Britain's post-war reconstruction and the identification of ex-colonies in the Caribbean and the Indian sub-continent as a source of such labour; and (d) the failure of the left and Trade Union movement to devise a strategy for extra social provision to match the influx of labour (Fryer, 1984; Miles and Phizacklea, 1987). As these new workers were recruited to Britain in increasing numbers during the 1950s, there was a question of whether they should be treated in terms of their class or their race. The ready availability of a racist discourse combined with the complete lack of any organization which would incorporate indigenous and migrant labour in a struggle for more housing and schooling and hospitals meant that, in time, racial classification became increasingly predominant (Miles and Phizacklea, 1987; Reicher, 1986).

It is important to stress that racist discourses and beliefs were both an independent and a dependent factor in this process. On the one hand, notions of Black inferiority and Black danger helped create a 'colour bar'. When Black migrants arrived in Britain they were denied housing by indigenous property owners and forced to congregate in multi-occupancy properties. When they tried to join social clubs, dance at dance halls, or even join Trade Unions they met opposition and any form of joint activity became increasingly difficult. On the other hand, the practical separation of people as a function of race made race seem more real. The subsequent creation of laws and policies which organized an increasing number of social domains along racial lines buttressed the use of racial categories and racist ideologies until it became a commonplace for all – left and right – that Black people had to be denied entry to Britain in order to forestall racial conflict in Britain (Dresser, 1986; Foot, 1969; Miles and Phizacklea, 1987).

There are profound implications here for many of the psychological approaches advanced in this book. Even the most cursory glance at history shows that the use of racial categories must be understood in relation to the organization of social reality and, moreover, that the incidence of racial categorization changes along with changing forms of social organization. This poses a challenge to those models which divorce (racial) categorization from social reality and see it as reflecting some invariant feature of the human psychological apparatus such as capacity limitation. If nothing else, it is an unduly pessimistic view of the human condition to see us as forever distorting information in order to cope through our meagre cognitive endowment. Rather, human beings are involved in the inherently constructive acts of weighing, selecting, and organizing data in order to create meanings. As Locke and Johnston argue in their chapter, such considerations have begun to shift the emphasis in social cognition research from people as 'cognitive misers' to people as 'motivated tacticians'. This is to be welcomed, however, when push comes to shove and we are dealing with complex social interactions – especially large-scale collective behaviour – it still tends to be argued that the weight of information simply overwhelms us and we slip back from being tacticians to being misers (Ostrom, 1994). In the domain where it is most important to address the categorization-reality relationship, social cognition theorists are most likely to deny that any such relationship exists.

If the importance of this relationship places a fundamental question mark over those who would ignore it, it must equally lead us to query those approaches which see the use of categories as set by early social experience but which ignore the impact of immediate social contexts. As Patrick Heaven acknowledges, this is possibly the most powerful objection to explanations of racial prejudice in terms of an authoritarian personality or equally a set social dominance orientation. If racialization, racial prejudice, and racism can change so rapidly as societies change (for instance, in Germany at the end of the Second World War), then what use are models which ascribe these phenomena to rigid individual structures? Moreover, as Billig (1976) has pointed out, what is the sense of conducting research on authoritarian personalities in the post-war US which had just fought a war against Nazism and then use it to explain the phenomena of Nazism? It may be that when extreme racism goes against public ideologies, when it is shunned by the mainstream, then it takes a particular type of person to join racist groups and express prejudiced beliefs. But the more racism becomes widespread, the more a racial worldview is taken for granted, the more that opposing racism may land you in trouble, then the less that a personality explanation is necessary. In short, the larger the problem of racism, the smaller the relevance of individualistic accounts. As soon as psychology breaks the link between categorization and context, it risks becoming an instance of ideology rather than contributing to our understanding of how ideology works. Having said this, the complexity of the relationship between categorization and context poses challenges to those approaches which rightly insist that category usage must be seen in relation to the structure of social reality.

On the one hand, discursive approaches consider what is accomplished by the use of categories in language. For them, it is through language that we make our worlds. On the whole, the focus is on the use of discourse in managing our micro-social worlds and interindividual relations: how we claim certain entitlements, how we avoid blame, and so on (see LeCouteur and Augoustinos, Chapter 13, or else Edwards and Potter, 1992). Yet it could be equally argued that 'race' language can serve to manage macro-social relations and intergroup relations: who is allowed access to resources or even allowed into the country, who is to blame for crime, for social conflict, or whatever? Thus racial discourse and the practices which flow from it are undoubtedly major factors in the creation of our social world. For instance, as I write there is a major conflict in Zimbabwe with the government of Robert Mugabe and activists of his ZANU party encouraging the seizure of farmland. There is a major debate as to whether the issue is one of 'race' (a landless Black majority against a minority of rich White farmers) or one of democracy (the unpopular Mugabe engineering a crisis which can lead him to clamp down on opposition politicians and delay an imminent election which he is likely to lose). If it is the former, then the majority belong on Mugabe's side against the Whites and those who challenge the way their land is seized. If it is the latter, then the majority belong in the opposition to Mugabe and his attempt to deny them their democratic choice. The future of the country hangs on the categories which are used to make sense of events.

But what then of the way in which the organization of our social worlds impacts upon the categories we use? Here, discursive approaches have less to say – if nothing else because of the philosophical concern that we can only describe the real world through language and that our use of descriptive language is never neutral but always oriented to some function. If our understanding of reality depends upon language use then trying to use 'reality' to explain language usage simply lands us in a never-ending loop. We can't escape that loop so our only option is to come clean about it and explicitly restrict our analyses to what people do with their discourse (cf., Edwards, 1997; Potter, 1996).

To argue this, however, is not to suggest that discourse analysts propose that there are no limits to the ways in which people use discourses to create their social worlds. Mark Rapley, as well as Amanda LeCouteur and Martha Augoustinos, stress the way in which 'interpretative repertoires' shape and limit the ways in which we can address social phenomena such as 'race'. Our cultures provide us with only so many ways of talking and hence of construing issues and it is through such linguistic restrictions that the larger culture impacts upon what we say and do as individuals. It should be noted that the notion of 'repertoires' has proved controversial even amongst discourse analysts, many of whom have tended to concentrate in recent years on the way in which utterances are flexibly used and organized within local conversational contexts rather than trying to relate talk to the wider cultural context (Antaki, 1994; Edwards, 1997; Potter, 1996). The problem is that interpretative repertoires are too cumbersome an instrument to explain the patterning of category usage. They relate to the broad cultural context and might explain the overall limits on what types of accounts we use, but they cannot explain how the categories we use vary from one setting to another within a given society. The problem is that discursive psychologists provide us with no alternative and we are therefore left between the devil and the deep blue sea. Either our talk of 'race' is governed by something too general to account for our specific uses or else it is governed by nothing but talk itself. All in all, the discursive approach provides a powerful means of addressing the link from (racial) categories to social organization but proves less helpful in addressing the link from social organization to (racial) categories.

Exactly the opposite can be said of work in the realistic conflict theory and self-categorization traditions. Consider again the situation during the 1950s and 1960s as people from the Caribbean and the Indian sub-continent came to Britain and the pressure on jobs and housing and social provision increased. In one sense it is entirely fair to say that there was a realistic conflict between indigenous and migrant workers and this led to increased hostility between them. But then note again that such competition was dependent upon the prior categorization of the migrant as an outgroup, and that this categorization impeded solidarity between newcomers and the longer-standing population, and that this in turn meant that the only game in town was to squabble over shares in the existing cake rather than fight for a bigger cake. A perfect illustration of such dependencies comes from Sherif's own boys' camp studies – albeit the one study that has been much neglected; the study conducted in 1953, just prior to 'Robber's Cave'. In this study, the two groups of boys realized that they were being set against each other and so they reconstrued the situation from being

'Group A' against 'Group B' to one of 'Boys' against 'Camp staff'. These new categories made the previous reality, in which boy competed against boy, seem irrelevant. The new reality was altogether too uncomfortable for the experimenters and so the study was abandoned and never fully written up (cf., Billig, 1976).

These examples show us that what appears at one point in time as an objective external reality which serves as an explanation of our subjective internal states (such as category usage, prejudice, and so on) is itself a product of prior organization of the social world based on the categories people use. There is nothing wrong in concentrating on how momentary forms of social organization affect subsequent forms of social categorization and relation between categories. Indeed, I have been arguing that such analysis is essential. It only becomes a problem if one begins to treat that social organization as a natural fact which determines human understanding but is not in turn determined by human understanding and action. That is, the problem is not that of analysing the path from social organization to (racial) categorization but of using it to substitute for the path from categorization to organization.

Similar points can be made about social identity and self-categorization theories (cf., Reicher, 1986; Reicher and Hopkins, in press). As is argued with particular verve in the chapter by Oakes and Haslam, along with that by Reynolds and Turner, the way we categorize the world derives from the ways people are positioned in relation to each other in reality. We see people in collective terms when people are actually organized in collective terms. If we don't like categories such as 'race' we should blame the ways our societies are organized, not the nature of the human psyche. If we want to change category usage we need to fight to restructure our societies and not seek to restructure the information load on individual minds. In short, groups don't subvert the quality of human thought. Rather, the collectivities in which we live provide the values, the understandings, and the perspectives that allow us to live and act within complex and ever-shifting social relations.

There is no doubt that self-categorization theory represents a powerful counterblast in contemporary social psychology to those in the social cognition tradition who would look at categorization without looking at the categorical structure of context – who would explain 'race' without reference to a racialized world. However, in order to hammer the point home, self-categorization theorists have laid the emphasis on how our categories 'fit' the world while devoting far less attention to how categories create the world. It would be unfair to describe self-categorization theory as conceptually one sided since there certainly is a recognition that people actively employ categories in order to affect how people relate to one another, who they see as friend and as foe, how they should act collectively, and so on (cf., Haslam, 2001). However, it certainly would be fair to say that, to date, the theory has been more concerned with looking at the way in which reality affects categorization than with looking at how categorization moves people to create reality.

In sum, the phenomena of racialization demand a two-sided approach to the relationship between racial categories and social reality. Some of our theories fail the challenge entirely by divorcing the two. Others have tended to emphasize one side of this relationship to the neglect of the other. It is a clear challenge to develop models which, by laying equal stress on both, can explain why sometimes we seem to be trapped into racialized patterns of thinking in a racialized world while at others we are able to forge new worlds through the use of new categories.

From Prejudiced Beliefs to Racial Theories

Racialization may well be a necessary condition for perceiving people in terms of their racial group membership, however, it is not sufficient to explain exactly how we see them and feel about them. Certainly, a study of the social scientific literature quickly reveals that people do not automatically revile all racial outgroups and even when they do the nature of that hostility varies considerably from case to case. Sometimes the racial outgroup is seen as noble and strong, sometimes as sly and untrustworthy, sometimes as stupid and lazy. There are almost as many views as there are relations between racialized groups (Balibar and Wallerstein, 1991; Miles, 1989; Thomas, 1994). In this section I will consider the nature of these views and what it is about them which may lead on to racist action. In the next section I will look at the links between racial beliefs and racist action more directly.

As will be apparent from the literature described in many chapters of this book, psychologists have tended to approach the issue of race-related beliefs and feelings in two general ways. First of all, they have assumed that these beliefs can be reduced to a simple and single form. To quote from the introduction of a fairly up-to-date edited collection which seeks, much like this book, to illustrate the diversity of research in the area of racism and racial prejudice: 'racism is a philosophy expressing the superiority of one race over another race' (van Oudenhoven and Willemsen, 1989: 15). Secondly, and as a consequence, it is generally assumed that we can measure racist stereotypes, racist attitudes, and racial prejudice by looking at the extent to which people consider that certain traits apply to members of racial groups: the racist is the individual who considers that 'they' are stupid, are lazy, are aggressive, and so on.

There is an obvious problem with all this which can be illustrated by reference to an extreme example. In recent years, some of the most rabid fascist groups in Britain, groups which advocate the expulsion of Black people from the country and who are associated with racist violence, have openly rejected the notion that Black people are inferior. They argue instead that racial groups have their own cultures and need to preserve their own identity. Any attempts to bring such groups together will inevitably lead to conflict and to decline and will therefore be to the detriment of all. For these fascists, 'we' don't denigrate Black people, 'we' simply don't want 'them' here. Such views are concisely expressed in the 1997 general election manifesto of the British National Party – currently Britain's largest fascist organization. They claim to be:

racial patriots who value our own racial heritage and want to maintain it intact. This has nothing to do with 'hating' other races – a pursuit which we believe is stupid and wrong ... Last year, some of our members even took part in a small demonstration in support of repatriation side by side with members of the ethnic minorities. Out of these small beginnings, we are confident that bigger things will come. This whole issue is not a matter of 'hate'. It is a matter of the mutual survival of our race and others, each in its own territory, each with its own identity, each to its own way of life. (taken from the BNP website – www.bnp.net)

More concisely, the BNP web page's mission statement declares that the Party aims: 'to promote a modern nationalism which emphasizes the fundamental right of all peoples to maintain their own societies, race and culture, without supremacist intentions towards others living within their own homelands'. The point about this example is that any definition which suggests that the BNP are not racist would self-evidently be absurd. However, a definition based on supremacism would do precisely this.

The response within the sociological literature has been to propose the emergence of a 'new racism' which is based on the idea of inherent difference and tension between racial groups rather than a natural hierarchy of races (e.g., Barker, 1981; Gilroy, 1987; Seidel, 1986). Similarly, as Iain Walker documents in this volume, psychologists have sought to distinguish between supremacist versus modern racism, or blatant versus ambivalent racism, or even between ambivalent and subtle forms of racism. Each of these dichotomies is opposed to the other and therefore it should not be thought that analysts acknowledge a wide range of forms of racism. Rather, psychologists have simply gone from one to two forms of racism and then argue about how exactly to label those two. Moreover, they tend to see one form as gradually replacing the other rather than seeing different forms of racism as co-existing at the same time. Two might be better than one even with this qualification, but it still isn't enough.

We come back to the observation that the nature of beliefs about racial outgroups is almost infinitely variable. Even where there is supremacism it can be expressed in many ways, as reflected in the different ideologies about different racial groups in Britain. Are the outgroup inferior because, like those of African origin, they lack intellectual qualities and are suitable only for physical labour and athletic endeavour? Or are the outgroup inferior because, like those of Asian origin, they lack moral qualities, they are untrustworthy, and their cleverness only makes them all the more dastardly (cf., Fryer, 1984). As Thomas puts it, in his analysis of colonialism's treatment of different colonized populations, racial ideas:

ought to be seen as a *discourse* that engages in conceptual and perceptual government, in its apprehension and legislation of types, distinctions, criteria for assessing proximity and distance, and in its more technical applications – in, for instance, notions stipulating that certain forms of labour are appropriate to one race but not another. (1994: 79, emphasis in the original)

It is not surprising, given this description, that Thomas does not in fact refer to racial ideas, but rather to racial *theory*. In this, he echoes Balibar (1991) who argues that our conceptions of race should not be reduced to a simple affective dimension or else to a set of discrete attitudes, but rather constitute an interconnected set of postulates which serve to characterize and explain the nature of our social world. Such theories are racial in the sense that they suggest that people relate to each other in terms of their membership of racial groups. As Thomas indicates, they then specify exactly how members of different racial groups inter-relate and the implications for the ways in which those groups should be governed, the positions which should be open to them, and the forms of contact which should be allowed between races. This conceptualization of our ideas about race as racial theories has a number of radical implications. It suggests a very different way of going about our study of the phenomena to that which flows from the use of constructs such as 'stereotype' or 'prejudice'.

To start with, it raises serious doubts about the use of the normal psychological toolkit with its preponderance of trait rating scales, semantic differentials, and attitude questionnaires. The difficulty is that the same trait term may have very different meanings when placed in the context of the wider theories from which they are taken. Or, to put it the other way round, we may lose the meaning of these terms when we abstract them from their theoretical contexts. As Schwarz (1982) has noted, the notion of a 'freedom-loving' Englishman acquires an entirely different meaning according to whether it is put in the context of the gallant English people standing up to Nazi invasion or else the English householder objecting to an Asian family moving in next door. In research I have conducted with Nick Hopkins on Scottish identity we see both left-wing and right-wing politicians agreeing that the Scots are 'communal', but for the one it is nested in an argument for a society based on strong welfare institutions whereas for the other it is used to advocate neighbourly support as a substitute for welfare provision (Hopkins and Reicher, 1997; Reicher and Hopkins, in press): the same term, but entirely different meanings based on entirely different models of social organization.

Similar points can be made in relation to evaluation. How do we know whether a particular term is positive or negative? Consider the most notorious term of all – the notion that Black children generally perform badly at school, that they obtain low scores on IQ tests, that they tend to be concentrated in jobs where they work by hand rather than work by brain. The problem is that subscribing to such a notion does not differentiate between those who do or do not view Black people negatively or between those who might be described (and describe themselves) as racists and anti-racists. I firmly believe all the statements made above to be true. Indeed it is precisely because I believe that the social practices of our society lead to disproportionate Black underachievement in the schools and at the workplace that I have been involved in anti-racist action, and because I believe that psychology has contributed to that underachievement through the use of discriminatory technologies like the IQ test that I was drawn to the area in order to contest received ideas. What is at issue between racists and anti-racists, then, is not whether Black people fail but why they fail. For me, it is not that Black people are a problem, but the racist practices in our society. Hence I reserve my hostility for those practices. If you want to get at my position and my feelings, you need to understand my theories, not my trait descriptions.

In order to emphasize the point, let us now take the opposite term – intelligent. It might seem that intelligent is a good thing, something which indicates a positive orientation towards a person or group. Hence, an individual who applies such a term towards a racial group might be considered as less racist for doing so. However, many racist theories consider an outgroup to be dangerous precisely because they are clever. According to certain forms of anti-semitism, it is the intelligence of Jews which allows them to overcome and subvert other groups. It was a staple form of British fascist thought in the 1970s and 1980s to argue that clever Jews use stupid Blacks in order to destroy White Britain (cf., Billig, 1978). Once again, the trait tells us nothing outside of its theoretical context. It simply makes no sense to try and evaluate a person's level of prejudice by totting up how many 'positive' and 'negative' traits they tick, firstly because one cannot tell whether traits are positive or negative in isolation and secondly because one element may change the meaning of all the others when placed in context. Fascists may see Jewish people as intelligent, as rich and as cultured. To find that they also see Jews as subversive obviously doesn't mean a 3 – 1 count in favour, it means that they see Jews as uniquely dangerous.

In contrast to a list of traits, then, a racial theory provides much more information. It provides a far richer account of how a group acts, it provides an explanation of why they act the way they do and hence allows us to predict both what they will do in particular circumstances and what they are able to do. This provides a link to my argument in the previous section: racial theories (unlike racial traits) are formulated in such a way as to provide a guide to practice in our social world. They both look backward and explain why particular racial groups occupy the place they do in society (that is, they justify existing social practices – cf., Tajfel, 1981a) and also look forward to tell us the place that racial groups should occupy in society (that is, they serve to create new social practices – cf., Reicher and Hopkins, in press). As the above quote from Thomas makes clear, racial theories relate to the governance of groups in society and hence the difference between racial theories can be related to different forms of governance. For instance, it could be claimed that notions of African stupidity relate to forms of direct rule in which people were forced off their land, forced into menial labour in colonies run by Europeans, whereas notions of Asian perfidy relate to forms of indirect rule in which commercial exploitation operated through the intermediary of indigenous client rulers (Fryer, 1984). Likewise, Thomas (1989) notes how the British regarded Fijians as far more advanced than Papuans or Solomon Islanders and that this was mirrored in forms of Fijian self-government.

All this now puts us in a position to address one outstanding issue. At the beginning of this section I argued that racialization does not inevitably lead on to racist action but that one also needs to take racist beliefs into account. I went on to argue that we should conceptualize racial beliefs in terms of theories and that the range of these theories is almost unlimited. However, the concept of a 'racial theory' makes it far harder to make a simple distinction between one sort of position which, uniquely, can be described as racist versus others that are not. Racist beliefs cannot be defined as those which say the racial outgroup is inferior, nor as those which contain a numerical preponderance of negative terms to describe a racial group. What then makes a racial theory a racist theory? In what ways are the 'new racism' and the 'old racism' both racist? How can a theory be equally racist whether it characterizes the outgroup as stupid or as intelligent?

Miles (1989) provides an answer. He argues that racism consists firstly of seeing a collectivity as inherently and irreparably different and then secondly representing the collectivity in terms that render it necessarily problematic for other racial groups – either because of its inherent nature or because of the consequences it induces for others. As Miles puts it: 'it follows that such a naturally defined collectivity constitutes a problematic presence: it is represented ideologically as a threat' (1989: 79). This meets the criteria set out above since a racial outgroup may be just as much of a problem for the ingroup by being inferior and hence threatening to drag standards down, as by being merely different and threatening to produce turmoil, or as by being intellectually superior and threatening to subvert the ingroup.

Another advantage of such a formulation is that it provides a means of addressing the affective dimension of racism which, as Baird and Duck demonstrate, is overlooked at our peril. However, rather than treating affect as an antecedent of prejudice and discrimination, the link here is from theory to feeling. That is, once a racial outgroup is constituted as a problem or a threat to the ingroup we may well begin to feel hostile to members of that outgroup. The point is made clearly by Thomas if we consider the continuation to his quotation concerning the colonizer's treatment of the colonized: 'racist discourse may often indeed be manifested personally, in responses of displeasure, fear or antipathy, but these should be understood as subjective internalizations of non-subjective ideologies, rather than the emotional springs from which the latter flow' (1994: 79) – although, of course, it should be clear from my argument that I also consider the identities, values, and norms implied in racial theories to be internalized and not just emotional reactions.

However, if the construction of an outgroup as providing a threat to the ingroup may lead to negative affect towards that outgroup, it need not necessarily do so, nor is actual discrimination necessarily dependent upon antipathy towards the target. Charles Husband, a well-known researcher on issues of 'race' in Britain, used to tell an anecdote from his own research into the matter. He was involved in talking to adolescent boys about racial issues, and one day he interviewed two very contrasting respondents one after the other. The first was the quintessential bigot. He expressed his hatred of Black people in the most foul terms. He virtually spat when he spoke of them and he concluded – venomously – that 'they' shouldn't be allowed into the country. The next boy was a charming liberal. He spoke of Black people as fellow human beings, he respected their culture, he deplored discrimination – but he sadly concluded that if too many Black people were in Britain there would surely be conflict and hence immigration laws must be used to limit entry. So ultimately, both had accepted the dominant ideology that the presence of Black people is a problem and that they must be excluded. However, the one proceeded with delight and the other with sorrow.

An altogether more chilling illustration of a similar point is provided in the autobiography of Rudolf Hoess, the Commandant of Auschwitz from 1940 until the end of 1943 (Hoess, 2000). In his time, Hoess presided over the systematic extermination of Jews and Gypsies alike. Hoess clearly sees both groups as a threat to the 'German people' and agrees that they should be destroyed rather than being allowed to destroy the Volk. It is clear throughout the book that he personally dislikes Jewish people, however in his comments on the Gypsies he sounds almost like a fond father of errant offspring who – sadly – must be punished. Hoess writes that:

> although they were a source of great trouble to me at Auschwitz they were nevertheless my best loved prisoners – if I may put it that way. They never managed to keep any job for long. They 'gypsied around' too much for that, whatever they did. Their greatest wish was to be in a transport company, where they could travel all over the place, and satisfy their endless curiosity, and have a chance of stealing. Stealing and vagrancy are in their blood and cannot be eradicated. (2000: 128)

And so on the night of 31st July – 1st August 1944, the 4,000-odd remaining gypsies in the camp were murdered. It was hard to drive them into the gas chambers, writes Hoess, because 'they were by their nature as trusting as children' (2000: 127).

In his introduction to Hoess's story, Primo Levi notes that it has no literary merit, that it is filled with evil and that reading it is agony. And yet it is one of the most instructive books ever written. One of the many things we learn is that the most extreme acts of racist barbarity may be performed without rancour against the victims. The difference between the way in which Hoess feels about Jews and Gypsies has to do with his different theories of threat. Jews are low and scheming and dangerous. They are to be despised as well as murdered. Gypsies are innocent and childlike and dangerous. They are to be liked, but they are still to be murdered. Thus, to use Taylor's terms, the relation between racial theories and affect depends upon the precise discourse of 'race' that is employed. However, whatever its basis, the fact of threat has certain consequences for action.

Because of its problematic presence, the racial outgroup cannot be allowed to express itself freely since that would inevitably damage the ingroup. Rather, the outgroup must be managed, controlled and constrained in ways that fit the ingroup. In other words, it must be subjected to racist action as I defined it at the outset of this chapter. If there is a general link between racial theories and practices around race, this definition provides the possibility of a link between racist theories and racist practices. What is more, it may be possible to the different variants of racist theory in terms of different types of racist practice.

Thus, Balibar suggests that any debate on whether there is such a thing as a 'neo-racism' must try to find: 'the connection between the newness of the doctrines and the novelty of the political situations and social transformations which have given them a purchase' (1991: 17).

One very rough explanation would be to argue that hierarchical racism is connected to the creation of difference and to creating the subordination of racial groups whereas the various forms of cultural and 'modern' racism serve to maintain those differences by obscuring them behind a discourse about universal individual rights. The implication – which mirrors Iain Walker's conclusion that 'modern' racism exists alongside 'old' racism rather than replaces it – is that any such temporal label is misleading. Rather, we should look how different forms of racial theory exist and develop in relation to the different practices that exist within a society. However, to argue that racist theories relate to racial practices is not to suggest that there is a seamless and automatic correspondence between the two. In order to understand when racist theories result in racist practices (and vice-versa) we must also understand when they do not. That is the task of the next section.

The Theory and the Practice of Racism

One of the more remarkable features of contemporary social psychology is the relative paucity of research which looks at how people actually act towards others. Indeed, there has been a marked decline in such work over recent years (Haslam and McGarty, 2001). Many explanations can be proposed for this phenomenon. In part it has to do with the 'cognitive revolution' leading to an emphasis on perception and judgement, on how we acquire and transform information. In part it has to do with our increasing reliance on experimental methods and the difficulty of getting people to do much more than say what they think and say what they would do in such situations. Even if it were possible to find ways of getting people to undertake intergroup interactions, the increasing sensitivity to ethical issues would place strict limits on exactly what we can get people to do. And so, if you look through the literature reported in this book and elsewhere, you will find a massive literature about what people think and feel about racial outgroups and you will find many studies reporting behavioural intentions. However, you will find very little in psychology which actually investigates racist action. Moreover, despite the fact that, from the very earliest studies, it was clear that what people say about racial outgroups and how they will treat them is often unrelated to what they do when confronted with members of those groups (LaPiere, 1934), there is still a tendency to suppose that demonstrations of stereotyping and prejudice are equivalent to demonstrations of racism. It is as if these are the best we can get, so they will have to do as an explanation of the phenomena which are at the basis of our investigation. Important as these phenomena are – or, to use the concepts I have argued for in this chapter, important as our racist theories may be – they are neither sufficient nor necessary for such action. That is, one can have racist theories without racist action and one can have racist action without racist theories.

The first and most obvious issue, one already intimated at in the first section of this chapter, has to do with power. As Ng (1980, 1982) has pointed out, the issue of power is much neglected throughout psychology and its absence from the study of intergroup relations is particularly surprising since such relations are so often both moulded by power and also revolve around issues of power. Ng argues that, whatever the motivation to discrimination against an outgroup, the act of discrimination depends upon having the 'usable power' to overcome the resistance and retaliation of the outgroup. Similarly, from my own work it is clear that the ability to express any aspect of one's identity depends upon whether such behaviour would be punished by the outgroup and whether the outgroup has the power to impose such punishment (Reicher and Levine, 1994a, 1994b; Reicher, Levine, and Gordijn, 1998, Reicher et al., 1995).

In our studies, we were particularly concerned with the effect of visibility relations within and between groups both upon the salience of group identities (and hence upon the adoption of group norms) and also upon power relations (and hence upon the expression of group norms). We reasoned that anonymity to the outgroup should decrease the ability of outgroup members to impose punishments while, conversely, anonymity to fellow ingroup members should decrease the sense of support and solidarity between members, decrease their power relative to the outgroup and hence increase the ability of outgroup to impose punishments. This underlines the argument made by Terry, Hogg, and Blackwood in their contribution that prejudiced positions only affect group action to the extent that they coincide with group norms. However, it suggests that this link may be due to a number of mechanisms. As well as cognitive accessibility one must also address the way in which a sense that a position is normative may affect the expectation of collective support and hence increase one's power to actually discriminate against the outgroup. More generally, we must always address how contextual factors affect not only our understanding of self and others but also our ability to enact those understandings (Reicher, 2000)

In terms of race, it is one thing to problematize a racial outgroup or to dislike that outgroup, but the expression of antagonism depends on the power relations between groups. A formulation that was widespread amongst anti-racist activists in the 1980s and 1990s was that discrimination = prejudice + power. In the terms used here, I am arguing that racist action depends upon racialization and outgroup problematization and power. That is, it need involve neither a sense of the other as inferior or a dislike of the other. But the inclusion of the power term is crucial. Attempts to address racism without including it get one into all sorts of difficulties. Most notably it creates a spurious equivalence between the oppressors and the oppressed.

It is certainly true that Black people and White people are equally human, that they have the same basic psychological processes and that they are equally capable of stereotyping and disliking other groups. However, they will differ in the expression of such ideas and feelings and, to the extent that there is such expression, its social dynamic will act in opposite ways. For the dominant group it will serve to perpetuate subordination, for the subordinate group it will serve to challenge their position. To reduce everything to a commonality of psychological predispositions once again fails to address how these dispositions both shape and are shaped by the structure of the world we live in. It rules out any understanding or any strategy to challenge social inequality. In particular, it fails to address the institutional bases of discriminatory action: the ways in which the laws, policies, and informal practices of organized bodies serve either to discriminate against particular groups or else facilitate certain groups discriminating against others. Thus, in the UK, one could argue that our immigration laws are systematically biased against Black people, that they have facilitated police action against Black people on the grounds that any Black person might be an 'illegal immigrant', and that a sense that the police might treat crimes by Black people more seriously than crimes against Black people has facilitated the expression of racist violence (Institute of Race Relations, 1987; Miles and Phizacklea, 1987).

Once one invokes the importance of institutions to racist practice a number of other issues must be considered. Whatever their original purposes and whatever the original bases on which they were organized, institutions tend to develop their own logics and their own autonomous interests. Most notably, they develop bureaucracies which seek to protect and perpetuate themselves irrespective of the ostensible reason why they were created in the first place. What is more, as Bauman (1991) argues, the combination of bureaucracy and technology in modern social organizations means both that there is an increasing distance between our actions and their consequences and also that our actions can bring about greater consequences than ever before. We concentrate on our narrow role as one small cog in the machine and fail to focus on what our ever more powerful machines are doing. Accordingly, Bauman describes much of our behaviour within institutions as 'adiaphoric' – that is, it is focused on technical rather than moral concerns. This has two important implications for the present argument. First of all, the bases on which people in institutions act may have little to do with the reasons why the institution exists in the first place. Secondly, one cannot infer the bases on which institutional members act from the consequences of their actions or else infer the consequences of action from the bases on which institutional members act. To put it more bluntly, people can act to sustain racial domination even when their concerns have little to do with race, racialization, or a concern with the problematized other.

Ogunsakin (1998) provides an excellent example of these disjunctions in his study of the relations between police and Black people. While undoubtedly police officers do problematize the Black other, their relations to Black people are primarily shaped by anti-racist policies. Officers are acutely aware of the danger of falling foul of these policies, of being accused of being racist, and of losing their careers as a result. Consequently, they use procedures to protect themselves. They will tail Black suspects in cars for far longer than White subjects before effecting a stop in order to check for information on the Police National Computer and ensure that they are not making a false search. Equally, when Black people are stopped, officers are far more likely to call out extra police in order to have corroboration should the suspect make accusations of maltreatment. Ironically, then, strategies of self-defence in relation to anti-racist policy produce highly discriminatory outcomes.

Bauman's own interest is in an altogether more extreme example of racist practice – the Nazi Holocaust. While it is certainly true that there were many sadistic and brutal racists who took great delight in the task of extermination, those who had far more effect in organizing the 'final solution' were often seemingly inoffensive figures – mild bureaucrats rather than slavering racists; people who were obsessed with their bureaucratic tasks such as ensuring that the requisite number of people were rounded up, that the trains were organized to deliver them to the camps and that the camps had the requisite technology to ensure that bodies could be disposed of in sufficient number.

The most famous example was Adolf Eichmann – chief adminstrator of the Nazi extermination process – whose capture and trial in 1961 gave rise to Hannah Arendt's chilling observations on 'the banality of evil' (Arendt, 1964). As she explained elsewhere: '[Evil] can spread over the whole world and lay waste precisely because it is not rooted anywhere … It was the most banal motives, not especially wicked ones (like sadism or the wish to humiliate or the will to power) which made Eichmann such a frightful evil-doer' (quoted in Novick, 2000: 135). More generally, Staub (1989) argues that the more people can compartmentalize their tasks and ignore the wider picture, the more they can specialize in one small area and the more they can focus on the bureaucratic aspect of their specialized task, the easier it is for them to participate in the process of genocide.

A similar argument can be applied to the German population as a whole, and not merely the functionnaries of the Holocaust. It is easy to assume that, because the most obvious aspect of the Third Reich to us was its murderous anti-semitism, such anti-semitism must have been equally prominent to those who voted for, who supported or who simply accepted the regime. Again, there is no doubt that some were attracted by the racist policies, but it was far from the dominant factor in Hitler's appeal (Abel, 1986). Moreover, there is evidence that active expressions of Nazi anti-semitism actually led to a drop in the popularity and prestige of the party (Kershaw, 1984). Thus we cannot infer that support for the murderous regime was due to its murderous policies. It was more that people were prepared to overlook the anti-semitism given other bases for supporting the regime. As Kershaw puts it, 'the road to Auschwitz was built by hate but paved by indifference' (1984: 277). This, of course, is not to remove moral responsibility from those who stood by while the millions were killed. However, it should lead us to use caution in projecting our concerns as the concerns of those whose behaviours we seek to explain and to be even more cautious in using them as the explanation of those behaviours.

The long and the short of it is that the search for racists and the search for racism should not be conflated with each other. If we only look for the expression of racist theories we will miss much, if not all, of the racism in our world and even where we find such theories we may not have found racist action.

Conclusion

As I stated at the outset, my aim in this chapter has been to provide some context which will make it easier for readers to evaluate the worth of psychological approaches to prejudice and racism. That is, I have sought to address the nature of the phenomena we are trying to explain in order to see whether our explanations are up to the job: what is 'race' in the first place; what is the nature of our understandings about 'race' and what makes such beliefs racist; what is the link between racist understandings and racist action? A number of specific conclusions can be derived from this exercise.

The first, and possibly the most important, is the need to remain ever vigilant that we do not take the category of 'race' for granted. We may live in a racialized world in which it is perfectly valid to start from the assumption that people will see others in terms of racial category memberships. However, if we too start from that assumption and if we presuppose 'race' in our dependent and independent variables, we are in danger of transforming a contingent feature of the social landscape into a natural fact. After all, if we – the experts – presuppose 'race' is it not all the more reasonable for our subjects to do likewise (cf., Hopkins et al., 1997; Reicher, 1986)? Our role must surely be to problematize the very category of 'race' (that is, to study racialization) rather than contribute to the conditions in which racial others are problematized.

The second conclusion is that any investigation of racialization must address the two-sided relationship between our use of racial categories and social reality. That means acknowledging both how our categories reflect the organization of social reality and also how the use of categories serves to create new forms of organization or protect old ones. It is a theoretical task of the first order to develop such a two-sided understanding. It may mean revisiting some of our most cherished concepts. It may mean synthesizing theoretical approaches which hitherto – in this book as well as elsewhere – have been seen (and have seen themselves) as in opposition. Whatever the case may be, we have not yet arrived at such an understanding.

My third conclusion is that our ability to address the phenomena which concern us will depend upon methodological as well as theoretical innovation. The subtleties of racial theories, the meanings of particular forms of description and the complex ways in which people construct racial categories are not always best captured by the use of quantitative scales. Indeed, the whole purpose of such scales is to ensure that they have a common meaning across context such that we can be sure that like is being compared with like and hence quantitative comparisons can be made. This fits ill with a conception of racial theories according to which the same term can have different meanings in different contexts and which – as in the case of the term 'intelligent' – may sometimes indicate racist beliefs, may sometimes indicate a repudiation of racist beliefs, and may sometimes have nothing to do with racist beliefs. If we rely on such scales alone we may therefore misunderstand the nature and the dynamics of racialized beliefs. We may even misrepresent the incidence of such beliefs.

For instance Connolly (1998) has argued that attempts to investigate the development of racial awareness have presupposed the form such awareness should take and codified it into measurement instruments. The failure to find racialized responses on these measures then leads to the conclusion that the children have not yet developed such awareness. However, it may simply be that they fail to capture the way in which 'race' and racialized understanding fit into the daily life of young people – something that may be captured by investigating how they interact and talk in context. Connolly's findings show that the dependence of theoretical development upon methodological sensitivity is just as acute within research on the development of prejudice than the larger body of research on prejudice in adults. This echoes some of the themes in the chapters by Nesdale and by Robinson, Witenberg, and Sanson. Understanding how racialized and racist understandings develop is clearly a matter of crucial importance and may help shed light on the fundamental socio-cognitive building blocks of prejudice and discrimination. For instance, it may not only be that ideas from social identity may shed light on how children become prejudiced, as Nesdale suggests, but also that the study of how children become prejudiced may show crucial conjunctions between the appearance of certain forms of categorical thinking and different forms of racist thought and action. However, in order to explore these conjunctions it becomes all the more important to base our investigations on how children use racial categories rather than presupposing the forms that their usage takes.

I should stress that this is not a plea to drop everything and rely exclusively on everyday talk. Experiments and surveys certainly do have their place. They may be particularly appropriate for looking at the ways in which certain structures of reality affect racial categorization and how the imposition of racial categories brings about certain consequences. They may be less appropriate for looking at the way in which people construe and use categories to make the social world. My point is more that a one-sided reliance on certain methods is likely to lead to a one-sided understanding of the phenomena at hand. We need to devise new methodological strategies and new combinations of methods in order to address the two-sided complexity of racial phenomena.

Fourthly, it is crucial that we place social psychological processes in their structural context. This was a point that was central to the way in which Tajfel and Turner conceptualized social identity processes and which is reiterated in the chapter by Reynolds and Turner. Contrary to many interpretations, we cannot understand racism simply by reference to processes of psychological differentiation between groups or indeed any other purely psychological tendency. Rather, we must investigate how such processes operate within our all too unequal world. One simple criterion for assessing any psychological model must be whether it allows such an articulation between levels or whether it seals one off from the other.

My fifth conclusion is that, for all the criticisms I have made, for all the limitations I have addressed, and for all my calls for future development, this volume demonstrates the liveliness, the relevance and the importance of contemporary social psychological research on prejudice and racism. There is no doubt that we have come a long way from the days in which the work of psychologists served to underpin ideas and policies based on racial difference. Equally, the weight of contemporary work undermines those who would gain comfort by casting out racists as disturbed individuals who are unlike the rest of us. Increasingly, we are aware of racism as a collective phenomenon and, instead of simply seeing collective behaviour as an aggregation of individual states, we are seeking to confront the complex questions of how individual psychology and collective life impinge on each other. These are certain matters of intense debate and this volume demonstrates that there is considerable discord. However, voices raised in argument are a sign of a live science and suggest the possibility of progress. They are certainly preferable to the silence of the grave.

If I have labelled these conclusions as specific, it is because of the way in which I have chosen particular phenomena against which to test the adequacy of psychological research and because I have chosen to discuss them in particular ways. Others may have made different choices and I would not defend mine as necessarily more valid than any alternatives. What I would defend – no, what I would insist on – is the more general procedure pointed to by Blumer's injunction that we must respect the nature of the empirical world and devise our studies accordingly. It is always easier and safer to narrow down our world so that our ideas seem big enough to fill it. When measured against previous experiments our own experiments may seem preferable. When measured against rival theories, our own theories may seem more powerful. But the real test is to measure our ideas against the phenomena they purport to explain. What are these phenomena? What criteria do they set for an adequate explanation? And do our existing accounts match up to those criteria?

One implication of this is that it becomes incumbent upon the social psychologists to be as aware and interested in the reality of racism and prejudice in the society around them as in the theories and models and practices of the discipline itself. As we walk through the library, we should not stop when we come to the end of the psychology section as if we had reached the end of the world. We should also explore the sociology and history and anthropology sections. We should go on to the current affairs sections and the daily newspapers. When out of the library we should attend to what is happening in our less and more extended communities. We should be curious about our world, knowledgeable about our world and rooted in our world. We might even want to be involved in anti-racist campaigns and initiatives rather than simply talking about the anti-racist potential of our ideas. These are the only ways of ensuring that our ideas and research will have any chance of matching up to the demands of our subject. They place heavy demands of us, but they hold out the possibility of making the psychology of prejudice and racism altogether more exciting and more worthwhile.

References

Abel, S. (1996) Wild Maori and tame Maori in television news. *New Zealand Journal of Media Studies*, **3**, 33-88.

Abel, T. (1986) *Why Hitler Came to Power*. Cambridge, MA: Harvard University Press.

Abele, A., Gendolla, G.H.E., and Petzold, P. (1998) Positive mood and in-group–out-group differentiation in a minimal group setting. *Personality and Social Psychology Bulletin*, **24**, 1343-1357.

Aboud, F.E. (1977) Interest in ethnic information: A cross-cultural developmental study. *Canadian Journal of Behavioural Science*, **9**, 134-146.

Aboud, F.E. (1980) A test of ethnocentrism with young children. *Canadian Journal of Behavioural Science*, **12**, 195-209.

Aboud, F.E. (1988) *Children and Prejudice*. Oxford: Basil Blackwell.

Aboud, F.E. and Doyle, A.-B. (1995) The development of in-group pride in Black Canadians. *Journal of CrossCultural Psychology*, **26**, 243-254.

Aboud, F.E. and Doyle, A.-B. (1996a) Does talk of race foster prejudice or tolerance in children? *Canadian Journal of Behavioural Science*, **28**, 161-170.

Aboud, F.E. and Doyle, A.-B. (1996b) Parental and peer influences on children's racial attitudes. *International Journal of Intercultural Relations*, **20**, 371-383.

Aboud, F.E. and Mitchell, F.G. (1977) Ethnic role taking: The effects of preference and self-identification. *International Journal of Psychology*, **12**, 1-17.

Abrams, D. and Hogg, M.A. (1988) Comments on the motivational status of self-esteem in social identity and intergroup discrimination. *European Journal of Social Psychology*, **18**, 317-338.

Achee, J., Tesser, A., and Pilkington, C. (1994) Social perception: A test of the role of arousal in self-evaluation maintenance processes. *European Journal of Social Psychology*, **24**, 147-160.

Adorno, T.W., Frenkel-Brunswik, E., Levinson, D.J., and Sanford, R.N. (1950/1982) *The Authoritarian Personality*. New York: Harper.

After the Removal (1996) Aboriginal Legal Service of Western Australia. Prepared by T. Buti.

Ajzen, I. (1987) Attitudes, traits, and actions: Dispositional prediction of behavior in personality and social psychology. In L. Berkowitz (ed.) *Advances in Experimental Social Psychology*, (Vol. 20. pp. 1-63). San Diego, CA: Academic Press.

Ajzen, I. (1988) *Attitudes, Personality, and Behavior*. Chicago, IL, USA: Dorsey Press.

Ajzen, I. (1991) The theory of planned behavior. *Organizational Behavior and Human Decision Processes*, **50**, 179-211.

Ajzen, I. and Fishbein, M. (1977) Attitude-behavior relations: A theoretical analysis and review of empirical research. *Psychological Bulletin*, **84**, 888-918.

Alinsky, S.D. (1971) *Rules for Radicals: A Pragmatic Primer for Realistic Radicals*. New York: Vintage Books.

Allen V.L. and Wilder, D.A. (1979) Group categorization and attribution of belief similarity. *Small Group Behaviour*, **10**, 73-80

Allport, F.H. (1962) A structuronomic conception of behaviour: Individual and collective. *Journal of Abnormal and Social Psychology*, **64**, 3-30.

Allport, G.W. (1954) *The Nature of Prejudice*. Cambridge, MA: Addison-Wesley.

Allport, G.W. and Postman, L. (1947) *The Psychology of Rumor*. New York: Henry Holt.

Altemeyer, B. (1981) *Right-Wing Authoritarianism*. Winnipeg: University of Manitoba Press.

Altemeyer, B. (1988) *Enemies of Freedom: Understanding Right-Wing Authoritarianism*. San Francisco: Jossey-Bass.

Altemeyer, B. (1994) Reducing prejudice in right-wing authoritarians. In M.P. Zanna and J.M. Olson (eds), *The Psychology of Prejudice: Ontario Symposium on Personality and Social Psychology* (Vol. 7. pp. 131-148). Hillsdale, NJ: Lawrence Erlbaum.

Altemeyer, B. (1996) *The Authoritarian Specter*. Cambridge, MA: Harvard University Press.

Altemeyer, B. (1998) The other 'authoritarian personality'. In M.P. Zanna (ed.), *Advances in Experimental Social Psychology*, (Vol. 30, pp. 47-92). London: Academic Press.

Amir, Y. and Ben-Arie, R. (1989) Enhancing intergroup relations in Israel: A differential approach. In D. Bar-Tal, C. Graumann, A. Kruglanski, and W. Stroebe (eds), *Stereotyping and Prejudice: Changing Conceptions*, (pp. 243-257). Berlin: Springer-Verlag.

Andreeva, G. (1984) Cognitive processes in developing groups. In L. H. Strickland (ed.), *Directions in Soviet Social Psychology*, (pp. 67-82). New York: Springer.

Antaki, C. (1994) *Explaining and Arguing: The Social Organisation of Accounts*. London: Sage.

Antaki, C., Condor, S., and Levine, M. (1996) Social identities in talk: Speaker's own orientations. *British Journal of Social Psychology*, **35**, 473-492.

Arendt, H. (1964) *Eichmann in Jerusalem*. New York: Viking.

Asch, S.E. (1952) *Social Psychology*. Englewood Cliffs, NJ: Prentice-Hall.

Asher, S.R. and Allen, V.L. (1969) Racial preference and social comparison processes. *Journal of Social Issues*, **25**, 157-167.

Ashmore, R. and DelBoca, F. (1981) Conceptual approaches to stereotypes and stereotyping. In D.L. Hamilton (ed.), *Cogntive Processes in Stereotyping and Intergroup Behaviour*, (pp. 1-36). Hillsdale, NJ: Erlbaum.

ATSIC (1998) *As a Matter of Fact: Answering the Myths and Misconceptions About Indigenous Australians*. Canberra: Aboriginal and Torres Strait Islander Commission. Available at http://www.atsic.gov.au/default_ns.asp

Augoustinos, M. (in press) Social categorisation: Towards theoretical integration. In K. Deaux and G. Philogene, *Social Representations: Introductions and Explorations*. Oxford: Blackwell.

Augoustinos, M., Ahrens, C., and Innes, J.M. (1994) Stereotypes and prejudice: The Australian experience. *British Journal of Social Psychology*, **33**, 125-141.

Augoustinos, M., Tuffin, K., and Rapley, M. (1999) Genocide or a failure to gel?: Racism, history and nationalism in Australian talk. *Discourse and Society*, **10**, 351-378.

Augoustinos, M., Tuffin, K., and Sale, L. (1999) Race talk. *Australian Journal of Psychology*, **51**, 90-97.

Augoustinos, M. and Walker, I. (1995) *Social Cognition: An Integrated Introduction*. London: Sage.

Augoustinos, M. and Walker, I. (1998) The construction of stereotypes within social psychology: From social cognition to ideology. *Theory and Psychology*, **8**, 629-652.

Aumack, L. (1955) The effects of imprisonment upon authoritarian attitudes. *American Psychologist*, **10**, 342.

Austin, J. (1962) *How to do Things With Words*. London: Oxford University Press.

Australian Psychological Society (1997) *Guidelines for the provision of psychological services for and the conduct of research with Aboriginal and Torres Strait Islander people of Australia*. Melbourne: Australian Psychological Society.

Avery, P.G. (1989) Adolescent political tolerance: Findings from the research and implication for educators. *High School Journal*, **72**, 168-174.

Azzi, A.E. (1992) Procedural justice and the allocation of power in intergroup relations: Studies in the U.S. and South Africa. *Personality and Social Psychology Bulletin*, **18**, 736-747.

Azzi, A.E. (1993) Implicit and category-based allocations of decision-making power in majority-minority relations. *Journal of Experimental Social Psychology*, **29**, 203-228.

Bagley, C., Verma, G., Mallick, K., and Young, L. (1979) *Personality, Self-esteem and Prejudice*. Westmead, England: Saxon House.

Bailey, S. (1993) Excerpt of a presentation delivered at the *Our Way: National Aboriginal Mental Health Conference*, Sydney, Australia.

Balibar, E. (1991) Racism and nationalism. In E. Balibar and I. Wallerstein (eds), *Race, Nation, Class* (pp. 37-67). London: Verso.

Balibar, E. and Wallerstein, I. (1991) *Race, Nation, Class*. London: Verso.

Banaji, M.R., Hardin, C., and Rothman, A.J. (1993) Implicit stereotyping in person judgment. *Journal of Personality and Social Psychology*, **65**, 272-281.

Bandura, A. (1977) *Social Learning Theory*. Englewood Cliffs, NJ: Prentice-Hall.

Banks, J. (1995) Multicultural education and the modification of students' racial attitudes. In W. Hawley and A. Jackson (eds), *Toward a Common Destiny: Improving Race and Ethnic Relations in America*, (pp. 315-340). San Francisco: Jossey-Bass.

Banton, M. (1999) Racism today: A perspective from international politics. *Ethnic and Racial Studies*, **22**, 606-615.

Bar-Tal, D. (1990) Causes and consequences of deligitimazaiton: Models of conflict and ethnocentrism. *Journal of Social Issues*, **46**, 65-81.

Bargh, J.A. (1989) Conditional automaticity: Varieties of automatic influence in social perception and cognition. In J.S. Uleman and J.A. Bargh (eds), *Unintended Thought*, (pp. 3-51). New York: The Guilford Press.

Bargh, J.A. (in press) The cognitive monster: The case against the controllability of automatic stereotype effects. In S. Chaiken and Y. Trope (eds), *Dual Process Theories in Social Psychology*. New York: Guilford Press.

Bargh, J.A., Chen, M., and Burrows, L. (1996) Automaticity of social behavior: Direct effects of trait construct and stereotype activation on action. *Journal of Personality and Social Psychology*, **71**, 230-244.

Barker, M. (1981) *The New Racism*. London: Junction Books.

Bass, B.M. (1955) Authoritarianism or acquiescence? *Journal of Abnormal and Social Psychology*, **51**, 616-623.

Bauman, Z. (1991) *Modernity and the Holocaust*. Oxford: Polity.

Baumeister, R.F., Smart, L., and Boden, J.M. (1996) Relation of threatened egotism to violence and aggression: The dark side of high self-esteem. *Psychological Review*, **103**, 5-33.

Baumgardner, A.H. and Arkin, R.M. (1988) Affective state mediates causal attributions for success and failure. *Motivation and Emotion*, **12**, 99-111.

Beggan, J.K., Platow, M.J., and McClintock, C.G. (1991) Social interdependence. In R. Baron and W. Graziano (eds), *Social Psychology*, 2nd edn (pp. 394-423). New York: Holt, Rinehart, and Winston.

Bennett, S. (1985) The 1967 referendum. *Australian Aboriginal Studies*, **2**, 26-31.

Berkowitz, L. (1989) Frustration-aggression hypothesis:Examination and reformulation. *Psychological Bulletin,* **106**, 59-73.

Berkowitz, L. (1990) On the formation and regulation of anger and aggression: A cognitive neoassociationist analysis. *American Psychologist,* **45**, 494-503.

Berkowitz, L. (1993) Towards a general theory of anger and emotional aggression: Implications of the cognitive-neoassociationistic perspective for the analysis of anger and other emotions. In R.S. Wyer and T. Srull (eds), *Advances in Social Cognition,* (Vol. 6, pp. 1-46). New Jersey: Erlbaum.

Berkowitz, L. and Troccoli, B.T. (1990) Feelings, direction of attention, and expressed evaulations of others. *Cognition and Emotion,* **4**, 305-325.

Berry, J. (1984) Multicultural policy in Canada: A Social psychological Analysis. *Canadian Journal of Behavioural Science,* **16**, 353-370.

Berry, J., Kalin, R., and Taylor, D. (1977) *Multiculturalism and Ethnic Attitudes in Canada.* Ottawa: Supply and Services Canada.

Beswick, D.G. and Hills, M.D. (1969) An Australian ethnocentrism scale. *Australian Journal of Psychology,* **21**, 211-225.

Bettencourt, B.A., Brewer, M.B., Croak, M.R., and Miller, N. (1992) Cooperation and the reduction of intergroup bias: The role of reward structure and social orientation. *Journal of Experimental Social Psychology,* **28**, 301-319.

Bhat, A., Carr-Hill, R., and Ohri, S. (1988) *Britain's Black Population.* Aldershot: Gower.

Bhavnani, K.K. and Phoenix, A. (1994) Shifting identities shifting racisms. *Feminism and Psychology,* **4**, 5-18.

Billig, M. (1973) Normative communication in a minimal intergroup situation. *European Journal of Social Psychology,* **3**, 339-44.

Billig, M. (1976) *Social Psychology and Intergroup Relations.* London: Academic Press.

Billig, M. (1978) *Fascists: A Social Psychological View of the National Front.* London: Academic Press.

Billig, M. (1979) *Psychology, Racism, and Fascism.* Birmingham: Searchlight and A.F.and R. Publications.

Billig, M. (1981) *L'Internationale Raciste.* Paris: Francois Maspero.

Billig, M. (1985) Prejudice, Categorization, and particularisation: >From a perceptual to a rhetorical approach. *European Journal of Social Psychology,* **15**, 79-103.

Billig, M. (1991a) Consistency and group ideology: Toward a rhetorical approach to the study of justice. In R. Vermunt and H. Steensma (eds). *Social Justice in Human Relations: Societal and Psychological Origins of Justice,* (Vol. 1, pp. 169-194). New York: Plenum Press.

Billig, M. (1991b) *Ideology, Rhetoric and Opinions.* London: Sage.

Billig, M. (1996) *Arguing and Thinking: A Rhetorical Approach to Social Psychology.* 2nd edn. Cambridge: Cambridge University Press.

Billig, M. (1997) Discursive, rhetorical and ideological messages. In C. McGarty and S.A. Haslam (eds), *The Message of Social Psychology,* (pp. 36-53). Oxford: Blackwell.

Billig, M., Condor, S., Edwards, M., Middleton, D., and Radley, A. (1988) *Ideological Dilemmas: A Social Psychology of Everyday Thinking.* London: Sage.

Billig, M. and Tajfel, H. (1973) Social categorization and similarity in intergroup behaviour. *European Journal of Social Psychology,* **3**, 27-52.

Bird, C., Monachesi, E.D., and Burdick, H. (1952) Infiltration and the attitudes of white and Negro parents and children. *Journal of Abnormal Social Psychology,* **47**, 688-689.

Black, H.D. (1987) Ethnocentrism in a pluralist society; children's perspectives. *Curriculum and Teaching,* **2**, 41-47.

Black-Gutman, D. and Hickson, F. (1996) The relationship between racial attitudes and social-cognitive development in children: An Australian study. *Developmental Psychology,* **32**, 448-456.

Blackwood, L., Terry, D.J., and Hogg, M.A. (1999) *Support for Multiculturalism: The Role of Group Norms and Group-Status Threat.* Unpublished manuscript. The University of Queensland.

Blair, I. and Banaji, M.R. (1996) Automatic and controlled processes in stereotype priming. *Journal of Personality and Social Psychology,* **70**, 1142-1163.

Blake, R. and Dennis, W. (1943) The development of stereotypes concerning the Negro. *Journal of Abnormal Social Psychology,* **38**, 525-531.

Blake, R.R. and Mouton, J.S. (1961) Reactions to intergroup competition under win-lose conditions. *Management Science,* **7**, 420-435.

Blake, R.R. and Mouton, J. S. (1962) Overevaluation of own group's product in intergroup competition. *Journal of Abnormal and Social Psychology,* **64**, 237-238.

Blake, R.R. and Mouton, J.S. (1986) From theory to practice in interface problem solving. In S. Worchel and W.G. Austin (eds) *Psychology of Intergroup Relations,* (pp. 67-82). Chicago: Nelson-Hall.

Blanchard, F. and Crosby, F. (eds) (1988) *Affirmative Action in Perspective.* New York: Springer-Verlag.

Blass, T. (1995) Right-wing authoritarianism and role as predictors of attributions about obedience to authority. *Personality and Individual Differences,* **19**, 99-100.

Blau, P.M. (1964) *Exchange and Power in Social Life.* New York: Wiley.

Blauner, R. (1972) *Racial Oppression in America.* New York: Harper and Row.

Blumer, H. (1969) *Symbolic Interactionism.* Berkeley: University of California Press.

Bobo, L. (1983) Whites' opposition to busing: Symbolic racism or realistic group conflict? *Journal of Personality and Social Psychology,* **45**, 1196-1210.

Bobo, L. (1988) Group conflict, prejudice, and the paradox of contemporary racial attitudes. In P.A. Katz and D.A. Taylor (eds), *Eliminating Racism: Profiles in Controversy* (pp. 85-116). New York: Plenum Press.

Bobo, L. and Hutchings, V.L. (1996) Perceptions of racial group competition: Extending Blumer's theory of group position to a multiracial social context. *American Sociological Review,* **61**, 951-972.

Bobo, L. and Licari, F.C. (1989) Education and political tolerance: Testing the effects of cognitive sophistication and target group effect. *Public Opinion Quarterly,* **53**, 285-308.

Bobo, L., Kluegel, J.R., and Smith, R.A. (1997) Laissez-faire racism: The crystallization of a kindler, gentler, antiblack ideology. In S.A. Tuch and J.K. Martin (eds), *Racial Attitudes in the 1990s: Continuity and Change,* (pp. 15-42). Westport, CT: Praeger.

Bochner, S. (1971) The use of unobtrusive measures in cross-cultural attitudes research. In R.M. Berndt (ed.), *A Question of Choice: An Australian Aboriginal Dilemma,* (pp. 107-115). Perth: UWA Press.

Bochner, S. (1972) An unobtrusive approach to the study of housing discrimination against Aborigines. *Australian Journal of Psychology,* **24**, 335-337.

Bochner, S. and Cairns, L.G. (1976) An unobtrusive measure of helping behaviour toward Aborigines. In G.E. Kearney and D.W. McElwain (eds), *Aboriginal Cognition: Retrospect and Prospect,* (pp. 344-356). Canberra: Australian Institute of Aboriginal Studies.

Bodenhausen, G.V. (1993) Emotion, arousal and stereotypic judgement: A heuristic model of affect and stereotyping. In D.M. Mackie and D.L. Hamilton (eds), *Affect, Cognition and Stereotyping: Interactive Processes in Group Perceptions*, (pp. 137-166). San Diego, CA: Academic Press.

Bodenhausen, G.V. and Macrae, C.N. (1998) Stereotype activation and inhibition. In R.S. Wyer (ed.), *Advances in Social Cognition*, (Vol. 11, pp. 1-52). Mahwah, NJ: Erlbaum.

Bogardus, E. (1925) Measuring social distance. *Journal of Applied Sociology*, **9**, 299-308

Bonacich, E. (1972) A theory of ethnic antagonism: The split labour market. *American Sociological Review*, **37**, 447-559.

Bonilla-Silva, E. (1996) Rethinking racism: Toward a structural interpretation. *American Sociological Review*, **62**, 465-480.

Borgida, E., Locksley, A., and Brekke, N. (1981) Social stereotypes and social judgement. In N. Cantor and J.F. Kilstrom (eds), *Personality, Cognition, and Social Interaction*, (pp. 153-169). Hillsdale, NJ: Lawrence Erlbaum.

Boulton, M. (1995) Patterns of bully/victim problems in mixed race groups of children. *Social Development*, **4**, 277-293.

Boulton, M.J. and Smith, P.K. (1993) Ethnic, gender partner, and activity preferences in mixed race schools in the U.K.: Playground observations. In C. Hart (ed.), *Children on Playgrounds: Research Perspectives and Applications*. New York: State University of New York Press.

Bower, G.H. (1981) Mood and memory. *American Psychologist*, **36**, 129-148.

Bower, G.H. (1991) Mood congruity in social judgments. In J.P. Forgas, (ed.), *Emotion and Social Judgments*, (pp. 31-54). Oxford: Pergamon Press.

Braddock, J.H., II, Dawkins, M.P., and Wilson, G. (1995) Intercultural contact and race relations among American youth. In W.D. Hawley and A.W. Jackson (eds), *Toward a Common Destiny*, (pp.237-256). San Francisco: Jossey-Bass.

Branch, C.W. and Newcombe, N. (1980) Racial attitude development among young Black children as a function of parental attitudes: A longitudinal and cross-section study. *Child Development*, **57**, 712-21.

Brand, E.S., Ruiz, R.A., and Padilla, A.M. (1974) Ethnic identification and preference: A review. *Psychological Bulletin*, 81, 860-890.

Branscombe, N.R. and Ellemers, N. (1998) Coping with group-based discrimination: Individualistic versus group-level strategies. In J.K. Swim and C. Stangor (eds), *Prejudice: The Target's Perspective*, (pp. 243-266). New York: Academic Press.

Branscombe, N.R. and Wann, D.L. (1994) Collective self-esteem consequences of outgroup derogation when a valued social identity is on trial. *European Journal of Social Psychology*, **24**, 641-657.

Brewer, M.B. (1979) Ingroup bias in the minimal intergroup situation: A cognitive-motivational analysis. *Psychological Bulletin*, **86**, 307-324.

Brewer, M.B. (1988) A dual process model of impression formation. In T.K. Srull and R.S. Wyer, Jr., (eds), *Advances in Social Cognition*, (Vol. 1, pp. 1-36). Hillsdale, NJ: Erlbaum.

Brewer, M.B. (1997) The social psychology of intergroup relations. *Journal of Social Issues*, **53**, 197-211.

Brewer, M.B. and Brown, R.J. (1998) Intergroup relations. In D.T. Gilbert, S.T. Fiske, and G. Lindzey (eds), *The Handbook of Social Psychology*, 4th edn (Vol 2, pp. 554-594). New York: Oxford University Press.

Brewer, M.B. and Kramer, R.M. (1985) The psychology of intergroup attitudes and behaviours. *Annual Review of Psychology*, **36**, 219-244.

Brewer, M.B. and Miller, N. (1984) Beyond the contact hypothesis: Theoretical perspectives on desegregation. In N. Miller and M.B. Brewer (eds), *Groups in Contact: The Psychology of Desegregation,* (pp. 281-302). San Diego: Academic.

Brewer, M.B. and Miller, N. (1988) Contact and Cooperation: When do they work? In P. Katz and D. Taylor (eds), *Eliminating Racism: Profiles in Controversy,* (pp. 315-326). New York: Plenum.

Brewer, M.B. and Miller, N. (1996) *Intergroup Relations.* Buckingham, England: Open University Press.

Brewer, M.B. and Silver, M. (1978) Ingroup bias as a function of task characteristics. *European Journal of Social Psychology,* **8**, 393-400.

Brewer, M.B. and Sneider, S. (1990) Social identity and social dilemmas: A double-edged sword. In D. Abrams and M. Hogg, (eds), *Social Identity Theory: Constructive and Critical Advances,* (pp. 169-184). London: Harvester Wheatsheaf.

Brigham, J.C. (1971) *Views of White and Black School Children Concerning Racial Personality Differences.* Paper presented to the Midwestern Psychological Association.

Brown, R.J. (1984) The effects of intergroup similarity and cooperative vs. competitive orientation on intergroup discrimination. *British Journal of Social Psychology,* 23, 21-33.

Brown, R.J. (1988) *Group Processes: Dynamics Within and Between Groups.* Oxford: Blackwell.

Brown, R.J. (1995) *Prejudice. Its Social Psychology.* Oxford, UK: Blackwell.

Brown, R.J. and Abrams, D. (1986) The effects of intergroup similarity and goal interdependence in intergroup attitudes and task performance. *Journal of Experimental Social Psychology,* **22**, 78-92.

Brown, R.J., Condor, S., Mathews, A., Wade, G., and Williams, J. (1986) Explaining intergroup differentiation in an industrial organisation. *Journal of Occupational Psychology,* **59**, 273-286.

Brown, R.J. and Turner, J.C. (1979) The criss-cross categorization effect in intergroup discrimination. *British Journal of Social and Clinical Psychology,* **18**, 371-383.

Brown, R.J. and Wade, G.S. (1987) Superordinate goals and intergroup behaviour: The effects of role ambiguity and status on intergroup attitudes and task performance. *European Journal of Social Psychology,* **17**, 131-142.

Brown, R.J. and Williams, J. (1984) Group identification: The same thing to all people. *Human Relations,* **37**, 547-564.

Bruner J.S. (1957) On perceptual readiness. *Psychological Review,* **64**, 123-152.

Camilleri, S.F. (1959) A factor analysis of the F scale. *Social Forces,* **37**, 316-323.

Campbell, D.T. (1965) Ethnocentrism and other altruistic motives. In D. Levine (ed.), *Nebraska Symposium on Motivation.* Lincoln, Nebr.: University of Kansas Press.

Carapetis, G. and Robinson, J.A. (1995) *Peer Preferences Among Pre-School Children From Different Ethnic Backgrounds.* Paper presented at the annual meeting of the Australian Psychological Society, Perth.

Carmichael, S. and Hamilton, C. (1967) *Black Power.* New York: Random House.

Carmines, E. and Merriman, W. (1993) The changing American dilemma: Liberal values and racial policies. In P. Sniderman, P. Tetlock, and E. Carmines (eds), *Prejudice, Politics, and the American Dilemma,* (pp. 237-255). Stanford, CA: Stanford University Press.

Carter, D.E., Detine-Carter, S.L., and Benson, F.W. (1980) Interracial acceptance in the classroom. In H.C. Foot, A.J. Chapman, and J.R. Smith (eds), *Friendship and Social Relations in Children,* (pp. 117-143). New Brunswick, NJ: Transaction Publishers.

Cherry, F. and Byrne, D.F. (1977) Authoritarianism. In T. Blass (ed.), *Personality Variables in Social Behavior* (pp. 109-133). Hillsdale, NJ: Lawrence Erlbaum Associates.

Chong, D. (1993) How people think, reason and feel about rights and liberties. *American Journal of Political Science, 37*, 867-899.

Christie, R. and Garcia, J. (1951) Subcultural variation in authoritarian personality. *Journal of Abnormal and Social Psychology, 46*, 457-469.

Christie, R., Havel, J., and Seidenberg, B. (1958) Is the F scale irreversible? *Journal of Abnormal and Social Psychology, 56*, 143-159.

Chyatte, C., Schaefer, D.F., and Spiaggia, M. (1951) Prejudice verbalisation among children. *Journal of Educational Psychology, 42*, 421-431.

Cialdini, R.B. and Trost, M.R. (1998) Social influence, social norms, conformity, and compliance. In Gilbert, D.G., Fiske, S.T. and G. Lindzey (eds), *The Handbook of Social Psychology,* 4th edn, (Vol. 2. pp. 151-192). Boston, MA: McGraw-Hill.

Clark, A., Hocevar, D., and Dembo, M.H. (1980) The role of cognitive development in childen's explanations and preferences for skin color. *Developmental Psychology,* 16(4), 332-339.

Clark, K.B. and Clark, M.K. (1939) Segregation as a factor in the racial identification of Negro pre-school children: A preliminary report. *Journal of Experimental Psychology, 8*, 161-163.

Clark, K.B. and Clark, M.K. (1947) Racial identification and preference in Negro children. In E.E. Maccoby, T.M. Newcomb, and E.L.Hartley (eds). *Readings in Social Psychology,* (pp. 551-560). London: Methuen.

Clark, M.S. and Isen, A.M. (1982) Towards understanding the relationship between feeling states and social behaviour. In A.H. Hastorf and A.M. Isen (eds), *Cognitive Social Psychology*. New York: Elsevier-North Holland.

Coe, P. (1993) Excerpt of a presentation delivered at the Our Way – National Aboriginal Mental Health Conference, Sydney.

Cohen, R.L. (1986) Power and justice in intergroup relations. In H.W. Bierhoff, R.L. Cohen, and J Greenberg (eds), *Justice in Social Relations,* (pp. 65-84). New York: Plenum Press.

Collier, G., Minton, H.L., and Reynolds, G. (eds) (1991) *Currents of Thought in American Social Psychology*. New York: Oxford University Press.

Colman, A.M. (1982) Experimental games. In A. Colman (ed.), *Cooperation and Competition in Humans and Animals,* (pp. 113-140). Wokingham: Van Nostrand Reinhold.

Connolly, P. (1998) *Racism, Gender Identities, and Young Children*. London: Routledge.

Cook, S. (1985) Experimenting on social issues: The case of school desegregation. *American Psychologist, 40*, 452-460.

Corenblum, B., Annis, R.C., and Tanaka, J.S. (1997) Influence of cognitive development, self-competency, and teacher evaluations on the development of children's racial identity. *International Journal of Behavioral Development, 20*, 269-286

Crawford, T. (1974) Sermons on racial tolerance and the parish neighbourhood context. *Journal of Applied Social Psychology, 4*, 1-23.

Crosby, F. and Clayton, S. (1990) Affirmative action and the issue of expectancies. *Journal of Social Issues, 46*, 61-79.

Crosby, F.J., Bromley, S., and Saxe, L. (1980) Recent unobtrusive studies of Black and White discrimination and prejudice: A literature review. *Psychological Bulletin, 87*, 546-563.

Cross, W.E. (1995) Oppositional identity and African American youth: Issues and prospects. In W. Hawley and A. Jackson (eds), *Toward a Common Destiny: Improving Race and Ethnic Relations in America,* (pp. 185-204). San Francisco: Jossey-Bass.

Cross, W.E. (1991) *Shades of Black: Diversity in African American Identity.* Madison, WI: University of Wisconsin Press.

Darley, J.M. and Gross, P.H. (1983) A hypothesis-confirming bias in labeling effects. *Journal of Personality and Social Psychology,* **44**, 20-33.

Davey, A.G. (1983) *Learning to be Prejudiced: Growing Up in Multi-Ethnic Britain.* London: Edward Arnold.

Davey, A.G. and Mullin, P.N. (1980) Ethnic identification and preference of British primary school children. *Journal of Child Psychology and Psychiatry,* **21**, 241-251.

David, B. and Turner, J.C. (1996) Studies in self-categorization and minority conversion: Is being a member of the outgroup an advantage? *British Journal of Social Psychology,* 35, 179-199. Special issue on minorities: Influence, processes and outcomes.

David, B. and Turner, J.C. (1999) Studies in self-categorization and minority conversion: The in-group minority in intragroup and intergroup contexts. *British Journal of Social Psychology,* **38**, 115-134.

de Benoist, A. (1999) What is racism? *Telos,* 114, 11-48.

De Cremer, D. and Van Vugt, M. (1999) Social identification effects in social dilemmas: A transformation of motives. *European Journal of Social Psychology,* **29**, 871-893.

de la Rey, C. and Raju P. (1996) Group relative deprivation: Cognitive versus affective components and protest orientation among Indian South Africans. *Journal of Social Psychology,* **136**, 579-588.

deGroot, A.M.B., Thomassen, J.W.M., and Hudson, P.T.W. (1986) Primed-lexical decision: The effect of varying the stimulus-onset asynchrony of prime and target. *Acta Psychologica,* **61**, 17-36.

Deschamps, J.-C. and Brown, R.J. (1983) Superordinate goals and intergroup conflict. *British Journal of Social Psychology,* **22**, 189-195.

Deschamps, J.-C. and Doise, W. (1978) Crossed category memberships in intergroup relations. In H. Tajfel (ed.), *Differentiation in Social Groups: Studies in the Social Psychology of Intergroup Relations,* (pp. 141-158). London: Academic.

Deutsch, M. (1985) *Distributive Justice: A Social Psychological Perspective.* New Haven: Yale University Press.

Devine, P.G. (1989) Stereotypes and prejudice: Their automatic and controlled components. *Journal of Personality and Social Psychology,* **56**, 5-18.

Devine, P.G. (1995) Prejudice and out-group perception. In A. Tesser (ed.), *Advanced Social Psychology,* (pp. 467-513). New York: McGraw-Hill.

Devine, P.G. and Monteith, M.J. (1993) The role of discrepancy-associated affect in prejudice reduction. In D.M. Mackie and D.L. Hamilton (eds), *Affect, Cognition and Stereotyping: Interactive Processes in Group Perceptions,* (pp. 317-344). San Diego, CA: Academic Press.

Diab, L.N. (1959) Authoritarianism and prejudice in near-Eastern students attending American universities. *Journal of Social Psychology,* **50**, 175-187.

Diab, L.N. (1963) Factors determining group stereotypes. *Journal of Social Psychology,* **61**, 3-10.

Diab, L N. (1970) A study of intragroup and intergroup relations among experimentally produced small groups. *Genetic Psychology Monographs,* **82**, 49-82.

Dickens, L. and Hobart, C. (1959) Parental dominance and offspring ethnocentrism. *Journal of Social Psychology,* **49**, 297-303.

Dickerson, P. (1997) 'It's not just me who's saying this...': The deployment of cited others in televised political discourse. *British Journal of Social Psychology*, **36**, 33-48.

Diehl, M. (1988) Social identity and minimal groups: The effects of interpersonal and intergroup attitudinal similarity on intergroup discrimination. *British Journal of Social Psychology*, **27**, 289-300.

Diehl, M. (1990) The minimal group paradigm: Theoretical explanations and empirical findings. In W. Stroebe and M. Hewstone (eds), *European Review of Social Psychology*, (Vol. 1, pp. 263-93). Chichester, England: John Wiley.

Dijksterhuis, A. and van Knippenberg, A. (1998) The relation between perception and behavior: Or how to win a game of trivial pursuit. *Journal of Personality and Social Psychology*, **74**, 865-877.

Dion, K.L. (1979) Intergroup conflict and intragroup cohesiveness. In W.G. Austin and S. Worchel (eds), *The Social Psychology of Intergroup Relations*. Monterey: Brooks/Cole.

Doise, W. (1978) *Groups and Individuals:Explanations in Social Psychology*. Cambridge: Cambridge University Press.

Doise, W., Csepeli, G., Dann, H.-D., Gourge, G.C., Larsen, K., and Ostell, A. (1972) An experimental investigation into the formation of intergroup representations, *European Journal of Social Psychology*, **2**, 202-204.

Doise, W., Deschamps, J.C., and Meyer, G. (1978) The accentuation of intercategory similarities. In H. Tajfel (ed.), *Differentiation Between Social Groups*, (pp. 159-168). London: Academic Press.

Dollard, J., Doob, L., Miller, M., Mowrer, O., and Sears, R. (1939) *Frustration and Aggression*. New Haven, CT: Yale University Press.

Donovan, R.J. and Leivers, S. (1993) Using paid advertising to modify racial stereotype beliefs. *Public Opinion Quarterly*, **57**, 205-218.

Doty, R.G., Winter, D.G., Peterson, B.E., and Kemmelmeier, M. (1997) Authoritarianism and American students' attitudes about the Gulf War, 1990-1996. *Personality and Social Psychology Bulletin*, **23**, 1133-1143.

Dovidio, J.F., Brigham, J., Johnson, J., and Gaertner, S. (1996) Stereotyping, prejudice, and discrimination: Another look. In N. Macrae, S. Strangor, and M. Hewstone (eds), *Stereotypes and Stereotyping*, (pp. 1276-1319). New York: Guilford Press.

Dovidio, J.F. and Gaertner, S.L. (1993) Stereotypes and evaluative intergroup bias. In D.M. Mackie and D.L. Hamilton (eds), *Affect, Cognition and Stereotyping: Interactive Processes in Group Perceptions*, (pp. 167-193). San Diego, CA: Academic Press.

Dovidio, J.F., Gaertner, S.L., and Validzic, A. (1998) Ingroup bias: Status, differentiation, and a common ingroup identity. *Journal of Personality and Social Psychology*, **75**, 109-120.

Dovidio, J.F., Kawakami, K., Johnson, C., Johnson, B., and Howard, A. (1997) On the nature of prejudice: Automatic and controlled processes. *Journal of Experimental Social Psychology*, **33**, 510-540.

Doyle, A.-B. (1982) Friends, acquaintances and strangers: The influence of familiarity and ethnolinguistic background on social interaction. In K.H. Rubin and H.S. Ross (eds), *Peer Relationships and Social Skills in Childhood*, (pp. 229-252). New York: Springer-Verlag.

Doyle, A.-B. and Aboud, F.E. (1995) A longitudinal study of white children's racial prejudice as a social-cognitive development. *Merrill-Palmer Quarterly*, **41**, 209-228.

Doyle, A.-B., Beaudet, J., and Aboud, F.E. (1988) Developmental patterns in the flexibility of children's ethnic attitudes. *Journal of Cross-Cultural Psychology*, **19**, 3-18.

Dresser, M. (1986) *Black and White on the Buses*. Bristol: Bristol Broadsides.

Duckitt, J. (1988) Normative conformity and racial prejudice in South Africa. *Genetic, Social, and General Psychology Monographs*, **114**, 413-437.

Duckitt, J. (1989) Authoritarianism and group identification: A new view if an old construct. *Political Psychology*, **10**, 63-84.

Duckitt, J. (1991) The development and validation of a subtle racism scale in South Africa. *South African Journal of Psychology*, **21**, 233-239.

Duckitt, J. (1992) Education and authoritarianism among English and Afrikaans-speaking white South Africans. *Journal of Social Psychology*, **132**, 701-708.

Duckitt, J. (1993) Right-wing authoritarianism among white South African students: Its measurement and correlates. *Journal of Social Psychology*, **133**, 553-563.

Duckitt, J. (1994) *The Social Psychology of Prejudice* (2nd edn). New York: Praeger.

Duckitt, J. (in press) Culture, personality, and prejudice. In S. Renshon and J. Duckitt (eds), *Political Psychology: Cultural and Cross-Cultural Foundations*. London: Macmillan.

Duckitt, J. and Farre, B. (1994) Right-wing authoritarianism and political intolerance among whites in the future majority-rule South Africa. *Journal of Social Psychology*, **134**, 735-741.

Duckitt, J. and Mphutning, T. (1998) Group identification and intergroup attitudes: A longitudinal analysis in South Africa. *Journal of Personality and Social Psychology*, **74**, 80-85.

Dudgeon, P. and Oxenham, D. (1989) The complexity of Aboriginal diversity: Identity and kindredness. *Black voices*, **5**.

Duncan, B. (1976) Differential social perception and attribution of intergroup violence: Testing the lower limits of stereotyping Blacks. *Journal of Personality and Social Psychology*, **34**, 590-598.

Durkin, K. (1995) *Developmental Social Psychology: From Infancy to Old Age*. Oxford: Blackwell.

Eagly, A.H. and Chaiken, S. (1993) *The Psychology of Attitudes*. CA: Harcourt Brace Jovanovich.

Eckermann, A., Dowd, T., Martin, M., Nixon., Gray, R., and Chong, E. (1992) *Binan Goonj – Bridging Cultures in Aboriginal Health*. Armidale: University of New England Press.

Edwards, D. (1991) Categories are for talking: On the cognitive and discursive bases of categorization. *Theory and Psychology*, **1**, 515-42.

Edwards, D. (1997) *Discourse and Cognition*. London: Sage.

Edwards, D. (1999) The relevant thing about her: Social identity categories in use. In C. Antaki and S. Widdicombe (eds), *Identities in Talk*. London: Sage.

Edwards, D. (in press) Analyzing racial discourse: A view from discursive psychology. In H. van den Berg, H. Houtkoop-Steenstra, and M. Wetherell (eds), *Analyzing Interviews on Racial Issues: Multidisciplinary Approaches to Interview Discourse*. Cambridge: Cambridge University Press.

Edwards, D., Ashmore, M., and Potter, J. (1995) Death and furniture: the rhetoric, politics and theology of bottom line arguments against relativism. *History of the Human Sciences*, **8**, 25-49.

Edwards, D. and Potter, J. (1992) *Discursive Psychology*. London: Sage.

Eisenberg, N. and Miller, P. (1990) The development of prosocial behavior versus nonprosocial behavior in children. In M. Lewis and S.M. Miller (eds), *Handbook of Developmental Psychopathology,* (pp. 181-188). NY: Plenum.

Eiser, J.R. (1996) Accentuation revisited. In P. Robinson (ed.) *Social Groups and Identities: Developing the Legacy of Henri Tajfel,* (pp. 121-142). Oxford: Butterworth-Heinemann

Eiser, J.R. and van der Pligt, J. (1982) Accentuation and perspective in attitudinal judgment. *Journal of Personality and Social Psychology,* **42**, 224-238.

Elder, B. (1988) *Blood on the Wattle: Massacres and Maltreatment of Australian Aborigines Since 1788.* Frenchs Forest, NSW: National Book Distributors.

Ellemers, N. (1993) The influence of socio-structural variables on identity management strategies. In W. Stroebe and M. Hewstone (eds), *European Review of Social Psychology,* (Vol. 4, pp. 27-57). Chichester, UK: Wiley.

Ellemers, N., Doosje, B., van Knippenberg, A., and Wilke, H. (1992) Status protection in high status minority groups. *European Journal of Social Psychology,* **22**, 123-40.

Ellemers, N, Spears, R, and Doosje, B. (eds) (1999) *Social Identity: Context, Commitment, Content.* Oxford: Blackwell.

Ellemers, N. van Knippenberg, A., de Vries, N., and Wilke, H. (1988) Social identification and permeability of group boundaries. *European Journal of Social Psychology,* **18**, 497-513.

Enright, R.D., Lapsley, D.K., Franklin, C.C., and Streuck, K. (1984) Longitudinal and cross-cultural validation of belief-discrepancy reasoning construct. *Developmental Psychology,* **20**, 143-149.

Epstein, I.M., Krupat, E., and Obudho, C. (1976) Clean is beautiful: Identification and preference as a function of race and cleanliness. *Journal of Social Issues,* **32**, 109-118.

Erber, R. and Erber, M.W. (1994) Beyond mood and social judgment: Mood incongruent recall and mood regulation. *European Journal of Social Psychology,* **24**, 79-88.

Essed, P. (1991) *Understanding Everyday Racism.* London: Sage

Esses, V.M., Haddock, G., and Zanna, M.P. (1993) Values, stereotypes, and emotions as determinants of intergroup attitudes. In D.M. Mackie and D.L. Hamilton (eds), *Affect, Cognition and Stereotyping: Interactive Processes in Group Perceptions,* (pp. 137-166). San Diego, CA: Academic Press.

Esses, V.M. and Zanna, M.P. (1995) Mood and the expression of ethnic stereotypes. *Journal of Personality and Social Psychology,* **69**, 1052-1068.

Eysenck, H.J. and Eysenck, S.B.G. (1976) *Psychoticism as a Dimension of Personality.* London: Hodder and Stoughton.

Eysenck, H.J. and Wilson, G.D. (eds) (1978) *The Psychological Basis of Ideology.* Lancaster: MTP Press.

Fairchild, H. and Gurin, P. (1978) Traditions in the social psychological analysis of race relations. *American Behavioral Scientist,* **21**, 757-778.

Fazio, R.H. (1986) How do attitudes guide behavior? In R.M. Sorrentino and E.T. Higgins (eds), *The Handbook of Motivation and Cognition: Foundations of Social Behavior,* (pp. 204-243). New York: Guilford.

Feather, N.T. (in press) Attitudes toward high achievers, self-esteem, and value priorities for Australian, American, and Canadian students. *Journal of Cross-Cultural Psychology.*

Feffer, M. and Gourevitch, V. (1960) Cognitive aspects of role-taking in children. *Journal of Personality,* **28**, 383-396.

Feldman, S. and Stenner, K. (1997) Perceived threat and authoritarianism. *Political Psychology,* **18**, 741-770.

Ferguson, C.K. and Kelley, H.H. (1964) Significant factors in overevaluation of own-group's product. *Journal of Abnormal and Social Psychology,* **69**, 223-228.

Finchilescu, G. (1986) Effect of incompatibility between internal and external group membership criteria on intergroup behaviour. *European Journal of Social Psychology,* **16**, 83-872.

Finkelstein, N.W. and Haskins, R. (1983) Kindergarten children prefer same-color peers. *Child Development,* **54**, 502-508.

Finman, R. and Berkowitz, L. (1989) Some factors influencing the effects of depressed mood on anger and overt hostility toward another. *Journal of Research in Personality,* **23**, 70-84.

Fishbein, H.D. and Imai, S. (1993) Preschoolers select playmates on the basis of gender and race. *Journal of Applied Developmental Psychology,* **14**, 303-316.

Fishbein, M. and Ajzen, I. (1975) *Belief, Attitude, Intention, and Behavior: An Introduction to Theory and Research.* Reading, Mass.: Addison-Wesley.

Fisher, R.J. (1990) *The Social Psychology of Intergroup and International Conflict Resolution.* New York: Springer-Verlag.

Fishman, J.A. (1956) An examination of the process and function of social stereoptyping. *Journal of Social Psychology,* **43**, 27-64.

Fiske, S.T. (1989) Examining the role of intent: Toward understanding its role in in stereotyping and prejudice. In S. Uleman and J.A. Bargh (eds) *Unintended Thought,* (pp.253-283). New York: The Guilford Press

Fiske, S.T. (1993) Social cognition and social perception. *Annual Review of Psychology,* **44**, 155-194.

Fiske, S.T. (1998) Stereotyping, prejudice, and discrimination. In D.T. Gilbert, S.T. Fiske, and G. Lindzey (eds), *The Handbook of Social Psychology,* 4th edn, (Vol. 2, pp. 357-411). Boston, MA: McGraw-Hill.

Fiske, S.T. and Neuberg, S.L. (1990) A continuum of impression formation, from category-based to individuating processes: Influences of information and motivation on attention and interpretation. In M.P. Zanna (ed.), *Advances in Experimental Social Psychology,* (Vol. 23, pp. 1-74). New York: Random House.

Fiske, S.T. and Ruscher, J.B. (1993) Negative interdependence and prejudice: Whence the affect? In D.M. Mackie and D.L. Hamilton (eds), *Affect, Cognition and Stereotyping: Interactive Processes in Group Perceptions,* (pp. 239-268). San Diego, CA: Academic Press.

Fiske, S.T. and Taylor, S.E. (1991) *Social Cognition.* (2nd edn). NewYork: McGraw Hill Book Company.

Flavell, J.H. (1963) *The Developmental Psychology of Jean Piaget.* New York: Litton Educational Publishing.

Flick, B. (1998) Health and land go hand in hand. *Australian Nursing Journal,* **5**, May: 16-17.

Foa, E.B. and Foa, U.G. (1980) Resource theory: Interpersonal behavior as exchange. In K.J. Gergen, M.S. Greenberg, and R.H. Willis (eds), *Social Exchange: Advances in Theory and Research,* (pp. 77-94). New York: Plenum Press.

Foot, P. (1969) *The Rise of Enoch Powell.* Harmondsworth: Penguin.

Forgas, J.P. (1991) *Emotion and Social Judgments.* Oxford: Pergamon Press.

Forgas, J.P. (1992) Affect in social judgments and decisions: A multi-process model. In M. Zanna (ed.), *Advances in Experimental Social Psychology,* (Vol. 24, pp. 134-167). New Jersey: Erlbaum.

Forgas, J.P. (1994) The role of emotion in social judgments: An introductory review and an affect infusion model (AIM). *European Journal of Social Psychology,* **24**, 1-24.

Forgas, J.P. (1995) Mood and judgment: The Affect Infusion Model (AIM). *Psychological Bulletin,* **116**, 39-66.

Forgas, J.P. and Bower, G.H. (1988) Affect in social judgments. *Australian Journal of Psychology,* **40**, 125-145.

Forgas, J.P. and Fiedler, K. (1996) Mood effects on intergroup discrimination: The role of affect in reward allocation decisions. *Journal of Personality and Social Psychology,* **70**, 28-40.

Foster-Carter, O. (1984) Racial bias in children's literature: A review of the research on Africa. *Sage Race Relations Abstracts,* **9**, 1-11.

Fowers, B. and Richardson, F. (1996) Why is multiculturalism good? *American Psychologist,* **51**, 609-621.

Fraser, C.O. and Islam, M.R. (1999) *Symbolic Racism in Australian Politics: Explaining the Rise of Pauline Hanson.* Unpublished manuscript. Monash University.

French, J.R.P., Jr. and Raven, B. (1960) The bases of social power. In D. Cartwright and A. Zander (eds), *Group Dynamics: Research and Theory,* 2nd edn, (pp. 607-623). New York: Harper and Row.

Frenkel-Brunswik, E. and Havel, J. (1953) Prejudice in the interviews of children: Attitudes toward minority groups. *Journal of Genetic Psychology,* **82**, 91-136.

Freud, S. (1901) *The Psychopathology of Everyday Life.* Hammondsworth: Penguin.

Frideres, J.S., Warner, L.G., and Albrecht, S.L. (1971) The impact of social constraints on the relationship between attitudes and behavior. *Social Forces,* **50**, 102-112.

Fryer, D. (1984) *Staying Power.* London: Pluto.

Gaertner, S.L. and Dovidio, J.F. (1977) The subtlety of white racism, arousal, and helping behavior. *Journal of Personality and Social Psychology,* **35**, 691-707.

Gaertner, S.L. and Dovidio, J.F. (1986) The aversive form of racism. In J.F. Dovidio and S.L. Gaertner (eds), *Prejudice, Discrimination, and Racism,* (pp. 61-90). Orlando, FL: Academic Press.

Gaertner, S.L. and Dovidio, J.F. (1986) Prejudice, discrimination, and racism: Problems, progress, and promise. In J.F. Dovidio and S.L. Gaertner (eds), *Prejudice, Discrimination, and Racism,* (pp. 315-332). Orlando, FL: Academic Press.

Gaertner, S.L., Dovidio, J.F., Anastasio, P.A., Bachman, B.A., and Rust, M.C. (1993) The common ingroup identity model: Recategorization and the reduction of intergroup bias. In W. Stroebe and M. Hewstone (eds), *European Review of Social Psychology,* (Vol. 4, pp. 1-26). Chichester, U.K.: Wiley.

Gaertner, S.L., Mann, J., Murrell, A., and Dovidio, J.F. (1989) Reducing intergroup bias: The benefits of recategorization. *Journal of Personality and Social Psychology,* **57**, 239-249.

Gaertner, S.L. and McLaughlin, J. (1983) Racial stereotypes: Associations and ascriptions of positive and negative characteristics. *Social Psychology Quarterly,* **46**, 23-30.

Gallois, C., Callan, V.J., and Parslow, L.A. (1982) Evaluations of four ethnic groups: Level of ethnocentrism, favourability, and social distance. *Australian Journal of Psychology,* **34**, 369-374.

Gallup Poll (June 4, 1974) *Aborigines are Treated Unjustly.* Australian Public Opinion Polls (The Gallup Method). North Sydney: McNair Anderson.

Gallup Poll (May 4, 1976) *Not Enough Being Done for Aborigines.* Australian Public Opinion Polls (The Gallup Method). North Sydney: McNair Anderson.

Gallup Poll (May 2, 1978) *Do More for Aborigines, Says Gallup Poll.* Australian Public Opinion Polls (The Gallup Method). North Sydney: McNair Anderson.

Gallup Poll (April 3, 1981) *Aborigines Most Subject to Discrimination.* Australian Public Opinion Polls (The Gallup Method). North Sydney: McNair Anderson.

Gallup Poll (September 1, 1981) *Give Aboriginals Land Rights.* Australian Public Opinion Polls (The Gallup Method). North Sydney: McNair Anderson.

Garcia Coll, C., Lamberty, G., Jenkins, R., McAdoo, H.P. Crnic, K., Wasik, B.H., and Vasquez Garcia, H. (1996) An integrative model for the study of developmental competencies in minority children. *Child Development, 67,* 1891-1914.

Genesee, F., Tucker, G.R., and Lambert, W.E. (1978) The development of ethnic identity and ethnic role-taking skills in children from different school settings. *International Journal of Psychology, 13,* 39-57.

George, D.M. and Hoppe, R.A. (1979) Racial identification, preference, and self-concept. *Journal of Cross-Cultural Psychology, 10,* 85-100.

Gerard, H.B. and Hoyt, M.F. (1974) Distinctiveness of social categorization and attitudes towards ingroup members. *Journal of Personality and Social Psychology,* **29,** 836-42.

Geras, N. (1996) *Solidarity in the Conversation of Humankind.* London: Verso.

Gergen, K.J. (1985) The social constructionist movement in modern psychology. *American Psychologist,* **40,** 266-75.

Gilbert, D.T. and Hixon, J.G. (1991) The trouble of thinking: Activation and application of stereotypic beliefs. *Journal of Personality and Social Psychology,* **60,** 509-517.

Gilroy, P. (1987) *There Ain't No Black in the Union Jack.* London: Hutchinson.

Gleeson, K. (1998) *The Effect of Three Physical Characteristics on Children's Preferences for Unknown Peers.* Unpublished Honours thesis, Flinders University of South Australia.

Glock, C., Wuthnow, R., Piliavin, J., and Spencer, M. (1975) *Adolescent Prejudice.* New York: Harper and Row.

Godin, G. (1993) The theories of reasoned action and planned behavior: Overview of findings, emerging research problems and usefulness for exercise promotion. *Journal of Applied Sport Psychology, 5,* 141-157.

Goertzel, T. (1987) Authoritarianism of personality and political attitudes. *Journal of Social Psychology,* **127,** 7-18.

Goldhagen, D.J. (1996) *Hitler's Willing Executioners: Ordinary Germans and the Holocaust.* London: Abacus/Little Brown and Co.

Goldstein, C.G., Koopman, E.J., and Goldstein, H.H. (1979) Racial attitudes in young children as a function of interracial contact in the public schools. *American Journal of Orthopsychiatry,* **49,** 89-99.

Goodman, M. (1946) Evidence concerning the genesis of interracial attitudes. *American Anthropologist,* **48,** 624-630.

Goodman, M. (1952) *Race Awareness in Young Children.* Cambridge, Mass.: Addison-Wesley.

Gopaul-McNicol, S. (1995) A cross-cultural examination of racial identity and racial preference of preschool children in the West Indies. *Journal of Cross-Cultural Psychology,* **26,** 141-152.

Grant, B. (1997) Introduction. In B. Grant (ed.), *Pauline Hanson: One Nation and Australian politics,* (pp.7-17). Armidale: University of New England Press.

Grant, P.R. and Brown, R.J. (1995) From ethnocentrism to collective protest: Responses to relative deprivation and threats to social identity. *Social Psychology Quarterly,* **58,** 195-211.

Graves, S.B. (1996) Diversity on television. In T.M. MacBeth (ed.), *Tuning in to Young Viewers,* (pp.61-86). Thousand Oaks, CA: Sage.

Greenberg, B.S. (1986) Minorities and the mass media. In J. Bryant and D. Zillmann (eds), *Perspectives on Media Effects,* (pp.165-188). Hillsdale, NJ: Lawrence Erlbaum

Greenwald, A.G. and Banaji, M.R. (1995) Implicit social cognition: Attitudes, self-esteem, and stereotypes. *Psychological Review,* **102**, 4-27.

Gregor, A.J. and McPherson, D.A. (1966) Racial attitudes among White and Negro children in a deep-south standard metropolitan area. *Journal of Social Psychology,* **68**, 95-106.

Grover, S.L. (1991) Predicting the perceived fairness of parental leave policies. *Journal of Applied Psychology,* **76**, 247-255.

Grube, J.W. and Morgan, M. (1990) Attitude-social support interactions: Contingent consistency effects in the prediction of adolescent smoking, drinking, and drug use. *Social Psychology Quarterly,* **53**, 329-339.

Haddock, G., Zanna, M.P., and Esses, V.M. (1993) Assessing the structure of prejudicial attitudes: The case of attitudes toward homosexuals. *Journal of Personality and Social Psychology,* **65**, 1105-1118.

Hage, G. (1998) White Nation: Fantasies of White Supremacy in Multicultural Australia. Pluto Press: Annandale, NSW.

Hall, R. (1998) *Black Armband Days: Truth from the Dark Side of Australia's Past.* Milsons Point, NSW: Random House.

Hamilton, D.L. (ed.) (1981) *Cognitive Processes in Stereotyping and Intergroup Behaviour.* Hillsdale, NJ: Erlbaum.

Hamilton, D.L. and Sherman, J.W. (1994) Stereotypes. In R.S. Wyer and T.K. Srull (eds), *Handbook of Social Cognition,* 2nd edn, pp. 1-68). Hillsdale, NJ: Erlbaum.

Hamilton, D.L. and Trolier, T.K. (1986) Stereotypes and stereotyping: An overview of the cognitive approach. In J.F. Dovidio and S.L. Gaertner (eds), *Prejudice, Discrimination, and Racism,* (pp. 127-163). NY: Academic Press.

Haralambos, M. (1980) *Sociology: Themes and Perspectives.* Slough: University Tutorial Press.

Harding, J., Proshansky, H.M., Kutner, B., and Chein, I. (1969) Prejudice and ethnic relations. In G. Lindzey and E. Aronson (eds), *The Handbook of Social Psychology,* (Vol. 5, pp. 1-76). Reading, MA: Addison-Wesley.

Harris, D.B., Gough, H.G., and Martin, W.E. (1950) Children's ethnic attitudes: 2. Relationship to parental belief concerning child training. *Child Development,* **21**, 169-181.

Harris, J.R. (1998) *The Nurture Assumption: Why Children Turn Out the Way They Do.* New York: Free Press.

Hart, I. (1957) Maternal child-rearing practices and authoritarian ideology. *Journal of Abnormal and Social Psychology,* **55**, 232-237.

Hartley, E.L., Rosenbaum, M., and Schwartz, S. (1948a) Children's perceptions of ethnic group membership. *Journal of Psychology,* **26**, 387-398.

Hartley, E.L., Rosenbaum, M., and Schwartz, S. (1948b) Children's use of ethnic frames of reference: An exploratory study of children's conceptualisations of multiple ethnic group membership. *Journal of Psychology,* **26**, 367-386.

Hartstone, M. and Augoustinos, M. (1995) The minimal group paradigm: Categorization into two versus three groups. *European Journal of Social Psychology,* **25**, 179-193.

Harding, J., Proshansky, H.M., Kuter, B., and Chein, I (1969) Prejudice and ethnic relations. In G. Lindzey and E Aronson (eds), *The Handbook of Social Psychology,* (Vol. 5, pp. 1-76). Reading MA: Addison-Wesley.

Hasher, L. and Zacks, R.T. (1979) Automatic and effortfull processes in memory. *Journal of Experimental Psychology: General,* **108**, 356-388.

Haslam, S.A. (2001) *Psychology in Organisations: The Social Identity Approach.* London: Sage.

Haslam, S.A. and McGarty, C. (2001) A hundred years of certitude? Social psychology, the experimental method, and the management of scientific uncertainty. *British Journal of Social Psychology*, **40**, 1-21.

Haslam, S.A. and Oakes, P.J. (1995) How context-independent is the outgroup homogeneity effect? A response to Bartsch and Judd. *European Journal of Social Psychology* **12**, 469-475.

Haslam, S.A., Oakes, P.J., Reynolds, K.J., and Mein, J. (1999) Rhetorical unity and social division: A longitudinal study of change in Australian self-stereotypes. *Asian Journal of Social Psychology*, **2**, 265-280.

Haslam, S.A., Oakes, P.J., Turner, J.C., and McGarty, C. (1995) Social categorization and group homogeneity: Changes in the perceived applicability of stereotype content as a function of comparative context and trait favourableness. *British Journal of Social Psychology*, **34**, 139-160.

Haslam, S.A., Oakes, P.J., Turner, J.C., and McGarty, C. (1996) Social identity, self-categorization and the perceived homogeneity of ingroups and outgroups: The interaction between social motivation and cognition. In: R.M. Sorrentino and E.T. Higgins (eds), *Handbook of Motivation and Cognition,* (Vol. 3, pp. 182-222) Guilford: New York.

Haslam, S.A. and Turner, J.C. (1992) Context-dependent variation in social stereotyping 2: The relationship between frame of reference, self-categorization and accentuation. *European Journal of Social Psychology*, **22**, 251-278.

Haslam, S.A. and Turner, J.C. (1995) Context-dependent variation in social stereotyping 3: Extremism as a self-categorical basis for polarized judgement. *European Journal of Social Psychology*, **25**, 341-371.

Haslam, S.A., Turner, J.C., Oakes, P.J., McGarty, C., and Hayes, B.K. (1992) Context-dependent variation in social stereotyping 1: The effects of intergroup relations as mediated by social change and frame of reference. *European Journal of Social Psychology*, **22**, 3-20.

Haslam, S.A., Turner, J.C., Oakes, P.J., McGarty, C., and Reynolds, K.J. (1998) The group as a basis for emergent stereotype consensus. In W. Stroebe and M. Hewstone (eds), *European Review of Social Psychology,* (Vol. 8, pp. 203-239). Chichester: Wiley.

Haslam, S.A. and Wilson, A. (2000) In what sense are prejudiced beliefs personal? The importance of ingroup shared stereotypes. *British Journal of Social Psychology*, **39**, 45-63.

Hastie, R. (1984) Causes and effects of causal attribution. *Journal of Personality and Social Psychology,* **46**, 44-56.

Hausenblaus, H.A., Carron, A.V., and Mack, D.E. (1997) Application of the theories of reasoned action and planned behavior to exercise behavior: A meta-analysis. *Journal of Sport and Exercise Psychology*, **19**, 36-51.

Hawley, W. (1995) Introduction: Our unfinished task. In W. Hawley and A. Jackson (eds), *Towards a Common Destiny: Improving Race and Ethnic Relations in America,* (pp. xi-xvii). San Francisco: Jossey-Bass.

Hawley, W.D. and Jackson, A.W. (eds) (1995) *Towards a Common Destiny: Improving Race and Ethnic Relations in America.* San Francisco: Jossey-Bass.

Heath, S. (1995) Race, ethnicity, and the defiance of categories. In W. Hawley and A. Jackson (eds), *Towards a Common Destiny: Improving Race and Ethnic Relations in America,* (pp. 39-70). San Francisco: Jossey-Bass.

Heaven, P.C.L (1983) Intraindividual versus intergroup explanations of prejudice among Afrikaners. *Journal of Social Psychology*, **121**, 201-210.

Heaven, P.C.L. (1984) Predicting authoritarian behaviour: Analysis of three measures. *Personality and Individual Differences*, **5**, 251-253.

Heaven, P.C.L., Greene, R.L., Stones, C.R., and Caputi, P. (in press) Levels of social dominance in three cultures. *Journal of Social Psychology*.

Herrnstein, R.J. and Murray, C. (1994) *The Bell Curve: Intelligence and Class Structure in American Life*. NY: Free Press.

Hester, S. and Eglin, P. (1997) *Culture in Action: Studies in Membership Categorisation Analysis*. Washington, DC: International Institute of Ethnomethodology and Conversation Analysis: University Press of America.

Hewstone, M. and Brown, R.J. (1986) Contact is not enough: An intergroup perspective on the 'Contact Hypothesis'. In M. Hewstone and R.J. Brown (eds), *Contact and Conflict in Intergroup Encounters,* (pp. 1-44). Oxford: Blackwell.

Hewstone, M., Hopkins, N., and Routh, D.A. (1992) Cognitive models of stereotype change: I. Generalization and subtyping in young people's views of the police. *European Journal of Social Psychology,* **22**, 219-234.

Hewstone, M., Johnston, L., and Aird, P. (1992) Cognitive models of stereotype change: II. Perceptions of homogeneous and heterogeneous groups. *European Journal of Social Psychology,* **22**, 235-249.

Hewstone, M., Macrae, C.N., Griffiths, R., Milne, A.B., and Brown, R.J. (1994) Cognitive models of stereotype change 5: Measurement, development, and consequences of subtyping. *Journal of Experimental Social Psychology,* **30**, 505-526.

Hites, R.W. and Kellogg, E.P. (1964) The F and social maturity scales in relation to racial attitudes in a deep south sample. *Journal of Social Psychology*, **62**, 189-195.

Hitler, A. (1969) *Mein Kampf*. London: Hutchinson.

Hitt, M. and Keats, B. (1984) Empirical identification of the criteria for effective affirmative action programs. *Journal of Applied Behavioral Science*, **20**, 203-222.

Hoess, R. (2000) *Commandant of Auschwitz*. London: Phoenix.

Hogg, M.A. and Abrams, D. (1988) *Social Identifications: A Social Psychology of Intergroup Relations and Group Processes*. London: Routledge.

Hogg, M.A. and Abrams, D. (1990) Social motivation, self-esteem and social identity. In D. Abrams and M.A. Hogg (eds), *Social Identity Theory: Constructive and Critical Advances,* (pp. 28-47). London: Harvester Wheatsheaf.

Hogg, M.A. and Abrams, D. (1993) Towards a single-process uncertainty-reduction model of social motivation in groups. In M.A. Hogg and D. Abrams (eds), *Group Motivation: Social Psychological Perspectives,* (pp. 173-190). London: Harvester Wheatsheaf.

Hogg, M.A. and Hornsey, M. (1998) *Pauline Hanson's One Nation: A Social Psychological Analysis*. Unpublished manuscript. The University of Queensland.

Hogg, M.A. and Mullin, B.A. (1999) Joining groups to reduce uncertainty: Subjective uncertainty reduction and group identification. In D. Abrams and M.A. Hogg (eds), *Social Identity and Social Cognition,* (pp. 249-279). Malden, MA, USA: Blackwell

Hogg, M.A. and Sunderland, J. (1991) Self-esteem and intergroup discrimination in the minimal group paradigm. *British Journal of Social Psychology*, **30**, 51-62.

Hogg, M.A. and Turner, J.C. (1985a) Interpersonal attraction, social identification and psychological group formation. *European Journal of Social Psychology,* **15**, 51-66.

Hogg, M.A. and Turner, J.C. (1985b) When liking begets solidarity: An experiment on the role of interpersonal attraction on psychological group formation. *British Journal of Social Psychology,* **24**, 267-281.

Hogg, M.A. and Turner, J.C. (1987) Intergroup behaviour, self-stereotyping and the salience of social categories. *British Journal of Social Psychology*, **26**, 325-340.

Hogg, M.A., Turner, J.C., Nascimento-Schulze, C., and Spriggs, D. (1986) Social categorization, intergroup behaviour and self-esteem: Two experiments. *Revista de Psicologia Social,* **1,** 23-37.

Holmes, R.M. (1996) *How Young Children Perceive Race.* Thousand Oaks, CA: Sage

Hopkins, N., Hewstone, M., and Hantzi, A. (1992) Police-schools liaison and young people's image of the police: An intervention evaluation. *British Journal of Psychology,* **83,** 203-220.

Hopkins, N. and Reicher, S. (1997) Constructing the nation and collective mobilisation: A case study of politicians' arguments about the meaning of Scottishness. In G. Barfoot (ed.), *Ethnic Stereotypes and National Purity,* (pp. 313-337). DQR Studies in Literature.

Hopkins, N., Reicher, S., and Levine, M. (1997) On the parallels between social cognition and the 'new racism'. *British Journal of Social Psychology,* **36,** 305-329.

Horowitz, D. (1985) *Ethnic Groups in Conflict.* Berkeley: University of California Press.

Horowitz, E.L. (1936) The development of attitude toward the Negro. *Archives of Psychology,* **194,** New York.

Horowitz, E.L. and Horowitz, R.E. (1938) Development of social attitudes in children. *Sociometry,* **1,** 301-338.

Houtkoop-Steenstra, H. (2000) *Interaction and the Standardized Survey Interview: The Living questionnaire.* Cambridge: Cambridge University Press.

Howard, J.W. and Rothbart, M. (1980) Social categorization and memory for in-group and out-group behaviour. *Journal of Personality and Social Psychology,* **38,** 301-310.

Howitt, D. and Owusu-Bempah, J. (1994) *The Racism of Psychology: Time for a Change.* Hemel Hempstead: Harvester Wheatsheaf.

Hraba, J. (1972) The doll technique: A measure of racial ethnocentrism? *Social Forces,* **50,** 522-527.

Hraba, J. and Grant, G. (1970) Black is beautiful: A reexamination of racial preference and identification. *Journal of Personality and Social Psychology,* **16,** 398-402.

Hughes, M. (1997) Symbolic racism, old-fashioned racism, and Whites' opposition to affirmative action. In S.A. Tuch and J.K. Martin (eds), *Racial Attitudes in the 1990s: Continuity and Change,* (pp. 45-75). Westport, CT: Praeger.

Human Rights and Equal Opportunity Commission (HREOC) (1997) *Bringing them home: Report of the National Inquiry into the Separation of Aboriginal and Torres Strait Islander Children from Their Families.* (Chair: Sir Ronald Wilson). Canberra: Australian Government Printing Service.

Hunsberger, B. (1978) Racial awareness and preference of white and Indian Canadian children. *Canadian Journal of Behavioural Science,* **10,** 176-179.

Hunter, J.A., Platow, M.J., Bell, L.M., Kypri, K., and Lewis, C.A. (1997) Intergroup bias and self-evaluation: Domain specific self-esteem, threats to identity and dimensional importance. *British Journal of Social Psychology,* **36,** 405-426.

Hunter, J.A., Platow, M.J., Howard, M.L., and Stringer, M. (1996) Social identity and intergroup evaluative bias: Realistic categories and domain specific self-esteem in a conflict setting. *European Journal of Social Psychology,* **26,** 631-647.

Hunter, J.A., Stringer, M., and Watson, R.P. (1991) Intergroup violence and intergroup attributions. *British Journal of Social Psychology,* **30,** 261-266.

Huo, Y.J., Smith, H.J., Tyler, T.R., and Lind, E.A. (1996) Superordinate identification, subgroup identification, and justice concerns: Is separatism the problem; is assimilation the answer? *Psychological Science,* **7,** 40-45.

Hyman, H.H. and Sheatsley, P.B. (1954) 'The authoritarian personality': A methodological critique. In R. Christie and M. Jahoda (eds), *Studies in the Scope and Method of 'The Authoritarian Personality',* (pp. 50-122). Glencoe, Illinois: The Free Press.

Ignatieff, M. (1995) *Blood and Belonging: Journeys into the New Nationalism.* London: Vintage.

Ignatieff, M. (1997) *The Warrior's Honour: Ethnic War and The Modern Conscience.* New York: Henry Holt and Co.

Inbar, D., Resh, N., and Adler, C. (1984) Integration and school variables. In Y. Amir, S. Sharan, and R. Ben-Arie (eds), *School Desegregation: Cross-Cultural Perspectives,* (pp. 119-132). Hillsdale, New Jersey: Erlbaum.

Insko, C.A., Schopler, J., Kennedy, J.F., Dahl, K.R., Graetz, K.A., and Drigotas, S.M. (1992) Individual-group discontinuity from the differing perspectives of Campbell's realistic group conflict theory and Tajfel and Turner's social identity theory. *Social Psychology Quarterly,* **55,** 272-291.

Institute of History, Prishtina (1997) Expulsions of Albanians and Colonisation of Kosovo. Available at http://www.kosova.com/expuls/contentx.htm.

Institute of Race Relations (1987) *Police Against Black People.* London: Institute of Race Relations.

Isen, A.M. (1984) Towards understanding the role of affect in cognition. In R.S. Wyer and T.K. Srull (eds), *Handbook of Social Cognition,* (Vol. 3, pp. 179-236). Hillsdale, NJ: Erlbaum.

Isen, A.M. (1987) Positive affect, cognitive processes, and social behavior. In L. Berkowitz (ed.), *Advances in Experimental Social Psychology,* (Vol. 20, pp. 203-253). San Diego, CA: Academic Press.

Jaccard, J., King, G.W., and Pomazel, R. (1977) Attitudes and behaviour: An analysis of specificity of attitudinal predictors. *Human Relations,* **30,** 817-824.

Jackson, J.W. (1993) Realistic group conflict theory: A review and evaluation of the theoretical and empirical literature. *The Psychological Record,* **43,** 395-414.

Jackson, S. and Ruderman, M. (eds) (1996) *Diversity in Work Teams.* Washington, DC: APA.

Jahoda, M. (1954) Introduction. In R. Christie and M. Jahoda (eds), *Studies in the Scope and Method of 'The Authoritarian Personality',* (pp. 11-23). Glencoe, Illinois: The Free Press.

James, C.L.R. (1989) *The Black Jacobins.* London: Alison and Busby.

Jayyusi, L. (1984) *Categorisation and Moral Order.* London: Routledge.

Jetten, J., Spears, R., and Manstead, A.S.R. (1996) Intergroup norms and intergroup discrimination: Distinctive self-categorization and social identity effects. *Journal of Personality and Social Psychology,* **71,** 1222-1233.

Johnson, C. (2000) *Governing Change: From Keating to Howard.* St. Lucia: University of Queensland Press.

Johnson, D.W. and Johnson, R.T. (1984) The effects of intergroup cooperation and intergroup competition on ingroup and outgroup cross-handicap relations. *Journal of Social Psychology,* **124,** 85-94.

Johnson, D.W., Johnson, R.T., Tiffany, M., and Zaidman, B. (1984) Cross-ethnic relationships: The impact of intergroup cooperation and competition. *Journal of Educational Research,* **78,** 75-79.

Johnston, L. (1996) Resisting change: Information-seeking and stereotype change. *European Journal of Social Psychology,* **26,** 799-825.

Johnston, L. (1998) *Moderation of stereotype-based judgments as a function of stereotype endorsement.* Manuscript under review.

Johnston, L. and Hewstone, M. (1992) Cognitive models of stereotype change: III. Subtyping and the perceived typicality of disconfirming group members. *Journal of Experimental Social Psychology,* **28**, 360-386.

Johnston, L., Hewstone, M., Pendry, L., and Frankish, C. (1994) Cognitive models of stereotype change 4. Motivational and cognitive influences. *European Journal of Social Psychology,* **24**, 237-265.

Johnston, L.C. and Macrae, C.N. (1994) Changing social stereotypes: The case of the information seeker. *European Journal of Social Psychology,* **24**, 581-592.

Jones, J.M. (1972) *Prejudice and Racism.* Reading, MA: Addison-Wesley.

Jones, J.M. (1997) *Prejudice and Racism* (2nd edn). New York: McGraw-Hill.

Jones, J.M. (1998) The essential power of racism: Commentary and conclusion. In J.L. Eberhardt and S.T. Fiske (eds), *Confronting Racism: The Problem and the Response,* (pp. 280 - 318). Thousand Oaks, CA: Sage.

Judd, C.M. and Park, B. (1988) Outgroup homogeneity: Judgements of variability at the individual and group level. *Journal of Personality and Social Psychology,* **54**, 778-788.

Judd, C.M. and Park, B. (1993) Definition and assessment of accuracy in social stereotypes. *Psychological Review,* **100**, 109-128.

Kahn, A. and Ryen, A.H. (1972) Factors influencing the bias towards one's own group. *International Journal of Group Tensions,* **2**, 33-50.

Kamin, L. (1977) *The Science and Politics of IQ.* Harmondsworth: Penguin.

Kamin, L. (1992) On the length of black penises and the depth of white racism. In L. Nicholas (ed.), *Psychology and Oppression* (pp. 35-54). Johannesburg: Skotaville.

Katz, I. (1978) *White Awareness: A Handbook for Anti-Racism Training.* Norman, Oklahoma: University of Oklahoma Press.

Katz, I. and Glass, D.C. (1979) An ambivalence-amplification theory of behavior toward the stigatized. In W.G. Austin and S. Worchel (eds), *The Social Psychology of Intergroup Relations,* (pp. 55-70). Monterey, CA: Brooks/Cole.

Katz, I. and Hass, R.G. (1988) Racial ambivalence and American value conflict: Correlational and priming studies of dual cognitive structures. *Journal of Personality and Social Psychology,* **55**, 893-905.

Katz, I., Wackenhut, J., and Hass, R.G. (1986) Racial ambivalence, value duality, and behavior. In J.F. Dovidio and S.L. Gaertner (eds), *Prejudice, Discrimination, and Racism* (pp. 35-59). Orlando, FL: Academic Press.

Katz, P.A. (1973) Stimulus Predifferentiation and Modification of Children's Racial Atittudes. *Child Developmental,* **44**, 232-237.

Katz, P.A. (1976) The acquisition of racial attitudes in children. In P.A. Katz (ed.), *Towards the Elimination of Prejudice,* (pp. 125-154). New York: Pergamon Press.

Katz, P.A. and Kofkin, J.A. (1997) Race, gender, and young children. In S.S. Luthar, J.A. Burack, D. Cicchetti, and J.R. Weisz (eds), *Developmental Psychopathology: Perspectives on Adjustment, Risk, and Disorder,* (pp. 51-74). New York: Cambridge University Press.

Katz, P.A., Sohn, M., and Zalk, S.R. (1975) Perceptual concomitants of racial attitudes in urban grade-school children. *Developmental Psychology,* **11**, 135-144.

Kawakami, K., Dion, K.L., and Dovidio, J.F. (1998) Racial prejudice and stereotype activation. *Personality and Social Psychology Bulletin,* **24**, 407-416.

Kawwa, T. (1968) Three sociometric studies of ethnic relations in London schools. *Race,* **10**, 173-180.

Kelley, H.H. and Thibaut, J.W. (1978) *Interpersonal Relations: A Theory of Interdependence.* New York: Wiley.

Kelly, C. (1988) Intergroup differentiation in a political context. *British Journal of Social Psychology*, **27**, 319-332.

Kelly, C. (1993) Group identification, intergroup perceptions and collective action. In W. Stroebe and M. Hewstone (eds), *European Review of Social Psychology,* (Vol. 4, pp. 59-83). Chichester, U.K.: Wiley.

Kelly, C. and Breinlinger, S. (1995) Identity and justice: Exploring women's participation in collective action. *Journal of Community and Applied Psychology*, **5**, 41-57.

Kerlinger, F. and Rokeach, M. (1966) The factorial nature of the F and D scales. *Journal of Personality and Social Psychology*, **4**, 391-399.

Kershaw, I. (1984) *Popular Opinion and Political Dissent in the Third Reich*. Oxford: Oxford University Press.

Kinder, D.R. and Sears, D.O. (1981) Prejudice and politics: Symbolic racism versus racial threats to the good life. *Journal of Personality and Social Psychology*, **40**, 414-431.

Kinder, D.R. and Sears, D.O. (1985) Public opinion and political action. In G. Lindzey and E. Aronson (eds), *Handbook of Social Psychology,* 3rd edn, (Vol. 2, pp. 659-741.). New York: Random House.

King, M.J., Jr. (1963) *Why We Can't Wait*. New York: Signet.

Klandermans, B. (1997) *The Social Psychology of Protest*. Cambridge: Blackwell.

Klein, J. (1996) Behavioral and personality correlates of cross-cultural sensitivity. *Psychology: A Journal of Human Behavior*, **33**, 52-55.

Kohlberg, L. (1976) Moral stages and moralisation: The cognitive-developmental approach. In T. Lickona (ed.), *Moral Development and Behaviou.r,* (pp. 31-53). New York: Holt, Rinehart and Winston.

Kohlberg, L. (1984) *The Philosophy of Moral Development:Essays on Moral Development* (Vol. 2). San Francisco: Harper and Row.

Konecni, V. J. (1979) The role of aversive events in the development of intergroup conflict. In W. G. Austin and S. Worchel (eds), *The Social Psychology of Intergroup Relations,* (pp. 85-102). Monterey: Brooks/Cole.

Kovel, J. (1970) *White Racism: A Psychohistory*. New York: Pantheon.

Krueger, J. and Rothbart, M (1990) Contrast and accentuation effects in category learning. *Journal of Personality and Social Psychology*, **59**, 651-663.

Krug, R.E. (1961) An analysis of the F scale. 1: Item factor analysis. *Journal of Social Psychology*, **53**, 285-291.

Kuhl, S. (1994) *The Nazi Connection*. New York: Oxford University Press.

Kunda, Z. and Oleson, K.C. (1995) Maintaining stereotypes in the face of disconfirmation: Constructing grounds for subtyping deviants. *Journal of Personality and Social Psychology,* **68**, 565-579.

Kunda, Z. and Oleson, K.C. (1997) When exceptions prove the rule: How extremity of deviance determines the impact of deviant examples on stereotypes. *Journal of Personality and Social Psychology,* **72**, 965-979.

Kunda, Z. and Sherman-Williams, B. (1993) Stereotypes and the construal of individuating information. *Personality and Social Psychology Bulletin*, **19**, 90-99.

Kunda, Z. and Thagard, P. (1996) Forming impressions from stereotypes, traits and behaviors: A parallel-constraint-satisfaction theory. *Psychological Review*, **103**, 284-308.

Kutner, B., Wilkins, C., and Yarrow, P.R. (1952) Verbal attitudes and overt behavior involving racial prejudice. *Journal of Abnormal and Social Psychology*, **47**, 649-652.

Lalonde, R.N. and Silverman, R.A. (1994) Behavioral preferences in response to social injustice: The effects of group permeability and social identity salience. *Journal of Personality and Social Psychology*, **66**, 78-85.

Lambert, W.E. and Taguchi, Y. (1956) Ethnic cleavage among young children. *Journal of Abnormal Psychology,* **53**, 380-382.

LaPiere, R.T. (1934) Attitudes vs actions. *Social Forces*, **13**, 230-237.

Larsen, K.S. (1978) White attitudes towards Aborigines: A working framework: *Australian Quarterly,* **50**, 94-113.

Larsen, K.S. (1981) White attitudes in Townsville: Authoritarianism, religiousity, and contact. *Australian Psychologist,* **16**, 111-122.

Lazarsfeld, P. and Stanton, F. (eds) (1949) *Communications Research, 1948-1949.* New York: Harper and Row.

LeCouteur, A., Rapley, M., and Augoustinos, M. (2001) 'This very difficult debate about Wik': Stake, voice and the management of category memberships in race politics. *British Journal of Social Psychology*, **40**, 35-57.

Lederer, G. (1993) Authoritarianism in German adolescents: Trends and cross-cultural comparisons. In W. Stone, G. Lederer, and R. Christie (eds), *Strength and Weakness: The Authoritarian Personality Today,* (pp. 182-198). New York: Springer-Verlag.

Leeson, P. and Heaven, P.C.L. (in press) Social attitudes and personality. *Australian Journal of Psychology*.

Leicester, M. (1989) *Multicultural Education: From Theory to Practice.* Windsor, England: NFER-Nelson.

Lemyre, L. and Smith, P.M. (1985) Intergroup discrimination and self-esteem in the minimal group paradigm. *Journal of Personality and Social Psychology,* **49**, 660-670.

Lepore, L. and Brown, R.J. (1997) Category and stereotype activation: Is prejudice inevitable? *Journal of Personality and Social Psychology,* **72**, 275-287.

Leudar, I. and Antaki, C. (1998) *Using Voices of Others in Parliamentary Argumentation.* Paper presented at the 6th International Pragmatics Association Conference, Reims, France, July.

Levine, R.A. and Campbell, D.T. (1972) *Ethnocentrism: Theories of Conflict, Ethnic Attitudes and Group Behaviour.* New York: Wiley.

Lewin, K. (1952) *Field Theory in Social Science.* New York: Harper and Row.

Lewis, V., Greive, N., Bell, R., and Bartlett, W. (in press) Measuring attitudes to women: Development of the Women in Society Questionnaire. *Australian Journal of Psychology.*

Leyens, J.-P., Yzerbyt, V., and Schadron, G. (1994) *Stereotypes and Social Cognition.* London: Sage.

Lindgren, H.C. and Harvey, J.H. (1981) *An Introduction to Social Psychology* (3rd edn). St Louis: The C.V. Cosby Company.

Linville, P.W. (1982) The complexity-extremity effect and age-based stereotyping. *Journal of Personality and Social Psychology*, **42**, 193-211.

Linville, P.W., Fischer, G.W., and Salovey, P. (1989) Perceived distributions of the characteristics of in-group and out-group members: Empirical evidence and a computer simulation. *Journal of Personality and Social Psychology*, **57**, 165-188.

Linville, P.W. and Jones, E.E. (1980) Polarized appraisals of outgroup members. *Journal of Personality and Social Psychology*, **38**, 689 - 703.

Lippmann, W. (1922) *Public Opinion.* New York: Harcourt Brace.

Liska, A. (1984) A critical examination of the causal structure of the Fishbein and Ajzen attitude-behavior model. *Social Psychology Quarterly*, **47**, 61-74.

Lo Coco, A., Pace, U., and Zappulla, C. (1998) *Ethnic Identification, Preferences, and Perceptions Among School Children: A Multiethnic Research.* Poster presented at the XVth Biennial ISSBD Meeting, Berne, Switzerland, July 1-4.

Locke, V., Macleod, C., and Walker, I. (1994) Automatic and controlled activation of stereotypes: Individual   differences associated with prejudice. *British Journal of Social Psychology,* **33**, 29-46.

Locke, V. and Walker, I. (1999) Stereotyping, processing goals, and social identity: Inveterate and fugacious characteristics of stereotypes. In D. Abrams and M.A. Hogg (eds), *Social Identity and Social Cognition,* (pp. 164-182). Oxford: Blackwells.

Long, K.M., Spears, R., and Manstead, A.S.R. (1994) The influence of personal and collective self-esteem on strategies of social differentiation. *British Journal of Social Psychology,* **33**, 313-319.

Longshore, D. and Prager, J. (1985) The impact of school desegregation: A situational analysis. *Annual Review of Sociology,* **11**, 75-91.

Loomis, C.P. (1943) Ethnic cleavages in the Southwest as reflected in two high schools. *Sociometry,* **6**, 7-26.

Louw-Potgieter, J., Kamfer, L., and Boy, R. (1991) Stereotype reduction workshop. *South African Journal of Psychology,* **21**, 219-224.

Lynch, T. and Reavell, R. (1997) Through the looking glass: Hanson, Howard and the politics of 'political correctness'. In B. Grant (ed.), *Pauline Hanson: One Nation and Australian Politics,* (pp. 29-49). Armidale: University of New England Press.

Maass, A. and Arcuri, L. (1996) Language and stereotyping. In N. Macrae, M. Hewstone, and C. Stangor (eds), *The Foundations of Stereotypes and Stereotyping,* (pp.193-226). New York: Guildford.

Mackie, D.M. and Hamilton, D.L. (1993) *Affect, Cognition, and Stereotyping.* San Diego: Academic Press.

Mackie, D.M. and Worth, L. (1991) Feeling good, but not thinking straight: The impact of positive mood on persuasion. In J.P. Forgas (ed.), *Emotion and Social Judgments,* (pp. 201-220). Oxford: Pergamon Press.

Mackie, M. (1973) Arriving at 'truth' by definition: The case of stereotype inaccuracy. *Social Problems,* **20**, 431-447.

MacLeod, C. and Rutherford, E.M. (1992) Anxiety and the selective processing of emotional information: Mediating roles of awareness, trait and state variables, and personal relevance of stimulus materials. *Behaviour Research and Therapy,* **30**, 479-491.

Macquarie Dictionary (1997) NSW, Australia: Macquarie Library.

Macrae, C.N., Bodenhausen, G.V., and Milne, A.B. (1998) Saying no to unwanted thoughts: Self-focus and the regulation of mental life. *Journal of Personality and Social Psychology,* **74**, 578-589.

Macrae, C.N. and Johnston, L. (1998) Help, I need somebody: Automatic action and inaction. *Social Cognition,* **16**, 400-417.

Macrae, C.N., Milne, A.B., and Bodenhausen, G.V. (1994) Stereotypes as energy saving devices: A peek inside the cognitive toolbox. *Journal of Personality and Social Psychology,* **66**, 37-47.

Madge, N.J.H. (1976) Context and the expressed ethnic preferences of infant school children. *Journal of Child Psychology and Psychiatry,* **17**, 337-344.

Maio, G. and Esses, V. (1998) The social consequences of affirmative action: Deleterious effects on the perception of groups. *Personality and Social Psychology Bulletin,* **24**, 65-74

Mama, A. (1995) *Beyond the Masks: Race, Gender, and Subjectivity.* London: Routledge.

Manne, R. (1998) Foreword. In N. Davidoff (ed.) *Two Nations: The Causes and Effects of the Rise of the One Nation Party in Australia,* (pp. 3-9). Melbourne: Bookman Press.

Manucia, G.K., Baumann, D.J., and Cialdini, R.B. (1984) Mood influences on helping: Direct effects of side effects? *Journal of Personality and Social Psychology,* **46**, 357-364.

Marjoribanks, K. and Jordan, D.F. (1986) Stereotyping among Aboriginal and Anglo-Australians: The uniformity, intensity, direction, and quality of auto- and heterostereotypes. *Journal of Cross-Cultural Psychology*, **17**, 17-28.

Marsh, A. (1970) Awareness of racial differences in West African and British children. *Race,* **11**, 289-302.

Martin, J. and Westie, F. (1959) The tolerant personality. *American Sociological Review*, **24**, 521-528.

McColsky, H. and Brill, A. (1983) *Dimensions of Tolerance: What Americans Believe About Civil Liberties.* New York: Russell Sage Foundation.

McConahay, J.B. (1982) Self-interest versus racial attitudes as correlates of anti-busing attitudes in Louisville: Is it the buses or the blacks? *Journal of Politics,* **44**, 692-720.

McConahay, J.B. (1986) Modern racism, ambivalence, and the modern racism scale. In J.F. Dovidio and S.L. Gaertner (eds), *Prejudice, Discrimination, and Racism,* (pp. 91-125). Orlando, FL: Academic Press.

McConahay, J.B., Hardee, B.B., and Batts, V. (1981) Has Racism declined in America? It depends on who is asking and what is asked. *Journal of Conflict Resolution*, **24**, 563-579.

McConahay, J.B. and Hough, J.C. (1976) Symbolic racism. *Journal of Social Issues,* **32**, 23-45.

McCreanor, T. (1993a) Mimiwhangata: Media reliance on Pakeha commonsense in interpretations of Maori actions. *Sites*, **26**, 79-90.

McCreanor, T. (1993b) Pakeha ideology of Maori performance: A discourse analytic approach to the construction of educational failure in Aoteoroa/New Zealand. *Folia Linguistica*, **27**, 293-314.

McCreanor, T. (1993c) Settling grievances to deny sovereignty: Trade goods for the year 2000. *Sites*, **27**, 45-73.

McFarland, S.G., Ageyev, V.S., and Abalakina-Paap, M.A. (1992) Authoritarianism in the former Soviet Union. *Journal of Personality and Social Psychology*, **63**, 1004-1010.

McGarry, J. and O'Leary, B. (1995) *Explaining Northern Ireland.* Oxford: Blackwell.

McGarty, C. (in press) *Categorization in Social Psychology.* London: Sage.

McGarty, C., Haslam, S.A., Hutchinson, K.J., and Turner, J.C. (1994) The effects of salient group membership on persuasion. *Small Group Research*, **25**, 267-293.

McGarty, C. and Penny, R.E.C. (1988) Categorization, accentuation and social judgement. *British Journal of Social Psychology*, **22**, 147-157.

McGarty, C. and Turner, J.C. (1992) The effects of categorization on social judgement. *British Journal of Social Psychology*, **31**, 253-268.

McGregor, J. (1993) Effectiveness of role playing and antiracist teaching in reducing student prejudice. *Journal of Educational Research,* **86**, 215-226.

Mead, G.H. (1934) *On Social Psychology.* Chicago: University of Chicago Press.

Medin, D.L. (1989) Concepts and conceptual structure. *American Psychologist,* **44**, 1469-1481.

Meertens, R.W. and Pettigrew, T.F. (1997) Is subtle prejudice really prejudice? *Public Opinion Quarterly,* **61**, 54-71.

Meloen, J. (1993) The F scale as a predictor of fascism: An overview of 40 years of authoritarianism research. In W. Stone, G. Lederer, and R. Christie (eds), *Strength and Weakness: The Authoritarian Personality Today,* (pp. 47-69). New York: Springer-Verlag.

Meloen, J. (in press) The political culture of state authoritarianism. In S. Renshon and J. Duckitt (eds), *Political Psychology: Cultural and Cross Cultural Foundations.* London: Macmillan.

Messick, D.M. and Mackie, D.M. (1989) Intergroup relations. *Annual Review of Psychology,* **40**, 45-81.

Messick, D.M. and Sentis, K.P. (1985) Estimating social and nonsocial utility functions from ordinal data. *European Journal of Social Psychology,* **15**, 389-399.

Middleton, R. (1960) Ethnic prejudice and susceptibility to persuasion. *American Sociological Review,* **25**, 679-686.

Migdal, M., Hewstone, M., and Mullen, B. (1998) The effects of crossed categorization on intergroup evaluations: A meta-analysis. *British Journal of Social Psychology,* **37**, 303-324.

Miles, R. (1989) *Racism.* London: Routledge.

Miles, R. and Phizacklea, A. (1987) *White Man's Country.* London: Pluto.

Milgram, S., Mann, L., and Harter, S. (1965) The lost-letter technique: A tool of social research. *Public Opinion Quarterly,* **29**, 437-438.

Miller, N. and Brewer, M.B. (1986) Social categorization theory and team learning procedures. In R.S. Feldman (ed.), *The Social Psychology of Education: Current Research and Theory,* (pp. 172-198). Cambridge: Cambridge University Press.

Miller, N., Brewer, M., and Edwards, K. (1985) Cooperative interaction in desegregated settings: A laboratory analogue. *Journal of Social Issues,* **41**, 63-79.

Miller, N.E. and Bugelski, R. (1948) Minor studies of aggression II: The influence of frustrations imposed by the in-group on attitudes expressed toward out-groups. *Journal of Psychology,* **25**, 437-442.

Milner, D. (1973) Racial identification and preference in 'black' British children. *European Journal of Social Psychology,* **3**, 281-295.

Milner, D. (1975) *Children and Race.* Harmondsworth, UK: Penguin.

Milner, D. (1983) *Children and Race: Ten Years On.* London: Ward Lock Educational.

Milner, D. (1996) Children and Racism: Beyond the value of the dolls. In W.P. Robinson, *Social Groups and Identities: Developing the Legacy of Henri Tajfel* (pp. 249-268). Butterworth Heinemann.

Minard, R.D. (1952) Race relations in the Pocahuntas coal field. *Journal of Social Issues,* **8**, 29-44.

Monteith, M.J. (1993) Self-regulation of prejudiced responses: Implications for progress in prejudice-reduction efforts. *Journal of Personality and Social Psychology,* **65**, 469-485.

Monteith, M.J., Sherman, J.W., and Devine, P.G. (1998) Suppression as a stereotype control strategy. *Personality and Social Psychology Review,* **2**, 63-82.

Moore, D.S. and McCabe, G.P. (1993) *Introduction to the Practice of Statistics* (2nd edn). New York: W.H. Freeman and Company.

Moore, J.W., Hauck, W.E., and Denne, T.C. (1984) Racial prejudice, interracial contact, and personality variables. *Journal of Experimental Education,* **52**, 168-173.

Moreland, R.L., Levine, J., and Cini, M. (1993) Group socialization: The role of commitment. In M.A. Hogg and D. Abrams (eds), *Group Motivation: Social Psychological Perspectives,* (pp. 104-129). Hemel Hempstead, UK: Harvester Wheatsheaf.

Morgan Poll (June 7, 1993) *Finding No. 2425: Australians off the Mark on Aborigines.* Mebourne: Roy Morgan Research Centre.

Morland, J.K. and Hwang, C.-H. (1981) Racial/ethnic identity of preschool children. *Journal of Cross-Cultural Psychology,* **12**, 409-424.

Morrison, B.E. (1997) *Social Cooperation: Redefining the Self in Self-Interest.* Unpublished Ph.D. Thesis, The Australian National University.

Morrison, B.E. (1999) Interdependence, the group and social cooperation: A new look at an old problem. In M. Foddy, M. Smithson, S. Schneider, and M.A. Hogg (eds), *Resolving Social Dilemmas: Dynamic, Structural, and Intergroup Approaches,* (pp. 295-308). Philadelphia: Psychology Press.

Moy, J. and Ng, S.H. (1996) Expectation of outgroup behaviour: Can you trust the outgroup? *European Journal of Social Psychology,* **26**, 333-340.

Mullen, B., Brown, R., and Smith, C. (1991) Ingroup bias as a function of salience, relevance and status: An integration. *European Journal of Social Psychology,* **22**, 103-122.

Muller-Hill, B. (1988) *Murderous Science.* Oxford: Oxford University Press.

Mummendey, A. and Wenzel, M. (1999) Social discrimination and tolerance in intergroup relations: Reactions to intergroup difference. *Personality and Social Psychology Review,* **3**, 158-174.

Myrdal, G. (1944) *An American dilemma: The Negro problem and American democracy.* New York: Harper.

Nairn, R. and McCreanor, T. (1990) Sensitivity and insensitivity: An imbalance in Pakeha accounts of Maori/Pakeha relations. *Journal of Language and Social Psychology,* **9**, 293-308.

Nairn, R. and McCreanor, T. (1991) Race talk and commonsense: Ideological patterns in Pakeha talk about Maori/Pakeha relations, *Journal of Language and Social Psychology,* **10**, 245-262.

National Inquiry into Racist Violence in Australia (1991) *Racist Violence: Report of the National Inquiry into Racist Violence in Australia.* Canberra: Australian Government Publishing Service.

National Inquiry into the Separation of Aboriginal and Torres Strait Islander Children from their Families (Australia) (1997) *Bringing Them Home: Report of the National Inquiry into the Separation of Aboriginal and Torres Strait Islander Children from their Families (Australia).* Sydney: Human Rights and Equal Opportunity Commission. Available at: http://www.austlii.edu.au/au/special/rsjproject/rsjlibrary/hreoc/stolen/

Neely, J.H. (1977) Semantic priming and retrieval from lexical memory: Roles of inhibitionless spreading activation and limited capacity attention. *Journal of Experimental Psychology,* **106**, 226-254 .

Neely, J.H. (1991) Semantic priming effects in visual word recognition: A selective review of current findings and theories. In D. Besner and G.W. Humphries (eds), *Basic Processes in Reading: Visual Word Recognition,* (pp. 264-336). Hillsdale, NJ: Erlbaum.

Nesdale, A.R. (in press-a) Developmental changes in children's ethnic preferences and social cognitions. *Journal of Applied Developmental Psychology.*

Nesdale, A.R. (in press-b) Social identity and ethnic prejudice in children. In P. Martin and W. Noble (eds), *Psychology and Society.* Australian Academic Press.

Nesdale, A.R. and Durkin, K. (1998) Stereotypes and attitudes: Implicit and explicit processes. In K. Kirsner, C. Speelman, M. Anderson, C. MacLeod, M. Maybery, and A. O'Brien-Malone (eds), *Implicit Processes in Psychological Science,* (pp. 219-232). Mahwah, NJ: Erlbaum.

Nesdale, A.R. and Flesser, D. (1999) *Social Identity and the Development of Children's Intergroup Attitudes*. Unpublished manuscript, Griffith University.

Nesdale, A.R. and McLaughlin, K. (1987) Effects of sex stereotypes on young children's memories, predictions and liking. *British Journal of Developmental Psychology,* **5**, 231-241.

Neuman, W.L. (1994) *Social Research Methods*. Boston: Allyn and Bacon.

Newman, M.A., Liss, M.B., and Sherman, F. (1983) Ethnic awareness in children: Not a unitary concept. *Journal of Genetic Psychology,* **143**, 103-112.

Ng, S.H. (1980) *The Social Psychology of Power*. London: Academic Press.

Ng, S.H. (1982) Power and intergroup discrimination. In H. Tajfel (ed.), *Social Identity and Intergroup Relations,* (pp. 179-206). Cambridge: Cambridge University Press.

Ng, S.H. (1985) Bias in reward allocation resulting from personal status, group status, and allocation procedure. *Australian Journal of Psychology,* **37**, 297-307.

Nielsen, H.D. (1977) *Tolerating Political Dissent: The Impact of High School Social Climates in the United States and West Germany*. Stockholm: Almqvist and Wiksell.

Nisbett, R.E. and Wilson, T.D. (1977) Telling more than we can know: Verbal reports on mental processes. *Psychological Review,* **84**, 231-259.

Novick, P. (2000) *The Holocaust and Collective Memory*. London: Bloomsbury.

Oakes, J. (1985) *Keeping Track: How Schools Structure Inequality*. New Haven, Conn., Yale University Press.

Oakes, P.J. (1987) The salience of social categories. In J.C. Turner, M.A. Hogg, P.J. Oakes, S.D. Reicher, and M.S. Wetherell (eds), *Rediscovering the Social Group,* (pp. 117-141). Oxford: Blackwell.

Oakes, P.J. (1996) The categorization process: Cognition and the group in the social psychology of stereotyping. In W.P. Robinson (ed.), *Social Groups and Identities: Developing the Legacy of Henri Tajfel,* (pp. 95-119). Oxford: Butterworth-Heinemann.

Oakes, P.J. (in press) The root of all evil in intergroup relations? Unearthing the categorization process. In R. Brown and S. Gaertner (eds), *Blackwell Handbook in Social Psychology Volume 4: Intergroup Processes*. Oxford: Blackwell.

Oakes, P.J., Haslam, S.A., Morrison, B.E., and Grace, D.M. (1995) Becoming an in-group: Reexamining the impact of familiarity on perceptions of group homogeneity. *Social Psychology Quarterly,* **58**, 52-60.

Oakes, P.J., Haslam, S.A., and Reynolds, K.J. (1999) Social categorization and social context: Is stereotype change a matter of information or meaning? In D. Abrams and M.A. Hogg (eds), *Social Identity and Social Cognition,* (pp. 55-79). Oxford: Blackwell.

Oakes, P.J., Haslam, S.A., and Turner, J.C. (1994) *Stereotyping and Social Reality*. Oxford: Blackwell.

Oakes, P.J. and Reynolds, K.J. (1997) Asking the accuracy question: Is measurement the answer? In R. Spears, P.J. Oakes, N. Ellemers, and S.A. Haslam (eds), *The Social Psychology of Stereotyping and Group Life,* (pp. 51-71). Oxford UK and Cambridge, MT: Blackwell.

Oakes, P.J., Reynolds, K.J., Haslam, S.A., and Turner, J.C. (1999) Part of life's rich tapestry: stereotyping and the politics of intergroup relations. In E.J. Lawler and S. Thye (eds), *Advances in Group Processes,* (Vol. 16, pp.125-160). JAI Press.

Oakes, P.J. and Turner, J.C. (1980) Social categorization and intergroup behaviour. Does minimal intergroup discrimination make social identity more positive? *European Journal of Social Psychology,* **10**, 295-301.

Oakes, P.J. and Turner, J.C. (1990) Is limited information processing capacity the cause of social stereotyping? In W. Stroebe and M. Hewstone (eds), *European Review of Social Psychology,* (Vol. 1, pp. 111-135). Chichester, UK: Wiley.

Oakes, P.J., Turner, J.C., and Halsam, S.A. (1991) Perceiving people as group members: The role of fit in the salience of social categorizations. *British Journal of Social Psychology* **30**, 125-144.

Obeng, S.G. (1997) Language and Politics: Indirectness in political discourse. *Discourse and Society,* **8**, 49-83.

Oeser, O.A. and Emery, F.E. (1954) *Social Structure and Personality in a Rural Community.* London: Routledge and Kegan Paul Ltd.

Oeser, O.A. and Hammond, S.B. (eds) (1954) *Social Structure and Personality in a City.* London: Routledge and Kegan Paul Ltd.

Ogunsakin, F. (1998) *Police and Black People.* Unpublished PhD thesis: University of Bristol.

Omi, M. and Winant, H. (1989) *Racial Formation in the United States.* New York: Routledge.

Operario, D. and Fiske, S.T. (1998) Racism equals power plus prejudice. In J.L. Eberhardt and S.T. Fiske (eds), *Confronting Racism: The Problem and the Response,* (pp. 33-53). Thousand Oaks, CA: Sage.

Opotow, S. (1990) Moral exclusion and injustice: An introduction. *Journal of Social Issues,* **46**, 1-20.

Orpen, C. (1970) Authoritarianism in an 'authoritarian' culture: The case of Afrikaans-speaking South Africa. *Journal of Social Psychology,* **81**, 119-120.

Orpen, C. (1971) Authoritarianism and racial attitudes among English-speaking South Africans. *Journal of Social Psychology,* **84**, 301-302.

Ostrom, T. (1994) Foreword to R.S. Wyer and T.K. Srull (eds), *Handbook of Social Cognition,* 2nd edn. Hillsdale, NJ: Lawrence Erlbaum.

Owen, D. and Dennis, J. (1987) Pre-adult development of political tolerance. *Political Psychology,* **8**, 547-561.

Park, B. and Rothbart, M. (1982) Perception of out-group homogeneity and levels of social categorization: Memory for the subordinate attributes of in-group and out-group members. *Journal of Personality and Social Psychology,* **42**, 1051-1068.

Patchen, M. (1982) *Black-White Contact in Schools: Its Social and Academic Effects.* West Lafayette, IN: Purdue University Press.

Pedersen, A. and Walker, I. (1997) Prejudice against Australian Aborigines: Old-fashioned and modern forms. *European Journal of Social Psychology,* **27**, 561-587.

Perdue, C.W., Dovidio, J.F., Gurtman, M.B., and Tyler, R.B. (1990) Us and them: Social categorization and the process of intergroup bias. *Journal of Personality and Social Psychology,* **59**, 475-486.

Perry, A. and Cunningham, W.H. (1975) A behavioral test of three F subscales. *Journal of Social Psychology,* **96**, 271-275.

Pescosolido, B.A., Grauerholz, E., and Milkie, M.A. (1997) Culture and conflict: The portrayal of Blacks in U.S. children's picture books through the mid- and late-twentieth century. *American Sociological Review,* **62**, 443-464.

Peterson, B.E., Doty, R.M., and Winter, D.G. (1993) Authoritarianism and attitudes toward contemporary social issues. *Personality and Social Psychology Bulletin,* **19**, 174-184.

Pettigrew, T.F. (1958) Personality and socio-cultural factors in intergroup attitudes: A cross-national comparison. *Journal of Conflict Resolution,* **2**, 29-42.

Pettigrew, T.F. (1998) Intergroup contact theory. *Annual Review of Psychology,* **49**, 65-85.

Pettigrew, T.F., Jackson, J.S., Ben Brika, J., Lemaine, G., Meertens, R., Wagner, U., and Zick, A. (1998) Outgroup prejudice in Western Europe. *European Review of Social Psychology,* **8**, 241-273.

Pettigrew, T.F. and Martin, J. (1989) Organizational inclusion of minority groups: A social psychological analysis. In J. van Oudenhoven and T. Willemsen (eds), *Ethnic Minorities: Social Psychological Perspectives,* (pp. 169-200). Amsterdam: Swets and Zeitlinger.

Pettigrew, T.F. and Meertens, R.W. (1995) Subtle and blatant prejudice in Western Europe. *European Journal of Social Psychology,* **25**, 57-75.

Phinney, J.S., Ferguson, D.L., and Tate, J.D. (1997) Intergroup attitudes among ethnic minority adolescents: A causal model. *Child Development,* **68**, 955-969

Platow, M.J., Harley, K., Hunter, J.A., Hanning, P., Shave, R., and O'Connell, A. (1997) Interpreting ingroup-favouring allocations in the minimal group paradigm. *British Journal of Social Psychology,* **36**, 107-118.

Platow, M.J., Hoar, S., Reid, S., Harley, K., and Morrison, D. (1997) Endorsement of distributively fair and unfair leaders in interpersonal and intergroup situations. *European Journal of Social Psychology,* **27**, 465-494.

Platow, M.J., McClintock, C.G., and Liebrand, W.B.G. (1990) Predicting intergroup fairness and ingroup bias in the Minimal Group Paradigm. *European Journal of Social Psychology,* **20**, 221-239.

Platow, M.J., O'Connell, A., Shave, R., and Hanning, P. (1995) Social evaluations of fair and unfair allocators in interpersonal and intergroup situations. *British Journal of Social Psychology,* **34**, 363-381.

Platow, M.J., Reid, S., and Andrew, S. (1998) Leadership endorsement: The role of distributive and procedural behaviour in interpersonal and intergroup contexts. *Group Processes and Intergroup Relations,* **1**, 35-47.

Porter, J.D.R. (1971) *Black Child, White Child: The Development of Racial Attitudes.* Cambridge, MS: Harvard University Press.

Posner, M.I. and Snyder, C.R.R. (1975) Facilitation and inhibition in the processing of signals. In P.M.A. Rabbit and S. Dornic (eds), *Attention and Performance,* (pp. 669-682). New York: Academic Press.

Potter, J. (1996) *Representing Reality: Discourse, Rhetoric and Social Construction.* London: Sage.

Potter, J. (1998) Cognition as context (whose cognition?) *Research on Language and Social Interaction,* **31**, 29-44.

Potter, J. and Wetherell, M. (1987) *Discourse and Social Psychology: Beyond Attitudes and Behaviour.* London: Sage.

Praat, A. (1998) *The Occupation of Moutoa Gardens-Pakaitore Marae: A Discourse Analysis.* Unpublished doctoral dissertation, Massey University.

Pratto, F., Sidanius, J., Stallworth, L., and Malle, B. (1994) Social dominance orientation: A personality variable predicting social and political attitudes. *Journal of Personality and Social Psychology,* **67**, 741-763.

Prentice, D.A. and Miller, D.T. (1996) Pluralistic ignorance and the perpetuation of social norms by unwitting actors. In M.P. Zanna (ed.), *Advances in Experimental Social Psychology,* (Vol. 29, pp. 161-209). San Diego, CA: Academic Press.

Proshansky, H.M. (1966) The development of intergroup attitudes. In L.W. Hoffman and M.L. Hoffman (eds), *Review of Child Development Research,* (pp. 311-371). New York: Russell Sage.

Pruegger, V.J. and Rogers, T.B. (1993) Development of a scale to measure cross-cultural sensitivity in the Canadian context. *Canadian Journal of Behavioural Science,* **25**, 615-621.

Quinton, W.J., Cowan, G., and Watson, B.D. (1996) Personality and attitudinal predictors of support of Proposition 187: California's anti-illegal immigrant initiative. *Journal of Applied Social Psychology*, **26**, 2204-2223.

Rabbie, J.M. (1982) The effects of intergroup competition and cooperation on intragroup and intergroup relationships. In V.J. Derlega and J. Grzelak (eds), *Cooperation and Helping Behavior*, (pp. 123-149). New York: Academic Press.

Rabbie, J.M. (1998) Is there a discontinuity or a reciprocity effect in cooperation and competition between individuals and groups? *European Journal of Social Psychology*, **28**, 483-507.

Rabbie, J.M., Benoist, F., Oosterbaan, H., and Visser, L. (1974) Differential power and effects of expected competitive and cooperative intergroup interaction on intragroup and outgroup attitudes. *Journal of Personality and Social Psychology*, **30**, 46-56.

Rabbie, J.M. and de Brey, J. (1971) The anticipation of intergroup cooperation and competition. *International Journal of Group Tensions*, **1**, 230-251.

Rabbie, J. M., Schot, J., and Visser, L. (1989) Social identity theory: A conceptual and empirical critique from the perspective of a behavioural interaction model. *European Journal of Social Psychology*, **19**, 171-202.

Rabbie, J.M., Visser, L., and van Oostrum, J. (1982) Conflict behavior of individuals, dyads and triads in mixed-motive games. In H. Brandstätter, J.H. Davis, and G. Stocker-Kreichgauer (eds), *Group Decision Making*, (pp. 315-343). London: Academic Press.

Rabbie, J.M. and Wilkins, G. (1971) Intergroup competition and its effect on intragroup and intergroup relations. *European Journal of Social Psychology*, **1**, 215-234.

Radtke, H.L. (1998) Introduction: Goldhagen's psychological thesis. *Theory and Psychology*, **8**, 673-706.

Radke, M.J., Sutherland, J., and Rosenberg, P. (1950) Racial attitudes of children. *Sociometry*, **13**, 154-171.

Radke, M.J. and Trager, H.G. (1950) Children's perceptions of the social roles of Negroes and whites. *Journal of Psychology*, **29**, 3-33.

Radke, M.J., Trager, H.G., and Davis, H. (1949) Social perceptions and attitudes of children. *Genetical Psychology Monograms*, **40**, 327-447.

Radke-Yarrow, M., Trager, H., and Miller, J. (1952) The role of parents in the development of children's ethnic attitudes. *Child Development*, **23**, 13-53.

Random House Dictionary (1987) New York: Ramndom House.

Rapley, M. (1998) 'Just an ordinary Australian': Self-categorisation and the discursive construction of facticity in 'racist' political rhetoric. *British Journal of Social Psychology*, **37**, 325-44.

Rapley, M. and Antaki, C. (1998) 'What do you think about..?': Generating views in an interview. *Text*, **18**, 587-608.

Ray, J.J. and Lovejoy, F.H. (1983) The behavioural validity of some recent measures of authoritarianism. *Journal of Social Psychology*, **120**, 91-99.

Reeves, F. (1983) *British Racial Discourse*. Cambridge: Cambridge University Press.

Reicher, S. (1986) Contact, action and racialization: Some British evidence. In M. Hewstone and R.J. Brown (eds), *Contact and Conflict in Intergroup Encounters: Social Psychology and Society*, (pp. 152-168). Oxford: Basil Blackwell.

Reicher, S. (1991) Politics of crowd psychology. *The Psychologist*, **4**, 487-491.

Reicher, S. (2000) Social identity definition and enactment: A broad SIDE against irrationalism and relativism. In T. Postmes, M. Lea, R. Spears, and S. Reicher (eds), *SIDE Issues Centre Stage*. Amsterdam: KNW.

Reicher, S. and Hopkins, N. (1996a) Seeking influence through characterising self-categories: An analysis of anti-abortionist rhetoric. *British Journal of Social Psychology*, **35**, 297-311.

Reicher, S. and Hopkins, N. (1996b) Self-category constructions in political rhetoric: An analysis of Thatcher's and Kinnock's speeches concerning the British miners' strike (1984-5). *European Journal of Social Psychology*, **26**, 353-371.

Reicher, S. and Hopkins, N. (in press) *Self and Nation*. London: Sage.

Reicher, S., Hopkins, N., and Levine, M. (1997) On the parallels between social cognition and the 'new racism'. *British Journal of Social Psychology*, **37**, 305-329.

Reicher, S. and Levine, M. (1994a) Deindividuation, power relations between groups and the expression of social identity: The effects of visibility to the out-group. *British Journal of Social Psychology*, **33**, 145-63.

Reicher, S. and Levine, M. (1994b) On the consequences of deindividuation manipulations for the strategic communication of self: Identifiability and the presentation of social identity. *European Journal of Social Psychology*, **24**, 511-524.

Reicher, S., Levine, M., and Gordijn, E. (1998) More on deindividuation, power relations between groups and the expression of social identity: Three studies on the effects of visibility to the ingroup. *British Journal of Social Psychology*, **37**, 15-40.

Reicher, S., Spears, R., and Postmes, T. (1995) A social identity model of deindividuation phenomena. *European Review of Social Psychology*, **6**, 161-198.

Reynolds, H. (1998) *This Whispering in our Hearts*. St. Leonards, NSW: Allen and Unwin.

Reynolds, K.J. (1996) *Beyond the Information Given: Capacity, Context and the Categorization Process in Impression Formation*. Unpublished PhD thesis, The Australian National University, Canberra, Australia.

Reynolds, K.J. and Oakes, P.J. (1999) Understanding the impression formation process: A self-categorization theory perspective. In T. Sugiman, M. Karasawa, J. Lui, and C. Ward (eds), *Progress in Asian Social Psychology Theoretical and Empirical Links*, (Vol. 2, pp. 213-235). Seoul, Korea: Kyoyook-Kwahak-Sa Publishing Co.

Reynolds, K.J. and Oakes, P.J. (2000) Variability in impression formation: Investigating the role of motivation, capacity and the categorization process. *Personality and Social Psychology Bulletin*, **26**, 355-373.

Reynolds, K.J, Oakes, P.J., Haslam, S.A., Nolan, M.A., and Dolnik, L. (in press) Responses to powerlessness: Stereotypes as an instrument of social conflict. *Group Dynamics: Theory, Research and Practice*.

Reynolds, K.J., Turner, J.C., and Haslam, S.A. (2000) When are we better than them and they worse than us? A closer look at social discrimination in positive and negative domains. *Journal of Personality and Social Psychology*, **78**, 64-80.

Reynolds, K.J., Turner, J.C., Haslam, S.A., and Ryan, M.K. (in press) The Role of Personality and Group Factors in Explaining Prejudice. *Journal of Experimental Social Psychology*.

Rice, A.S., Ruiz, R.A., and Padilla, A.M. (1974) Person perception, self-identify, and ethnic group preference in Anglo, Black and Chicano preschool and third grade children. *Journal of Cross-Cultural Psychology*, **5**, 100-108.

Richards, G. (1997) *'Race' Racism and Psychology*. London: Routledge.

Richardson, S.A. and Royce, J. (1968) Race and physical handicap in childrens' preferences for other children. *Child Development*, **39**, 467-480.

Riemann, R., Grubich, C., Hempel, S., Mergl, S., and Richter, M. (1993) Personality and attitudes towards current political topics. *Personality and Individual Differences*, **15**, 313-321.

Riessman, C.K. (1993) *Narrative Analysis*. Newbury Park: Sage.

Robinson, J.A. (1998) The impact of race and ethnicity on children's peer relations. In K. Rigby and P. Slee (eds), *Children's Peer Relations*, (pp.76-88). London: Routledge.

Robinson, J.A. and Maine, S. (1998) *The Influence of the Ethnicity and Play Preferences of Unknown Peers on the Preferences of Children from Different Ethnic Backgrounds Who Live in Australia*. 15th Biennial Meeting of the International Society for the Study of Behavioral Development, Berne, Switzerland, July 1-4.

Rokeach, M. (1973) *The Nature of Human Values*. New York: Free Press.

Rokeach, M., Smith, P., and Evans, R. (1960) Two kinds of prejudice or one? In M. Rokeach (ed.), *The Open and the Closed Mind*, (pp. 132-168). New York: Basic Books.

Rorer, L.G. (1965) The great response style myth. *Psychological Bulletin*, **63**, 129-156.

Rosch, E. (1978) Principles of categorization. In E. Rosch and B.B. Lloyd (eds), *Cognition and Categorization*, (pp.28-49). Hillsdale, NJ: Erlbaum.

Rose, S., Lewontin, R., and Kamin, L. (1984) *Not in Our Genes*. Harmondsworth: Penguin.

Ross, M. (1993) *The Culture of Conflict*. New Haven: Yale.

Rothbart, M. and Taylor, M. (1992) Category labels and social reality: Do we view social categories as natural kinds? In G.R. Semin and K. Fiedler (eds), *Language, Interaction, and Social Cognition*, (pp. 11-36). London: Sage Publications,

Royal Commission into Aboriginal Deaths in Custody (1991) *National Report (Commissioner Elliot Johnston)*. Canberra: Australian Government Printing Service.

Rubin, M. and Hewstone, M. (1998) Social identity theory's self-esteem hypothesis: A review and some suggestions for clarification. *Personality and Social Psychology Review*, **2**, 40-62.

Runciman, W.G. (1966) *Relative Deprivation and Social Justice*. London, UK: Routledge.

Rusbult, C.E. and Martz, J.M. (1995) Remaining in an abusive relationship: An investment model analysis of nonvoluntary dependence. *Personality and Social Psychology Bulletin*, **21**, 558-571.

Rusbult, C.E. and van Lange, P.A.M. (1996) Interdependence processes. In E.T. Higgins and A.W. Kruglanski (eds), *Social Psychology: Handbook of Basic Principles*, (pp. 564-596). New York: Guilford Press.

Ruscher, J.B., Fiske, S.T., Miki, H., and van Manen, S. (1991) Individuating processes in competition: Interpersonal versus intergroup. *Personality and Social Psychology Bulletin*, **17**, 595-605.

Rushton, J.P. (1994) *Race, Evolution, and Behaviour: A Life History Perspective*. New Brunswick, NJ: Transaction Publishers.

Ryen, A.H. and Kahn, A. (1975) Effects of intergroup orientation on group attitudes and proxemic behavior. *Journal of Personality and Social Psychology*, **31**, 302-310.

Ryle, G. (1949) *The Concept of Mind*. London: Hutchinson

Sachdev, I. and Bourhis, R.Y. (1985) Social categorization and power differentials in group relations. *European Journal of Social Psychology*, **15**, 415-434.

Sachdev, I. and Bourhis. R.Y. (1987) Status differentials and intergroup behaviour. *European Journal of Social Psychology*, **17**, 277-293.

Sachdev, I. and Bourhis. R.Y. (1991) Power and status differentials in minority and majority group relations. *European Journal of Social Psychology*, **21**, 1-24.

Sacks, H. (1992) *Lectures on Conversation, Volumes 1 and 2*. G. Jefferson (ed.). Oxford: Basil Blackwell.

Sacks, H. (1995) 'Hotrodders' as a revolutionary category. Lecture 18 in G. Jefferson (ed.) *Harvey Sacks' Lectures on Conversation*, (Vol. 1, pp. 396-403). Oxford: Blackwell.

Sagar, H.A. and Schofield, J.W. (1980) Racial and behavioral cues in Black and White children's perceptions of ambiguously aggressive acts. *Journal of Personality and Social Psychology*, **39**, 590-598.

Sahakian, W.S. (1982) *History and Systems of Social Psychology* (2nd edn). Washington, DC: Hemisphere Publishing Corporation.

Saharso, S. (1989) Ethnic identity and the paradox of equality. In J. van Oudenhoven and T. Willemsen, (eds), *Ethnic Minorities: Social Psychological Perspectives,* (pp. 97-114). Amsterdam: Swets and Zeitlinger.

Samelson, F. (1978) From 'race psychology' to 'studies in prejudice': Some observations on the thematic reversal in social psychology. *Journal of the History of the Behavioral Sciences*, **14**, 265-278.

Sanson, A., Augoustinos, M., Gridley, H., Kyrios, K., Reser, J., and Turner, C. (1998) Racism and prejudice: An APS Position Paper. *Australian Psychologist,* **33**, 161-182.

Schegloff, E.A. (1989) Harvey Sacks – lectures 1964-1965: An introduction/memoir. *Human Studies*, **12**, 185-209.

Schegloff, E.A. (1997) Whose text? Whose context? *Discourse and Society*, **8**, 165-187.

Schneider, W. and Shiffrin, R.M. (1977) Controlled and automatic human information processing I: Detection, search and attention. *Psychological Review,* **84**, 1-66.

Schofield, J.W. (1975) Effects of norms, public disclosure, and need for approval on volunteering behavior consistent with attitudes. *Journal of Personality and Social Psychology*, **31**, 1126-1133.

Schofield, J.W. (1986) Causes and consequences of the colorblind perspective. In J.F. Dovidio and S.L. Gaertner (eds), *Prejudice, Discrimination, and Racism,* (pp. 231-254). Orlando, FL: Academic.

Schofield, J.W. (1995) Promoting positive intergroup relations in school settings. In W.D Hawley and A.W. Jackson (eds), *Toward a Common Destiny: Improving Race and Ethnic Relations in America,* (pp. 257-289). San Francisco, CA: Jossey-Bass Inc, Publishers.

Schopler, J. and Insko, C.A. (1992) The discontinuity effect in interpersonal and intergroup relations: Generality and mediation. In W. Stroebe and M. Hewstone (eds), *European Review of Social Psychology,* (Vol. 3, pp. 121-151). New York: Wiley.

Schopler, J. and Insko, C.A. (1999) The reduction of the interindividual-intergroup discontinuity effect: The role of future consequences. In M. Foddy, M. Smithson, S. Schneider, and M.A. Hogg (eds), *Resolving Social Dilemmas: Dynamic, Structural, and Intergroup Approaches,* (pp. 281-293). Philadelphia: Psychology Press.

Schopler, J., Insko, C.A., Graetz, K.A., Drigotas, S.M., Smith, V.A., and Dahl, K. (1993) Individual-group discontinuity: Further evidence for mediation by fear and greed. *Personality and Social Psychology Bulletin*, **19**, 419-431.

Schuman, H., Steeh, C., and Bobo, L. (1985) *Racial Attitudes in America: Trends and Interpretations*. Cambridge, MA: Harvard University Press.

Schwarz, B. (1982) 'The people' in history: the Communist Party Historians' Group, 1946-56. In Centre for Contemporary Cultural Studies, *Making History: Studies in History Writing and Politics*. London: Hutchinson.

Schwarz, N. (1990) Feelings as information: Informational and motivational functions of affective states. In R. Sorrentino and E.T. Higgins (eds), *Handbook of Motivation and Cognition,* (Vol. 2, pp. 527-561). New York, Guilford Press.

Schwarz, N. and Clore, G.L. (1983) Mood misattribution and judgments of well-being: Informative and directive functions of affective states. *Journal of Personality and Social Psychology,* **45**, 513-523.

Schwarz, N. and Clore, G.L. (1988) How do I feel about it? The informative function of affective states. In K. Fiedler and J.P. Forgas (eds), *Affect, Cognition, and Social Behavior,* (pp. 44-62). Toronto: Hogrefe.

Sears, D.O. (1988) Symbolic racism. In P.A. Katz and D.A. Taylor (eds), *Eliminating Racism: Profiles in Controversy,* (pp. 53-84). New York: Plenum Press.

Sears, D.O. and Kinder, D.R. (1971) Racial tensions and voting in Los Angeles. In W.Z. Hirsch (ed.), *Los Angeles: Viability and Prospects for Metropolitan Leadership,* (pp. 51-88). New York: Praeger.

Sears, D.O. and McConahay, J.B. (1973) *The Politics of Violence: The New Urban Blacks and the Watts Riot.* Boston: Houghton Mifflin.

Segall, M. (1998) *On the Pernicious Concept of 'Race' or Why Do We Still Have Racism if There Are No Such Thing as Races?* Presidential Address to the International Association for Cross-Cultural Psychology Fourteenth International and Silver Jubilee Congress. Western Washington University, Bellingham, Washington, USA.

Seidel, G. (1986) *The Holocaust Denial.* Leeds: Beyond The Pale Collective.

Selman, R.L. and Byrne, D.F. (1974) A structural-developmental analysis of levels of role-taking in middle childhood. *Child Development,* **45**, 803-806.

Selznick, G. and Steinberg, S. (1969) *The Tenacity of Prejudice.* New York: Harper and Row.

Serbian Ministry of Information (1998) Facts about Kosovo and Metohia: History. In SerbiaInfo. Available at http://www.serbia-info.com/news/kosovo/facts/history.html.

Sharan, S. (ed.) (1990) *Cooperative Learning: Theory and Research.* New York: Praeger.

Sharan, S. and Rich, Y. (1984) Field experiments on ethnic integration in Israeli schools. In Y. Amir, S. Sharan, and R. Ben-Arie (eds), *School Desegregation: Cross-Cultural Perspectives,* (pp. 189-218). Hillsdale, New Jersey: Erlbaum.

Sheehan, P. (1998) *Among the Barbarians: The Dividing of Australia.* Milsons Point, NSW: Random House.

Sheppard, B.H., Hartwick, J., and Warshaw, P.R. (1988) The theory of reasoned action: A meta-analysis of past research with recommendations for modification and future research. *Journal of Consumer Research,* **15**, 325-343.

Sherif, M. (1966/1967) *Group Conflict and Co-operation: Their Social Psychology.* London: Routledge and Kegan Paul. (Originally published in 1966 as *In Common Predicament: Social Psychology of Intergroup Conflict and Cooperation.* Boston: Houghton Mifflin).

Sherif, M., Harvey, O.J., White, B.J., Hood, W.R., and Sherif, C. (1961) *Intergroup Conflict and Cooperation: The Robber's Cave Experiment.* Norman: University of Oklahoma Press.

Sherif, M. and Sherif, C. (1953) *Groups in Harmony and Tension: An Integration of Studies in Intergroup Relations.* New York: Harper.

Sherif, M. and Sherif, C. (1969) *Social Psychology.* New York: Harper and Row.

Sherif, M., White, B.J., and Harvey, O.J. (1955) Status in experimentally produced groups. *American Journal of Sociology,* **60**, 370-379.

Sidanius, J. (1993) The psychology of group conflict and the dynamics of oppression: A social dominance perspective. In S. Iyengar and W. McGuire (eds), *Explorations in Political Psychology,* (pp. 183-219). Durham, NC: Duke University Press.

Sidanius, J., Devereux, E., and Pratto, F. (1992) A comparison of symbolic racism theory and social dominance theory as explanations for racial policy attitudes. *Journal of Social Psychology,* **132**, 377-395.

Sidanius, J. and Liu, J. (1992) Racism, support for the Persian Gulf war, and the police beating of Rodney King: A social dominance perspective. *Journal of Social Psychology*, **132**, 685-700.

Siegel, A.E. and Siegel, S. (1957) Reference groups, membership groups, and attitude change. *Journal of Abnormal and Social Psychology*, **55**, 360-364.

Siegelman, C.K. and Toebben J.L. (1992) Tolerant reactions to advocates of disagreeable ideas in childhood and adolescence. *Merrill-Palmer Quarterly*, **38**, 542-557.

Siegman, A.W. (1961) A cross-cultural investigation of the relationship between ethnic prejudice, authoritarian ideology, and personality. *Journal of Abnormal and Social Psychology*, **63**, 654-655.

Silberman, L. and Spice, B. (1950) *Colour and Class in Six Liverpool Schools*. Liverpool: Liverpool University Press.

Simon, B. (1992) The perception of ingroup and outgroup homogeneity: Reintroducing the social context. *European Review of Social Psychology*, **3**, 1-30.

Simon, B. (1993) On the asymmetry in the cognitive construal of ingroup and outgroup: A model of egocentric social categorization. *European Journal of Social Psychology*, **23**, 131-147.

Simon, B. (1995) The perception of ingroup and outgroup homogeneity: On the confounding of group size, level of abstractness and frame of reference: A reply to Bartsch and Judd. *European Journal of Social Psychology*, **12**, 463-468.

Simon, B. and Brown, R.J. (1987) Perceived homogeneity in minority-majority contexts. *Journal of Personality and Social Psychology*, **53**, 703-711.

Simpson, G.E. and Yinger, J.M. (1985) *Racial and Cultural Minorities: An Analysis of Prejudice and Discrimination* (5th edn). New York: Plenum Press.

Singleton, L.C. and Asher, S.R. (1979) Racial integration and children's peer preferences: An investigation of developmental and cohort differences. *Child Development*, **50**, 936-941.

Slavin, R. (1990) *Cooperative Learning: Theory, Research, and Practice*. Englewood Cliffs, NJ: Prentice-Hall.

Slavin, R. (1995) Enhancing intergroup relations in schools: Cooperative learning and other strategies. In W. Hawley and A. Jackson (eds), *Toward a Common Destiny: Improving Race and Ethnic Relations in America*, (pp. 291-314). San Francisco: Jossey-Bass.

Smith, A.W. (1981) Tolerance of school desegregation, 1955-1977. *Social Forces*, **59**, 1256-1274.

Smith, H.J. and Tyler, T.R. (1996) Justice and power: When will justice concerns encourage the advantaged to support policies which redistribute economic resources and the disadvantaged to willingly obey the law? *European Journal of Social Psychology*, **26**, 171-200.

Smith, P. and Bond, M. (1993) *Social Psychology Across Cultures: Analysis and Perspectives*. New York: Harvester Wheatsheaf.

Sniderman, P.M. and Piazza, T. (1993) *The Scar of Race*. Cambridge, MA: Harvard University Press.

Sniderman, P.M. and Tetlock, P.E. (1986) Symbolic racism: Problems of motive attribution in political analysis. *Journal of Social Issues*, **42**, 129-150.

Solomon, S., Greenberg, J., and Pyszczynski, T. (1991) A terror management theory of social behavior: The psychological functions of self-esteem and cultural worldviews. In M.P. Zanna (ed.), *Advances in Experimental Social Psychology*, (Vol. 24, pp. 93-159) Orlando, FL: Academic Press.

Spence, J., Helmreich, R., and J Stapp. (1973) A short version of the Attitudes toward Women Scale (AWS). *Bulletin of the Psychonomic Society, 2*, 219-220.

St. Claire, L. and Turner, J.C. (1982) The role of demand characteristics in the social categorization paradigm. *European Journal of Social Psychology, 12*, 307-314.

St. John, N.H. and Lewis, R.G. (1975) Race and the social structure of the elementary classroom. *Sociology of Education, 48*, 346-368.

Stangor, C. and Lange, J.E. (1994) Mental representations of social groups: Advances in understanding stereotypes and stereotyping. In M.P. Zanna (ed.), *Advances in Experimental Social Psychology,* (Vol. 26, pp. 357-416) New York: Academic Press.

Stangor, C., Sullivan, L.A., and Ford, T.E. (1991) Affective and cognitive determinants of prejudice. *Social Cognition, 9*, 359-380.

Staub, E. (1989) The Roots of Evil: The Origins of Genocide and Other Group Violence. Cambridge: Cambridge University Press.

Steensma, H. and Vermunt, R. (eds) (1991) Social Justice in Human Relations: Society and Psychological Consequences of Justice and Injustice (Vol. 2). New York: Plenum Press.

Stephan, W.G. (1985) Intergroup relations. In G. Lindzey and E. Aronson (eds), *Handbook of Social Psychology.* New York: Random House.

Stephan, W.G. (1987) The contact hypothesis in intergroup relations. In C. Hendrick (ed.), *Group Processes and Intergroup Relations: Review of Personality and Social Psychology,* (Vol. 9, pp. 13-40). Newbury Park: Sage.

Stephan, W.G. and Rosenfield, D. (1979) Black self-rejection: Another look. *Journal of Educational Psychology, 71*, 708-716.

Stephan, W.G. and Rosenfield, D. (1982) Racial and ethnic stereotypes. In A.G. Miller (ed.), *In the Eye of the Beholder: Contemporary Issues in Stereotyping.* New York: Praeger.

Stephan, W.G. and Stephan, C.W. (1985) Intergroup anxiety. *Journal of Social Issues, 41*, 157-175.

Stephan, W.G. and Stephan, C.W. (1993) Cognition and affect in stereotyping: Parallel interactive networks. In D.M. Mackie and D.L .Hamilton (eds), *Affect, Cognition, and Stereotyping: Interactive Processes in Group Perception,* (pp. 111-136). San Diego: Academic Press.

Stephan, W.G., Ybarra, O., Martinez-Martinez, C., Schwarzwald, J., and Tur-Kaspa, M. (1998) Prejudice toward immigrants to Spain and Israel: An integrated threat theory analysis. *Journal of Cross-Cultural Psychology, 29*, 559-576.

Stevenson, H.W. and Stevenson, N.G. (1960) Social interaction in an interracial nursery school. *Genetic Psychology Monographs, 61*, 37-75.

Stone, S. (ed.) (1974) *Aborigines in White Australia: A Documentary History of the Attitudes Affecting Official Policy and the Australian Aborgine, 1697-1973.* South Yarra, VIC: Heinemann Educational Books.

Stroessner, S.J., Hamilton, D.L., and Mackie, D.M. (1992) Affect and stereotyping: The effect of induced mood on distinctiveness-based illusory correlations. Journal of Personality and Social Psychology, *62*, 564-576.

Strutch, N. and Schwartz, S.H. (1989) Intergroup aggression: Its predictors and distinctiveness from ingroup bias. *Journal of Personality and Social Psychology, 56*, 364-373.

Sullivan, J. and Transue, J. (1999) The psychological underpinnings of democracy: A selective review of research on political tolerance, interpersonal trust, and social capital. *Annual Review of Psychology, 50*, 625-650.

Swim, J.K., Aikin, K.J., Hall, W.S., and Hunter, B.A. (1995) Sexism and racism: Old-fashioned and modern prejudices. *Personality and Social Psychology Bulletin*, **22**, 507-519.

Taft, R. (1970) Attitudes of Western Australians towards Aborigines. In R. Taft, J.L.M. Dawson, and P. Beasley (eds), *Attitudes and Social Conditions,* (pp. 3-72). Canberra: Social Science Research Council of Australia.

Tajfel, H. (1969) Cognitive aspects of prejudice. In G.A. Harrison and J. Peel (eds), *Biosocial Aspects of Race,* (pp. 173-191). Oxford and Edinburgh: Blackwell. Reprinted in *Journal of Social Issues*, **25**, 79-97.

Tajfel, H. (1970) Experiments in intergroup discrimination. *Scientific American,* **223**, 96-102.

Tajfel, H. (1972) Social Categorization. In S. Moscovici (ed.), *Introducion a la Psychologie Sociale* (pp. 272-302). Paris: Larousse.

Tajfel, H. (1974) Social identity and intergroup behaviour. *Social Science Information*, **13**, 65-93.

Tajfel. H. (1978a) The achievement of group differentiation. In H. Tajfel (ed.), *Differentiation Between Social Groups: Studies in the Social Psychology of Intergroup Relations,* (pp.77-100). London: Academic Press.

Tajfel, H. (ed.) (1978b) *Differentiation Between Social Groups: Studies in the Social Psychology of Intergroup Relations*. London: Academic Press.

Tajfel. H. (1978c) Interindividual behaviour and intergroup behaviour. In H. Tajfel (ed.) *Differentiation Between Social Groups: Studies in the Social Psychology of Intergroup Relations,* (pp. 27-60). London: Academic Press.

Tajfel, H. (1981a) *Human Groups and Social Categories: Studies in Social Psychology*. Cambridge: Cambridge University Press.

Tajfel, H. (1981b) Social Stereotypes and Social Groups. In J.C. Turner and H. Giles. *Intergroup Behaviour,* (pp. 144-167). Oxford: Blackwell.

Tajfel, H. (1982a) Introduction. In H. Tajfel (ed.), *Social Identity and Intergroup Relations,* (pp. 1-14) Cambridge: Cambridge University Press.

Tajfel, H. (1982b) Social psychology of intergroup relations. *Annual Review of Psychology,* **33**, 1-39.

Tajfel, H., Flament, C., Billig, M.G., and Bundy, R.P. (1971) Social categorisation and intergroup behaviour. *European Journal of Social Psychology,* **1**, 149-178.

Tajfel, H., Jahoda, G., Nemeth, C., Rim, Y., and Johnson, N.B. (1972) The devaluation by children of their own national and ethnic group: Two case studies. *British Journal of social and Clinical Psychology,* **11**, 235-243.

Tajfel, H., Jaspars, J.M.F., and Frazer, C. (1984) The social dimension in European social psychology. In H. Tajfel (ed.), *The Social Dimension: European Developments in Social Psychology*. Cambridge: Cambridge University Press.

Tajfel, H., Sheikh, A.A., and Gardner, R.C. (1964) Content of stereotypes and the inference of similarity between members of stereotyped groups. *Acta Psychologica*, **22**, 191-201.

Tajfel, H. and Turner, J.C. (1979) An integrative theory of intergroup conflict. In W.G. Austin and S. Worchel (eds), *The Social Psychology of Intergroup Relations,* (pp. 33-47). Monterey, CA: Brooks/Cole.

Tajfel, H. and Turner, J.C. (1986) The social identity theory of intergroup behavior. In S. Worchel and W.G. Austin (eds), *Psychology of Intergroup Relations,* (pp. 7-24). Chicago: Nelson Hall.

Tajfel, H. and Wilkes, A.L. (1963) Classification and quantitative judgement. *British Journal of Psychology*, **54**, 101-114.

Tatz, C. (1999) *Genocide in Australia.* Canberra: Australian Institute of Aboriginal and Torres Strait Islander Studies. Available at: http://aiatsis.gov.au/research/dp/8/genocide.html.

Taylor, D.A. and Moriarty, B.F. (1987) Ingroup bias as a function of competition and race. *Journal of Conflict Resolution,* **31**, 192-199.

Taylor, D.M. and Moghaddem, F.M. (1994) *Theories of Intergroup Relations: International Social Psychological Perspectives* (2nd edn). London: Praeger.

Taylor, D.M., Moghaddam, F.M., Gamble, I., and Zellerer, E. (1987) Disadvantaged group responses to perceived inequality: From passive acceptance to collective action. *Journal of Social Psychology,* **127**, 259-272.

Taylor, S.E., Fiske, S.T., Etcoff, N.L., and Ruderman, R.L. (1978) Categorical and contextual bases of person memory and stereotyping. *Journal of Personality and Social Psychology,* **36**, 778-793.

Taylor, S.E. (1981) The categorization approach to stereotyping. In D.L. Hamilton (ed.), *Cognitive Processes in Stereotyping and Intergroup Behaviour,* (pp. 88-114). Hillsdale, NJ: Erlbaum.

Taylor, S.E. and Repetti, R.L. (1997) Health psychology: What is an unhealthy environment and how does it get under the skin? *Annual Review of Psychology,* **48**, 411-447.

Taylor, T.J. and Cameron, D. (1987) *Analyzing Conversation: Rules and units in the Structure of talk.* Oxford: Pergamon Press.

Telling Our Story (1995) Aboriginal Legal Service of Western Australia.

Terry, D.J., Gallois, C., and McCamish, M. (1993) The theory of reasoned action and health behaviour. In D.J. Terry, C. Gallois, and M. McCamish (eds), *The Theory of Reasoned Action: Its Application to AIDS-Preventive Behaviour,* (pp. 1-27). Oxford, UK: Pergamon.

Terry, D.J. and Hogg, M.A. (1996) Group norms and the attitude-behavior relationship. A role for group identification. *Personality and Social Psychology Bulletin,* **22**, 776-793.

Terry, D.J., Hogg, M.A., and Duck, J. (1999) Group membership, social identity, and attitudes. In D.A. Abrams and M.A. Hogg (eds), *Social Identity and Social Cognition,* (pp. 280-314). Oxford, UK: Blackwell.

Terry, D.J., Hogg, M.A, and McKimmie, B.M. (in press) Group salience, norm congruency, and mode of behavioral decision-making: The effect of group norms on attitude-behavior relations. *British Journal of Social Psychology.*

Terry, D.J., Hogg, M.A., and White, K.A. (1999) Group norms, social identity, and attitude-behavior relations. In D.J. Terry and M.A. Hogg (eds), *Attitudes, Behavior, and Social Context: The Role of Norms and Group Membership,* (pp. 67-94). NJ: Erlbaum.

Terry, D.J., Hogg, M.A., and White, K.M. (in press) The theory of planned behavior: Self-identity, social identity, and group norms. *British Journal of Social Psychology.*

Terry, D.J. and Johnson, D.W. (1999) *Prejudice Among Majority Group Members: The Role of Group Norms and Intergroup Beliefs.* Paper presented at the 4th Meeting of the Society of Australasian Social Psychologists, Coolum, April, 1999.

The Advertiser (1998) 'Yellowfellas rort' system., 27th July, 1998.

The Cairns Post (1999) Political correctness drags bush to its knees. Letters to the Editor.

Thomas, N. (1994) *Colonialism's Culture.* Oxford: Polity.

Thomas, N. (1989) *Out of Time: History and Evolution in Anthropological Discourse.* Cambridge: Cambridge University Press.

Titus, H.E. (1968) F scale validity considered against peer nomination criteria. *Psychological Record*, **18**, 395-403.

Titus, H.E. and Hollander, E.P. (1957) The California F scale in psychological research: 1950-1955. *Psychological Bulletin*, **54**, 47-64.

Törnblom, K.Y. and Foa, U.G. (1983) Choice of distribution principle: Cross-cultural evidence on the effects of resources. *Acta Sociologica*, **26**, 161-173.

Torney-Purta, J. (1995) Education in multicultural settings. In W. Hawley and A. Jackson (eds), *Toward a Common Destiny: Improving Race and Ethnic Relations in America*, (pp. 341-370). San Francisco: Jossey-Bass.

Tougas, F., Brown, R., Beaton, A.M., and Joly, S. (1995) Neo-sexism: Plus ca change, plus c'est pareil. *Personality and Social Psychology Bulletin*, **21**, 842-849.

Trope, Y. (1989) Stereotypes and dispositional judgment. In D. Bar-Tal, C.F. Graumann, A.W. Kruglanski, and W. Stroebe (eds), *Stereotyping and Prejudice: Changing Conceptions*, (pp. 133-149). New York: Springer-Verlag.

Turner, J.C. (1975) Social comparison and social identity: Some prospects for intergroup behaviour. *European Journal of Social Psychology*, **5**, 5-34.

Turner, J.C. (1978) Social categorization and social discrimination in the minimal group paradigm. In H. Tajfel (ed.), *European Monographs in Social Psychology*, (Vol. 14, pp. 101-140). London: Academic Press.

Turner, J.C. (1981) The experimental social psychology of intergroup behaviour. In J.C. Turner and H. Giles (eds), *Intergroup Behaviour*, (pp. 66-101). Oxford: Blackwell.

Turner, J.C. (1982) Towards a cognitive redefinition of the social group. In H. Tajfel (ed.), *Social Identity and Intergroup Relations*, (pp 15-40). Cambridge: Cambridge University Press.

Turner, J.C. (1983) Some comments on ... 'the measurement of social orientations in the minimal group paradigm'. *European Journal of Social Psychology*, **13**, 351-367.

Turner, J.C. (1984) Social identification and psychological group formation. In H. Tajfel (ed.), *The Social Dimension: European Developments in Social Psychology*, (Vol. 2, pp. 518-538). Cambridge: Cambridge University Press and Paris: Editions de la Maison des Sciences de l'Homme,.

Turner, J.C. (1985) Social categorization and the self-concept: A social cognitive theory of group behaviour. In E.J. Lawler (ed.), *Advances in Group Processes*, (Vol. 2, pp. 77-121). Greenwich, CT: JAI Press.

Turner, J.C. (1987) Rediscovering the social group. In J.C. Turner, M.A. Hogg, P.J. Oakes, S.D. Reicher, and M.S. Wetherell (eds), *Rediscovering the Social Group: A Self-Categorization Theory*, (pp. 19-41). Oxford: Blackwell.

Turner, J.C. (1991) *Social Influence*. Buckingham, UK: Open University Press.

Turner, J.C. (1996) *Fifty Years' Research on Intergroup Relations: Advances and prospects*. Invited plenary paper presented to Symposium on 'Social psychology over the last 50 years', at the 2nd Annual Meeting of the Society of Australasian Social Psychologists, Canberra, ACT, May 2-5.

Turner, J.C. (1999a) *The Prejudiced Personality and Social Change: A Self-Categorization Perspective*. The Tajfel Lecture at European Association of Experimental Social Psychology, Oxford, July 7-11.

Turner, J.C. (1999b) Some current themes in research on social identity and self-categorization theories. In N. Ellemers, R. Spears, and B. Doosje (eds), *Social Identity: Context, Commitment, Content*, (pp. 6-34). Oxford: Blackwell.

Turner, J.C. and Bourhis, R.Y. (1996) Social identity, interdependence and the social group: A reply to Rabbie et al.. In W.P. Robinson (ed.), *Social Groups and Identities: Developing the Legacy of Henri Tajfel*, (pp. 25-63). Oxford: Butterworth Heinemann.

Turner, J.C. and Brown, R.J. (1978) Social status, cognitive alternatives and intergroup relations. In H. Tajfel (ed.), *Differentiation Between Social Groups: Studies in the Social Psychology of Intergroup Relations,* (pp. 201-234). London: Academic Press.

Turner, J.C. and Giles, H. (eds) (1981) *Intergroup Behaviour.* Oxford: Basil Blackwell and Chicago: University of Chicago Press.

Turner, J.C., Hogg, M.A., Oakes, P.J., Reicher, S.D., and Wetherell, M.S. (1987) *Rediscovering the Social Group: A Self-Categorization Theory.* Oxford and New York: Basil Blackwell.

Turner, J.C. and Oakes, P.J. (1986) The significance of the social identity concept for social psychology with reference to individualism, interactionism and social influence. *British Journal of Social Psychology,* **25**, 237-252. Special issue on the Individual/Society Interface.

Turner, J.C. and Oakes, P.J. (1989) Self-categorization theory and social influence. In P.B. Paulus (ed.), *The Psychology of Group Influence,* 2nd edn, (pp. 233-275). Hillsdale, NJ: Erlbaum.

Turner, J.C. and Oakes, P.J. (1997) The socially structured mind. In C. McGarty and S.A. Haslam (eds), *The Message of Social Psychology,* (pp. 355-373). Oxford, UK: Blackwells.

Turner, J.C., Oakes, P.J., Haslam, S.A., and McGarty, C. (1994) Self and collective: Cognition and social context. *Personality and Social Psychology Bulletin,* **20**, 454-463.

Turner, J.C. and Onorato, R.S. (1999) Social identity, personality and the self-concept: A self-categorization perspective. In T.R. Tyler, R. Kramer, and O. Johns (eds), *The Psychology of the Social Self,* (pp. 11-46). Hillsdale, NJ: Lawrence Erlbaum.

Turner, J.C. and Reynolds, K.J. (in press) The social identity perspective in intergroup relations: Theories, themes and controversies. To appear in R.J. Brown and S. Gaertner (eds), *Blackwell Handbook in Social Psychology, Volume 4: Intergroup Processes.* Oxford: Blackwell.

Turner, J.C., Reynolds, K.J., and Haslam, S.A. (1998) *The Social Psychology of Intergroup Relations: Investigating the Role of Individual and Group Factors in Explaining Ethnocentrism, Prejudice and Discrimination.* Grant Proposal to the Australian Research Council, The Australian National University, Canberra, February.

Twiss, C., Tab, S., and Crosby, F. (1988) Affirmative action and aggregate data: The importance of patterns in the perception of discrimination. In F. Blanchard and F. Crosby (eds), *Affirmative Action in Perspective,* (pp. 159-167). New York: Springer-Verlag.

Tyack, D. (1995) Schooling and social diversity: Historical reflections. In W. Hawley and A. Jackson (eds), *Toward a Common Destiny: Improving Race and Ethnic Relations in America,* (pp. 3-38). San Francisco: Jossey-Bass.

Tyerman, A. and Spencer C. (1983) A critical test of the Sherifs' Robber's Cave experiments: Intergroup competition and cooperation between groups of well-acquainted individuals. *Small Group Behavior,* **14**, 515-531.

Tyler, T.R. (1984) The role of perceived injustice in defendants' evaluations of their courtroom experience. *Law and Society Review,* **18**, 51-74.

Tyler, T.R. (1994) Psychological models of the justice motive: Antecedents of distributive and procedural justice. *Journal of Personality and Social Psychology,* **67**, 850-863.

Tyler, T.R. and Dawes, R.M. (1993) Fairness in groups: Comparing the self-interest and social identity perspectives. In B.A. Mellers and J. Baron, Jonathan (eds), *Psychological Perspectives on Justice: Theory and Application,* (pp. 87-108). New York: Cambridge University Press.

Tyler, T.R. and Folger, R. (1980) Distributional and procedural aspects of satisfaction with citizen-police encounters. *Basic and Applied Social Psychology,* **1**, 281-292.

Tyler, T.R. and Lind, E.A. (1992) A relational model of authority in groups. In M.P. Zanna (ed.), *Advances in Experimental Social Psychology,* (Vol. 25, pp. 115-191). New York: Academic Press.

Tyler, T.R. and Smith, H.J. (1998) Social justice and social movements. In D.T. Gilbert, S.T. Fiske, and G. Lindzey (eds), *The Handbook of Social Psychology,* 4th edn, (Vol. 2, pp. 595-629). Boston, MA: McGraw Hill.

UNESCO (1983) *Racism, Science, and Pseudo-Science.* Paris: UNESCO.

van Ausdale, D.V. and Feagin, J.R. (1996) Using racial and ethnic concepts: The critical case of very young children. *American Sociological Review,* **61**, 779-793.

Van den Heuvel, H. and Meertens, R.W. (1989) The culture assimilator: Is it possible to improve interethnic relations by emphasizing ethnic differences? In J. van Oudenhoven and T. Willemsen (eds), *Ethnic Minorities: Social Psychological Perspectives,* (pp. 221-236). Amsterdam: Swets and Zeitlinger.

van Dijk, T.A. (1984) *Prejudice in Discourse.* Amsterdam: Benjamins.

van Dijk, T.A. (1985) Cognitive situation models in discourse processing: The expression of ethnic situation models in prejudiced stories. In J.P. Forgas (ed.), *Handbook of Discourse Analysis,* (Vol. 2, pp. 103-136). New York: Springer.

van Dijk, T.A. (1987) *Communicating Racism: Ethnic Prejudice in Thought and Talk.* Newbury Park, CA: Sage.

van Dijk, T.A. (1991) *Racism and the Press.* London: Routledge.

van Dijk, T.A. (1992) Discourse and the denial of racism. *Discourse and Society,* **3**, 87-118.

van Dijk, T.A. (1993) *Elite Discourse and Racism.* Newbury Park, CA: Sage.

Van Hiel, A. and Mervielde, I. (1996) Personality and current political beliefs. *Psychologica Belgica,* **36**, 221-226.

van Knippenberg, A., van Twuyver, M., and Pepels, J. (1994) Factors affecting social categorization processes in memory. *British Journal of Social Psychology,* **33**, 419-431.

van Oudehoven, J. and Willemsen, T. (1989) *Ethnic Minorities: Social Psychological Perspectives.* Amsterdam: Swets and Zeitlinger.

van Oudenhoven, J. and Willemsen, T. (1989) Towards a useful social psychology for ethnic minorities. In J. van Oudenhoven and T. Willemsen, (eds), *Ethnic Minorities: Social Psychological Perspectives,* (pp. 237-251). Amsterdam: Swets and Zeitlinger.

Vanneman, R.D. and Pettigrew, T.F. (1972) Race and relative deprivation in urban United States. *Race,* **13**, 461-486.

Vaughan, G.M. (1963) Concept formation and the development of ethnic awareness. *Journal of Genetic Psychology,* **103**, 93-103.

Vaughan, G.M. (1964a) The development of ethnic attitudes in New Zealand school children. *Genetic Psychology Monographs,* **70**, 135-175.

Vaughan, G.M. (1964b) Ethnic awareness in relation to minority group membership. *The Journal of Genetic Psychology,* **105**, 119-130.

Vaughan, G.M. (1987) A social psychological model of ethnic identity development. In J.S. Phinney and M.J. Rotheram (eds), *Children's Ethnic Socialisation,* (pp. 73-91). London: Sage.

Vaughan, G.M. (1988) The psychology of intergroup discrimination. *New Zealand Journal of Psychology,* **17**,1-14.

Vaughan, G.M., Tajfel, H., and Williams, J.A. (1981) Bias in reward allocation in an intergroup and an interpersonal context. *Social Psychology Quarterly,* **44**, 37-42.

Vaughan, G.M. and Thompson, R.H.T. (1961) New Zealand children's attitudes toward Maoris. *Journal of Abnormal Social Psychology,* **62**, 701-704.

Verkuyten, M. and Hagendoorn, L. (1998) Prejudice and self-categorization: The variable role of authoritarianism and in-group stereotypes. *Personality and Social Psychology Bulletin*, **24**, 99-110.

Verkuyten, M. and Masson, K. (1995) 'New Racism', Self esteem, and ethnic relations among minority and majority youth in the Netherlands. *Social Behaviour and Personality*, **23**, 2, 137-154.

Vogt, W.P. (1997) *Tolerance and Education: Learning to Live with Diversity and Difference*. Thousand Oaks, CA: Sage Publications.

von Hippel, W., Sekaquaptewa, D., and Vargas, P. (1995) On the role of encoding processes in stereotype maintenance. In M.P. Zanna (ed.), *Advances in Experimental Social Psychology*, (Vol. 27, pp. 117-254). San Diego, CA: Academic Press.

Wagner, U., Lampen, L., and Syllwasschy, J. (1986) Ingroup inferiority, social identity and outgroup devaluation in a modified extended minimal group study. *British Journal of Social Psychology*, **25**, 15-24.

Wainryb, C., Shaw, L.A., and Maianu, C. (1998) Tolerance and intolerance: Children's judgments of dissenting beliefs, speech, persons, and conduct. *Child Development*, **69**, 1541-1555.

Walker, I. (1994) Attitudes to minorities: Survey evidence of Western Australians' attitudes to Aborigines, Asians, and women. *Australian Journal of Psychology*, **46**, 137-143.

Walker, I. and Crogan, M. (1998) Academic performance, prejudice, and the Jigsaw classroom: New pieces to the puzzle. *Journal of Community and Applied Social Psychology*, **8**, 381-393.

Walker, I. and Mann, L. (1987) Unemployment, relative deprivation, and social protest. *Personality and Social Psychology Bulletin*, **13**, 275-283.

Walker, I. and Pettigrew, T.F. (1984) Relative deprivation theory: An overview and conceptual critique. *British Journal of Social Psychology*, **23**, 301-310.

Walker, P and Antaki, C. (1986) Sexual orientation as a basis for categorization in recall. *British Journal of Social Psychology*, **25**, 337-339.

Walster, E. and Walster, G.W. (1975) Equity and social justice. *Journal of Social Issues*, **31**, 21-43.

Warren, R.E. (1972) Stimulus encoding and memory. *Journal of Experimental Psychology*, **94**, 90-100.

Weber, R. and Crocker, J. (1983) Cognitive processes in the revision of stereotypic beliefs. *Journal of Personality and Social Psychology*, **45**, 961-977.

Weigel, R.H. and Howes, P.W. (1985) Conceptions of racial prejudice: Symbolic racism reconsidered. *Journal of Social Issues*, **41**, 117-138.

Weigl, B. (1995) Similarity between parents' and children's social stereotypes. *Polish Psychological Bulletin*, **26**, 161-174

Wellen, J.M., Hogg, M.A., and Terry, D.J. (1998) Group norms and attitude-behaviour consistency: The role of group salience and mood. *Group Dynamics: Theory, Research and Practice*, **2**, 48-56.

Wells, D. (1997) One Nation and the politics of populism. In B. Grant (ed.), *Pauline Hanson: One Nation and Australian Politics*, (pp. 18-28). Armidale: University of New England Press.

Werth, J. and Lord, C. (1992) Previous conceptions of the typical group member and the contact hypothesis. *Basic and Applied Social Psychology*, **13**, 351-369.

Western, J.S. (1969) What white Australians think. *Race*, **10**, 411-434.

Wetherell, M. (1998) Positioning and interpretative repertoires: Conversation analysis and post-structuralism in dialogue. *Discourse and Society*, **9**, 387-412.

Wetherell, M. (1999) *Discursive Psychology and Psychoanalysis: Theorising Masculine Subjectivities*. Paper presented at the Millenium World Conference of Critical Psychology, University of Western Sydney, Australia. May.

Wetherell, M. and Potter, J. (1988) Discourse analysis and the identification of interpretative repertoires. In C. Antaki (ed.), *Analysing Everyday Explanation*, (pp. 168-183). London: Sage.

Wetherell, M. and Potter, J. (1992) *Mapping the Language of Racism: Discourse and the Legitimation of Exploitation*. London: Harvester Wheatsheaf.

Whitley, B.E., Schofield, J.W., and Snyder, H.N. (1984) Peer prefernces in a desegregated school: A round robin analysis. *Journal of Personality and Social Psychology,* **46**, 799-810.

Wicker, A.W. (1969) Attitudes versus actions: The relationship of verbal and overt behavioral responses to attitude objects. *Journal of Social Issues*, **25**, 41-78.

Wilder, D.A. (1978) Perceiving persons as a group: Effects on attributions of causality and beliefs. *Social Psychology*, **41**, 13-23.

Wilder, D.A. (1981) Perceiving persons as a group: Categorization and intergroup relations. In D.L. Hamilton (ed.), *Cognitive Processes in Stereotyping and Intergroup Behaviour* (pp. 213-257). Hillsdale, NJ: Erlbaum.

Wilder, D.A. (1984) Intergroup contact: The typical member and the exception to the rule. *Journal of Experimental Social Psychology*, **20**, 177-194.

Wilder, D.A. (1986) Social categorization: Implications for creation and reduction of intergroup bias. In L. Berkowitz (ed.), *Advances in Experimental Social Psychology,* (Vol. 19, pp. 291-355). New York: Academic Press.

Wilder, D.A. (1993) The role of anxiety in facilitating stereotypic judgment of outgroup behavior. In D.M. Mackie and D.L. Hamilton (eds), *Affect, Cognition and Stereotyping: Interactive Processes in Group Perceptions,* (pp. 87-109). San Diego, CA: Academic Press.

Wilder, D.A. and Shapiro, P.N. (1989) Role of competition induced anxiety in influencing the beneficial impact of positive behaviour by an outgroup member. *Journal of Personality and Social Psychology*, **56**, 60-69.

Williams, D.R. and Collins, C. (1995) US socioeconomic and racial differences in health. *Annual Review of Sociology,* **21**, 349-386.

Williams, J.E. and Best, D.L. (1982 *Measuring Sex Stereotypes: A Thirty-Nation Study*. Beverly Hills, CA: Sage.

Williams, J.E. and Best, D.L. (1990) *Measuring Sex Stereotypes : A Multination Study*. California: Sage.

Williams, J.E., Best, D.L., and Boswell, D.A. (1975) The measurement of children's racial attitudes in the early school years. *Child Development,* **46**, 494-500.

Williams, J.E. and Morland, J.K. (1976) *Race, Color, and the Young Child*. Chapel Hill, NC: University of North Carolina Press.

Williams, J.E. and Roberson, J.K. (1967) A method for assessing racial attitudes in preschool children. *Educational and Psychological Measurement*, **27**, 671-689.

Wilson, W., Chun, N., and Kayatani, M. (1965) Projection, attraction, and strategy choices in intergroup competition. *Journal of Personality and Social Psychology*, **2**, 432-435.

Windemeyer, R. (1842) *On the rights of the Aborigines of Australia*. Public Lecture. Original Manuscript held in the Mitchell Library, Sydney, Australia.

Witenberg, R.T. (1998) *The Role of Reasoning Strategies, Cognitive Operational Level and Prior Knowledge in Moral and Social Conventional Dilemmas*. The 15th Biennual Meeting of the Society for the Study of Behavioural Development, Berne, Switzerland, July 1-4.

Wittgenstein, L (1953) *Philosophical Investigations*. NY: Macmillan.

Worchel, S., Andreoli, V.A., and Folger, R. (1977) Intergroup cooperation and intergroup attraction: The effect of previous intersection and outcome combined effort. *Journal of Personality and Social Psychology*, **13**, 131-140.

Worchel, S., Axsom, D., Ferris, F., Samaha, G., and Schweizer, S. (1978) Determinants of the effect of intergroup cooperation on intergroup attraction. *Journal of Conflict Resolution*, **22**, 429-439.

Worchel, S. and Norvell, N. (1980) Effect of perceived environmental conditions during cooperation on intergroup attraction. *Journal of Personality and Social Psychology*, **38**, 764-772.

Wright, S.C., Taylor, D.M., and Moghaddam, F.M. (1990) Responding to membership in a disadvantaged group: From acceptance to collective protest. *Journal of Personality and Social Psychology*, **58**, 994-1003.

Wyer, R.S. and Srull, T.K. (1989) *Memory and Cognition in its Social Context*. Hillsdale, NJ: Erlbaum.

Wylie, L. and Forest, J. (1992) Religious fundamentalism, right-wing authoritarianism and prejudice. *Psychological Reports*, **71**, 1291-1298.

Yee, M.D. and Brown, R.J. (1992) Self-evaluations and intergroup attitudes in children aged three to nine. *Child Development*, **63**, 619-629.

Yzerbyt, V.Y. and Leyens, J.-P. (1991) Requesting information to form an impression: The influence of valence and confirmatory status. *Journal of Experimental Social Psychology*, **27**, 334-356.

Yzerbyt, V.Y, Rocher, S, and Schadron, G. (1997) Stereotypes as explanations: A subjective essentialistic view of group perception. In R. Spears, P.J. Oakes, N. Ellemers, and S.A. Haslam (eds), *The Social Psychology of Stereotyping and Group Life*, (pp. 20-50). Oxford UK and Cambridge, MT: Blackwell.

Yzerbyt, V.Y., Rogier, A., and Fiske, S.T. (1998) Group entitativity and social attribution: On translating situational constraints into stereotypes. *Personality and Social Psychology Bulletin*, **24**, 1090-1104.

Zawadzki, B. (1948) Limitations on the scapegoat theory of prejudice. *Journal of Abnormal and Social Psychology*, **43**, 127-141.

Zeichner, K. (1995) Preparing educators for cross-cultural teaching. In W.D. Hawley and A.W. Jackson (eds), *Toward a Common Destiny: Improving Race and Ethnic Relations in America*, (pp. 397-419). San Francisco: Jossey-Bass.

Zellman, G.L. and Sears, D.O. (1971) Childhood origins of tolerance for dissent. *Journal of Social Issues*, **27**, 109-135.

Zimbardo, P. (1970) The human choice: Individuation, reason, and order versus deindividuation, impulse, and chaos. In W.J. Arnold and D. Levine (eds) *Nebraska Symposium on Motivation*, (pp. 237-307) . Lincoln: University of Nebraska Press.

Zimbardo, P. and Leippe, M. (1991) *The Psychology of Attitude Change and Social Influence*. New York: McGraw-Hill.

Zinser, O., Rich, M.C., and Bailey, R.C. (1981) Sharing behaviour and racial preference in children. *Motivation and Emotion*, **5**, 179-187.

Zuckerman, M. (1979) Attribution of success and failure revisited, or: The motivational bias is alive and well in theory. *Journal of Personality*, **47**, 245-287.

Author Index

Subject Index